The Frontiers of Women's Writing

The Frontiers of

Brigitte Georgi-Findlay

Women's Writing

Women's Narratives and

the Rhetoric of Westward Expansion

The University of Arizona Press   Tucson

The University of Arizona Press
© 1996
The Arizona Board of Regents
All Rights Reserved

01   00   99   98   97   96   6   5   4   3   2   1

Library of Congress Cataloging-in-Publication Data
Georgi-Findlay, Brigitte.
The frontiers of women's writing : women's narratives and the
rhetoric of westward expansion / Brigitte Georgi-Findlay.
p.   cm.
Includes bibliographical references and index.
ISBN 0-8165-1596-4 (cloth : alk. paper). — ISBN 0-8165-1597-2
(paper : alk. paper)
1. American prose literature—Women authors—History and
criticism.   2. Frontier and pioneer life in literature.   3. Women
pioneers in literature.   4. American prose literature—West (U.S.)—
History and criticism.   5. United States—Territorial expansion—
Historiography.   6. Women and literature—United States—History.
7. Literature and anthropology—United States—History.   8. Indians
of North America in literature.   9. Culture conflict in literature.
10. White women in literature.   I. Title.
PS366.F76G46   1996
810.9'3278'082—dc20   95-32502

British Cataloguing-in-Publication Data
A catalogue record for this book is available from the British Library.

For Jay, Theresia, and Eugen

Contents

Preface

In the annals of American culture, the frontier experience and the national expansion westward beyond the Mississippi have long assumed a mythical status as formative events, providing generations of Americans with a collective cultural history and tradition, themes for a national epic, and a space for fantasy. Within this story of empire building there has been little room for women. Neither leading actors in the drama nor agents in history, women were assigned to the margins of a cultural plot in which gender played a significant role: westward expansion has been encoded as a male activity, and the American West has served as a generating force and a proving ground for the definition of American manhood.

This study began as a search for the female voices that seemed to be missing from the story of westward expansion as told in the literature of frontier heroes, western discovery, exploration, and travel, and in the stories, novels, and movies that comprise the genre of the Western. Historical studies of women in the West provided an important starting point. Over the past two decades, researchers not only have established the presence of women on all western frontiers, but they have also brought to light a body of texts written by nineteenth-century women on the American West, initiating a rediscovery of previously published writings and bringing unpublished archival material into print.

On the basis of this wealth of material—published and unpublished letters; diaries and journals; narratives of travel, exploration, and settlement; memoirs and reminiscences; stories and novels—it became possible to reconstruct the frontier narrative from a female point of view. The more of these writings I read, however, the more my initial focus began to shift. Like many of the women's historians dealing with the American West, I had to confront my own naive assumption that, owing to nineteenth-century women's marginal political status, I would find in their texts a more detached and perhaps critical narrative of westward expansion that could bring into focus the problematic legacy of violence and disenfranchisement that accompanied the Euro-American move west. The more I read, however, the more complicit these women appeared. At the same time, I became increasingly aware of the discursive pressures at work in women's western narratives. In their struggle with both the rhetoric that defined American claims to the West and the discourses that circumscribed women's roles within that enterprise, these texts negotiated complicated questions of authority, power, and ideology that needed to be addressed.

Women's western narratives demanded a revisioning of my initial, almost exclusive focus on gender issues. They required a rethinking of the West as a contested space in which people of different classes, genders, and cultures—white, Indian, Hispanic, black, Chinese—met, interacted, and often clashed within highly asymmetrical relations of power and authority. The sisterly category of "women in the West" that had initially informed my study began to crumble and dissolve. By subsuming all women—despite differences of race, class, and historical circumstances—into one common story, it had filtered relations of unequal power out of the picture and exposed its ethnocentric foundations, veiling the fact that most of the women who wrote about the nineteenth-century West were white, literate, middle- to upper-class women who asserted their own kind of cultural authority over the lands and people they encountered. Their accounts, I realized, not only had to be set in relation to a masculinist frontier myth but also needed to be probed for clues about women's own involvement with territorial expansion.

In the following study of American women's narratives dealing with the westward movement and the West roughly between 1830 and 1930, white women emerge as authors and agents of territorial expansion, positioned ambiguously within systems of power and authority. Defining the rhetoric of American westward expansion, as have other recent revisionist critics of the "frontier myth," as a range of cultural discourses ordering relations of race, class, and gender, I will explore the various ways in which women as writers actively engaged with, contributed to, and at times rejected the development of a national narrative associated with the American West. Focusing particularly on women's personal narratives of traveling and living in the nineteenth-century West, I will show how women's accounts are implicated in expansionist processes at the same time that they formulate positions of innocence and detachment. However, these accounts also reveal that women writers often subverted their claims to cultural authority, exposing in their own unstable positioning the shaky foundations of discourses of empire building and colonization.

In the introduction, I will develop the methodological premises and questions informing my discussion, drawing on Americanist scholarship on frontier mythology and the literature of national self-creation, feminist criticism, and studies of colonial discourse. The latter field, which has devoted itself recently to reexamining the history, politics, psychology, and language of colonization in the aftermath of European colonialism, may seem an odd choice in a study of the American rhetoric of westward expansion, which so strongly invokes its own anticolonialist roots. However, while reading women's western narratives, I sometimes felt transported into the realm of colonialism, for the West often emerges as a dark, alienating space in desperate need of control, or as a site for the establishment of a benign patriarchal/matriarchal authority over "natives" in need of white help and intervention.

Considering that the rhetoric of American national self-creation rests on the unresolved contradictions between the struggle for independence from colonial domination and the quest for imperial power, I believe that studies of colonial discourse, which have illuminated the textual processes of what will be referred to as "imperial meaning-making," can also help to gain insight into the rhetoric of American westward expansion. The creation of innocent yet imperial narrative presences, the naturalization of colonial space, and the de-humanizing of indigenous inhabitants are rhetorical strategies that can be found in both European and Euro-American travel writing. Women's western texts, I will argue, relate not so much to a masculinist frontier myth but to the discourses that have created the male subject of westward expansion and that have produced and consolidated knowledge about the

American West in the narratives of western discovery, exploration, travel, and adventure.

Chapters 1 and 2 focus on women's texts that were generated by the westward movements between 1830 and 1860. I begin my discussion with women's accounts of traveling and settling in the prairie states of today's Midwest, which had been newly opened to white settlement and travel. These accounts provide important parameters for the study of many of the later texts dealing with the trans-Mississippi frontier. The narratives of Caroline Kirkland, Eliza Farnham, Eliza Steele, Margaret Fuller, and Anna Jameson, which were published in the 1830s and 1840s, map the geographies of gender, class, and culture on the new western frontiers, surveying the terrain for women's writings about the West.

Kirkland's works serve as a point of entry into my subject. Staking the boundaries of a woman's western text, they reveal a woman writer's unstable and ambiguous positioning between cultural affirmation and cultural critique. They are also useful in reconsidering the feminist practice of privileging the personal and domestic in women's texts as arenas for affirming counterhegemonic insights. I consequently read configurations of femininity and domesticity in Kirkland's narratives not only as female countervisions to male fantasies of conquest and possession but also as complements to them: the ideal of domesticity, read in the context of expansionism, potentially functions as an instrument of cultural and social control and order imposed on western disorder. The same reading applies to the western narratives of Fuller and Jameson, in which imperial conventions are reinforced by the creation of an innocent female subject of romantic individualism, and the projection of domestic and familial fantasies upon the western landscape—which both obscure the historical processes that led to Native American dispossession and environmental destruction.

Fuller's and Jameson's narratives also introduce a major concern addressed throughout the book: the negotiation of issues of gender, race, and culture in representing encounters with Native Americans. The rhetorical deployment of femininity and domesticity in such descriptions often highlights the ironic ambiguity of white women's attempts to represent and assert authority over the cultural/racial other. The privilege and power of the gaze—of inspecting, examining, and looking at the "natives"—tend to dissolve as mere illusions: ultimately the gaze falls back on the white woman, who stands exposed as the object of Indian curiosity and critical scrutiny.

Representations of the other are intimately tied to the problems of female self-representation. In some women's narratives, the description of scenes of contact seems to mark a crisis that temporarily subverts generalizing monologues on Native and Hispanic Americans, timidly opening the texts up to other voices. However, this does not resolve the basic contradiction in women's texts, where visions of reciprocity compete with female versions of asserting and affirming cultural authority.

Chapter 2 introduces a different group of women writers: the diarists of the overland trails. Writing semipublic accounts of their journeys for a limited audience of friends and relatives, they struggled with language and representation in a more essential and concrete way than the highly literate women writing about the prairie West. Although some accounts superimpose a narrative design upon the westward move, these women's representations of western landscapes and people are inconsistent and shifting, reflecting the writers' efforts to make sense of what they saw and experienced. Female overland diarists were also on insecure ground as travelers, seeing themselves one day as trespassers in a country they perceived as foreign, alienating, and unsafe, a land in which American claims were fiercely contested by indigenous inhabitants, and the next day casting themselves as tourists on a pleasure trip, innocently passing through, and imposing aesthetic designs upon, the land.

In the work of the diarists, discourses of femininity again complicate women writers' access to an imperial voice. Attempts to adopt scientific or artistic modes of description often end in declarations of incompetence or in self-parodic mockery. Fashioning feminine selves who enter into nonappropriative relations with their surroundings, women diarists often detached themselves from an expansionist enterprise with doubtful purpose and results and assumed the role of critical observers. In the process, they established the Indian presence as an important factor determining the journey's outcome, deflating images of courageous pioneers in conflict with fierce warriors and drawing attention instead to the daily interactions between travelers and Native Americans.

Chapters 3 and 4 deal with the heterogeneous body of women's texts written since the 1860s that were generated by the emergence, or closure, of the many disparate western frontiers that developed simultaneously during the second half of the nineteenth century. I will first focus on the large and still relatively homogeneous group of writings that revolve around women's western experiences as wives of frontier army officers during the Indian wars: private diaries and letters, accounts published in the 1850s and 1860s, and reminiscences that appeared from the 1880s through the first decades of the twentieth century. I especially aim to show how women's narratives of western army life engage with the controversies over Indian wars and with discussions that shaped the development of a national Indian policy as part of the federal government's increasing involvement in the management of the American West. I also set these texts in relation to the late-nineteenth-century voices in politics, literature, and culture that called for the revitalization and remasculinization of America, deploying highly gendered visions of the American West as a source of cultural identity and unity.

Despite professions of detachment, women's narratives of army life were necessarily implicated in the politics of managing the West, revealing the dynamics of power not only within the social microcosm of the frontier army but also in the army's relationships with the western world "outside"—the world of Native Americans, Hispanics, and Euro-American settlers. They created images of frontier officers as innocents with marginal cultural power in a West in which American territorial claims were extremely tenuous and still had to be established and legitimated against Indian nations—a West that these women writers could claim only sporadically as pure "Nature." Neither can the Indian presence be easily obscured in visions of an empty, inviting land. Although women described this West as a space of physical freedom and expansion, it emerges simultaneously as a culturally contested terrain, the enjoyment of which required the pacification of Native Americans.

The representation of interactions with Indians reflects a sense of insecurity accompanied by an emphasis on domestication and control (over self and others). Relations between white women and Indians revolved not only around their homes and their children but also around such events as Indian dances and distributions of annuities, both perceived as being highly charged with potential violence. Hierarchies of race were dangerously subverted, especially by hierarchies of gender, in relations between white women and Indian men. They could be reinstated and upheld only by rhetorically domesticating the Indian man, a strategy that maintains racial inequality and significantly counters female professions of powerlessness. The way Indian men are aestheticized and feminized in women's texts illustrates how discursive conventions of colonialism can work in the service of women's empowerment. Together with the representation of Indian women as victims of Indian patriarchy, the description of Indian men as effeminate dandies or as aesthetic objects forms part of the rhetorical de-legitimation of Indian cultures and lifeways in white women's western writings. Nevertheless, I also aim to demonstrate how white women's narratives of personal encounters with Indian men and women may simultaneously disrupt women's visions of control—of the self and others—by exposing the white woman as the vulnerable target of Indian scrutiny, and by presenting Indians as speakers, commentators, and actors who assert power over their own lives.

At the same time as women bound to the army by marriage were encountering the American West as a site of cultural conflict, other women were writing accounts of travel on new touristic frontiers, embracing the West as a cornerstone for professional writing careers. Those who had come to live there found professional opportunities in the emerging regional publishing cultures, engendering regional traditions in their travel narratives, journalistic writing, and fiction. Chapter 4 charts this emergence of the West as a kind of female vocation in women's narratives of the 1870s and 1880s. Whereas chapter 3 revolves around one thematic center, this chapter is organized by a more historicist concern with the relations between women's western writing and cultural discourses on the West within a certain time period. Although the initial focus is the touristic frontier, my main goal is to trace the diversification of women's interests in the West and to illustrate how women writers in various genres and regional contexts emerged, despite problems of authority and patronage, as influential mythmakers who left their imprint, at least temporarily, on cultural narratives associated with the West. The chapter concentrates on the public writings of Sara Lippincott (Grace Greenwood), Helen Hunt Jackson,

Jessie Benton Frémont, Frances Fuller Victor, Josephine Clifford, Susan Wallace, and Caroline Leighton, as well as on some private diaries.

American westward expansion, with its official proclamations of manifest destiny and mission, entailed not only a history of war with Indian nations but also, especially since the last quarter of the nineteenth century, a legacy of policies designed to incorporate Indians as individuals into the nation by way of Christianization and what may be called "Americanization." Within this context of Indian reform and transformation, women and ideologies of womanhood were to play significant and conflicting roles as both agents and tools of cultural change. Chapter 5 focuses on women's participation in the development and implementation of federal Indian policies, where the transformation of Indian gender identities and gendered work roles, as well as tribal conceptions of kinship, family, and marriage, became increasingly crucial. Studying the narratives of female missionaries and teachers on Indian reservations in the American West, I analyze how these writers engaged with both the rhetoric of Indian transformation and the discourses that configured the American West as "wild": the conflicting, but at times complementary, ideals and ideologies of home mission and strenuosity and of progressivism and primitivism that existed side by side in late-nineteenth-century American culture. My aim is to show how women writers participated continuously in the cultural task of defining the boundaries and hierarchies of race, gender, nationality, and culture.

These women's accounts highlight the ironic fact that since the 1870s an increasing number of single women embraced the missionary service and work for the Indian Bureau in the West as professional opportunities and alternatives to female domesticity, thus contradicting in their personal and professional lives the domestic ideology they were to propagate among Indians and Hispanics. As church and government officials, they contested Indians' ability to manage their own lives, their homes, and the education of their children, and they established themselves as maternalist colonizers and transformers. In their personal narratives, however, they distanced themselves from the official home-mission rhetoric and struggled with the ideological constructions of womanhood that lay at the basis of their task. Writing about their work on Indian reservations, they assumed an ambiguous position toward their mission of Americanization, often focusing on a personal process of learning and the quest for independence rather than on the work of transforming the Indians. Again, the descriptions of personal encounters with Native Americans, always closely tied to strategies of feminine self-representation, work as a destabilizing element, exposing the shaky foundations of the Indian-reform ideology.

Women's western writings create conflicting versions of westward expansion and the American West, and the writers engaged with discourses of femininity (and feminism) in often very different ways. This underscores the questionable usefulness of an approach that seeks to impose a narrative of linear development on women's western writings. Nevertheless, I have identified a network of common tropes and rhetorical gestures that join women's texts together, locating them not only in a context of westward expansion but within a more global framework of expansion and empire building.

Despite my efforts to organize this study along a rough chronological outline, I have not intended to write a complete literary history of women's western writings. My discussion cannot lay claim to completeness; it is admittedly selective and full of exclusions, due to both my thematic focus and the large and ever-increasing number of women's western texts available for study. The writings of such well-known western writers as Mary Hallock Foote and Mary Austin, for example, have by necessity been relegated to the status of reference texts, while more obscure, lesser-known writers were foregrounded. Neither have I included a discussion of the western novels written by women in the twentieth century, because this would have required a new methodological framework.

There are other regrettable exclusions. Although in all parts of my analysis I have aimed to establish the copresence of Native and Hispanic Americans as crucial to the formation of cultural discourses about westward expansion and the American West, my approach has an obvious and problematic flaw: it still puts white women first. With a few exceptions, there are no Native American, Hispanic, or black women's voices heard in my account. Speaking through white women's words, these other women only exist, so to speak, as translations. This is due to the limited number of nineteenth-century minority women's written autobiographical or autoethnographical texts available for a comparative study of cultural narratives of westward expansion. Indian women's voices have been preserved in the tradition of their oral cultures, and only a few have been able to authorize their own written narratives. Hispanic women's texts additionally confront us with a language barrier. Although I have attempted to refer to and discuss the available texts written in English as far as possible, I feel that they could be done better justice in a study that takes into account the material collected in oral-history projects.

Acknowledgments

This book could not have been written without the generous support of many individuals and institutions. I would like to thank the American Council of Learned Societies and the German Research Association, whose research fellowships have enabled me to chart the frontiers of women's writings during a research leave from the John F. Kennedy Institute for North American Studies at the Free University of Berlin, Germany.

Although the project was conceived in Germany, it received its present form during two inspiring years spent as a visiting scholar at the University of Arizona. I am deeply indebted to friends and colleagues in Germany and the United States, many of whom patiently read earlier, rather voluminous drafts of the manuscript. Eve Keitel accompanied the work in all its stages as a special friend and ideal critic. Barbara Babcock and Judy Nolte Temple shared their work and ideas with me and smoothed the way into the unfamiliar environment of an American university. Barbara led me on the right path by drawing my attention to studies of colonial discourse. Heinz Ickstadt has been a supportive mentor whose work on American westward expansion has probably started it all. I am particularly indebted to Annette Kolodny, whose stimulating work has opened the literary terrain of women's western writings, guiding me on the often-arduous path of women's western journeys. Her presence at the University of Arizona drew me to Tucson, and I am grateful for her support and for sharing her time and ideas with me. I also want to thank Maria Diedrich and Ursula Brumm for providing encouragement, advice, and criticism. My editors,

Joanne O'Hare and Alexis Noebels, and the readers of the University of Arizona Press have been extremely helpful by offering constructive criticism and practical advice. Finally, I want to express my deepest gratitude to my husband and my whole family for their patience, encouragement, and nurturing presence.

The Frontiers of Women's Writing

American Literature, Westward Expansion, and Imperial Meaning-Making

American westward expansion and the experience of the frontier—the dividing line between white settlements and the unknown, "empty" land beyond—have for a long time served as important frameworks for the explanation and definition of a specific U.S. American history and culture. In his paper "The Significance of the Frontier in American History," presented in 1893, Frederick Jackson Turner designated the moving frontier as the most significant factor in shaping American political and social institutions and in forming a specifically American national character. Turner's frontier paradigm—although continually contested and revised—would dominate the study of American history, literature, and culture long into the twentieth century. In 1950, Henry Nash Smith defined the notion that American society has been shaped by "the pull of a vacant continent" as one of the most persistent generalizations concerning American life and character. Taking up Turner's idea of empty space as a main determinant of American culture, Smith described his *Virgin Land* as a study that "traces the impact of the West, the vacant continent beyond the frontier, on the consciousness of Americans" (3–4).

In a recent reconsideration of his study, however, Smith criticized the premises of his earlier work, admitting that his own attitudes "were influenced by the basic myth or ideology of America" more than he had realized. He had failed to fully comprehend the assumptions underlying Turner's view of American history, which revolved around "the celebrated declaration that 'the existence of an area of free land, its continuous recession, and the advance of American settlement westward explain American development.'"

Thus he had taken over from Turner "the attitude that Ursula Brumm has found to be characteristic of American culture, a refusal to acknowledge the guilt intrinsic to the national errand into the wilderness." Like his teachers and academic colleagues, he had "lost the capacity for facing up to the tragic dimensions of the Westward Movement." He had acquired "an even more important contagion from Turner's conception of the wilderness beyond the frontier as free land: the tendency to assume that this area was in effect devoid of human inhabitants."[1]

The Innocent Hero and the Naturalization of America

As Bruce Greenfield has pointed out, the idea that Euro-Americans moving westward were dealing with a primordial space rather than inhabited foreign countries still informs twentieth-century scholarship on American literature and American westward expansion. This scholarship, however, has mostly failed to question this construction of an empty, natural America as a crucial factor in the culture.[2] Indeed, American literary and cultural criticism has long been shaped and dominated by the images and symbols of the "myth of America." Scholars have not only accepted the idea of America as a promised land of regeneration, interpreting it as the basic theme in shaping an American national identity, but they have also emphasized the idea of innocence: America, envisioned by Europe as the unspoiled Virgin Land, a pastoral New World garden, was inhabited by the American Adam, a heroic figure who began human history all over again.[3]

Since the 1960s, however, scholars have revealed this myth of America as part of a broader ideology, and they have started to expose its problematic aspects in terms of unspoken assumptions about class, race, and gender. Already in the 1950s, some western historians challenged the paradigm that the explanation for American history and culture lay in the West. Instead, they argued, developments in the American West should be seen as extensions of Eastern and European economic, political, and cultural processes. Far from being a formative space for an American avant-garde, the West had been a colony.[4] Richard Slotkin, Michael Rogin, Bruce Greenfield, and others have exposed the naturalization and de-historicization of America and the American West as essentially a masking of the economic, ecological, and cultural consequences of westward expansion. In fact, the idea of an uninhabited, primordial, natural America reflected in 1830s and 1840s literary and political discourse, and especially in landscape painting, coincided with the beginnings of industrialization, the massive destruction of the American landscape, and the removal of Native Americans. It was during these years that women's public writings on the American West in the form of travel and settlement narratives appeared on the scene of American literature.

By the 1830s, the image of the West implied not only primeval, untouched nature promising spiritual regeneration, but also natural abundance to be cultivated and exploited by an agrarian civilization—obvious contradictions that were difficult to reconcile. Having linked their sense of national identity to primordial nature, Euro-Americans began to feel threatened by their own destructive efforts to build an empire.[5] Greenfield traces the emergence of the definition of America as "Nature's Nation" to cultural tensions related to Americans' anxieties about the past, particularly about their relationships with those having prior claims to the land. After their independence from European sponsors and institutions, they needed a new basis for their continued expansion on the continent. One such basis was "the idea of the place itself, at least once they could conceive of it as natural, empty, uncivilized, or virgin. For after America had become 'natural,' Euro-Americans were no longer cohabitants of a continent whose peoples they had conquered; instead, they could see the primordial land itself as the explanation and justification for their presence in it."[6]

It is therefore no coincidence that American literary and artistic romanticism flourished during the nation's first great territorial expansion, a period in which Native Americans were dispossessed and removed from their lands by legal and military force on a scope never known before. In the 1830s, the Jacksonian Removal Act forced most Indian tribes from their lands east of the Mississippi, and Michael Rogin argues that this Indian dispossession initiated and shaped the period, which has become known as the "Age of Jackson." Beginning in 1819, "Jackson, Indians, and westward expansion, not slavery and Negroes, structured American politics for the next generation."[7]

Richard Slotkin identifies the "myth of regeneration through violence" as the major and persistent force shaping Americans' interpretations of their history, present, and future.[8] Like Roy Harvey Pearce, Slotkin sees American national and personal identity defined not by its self-assertion against Europe but by the encounter with the Indian "other," who represents an "inescapable presence" to the colonists as "the primitive proprietor of the land and . . . the human product of the New World." Early colonists tended to minimize this human presence by treating it simply "as an aspect of the inanimate world, a natural obstacle to acquisition." What Slotkin calls the "myth of the Indian wars" can therefore be seen as a cultural act of legitimation that translates "a human drama of dispossession into one in which resources are innocently appropriated directly from nature, without human cost." Consequently, the myth of a pastoral New World garden inhabited by a solitary, innocent, male American hero needs to be historicized as an obfuscation of the act and cost of conquest. The concept of the frontier essentially masks actual social and economic conflicts and deflects or displaces them into the world of myth.[9]

This myth of the frontier West as "the garden republic" thus served as a much-needed cultural legitimation for American westward expansion, which in the words of Heinz Ickstadt, "responded to the needs of an expanding capitalist economy and represented at the same time a continuous act of national self-creation throughout the nineteenth century."[10] As Michael Rogin has put it, the myth of the West, which veiled the economic, social, and cultural basis and contradictions of westward expansion, developed "in flight from the significance of capitalist expansion" and "helped form the politics and culture of American capitalism."[11]

Enter Eve: The Woman in the Frontier Myth

Scholarship has shown how the myth of the innocent in the New World garden conceals human intention and authorship by transforming the historically made into the naturally given. But which discourses authorize this naturalization and denial of human responsibility into myth? Who or what authorizes this collective

self-interpretation?[12] Was this mythical narrative of solitary, innocent (male) heroes the only story that people told in nineteenth-
century America?

Annette Kolodny has pointed out that scholars deconstructing
the frontier myth "tend to ignore the fact (and significance) of
women as readers as much as they tend to ignore the potentially
symbolic significations of gender within a text." They persistently
ignore not only the impact of the frontier mythology on women but
also the possibility that women, too, "required imaginative constructs through which to accommodate themselves to the often
harsh realities of the western wilderness."[13] Indeed, studies of the
frontier myth more often than not use economy and class as a
metalanguage that orders other relations like those of gender and
race. Also, at the basis of most studies of the frontier myth is the
idea of a cultural, ideological consensus. Sacvan Bercovitch has
defined ideology as "the ground and texture of consensus. In its
narrowest sense, this may be a consensus of a marginal or maverick
group. In the broad sense in which I use the term here (in conjunction with the term 'America'), ideology is the system of interlinked
ideas, symbols, and beliefs by which a culture—any culture—seeks
to justify and perpetuate itself; the web of rhetoric, ritual, and
assumption through which society coerces, persuades, and co-
heres. So considered, ideology is basically conservative; but it is
not therefore static or simply repressive."[14]

For Bercovitch, America exemplifies the ideology of consensus
rooted in the Puritan sense of mission and destiny in the wilderness, an ideology envisioning a redeeming world that offers the
potential for individual spiritual renewal and moral regeneration.
He argues that the rhetoric of the Puritan jeremiad, containing
a summons to radical individualism and dissent, preempts the
threat of radical alternatives and persistently structures an American ideology that both dominant and marginal social and ethnic
groups can relate to, incorporating them into the American mission, confining them in their freedom to the terms of the American
myth, and enlisting them in the cause of "the American way."[15]

Yet even if Bercovitch asserts radical individualism and dissent
as the essence of an American ideology that represents and incorporates both dominant and marginal voices, he does so by gathering both female and ethnically diverse voices under an intellectual

umbrella opened by white male voices who authorized themselves as speakers for a unified American culture. But what if the purported rules governing the frontier myth were not shared by all participants in the game?[16] What does it mean that lettered, male, eastern and western authors in the nineteenth century created an American hero who is often unlettered and immature, both innocent and imperial, who claims possession of America yet denies claiming it, and who keeps women from entering the New World garden?

Feminist critics have targeted the frontier myth not only as a basically patriarchal story but also as the expression of a Euro-American totalizing perspective that subsumes all human experience under the unmarked category "man," claiming to speak "as the One prophetic voice for all Mankind."[17] They argue that by establishing the centrality of the frontier myth in defining the essential "American-ness" of American literature—and by locating it in the story of the male innocent who escapes from civilization into the wilderness to become a man, free from the constraints of tradition and authority—cultural and literary studies have privileged the story of radical individualism to the exclusion of all other formulations of the American self. Within this privileged narrative of cultural self-definition, white women are assigned a symbolic role as the hero's other, made to stand for the repressive rules and constraints of white civilization, inimical to adventure, independence, and freedom.

Leslie Fiedler, for instance, defines the West of the classic American story as the place "to which White male Americans flee from their own women into the arms of Indian males, but which those White women, in their inexorable advance from coast to coast, destroy."[18] What has come to be defined as the quintessential American plot—and what Nina Baym has called the "melodrama of beset manhood"[19]—reveals itself as a story based on a rigid dichotomy of sex roles that not only denies women active, heroic roles but defines them as obstacles to the male hero's freedom. It is, in the words of Wallace Stegner, a story of "male freedom and aspiration versus female domesticity, wilderness versus civilization, violence and danger versus the safe and tamed."[20] Thus the frontier myth has been exposed as a patriarchal story formulated from the male point of view, "as if the male is the subject of all experience, the female an object in his story, the antagonist to the story's implicit values."[21] As a story of male individuation, dealing with both the rejection and assertion of patriarchal values, the frontier myth also necessarily encodes the conquest of the continent as an exclusively male adventure.[22]

Kolodny has shown in *The Lay of the Land* how American male writers have identified the American land metaphorically as feminine, casting it as a woman invested with both "the regressive pull of maternal containment and the seductive invitation to sexual assertion," and triggering conflicting desires that shape man's relation to the land. At the same time that man desires to conquer, master, and transform the land, he wishes to become its son and lover, its owner and husbandman. It is this fantasy of a feminine landscape, promising both filial contentment and erotic mastery, that Kolodny identifies as the basis of Americans' destructive behavior toward the American land. The myth of the frontier is revealed as a historical account of conquest that is intrinsically gender coded, linked as it is to the psychological tale of masculine individuation, separation, and schism.[23] Within this story, generic Woman is naturalized and neutralized: "Hers is a double bind; she is the female who keeps him from the land, and she is the female embodiment of the land. Metonymically she becomes home and mother; metaphorically she stands for all he fears and all he desires. In either manifestation, she can't win."[24]

Dawn Lander has linked the representation of women within the frontier myth to the male guilt of conquest. White women, she suggests, function in American literature and scholarship as they do in biblical tradition: as the scapegoats responsible for the loss of Paradise. If women are identified with religion and civilization, they are at the same time antithetical to the wilderness, obstructing man's longing for "an untamed wilderness of desire." As the white man's racist and imperialist atrocities increase, Lander argues, "so does his need to idealize the white woman, to symbolize his finer intentions. The mere presence of the married white female is considered to be sufficiently potent to dispel the wilderness and to constitute the establishment of white civilization." In the American tradition, the white woman is a prohibitive moral figure, "and the fury the white male may feel against his own passions and prejudices is vented against the white female: she becomes the cause of racism, of the destruction of the wilderness, and of the psychic crippling of the American male. The figure which was, in civilization, on an asexual pedestal, becomes, in the wilderness, a scapegoat."[25]

The studies of historian Carroll Smith-Rosenberg further illuminate and historicize this phenomenon. Exploring the ways in which gender has persistently structured definitions of American identity, she has shown how fears of an invasive female power entered nineteenth-century political discourse not only in debates over women's rights but also in the regulation of women's intimate lives; for example, in medical discourse and in the folklore and mythology of the American frontier. Analyzing the Davy Crockett myth that flourished in the Jacksonian period, Smith-Rosenberg points to the irony that the Crockett stories, which celebrate an adolescent escape from family restraint and female influence into western, racial violence, appeared at the very time "when institutions in the service of commercial and industrial capitalism and, often, with the specific purpose of socializing and controlling the youthful population, first proliferated." At the same time as the Crockett myth celebrated the adolescent innocent beyond institutional boundaries, "formal institutions, indeed state institutions, had increasingly begun to replace the informal and domestic modes of social control which had characterized traditional eighteenth-century society." America, she concludes, "had never been so mythically free and so actually institutionalized."[26] The Davy Crockett myth not only encodes the American West as a space for male adolescent, fraternal competition, but also prepares the ground for a maturing paternalistic authority.

The feminist revision of the frontier myth has exposed the androcentric bias underlying the pastoralization of America—a bias that either neutralizes women completely or colonizes them as captives within the story of the male innocent. Feminist scholars have also drawn attention to the ways gender and sexuality constitute national identity. Nevertheless, in their focus on gender issues, feminist critics have at times tended to overlook the racial politics that prompted the pastoral myth, in which the white self was also defined against racial others—a quest in which white women were enlisted as much as, sometimes even more than, white men.

The quintessential American plot cannot be explained solely in terms of the sex-gender system. Rather, gender must be explored together with race and class to understand the formulation of an American identity that allegedly has at its center a solitary, innocent, male hero who disclaims responsibility for both civilization and conquest. Moreover, it is important to establish not only how women were subsumed within the story of the male innocent, but also how they, as writers and mythmakers, contributed to or resisted the creation of a frontier mythology as part of a national narrative.[27]

Women Writing the West: An Alternative Myth?

How could women, positioned as they were in a language and a literary tradition seemingly dominated by men, write about the West, a terrain so laden with symbolic claims and serving as the embodiment of the American national narrative? What did they write?

Women's secondary presence within the frontier myth has been attributed not only to the patriarchal impulse in nineteenth-century American culture but also to the exclusion of women's texts in the formative studies of American literary and cultural criticism. Of course, one could also speculate that the meager presence of women and their seldom-active role in the literature formulating the frontier myth mirror the historical fact that women participated in the westward movements in comparatively fewer numbers than men. One could also reason that literary and cultural studies of the frontier mythology failed to include women's voices due to the scarcity of women's writings on westward expansion. This seeming scarcity has led some feminist literary critics to identify an alternative female tradition to the male frontier fantasy in the sentimental or domestic novels, locating women's concerns and culture in a domestic context decidedly and programmatically antithetical to the male preoccupation with the (more or less symbolic) frontier.[28]

Within the last two decades, however, historians have established women's presence on all western frontiers, and they have unearthed a wealth of texts revealing women's continuing engagement with the issues surrounding westward expansion.[29] They found that female writers most often formulated their concerns in published and unpublished letters, diaries, journals, travel narratives, autobiographies and memoirs, and only sometimes in stories and novels.[30] Women's historians have read westering women's texts against the male frontier myth, revealing a female perspective on the frontier experience organized by the search for home and stability, for the reestablishment of familiar social and familial patterns—for the old rather than the new. Hoping to discover whether the move west was a liberating experience for women, some historians found that instead of freeing women from social constraints, the West "isolated women from other women, heightened their vulnerability to men, and increased their domestic work load." Western women's history debunked the myth of the West as a place more democratic, egalitarian, and individualistic than the East.[31] However, in their search for the "real" women behind the stereotypical female images of the masculinist frontier myth, and in their efforts to accord women a place in the "taming of the wilderness" or the "conquest" of the West, women's historians have at times forgotten to question the ideological assumptions about westward expansion underlying their studies. Some have corrected rather than explained stereotypical representations of westering women without considering how women's westering texts might fit into the larger cultural context of ideas relating to westward expansion.

Feminist theory has studied women's personal narratives in their own right as formulations of a female individuation process and a female identity, which function both as "sources of counter-hegemonic insight" and as "part of a dialogue of domination."[32] Personal narratives have thus become, in women's studies, newly prominent and central in the critical debate on the status of self, the nature of self-representation, and the relationship between experience and representation.[33]

But how do women's texts relate to the frontier mythology and the cultural discourses on westward expansion? In *The Land Before Her*, Annette Kolodny has shown how women's western narratives, whether private or public, engage with the male myth of the frontier. Focusing on the imaginative constructs women have projected onto the western frontiers, she traces "the sequence of fantasies" through which generations of women "came to know and act upon the westward-moving frontier." She suggests that "[i]n the process of projecting resonant symbolic contents onto otherwise unknown terrains—a process I designate here as fantasy—women made those terrains their own." Fantasy, Kolodny argues, "allowed women to enact relational paradigms on strange and sometimes forbidding landscapes" (xii). Having noted in *The Lay of the Land* how male fantasies had taken hold from the beginnings of exploration and had governed subsequent Euro-American relations with the landscape, she had turned to women's materials "hoping to discover some alternative metaphorical design—one that would lead us away from our destructive capacities" (xiii).

What Kolodny found both confirmed and disappointed her initial assumptions. If women shared in the economic motives behind emigration and, like the men, also dreamed of transforming the wilderness, the emphases were still different. On the wooded frontiers of the Northeast and the Ohio Valley, women "quite literally set about planting gardens in these wilderness places." Later, when white settlers moved onto the open prairies of Texas and Illinois, women embraced these spaces "as a garden ready-made. Avoiding for a time male assertions of a rediscovered Eden, women claimed the frontiers as a potential sanctuary for an idealized domesticity. Massive exploitation and alteration of the continent do not seem to have been part of women's fantasies. They dreamed, more modestly, of locating a home and a familial human community within a cultivated garden." Kolodny suggests that in captivity narratives, diaries, and travel narratives, as well as in domestic novels, women as writers and readers were able "to evade the power and cultural pervasiveness of male fantasy structures" and to challenge "outright the nation's infatuation with a wilderness Adam" (xiii).[34]

Assuming the centrality of a male frontier fantasy in American culture, Kolodny sees women's western texts engaging with the premises of the frontier myth. But how pervasive and homogeneous is this male fantasy? Approaching her study with a feminist insight into white women's double positioning, at once inside and outside of the dominant culture, Kolodny is well aware of the problem of presenting male and female fantasies as essentially antithetical. Still, it had been important for her to show that women, although restricted by the constraints of gender ideology, have never been held captive—at least not completely—within men's imagination.

It is, of course, tantalizing to speculate with Kolodny that "had women's fantasies been in control (rather than men's), westward migration might have taken a different course" (11). But then, some of Kolodny's findings in women's narratives sound like echoes of the innocent in the garden, giving rise to suspicions that women's fantasies were at times less alternative than complementary to the Adamic myth. Thus Kolodny suggests that women may have "avoided male anguish at lost Edens and male guilt in the face of the raping of the continent by confining themselves, instead, to the 'innocent . . . amusement' of a garden's narrow space" (7).

The following study modifies the discussion that Kolodny began, by challenging the concept of a homogeneous male myth of the frontier. Assuming the existence of heterogeneous discourses on the frontier and on westward expansion that engage, complement, or contest one another, I am interested in how women locate themselves in relation to these discursive frameworks: How do they authorize their own writing, and how do they authorize westward expansion? In the context of women's involvement with territorial expansion, their texts relate not so much to a male hero figure but to the modes of discourse that created him as the subject of westward expansion. The differences between men's and women's western writing are also related to the discursive constraints produced by cultural definitions of womanhood and women's writing, which complicate women's access to discourses of empire building and colonization.

Personal narratives of travel and adventure by frontier heroes, explorers, and travelers have produced and consolidated knowledges about the American West and created the (male) subject of westward expansion. Because it is especially in personal narratives that women engaged with the discourses that have produced the West for a Euro-American audience, those narratives are the focus of this study. Even though it has often been observed that women's access to writing moves along generic lines, with women usually accorded the task of novel writing,[35] women writing on the West produced narratives of travel, discovery, and "adventurous enterprise,"[36] a journalistic kind of writing seldom associated with female writers. It is this genre of writing that shows women positioned ambiguously within relations of power and authority.

This focus on personal narratives also entails a revisioning of such concepts as "the frontier" and "westward expansion," and establishes the American West as a conflicted and contested cultural space marked by asymmetrical relations of power and authority between people of different cultures, classes, and genders. Set within this context, white women's western narratives do assume a role in the affirmation of cultural power and, in fact, establish maternalist versions of an American West.

Travel Writing and Expansion

Male narratives of discovery, exploration, and travel could authorize themselves by way of several discursive modes: the scientific discourse of natural history; the language of discovery, adventure, and commerce; the political discourse of federal Indian policy; and the narrative of personal aesthetic experience. With the exception of the latter, these discursive modes are strategies for claiming authority that, on account of cultural definitions of womanhood, were potentially problematic for female writers; moreover, women's access to these discourses was itself controversial because narratives of travel, discovery, and adventurous enterprise address questions of authority connected with the production of knowledge and the assumption of power. Since women were traditionally excluded from certain knowledges and discourses, even writing travel narratives may have placed them in inherently transgressive positions of authority and knowledge.

As Bruce Greenfield has shown, Euro-American travelers writing accounts of exploratory journeys in North America needed to address a problem of authority: the authority that enabled them to claim what was by generic definition alien territory. Discovery narratives, he suggests, "do, as a matter of course, construe European action in America as being in conflict with existing peoples, even though, over the years, they developed rhetorical strategies for mitigating and marginalizing this conflict (since the late seventeenth century, they have presented themselves as scientific discourse)." He regards it as commonsensical to include North

American–discovery narratives in the realm of what Edward Said, Peter Hulme, and Mary Pratt, among others, have defined as colonial discourse: "an ensemble of linguistically-based practices unified by their common deployment in the management of colonial relationships."[37] To "make discoveries" was to travel and to observe, but it also meant that the traveler participated in European expansionism and the extension of European authority over unfamiliar regions. Through the well-established conventions of the discovery narrative, individual adventurers allied themselves with the power of European and Euro-American institutions. To validate individual experience, travelers sought to transform adventures into history, and even fictional adventure stories reflected and served the West's cult of expansion.[38]

Greenfield argues that in the North American narratives of discovery, relationships with native peoples are crucial. When reading these narratives, one not only recognizes afresh the importance of these relationships in Euro-American culture, but one can also see the emerging role of American nature, which developed, at least in part, out of the painful conflicts between Euro-Americans and Native Americans. Narratives of travel, discovery, and exploration also challenge us to revise assumptions that the frontier was both a space and a process determined exclusively by the interests of white Euro-American culture. Mary Pratt's idea of "contact zones," the "social spaces where disparate cultures meet, clash, and grapple with each other, often in contexts of highly asymmetrical relations of domination and subordination—like colonialism, slavery, or their aftermaths," is intended in part to revise these assumptions. Her "contact zone" concept is an attempt "to invoke the spatial and temporal copresence" of people and cultures previously separated by geography and history, who now share—and contest— a common space. By using this term, she aims to foreground the "interactive, improvisational dimensions of colonial encounters so easily ignored or suppressed by diffusionist accounts of conquest and domination. A 'contact' perspective emphasizes how subjects are constituted in and by their relations to each other."[39]

Recently, Kolodny has also reconsidered her frontier concept by redefining it as "the borderlands, that liminal landscape of changing meanings on which distinct human cultures first encounter one another's 'otherness' and appropriate, accommodate, or domesticate it through language." She now envisions the frontier as "a multiplicity of ongoing first encounters over time and land, rather than as a linear chronology of successive discoveries and discrete settlements." Consequently, the literature of the frontier may be seen as encoding "some specifiable first moment in the evolving dialogue between different cultures and languages and their engagement with one another and with the physical terrain."[40]

In *Imperial Eyes,* a study of European travel writing in South America and Africa, Mary Pratt sets these narratives in the context of European expansion and the dynamics of what she calls imperial "meaning-making." She shows how travel books by Europeans about non-European parts of the world go about creating the domestic subject of European imperialism, and how they have engaged metropolitan reading publics with (or to) expansionist enterprises (5). Using the term "anti-conquest" to refer to the strategies of representation whereby "European bourgeois subjects seek to secure their innocence in the same moment as they assert European hegemony," she argues that in travel and exploration writing, "these strategies of innocence are constituted in relation to older imperial rhetorics of conquest." The main protagonist of Pratt's anti-conquest is "the 'seeing-man,' an admittedly unfriendly label for the European male subject of European landscape discourse— he whose imperial eyes passively look out and possess" (7).

Bruce Greenfield identifies similar tropes in North American narratives of discovery where merely visual contact with the land creates a transcendental romantic subject, another anti-conquest hero constructed as a noninterventionist presence. For Greenfield, one of the most powerful assertions of authority is the trope of aesthetic appropriation, often expressed in what Pratt has termed the "monarch-of-all-I-survey" scene, with explorers placing themselves on hilltops and mountain peaks to gain a sweeping view of the surrounding country—a position that increasingly provided the privileged perspective for American landscape painting.[41] He also shows how a romantic discourse of discovery became part of the narrative of American identity, in which the voice of personal aesthetic experience and self-discovery tended to silence commentaries on the historical processes and politics of exploration, conquest, and settlement.[42]

Mary Pratt's and Bruce Greenfield's analyses of European and

North American travel writing point to rhetorical strategies that create innocent yet imperial narrative presences and affirm the authority of the narrator-traveler at the same time his/her complicity in the transformative project of expansion is denied. The issues and questions opened up by studies of colonial discourse, by the recent rediscovery of travel writing, and especially by Pratt's study, are provoking also in the context of American travel writing and westward expansion, where we need to address questions of authorization as well as the themes of innocence and responsibility. For example, William Goetzmann and Earl Pomeroy have shown how exploration and travel narratives have not only created the West for eastern audiences, but have also been implicated in the development of expansionist patterns and policies.[43] Frontier narratives did not simply record American expansion beyond the frontiers. They authorized, and legitimized, and were in turn generated by an expansionist history, producing the rest of America for readers and thus playing an active role in managing relationships between cultural centers and margins.

Both Pratt and Greenfield have illuminated the importance of the discursive processes and rhetorical strategies that create meaning in the realm of empire building. When focusing on the American hero, scholarship has often tended to neglect these crucial issues of textual meaning-making. Scholars have not paid enough attention to how texts authorize themselves and how rhetorical strategies create the American self as white and male, innocent and imperial—issues that become particularly significant for interpreting women's western writings.

This study aims to analyze women's western narratives within the discursive context of territorial expansion, assuming that women's accounts, like those of their male contemporaries, were implicated in expansionist processes, although in a different way than men's. Many of the women who wrote accounts of western life and travel authorized their narratives through their experiences as the wives of traders, military officers, and government officials. Thus, due to their nearness to positions of power, they were never completely innocent travelers and sojourners. However, being in proximity to power is certainly not the same as having it, and women writers often took complex and ambiguous stances toward questions of power, authority, and ideology.

Other women traveled and wrote as settlers, as the wives and daughters of homesteaders, merchants, and professionals. They also came west as teachers in white communities and on Indian reservations, as missionaries, and later in the century, as field matrons on Indian reservations. In all of these roles, but especially the latter, they participated in asserting Euro-American cultural claims over different cultures and lifestyles. Women also traveled and wrote as anthropologists, naturalists, and historians—members of professional groups who increasingly affirmed their scientific authority over the American West. Thus, within the discursive frameworks of westward expansion, women were not only objects of representation and control but also participants in the exercise of control.

In this context, the comparative perspective provided by studies of gender and colonialism in European women's writing is particularly helpful. In her book *Discourses of Difference,* Sara Mills has set European women's travel narratives within the context of colonialism instead of studying them as marginal to it. She suggests that it is possible to discover the specificity of women's travel writing and also, at the same time, the elements that it shares with men's writing. Women's writing and their involvement in colonialism was markedly different from men's, with their work informed by different discursive frameworks and pressures. Because of the way that discourses of femininity circulated within European cultures, Mills argues, "women travel writers were unable to adopt the imperialist voice with the ease with which male writers did" (3). I would add that women's access to the imperialist voice is even more complicated by their potentially limited access to the knowledge necessary to produce imperialist statements. As Mills suggests, it is in their struggle with the discourses of imperialism and femininity, "neither of which they could wholeheartedly adopt, and which pulled them in different textual directions, that their writing exposes the unsteady foundations on which it is based" (3).

Thus the differences between men's and women's writing can be seen as resulting from a range of discursive pressures on both production and reception, which female writers had to negotiate differently than male writers. The women travelers whose writings Mills analyzes "constructed their texts within a range of power nexuses: the power of patriarchy which acted upon them as middle-class women, through discourses of femininity: and the power of colonialism which acted upon them in relation to the people of the countries they describe in their books" (18). It is the convergence and conflict of these power systems, she claims, that determine the style and content of women's writings, which Mills sees as "textual constructs emanating from a range of discourses in conflict" (20).

Within the context of territorial expansion, American women's narratives of travel, contact, and settlement in the American West can be seen engaging with discourses of femininity and of empire building and colonization, which are at least partially indebted to the rhetorical conventions informing what has been called (European) colonial discourse. In fact, once the American West is defined as a cultural contact zone, what has been innocently termed the "frontier experience" manifests itself as a prototypical colonial situation, characterized by "the domination imposed by a foreign minority, 'racially' and culturally different, over a materially weaker indigenous majority in the name of a racial (or ethnic) and cultural superiority."[44]

Of course, talking about nineteenth-century America in terms of colonialism has its obvious pitfalls, considering that the master narratives defining the American national identity draw on the rhetoric of liberation and emancipation from English colonial oppression. Moreover, the history of white colonization in North America does not, at least not consistently, follow the classic colonialist pattern of a foreign minority ruling and extending its laws over an indigenous majority. However, as revisionists of the frontier myth have shown, the figure of the innocent American Adam in the New World garden, rebelling against Old World convention, implicitly asserts his own version of imperial control and draws on the notion of a savage Indian other for his own self-definition. American narratives of discovery, exploration, and travel, in describing and interpreting white Euro-American presence in the unfamiliar world of the American West, establish their own American version of colonial discourse that can assume various rhetorical forms, whether drawing authority from the objectivist claims of science or from the privileging of personal aesthetic experience.[45]

part 1

Surveyors of the Terrain, 1830–1860

Recent research on frontier women's history has shown that Euro-American white women were present in all phases of American expansion to the West. True, it was men who took the lead as explorers and trail blazers, and men, more often than not, who made the decision for their families to move west. Men mined gold and other mineral resources, built railroads, ordered and fought wars against tribal people, and designed policies to contain them on reservations. But women, white and non-white, were there on all frontiers. Moreover, white, literate women wrote copiously in, on, and about the western frontiers—in letters and diaries, travel and settlement narratives, reminiscences and autobiographies, and poems, stories, and novels.

Among those who in the 1830s began writing books about their travels and experiences as settlers in the American West were Englishwomen Frances Trollope and Harriet Martineau, who explored and mapped American society, including its western fringes, for European readers.[1] They were succeeded by other European women travelers such as Fredrika Bremer, Ida Pfeiffer, and Isabella Bird. In 1833, the American Mary Austin Holley recorded the first stage of settlement in Stephen Austin's Texas colony in a work entitled *Texas,*[2] a promotional account of the author's visit in 1831. In 1839, Caroline Kirkland published *A New Home— Who'll Follow? Or, Glimpses of Western Life* under the pseudonym of "Mrs. Mary Clavers, An Actual Settler." Two years earlier she had moved with her husband and children to a new settlement in Michigan, which did not take favorably to being the obvious model for Mrs. Clavers' fictional frontier settlement: although hailed with enthusiasm by eastern readers, the book created an outcry among Kirkland's neighbors, who objected to having become the unwitting objects of her satire. Nevertheless, it was followed in 1842 by *Forest Life,* in which Kirkland responded to the controversial reception of her first book by shifting the perspective of her writing: the eastern outsider had become a western insider. None of this sort of corrective seemed to have been necessary for Eliza Farnham, who reconciled the two positions in *Life in Prairie Land* (1846), an account of settling in Illinois in the late 1830s.

Most of these early works stretched the generic conventions of travel writing by accommodating new modes of writing—narrative forms that anticipated the increasing numbers of regionalist and local-color stories appearing after the Civil War. American women also wrote in the more conventional variety of travel writing, as tourists, and in fact the 1840s seem to have been the decade of women travelers who followed an almost-canonical tourist itinerary.[3] This itinerary led women from New York to Niagara Falls and the Great Lakes, then through Michigan and/or Wisconsin onto the prairies of Illinois and Indiana, and then back to the East.

One of these female tourists, Eliza Steele, published her view of *A Summer Journey in the West* in 1841. She was followed by Catherine Stewart, who traveled extensively in Michigan and Illinois for more than a decade. In 1843, Stewart published, with obvious reference to Kirkland's *New Home,* an exuberant *New Homes in the West.* In 1844, Margaret Fuller's *Summer on the Lakes* appeared. At the same time, in Canada, the 1830s saw the publication of Catharine Parr Traill's narrative of settlement, *The Backwoods of Canada* (1836), followed two years later by Anna Jameson's *Winter Studies and Summer Rambles in Canada,* the travel narrative of an adventurous Irishwoman who had come to live in Canada. Traill's sister Susanna Moodie produced *Roughing It in the Bush* (1852), a settlement and travel narrative that has become one of the classics of Canadian literature.

chapter 1

Traveling and Settling on the Prairies

Some of the texts about regions east of the Mississippi and published in the 1830s and 1840s provide important parameters for many of the later texts dealing with the trans-Mississippi frontier. The sheer volume in these years of women's published writings about the western frontiers proves that women took part in developing the narrative paradigms that made traveling and settling on the American frontiers writable and readable. Many more women wrote private letters, diaries, and reminiscences that were never published but were read by family and friends. Some of these texts, like the letters and diaries of the Oregon missionaries Narcissa Whitman, Eliza Spalding, and Mary Richardson Walker, were part of a public discourse in the eastern United States about Indian mission activities and white settlement in Oregon, as well as about the significance of white women's presence in the "wilderness." Other private texts draw their significance from the exclusivity of private communication over long distances of space and time.

The way that many female writers of western travel narratives described their work suggests that various discursive constraints and pressures influenced the production and reception of their texts, leading to the divisions of labor between male and female writing proclaimed by authors of both sexes. Frances Trollope, in her book *Domestic Manners of the Americans,* purports to restrict her observations in the western part of America exclusively to the study of "the influence which the political system of the country has produced on the principles, tastes, and manners of its domestic life." What she explicitly excludes and leaves to "abler pens" is "the more ambitious task of commenting on the democratic form of the American government." Yet, while professing disinterest in the area of politics, her aim is nevertheless political: by aiming to faithfully describe everyday, ordinary life in America, she also attempted to show "how greatly the advantage is on the side of those who are governed by the few, instead of the many" (v).

Trollope also defines her work in opposition to that of her predecessor and countryman Basil Hall, whose *Travels in North America* was published in 1829. Whereas Hall "saw the country to the greatest possible advantage . . . in full dress" and "had certainly excellent opportunities of making himself acquainted with the form of the government and the laws," she herself was involved in "the ordinary working-day intercourse of life (222–23). In a country in which, as Trollope repeatedly observes, the separation of the sexes is so striking, women seem to have no access to political life and stand apart in a world of their own.

Trollope's belittling of her "gossiping pages" (64) can be identified as part of a tradition of apologia in women's writing. She declares herself incompetent to judge American political institutions, but if she should occasionally touch upon these issues as they meet her "superficial glance," this will be done "in the spirit and with the feeling of a woman, who is apt to tell what her first impressions may be, but not apt to reason back from effects to their causes. Such observations, if they be unworthy of much attention, are also obnoxious to little reproof" (66). By speaking the language of the powerless, Trollope simultaneously claims the power of marginality assigned to women, defining it as a position of irresponsibility and innocence:

> All the freedom enjoyed in America, beyond what is enjoyed in England, is enjoyed solely by the disorderly at the expense of the orderly; and were I a stout knight, either of the sword or of the pen, I would fearlessly throw down my gauntlet, and challenge the whole Republic to prove the contrary; but being, as I am, a feeble looker-on, with a needle for my spear, and 'I talk' for my device, I must be contented with the power of stating the fact, perfectly certain that I shall be contradicted by one loud shout from Maine to Georgia. (148)[1]

American women writers of western travel and settlement narratives follow a similar strategy of feminine understatement. Caroline Kirkland describes the concerns of her writing in *Forest Life* as "the very ordinary scenes, manners and customs of Western Life. No wild adventures,—no blood-curdling hazards,—no romantic incidents,—could occur within my limited and sober sphere. No new lights have appeared above my narrow horizon. Commonplace all, yet I must tell it" (10). In the process, she defines the parameters of her work—in opposition to male writing in the adventurous mode—as following the ethnographic, or rather sociographic, mode of a "manners-and-customs" narrative.[2] "'Tis true," Kirkland's narrator confesses in *A New Home*, "there are but meagre materials for anything which might be called a story. I have never seen a cougar—nor been bitten by a rattlesnake." The reader is therefore asked to expect "nothing but a meandering recital of common-place occurrences—mere gossip about every-day people, little enhanced in value by any fancy or ingenuity of the writer, in short, a very ordinary pen-drawing; which, deriving no interest from colouring, can be valuable only for its truth" (3).

In *Forest Life,* Kirkland suggests that a woman writer can choose neither the form nor the topic of her writing: "Politics and statistics are work for wiser heads, and abler hands, and more extensive information. But views of society have been thought to come legitimately within the feminine province, and for this purpose the humblest form has been adopted" (2:232). Like Trollope, Kirkland defines her work as marginal by professing to present "only rambling impressions, not a sober view, the result of deliberate and discriminating judgment." Invoking what she calls women's "precious privilege of irresponsibility," she relates the style of her writing to her marginality as a woman, thus claiming, like Trollope, its subversive power (14).

Most nineteenth-century women's travel and settlement narratives were published in occasional forms such as letters and journals. Kirkland's introduction to *A New Home* is paradigmatic for the almost-conventional disclaimers in women's writing to autonomous and public authorship: "Our friends in the 'settlements' have expressed so much interest in such of our letters to them, as happened to convey any account of the peculiar features of western life, and have asked so many questions . . . [that] I have determined to give them to the world, in a form not very different from that in which they were originally recorded, for our private delectation" (7–8). Of course, this epistolary form of travel writing is not restricted to women's writing but is assumed by male travel writers as well.[3]

Nevertheless, women writers of the 1830s and 1840s could use these disclaimers strategically to authorize their texts. Thus, although Anna Jameson's "little book" (published in three volumes, containing more than a thousand pages!) was "never intended to go before the world in its present crude and desultory form," it derives its authority from the exceptional status of a woman's travel experience: "While in Canada, I was thrown into scenes and regions hitherto undescribed by any traveller . . . and into relations with the Indian tribes, such as few European women of refined and civilised habits have ever risked, and none have recorded" (iv).

However differently these women writers may stake the boundaries of their literary terrain, all profess to distance themselves from politics and statistics—defined as explicitly unfeminine practices—as well as from imperial visions of adventurous enterprise. Moreover, they present their writings as decidedly personal narratives, framed by a subjective and necessarily limited vision. This restriction to the personal is, of course, linked to the epistolary and journalistic forms in which the narratives are presented.

The concern with the personal, the domestic, and the quotidian has been regarded by scholars as the characteristic aspect that distinguishes women's from men's travel writing. As Catherine Stevenson has argued, both the circumstances of women's travel (they seldom traveled on official business), and the narrative structures in which they cast their journeys, point to basic differences in men's and women's writing. Furthermore, most scholars infer that female travel writers are less openly implicated in a colonial context.[4] In general, Marion Tinling claims in *Women into the Unknown*, women show less interest in politics and the introduction of European ideas and technology than do men; they are, so to speak, the anthropologists of everyday life: "They observe more closely the rhythm of daily life—birth, marriage, child-rearing, death, and household economy. These matters, so much a part of everywoman's life, are basic and universal, enduring through all political changes" (xxiv–xxv). Jane Robinson suggests that women writers left the facts and figures of foreign travel to the men and dwelt instead on the personal practicalities of getting from A to B, and on their personal impressions.[5]

However, personal narratives and the privileging of the personal aesthetic mode of narration, which often masks histories of conquest, have also been significant factors in the representation of the American West for Euro-American audiences. As Michel Foucault has suggested, the epistolary and autobiographical forms that emerged in the eighteenth century can be seen as part of what he calls a new "economy" of power, "procedures which allowed the effects of power to circulate in a manner at once continuous, uninterrupted, adapted and 'individualised' throughout the entire social body."[6] Before privileging the personal and private as the characteristic representation of women's perspectives, we should consider that confessional forms such as diary and letter writing function as culturally sanctioned expressions of individualism in Western cultures.[7] Consequently, Sara Mills, in *Discourses of Difference,* proposes that women's travel writing "can be seen as a response to disciplinary pressure, tending to exhibit a concern with displaying the 'self' " (19).

Traveling and writing actually empowered women who at home were intellectually and experientially excluded from the world of politics, but then found themselves at the center of intense political activity.[8] Regardless of their professions of self-restriction, traveling and writing authorized women as the possessors of exotic knowledge and experience. Moreover, because the travel narrative is a mixed genre, "offering hard facts about geography, history, botany, zoology, medicine, and ethnology,"[9] it is difficult to imagine that these writers did not have to transgress the boundaries outlined in their writings.

I agree with Sara Mills that women's travel writing, although generally not given authoritative status or considered a substantial source of knowledge in the context of colonial expansion, nevertheless adds "to the affirming and contesting of knowledges about the empire," since women travel writers are "caught between the conflicting demands of the discourse of femininity and that of imperialism" (21). In *Imperial Eyes,* Mary Pratt points to the same implication of women's travel writing in the colonialist and expansionist enterprise, arguing that by the nineteenth century, women's travel writing emerged "to create specifically female relationships to North European expansionism, a female domestic subject of empire, and forms of female imperial authority in the contact zone" (170).

Some of the women's travel narratives considered in the following chapters have already been discussed by Annette Kolodny in terms of how they project alternative paradigms upon western landscapes. The goal of this study is to show that these narratives can also be read within an expansionist context as narratives of the contact zone. What happens when women write in/on the contact zones of frontiers, where they are simultaneously part of an expansionist enterprise and members "of that group itself most thoroughly colonized by patriarchal 'civilization'"?[10] Susan Hardy Aiken has engaged this issue in her study of the writer Isak Dinesen, assuming that even a woman who consciously seeks to ratify the claims of the patriarchal/colonial system "must at the very least position herself differently than a man, must engage in a more complicated process of rationalization and self-construction in order to identify with its dominant ideologies" (28–29). Aiken asks us to consider the import of the woman writer's double positioning as at once subject and object within the imperialist frame of reference (38–39).

Comparisons between American westward expansion and European colonialism in Africa and Asia, and between American and European women travelers on the frontiers and in the colonies, should be made with caution, since American national self-definition has traditionally rested on the unresolved contradictions between the struggle for independence from colonial domination and the quest for imperial power.[11] Nevertheless, such comparisons show how the American rhetoric of westward expansion is, in a more global sense, part of Western colonialist discourses.

Mills points out that considering women's travel narratives within colonial contexts as emanating from a range of discourses in conflict "enables us to see oppositional forces at work in colonial texts." Thus, what are generally regarded as limitations on women's writing "can in fact be seen to be discursively productive, in that these constraints enable a form of writing whose contours both disclose the nature of the dominant discourses and constitute a critique from its margins."[12] The same argument can be applied to American women's western writings, once they are set within the framework of an expansionist history.

Caroline Kirkland and the Mapping of Social Space

When Kirkland's *New Home* was published in 1839, reviewers read it as a realistic text, although Westerners objected to Kirkland's often-satirical portrayals.[13] In contrast, the eastern press hailed the book as original, without "the usual trimmings" of romance, at last giving "some reality to [American] fiction." Edgar Allan Poe praised the book especially for its "truth and novelty" and for the "fidelity and vigor that prove[d] her pictures to be taken from the very life."[14]

Kirkland's description of her narrator's journey to the new village of Montacute and her new life as a western settler deliberately deflates the expectations produced by male narratives of western adventure. The journey to Michigan is cast as decidedly uneventful save for "one night passed in a wretched inn," which "was not without its terrors, owing to the horrible drunkenness of the master of the house, whose wife and children were in constant fear of their lives, from his insane fury" (7). For most of the journey, however, the female traveler has to revise the notions gleaned from men's travel narratives:

> When I first "penetrated the interior" (to use an indigenous phrase) all I knew of the wilds was from Hoffman's tour or Captain Hall's "graphic" delineations: I had some floating idea of "driving a barouche-and-four anywhere through the oak-openings"—and seeing "the murdered Banquos of the forest" haunting the scenes of their departed strength and beauty. But I confess, these pictures, touched by the glowing pencil of fancy, gave me but incorrect notions of a real journey through Michigan. (6)

Kirkland's narrative also runs counter to male notions of empire building. When Mrs. Clavers' husband takes a tour with other male guests of a Detroit hotel, "with a view to the purchase of one or two cities" (25), the deflationary tone used to describe this "adventurous enterprise"—which obviously refers to Washington Irving's *Tour on the Prairies* (1835) and Charles F. Hoffman's *Winter in the*

West (1835)—makes it clear the venture will fail. Upon their return, the tired men are silent: "No word of adventures, no boasting of achievements, not even a breath of the talismanic word 'land,' more interesting to the speculator of 1835–6 than it ever was to the ship-wrecked mariner" (26). They had bought land after having seen "reflected in the now glassy wave the towers and masts of a great commercial town" (28), only to find that they had "staked their poor means on strips of land which were at that moment a foot under water" (31).

By using satire in a novelistic manner, Kirkland was able to critique an imperial, "improving" vision, which she portrays as explicitly male and naive. This mythic vision is not only stimulated by land speculators but underscored and reproduced by travel narratives like Captain Hall's *Travels in North America* (Kirkland possibly also refers to Judge James Hall's *Legends of the West* of 1832) and Charles Hoffman's *Winter in the West*. Such "elegant sketches of western life" only delude female readers like the narrator herself:

> The circumstance of living all summer, in the same apartment with a cooking fire, I had never happened to see alluded to in any of the elegant sketches of western life which had fallen under my notice. . . . I had, besides the works to which I have alluded, dwelt with delight on Chateaubriand's *Atala,* where no such vulgar inconvenience is once hinted at; and my floating visions of a home in the woods were full of important omissions . . . The inexorable dinner hour, which is passed *sub silentio* in imaginary forests, always recurs, in real woods, with distressing iteration, once in twenty-four hours, as I found to my cost. And the provoking people for whom I had undertaken to provide, seemed to me to get hungry oftener than ever before. (83–84)

In *Winter in the West,* Hoffman represented Michigan as a playground for the traveler who likes to "plunge . . . into the wilderness" (167) and exults in hunting wildlife in the "garden of the Union" (139). It is a place where growth is attained "from almost nothing" (155), a tempting field for speculation: "in a country where you may drive a barouche-and-four for hundreds of miles in any direction through the woods, the expense of constructing more artificial ways will be comparatively trivial" (183). These and similar passages reveal that Hoffman indulged in personal fantasies of a garden and also claimed the truth-value of his observations by virtue of personal experience. Kirkland sets her own narrative apart from such male literary practices, not only criticizing the celebration of the West as "Nature," but also, as Zagarell notes in her introduction to *A New Home,* exposing male representations of the West as inherently indebted to androcentric romantic conventions, whether French, British, or American (xxvii).

To be sure, scholars have also criticized Kirkland's own efforts to create an alternative West as being equally marred by "obvious efforts to impose conventional plots on Western material."[15] Henry Nash Smith has seen the "contradictions between her high-flown theory and her instinctive revulsion from the crudities of backwoods Michigan . . . reflected in her vain struggle to find a satisfactory literary form."[16] Only since the 1970s has Kirkland (again) been accorded the status of a pioneer realist, and feminist scholars have shown that Kirkland explicitly drew on a woman's perspective to take popular representations of western life to task and to reveal the consequences of life in the West for women settlers.[17] But Kirkland's realistic strategy, I would argue, was as much indebted to the generic conventions of the travel narrative as it served to authorize the special perspective of a woman's text, and the tension between the two discursive strains makes *A New Home* a rather complex text. Although Kirkland's claim to truth is based on the authority of personal experience as an "actual settler," she consistently undermines her narrator's authority by making repeated references to her marginality as a woman, and just as importantly, by invoking humor and self-mockery.[18]

Kirkland's West is a social space in which different classes of settlers interact, and power relations, based on differences of class and gender, are set in motion. Class-based definitions of womanhood and standards of domesticity—the establishment of a middle-class home in the West—form the centers around which these power relations revolve. Houses and their interiors, standards of domestic comfort, and manners (especially table manners) provide important indicators for the cultural "domestication" of an eccentric West that defines itself by its rhetoric, but not its practice, of egalitarian democracy. Here, the domestic can be read not only as the basis for a female countervision to male fantasies of conquest and possession, but as in fact complementary to them: the ideal of domesticity, read in a context of empire building, also functions as an instrument for imposing cultural and social control and order upon the "disorderly" classes of the West.

As Sandra Zagarell has pointed out, the difference between Kirkland's model (Mary Russell Mitford's sketches of village life) and her own material was that she was not writing about an established village and culture but about the creation of both.[19] Kirkland's book is about a complex process of community building, about a society in the making, always in flux and formed by disparate populations. The phases of frontier development, described by Frederick Jackson Turner as successive phases, are played out as conflicts and accommodations between heterogeneous groups: the first-comers, unlettered individualistic farmers and woodsmen, described by Kirkland as "indigenous" settlers or "natives," are followed by a new wave of eastern immigrants whose middle-class values align them with the genteel culture of the Northeast—town planners, real estate brokers, lawyers, men of capital—a heterogeneous group in itself. Moreover, as the role of American Indians seems to have been taken over by white, lower-class "natives" or "indigenous" settlers, these groups play out the scenario of westward expansion as a contest between classes and cultures in a contact zone where the history of racial conflict has already been suppressed or sublimated.

In *A New Home,* Kirkland's narrator, a lettered, cultivated middle-class member of the second wave of immigrants, defines herself through, or in contrast to, her various others—simple rural folk, greedy land speculators, and upper-class gentility. Her positioning is flexible, however, as she experiences the changes associated with participating in community and culture formation, the central action of her narrative. Mary Clavers' others are not held in her gaze but speak in their own western vernacular; her observations are rendered playfully through the medium of novelistic story-telling. Voice is privileged over vision, narrative over description. But even if the others speak in Kirkland's seemingly multivocal text, they speak under the direction of a narrating subject who ironically defines herself as powerless, who mocks and satirizes herself, and who assumes no control over her rambling, associative, digressing fragments of a story.

Henry Nash Smith has described the structure of Kirkland's

book as "extremely simple. She writes as if she were keeping a travel diary in which, as a cultivated outsider, she makes notes concerning the natives of a strange land. The form is that which comes naturally to the first explorers of a new area."[20] Kirkland's book is much more complex than Smith suggests, however, due in part to the dynamic relation between self-representation and the representation of others.

In the first chapters, the Clavers family present a comic picture as eastern tenderfeet in "the woods." In symbolic anticipation of the reversal of social hierarchies, they repeatedly have to rely on the help of exotic frontier figures. The narrator casts herself as an innocent wearing inappropriate paper-soled shoes, picking flowers, and enduring hardships connected with frontier "accommodations" (or, rather, the lack of any). Satirizing an eastern-based vision of the West as unspoiled nature, at the same time Kirkland establishes the existence of an indigenous western culture[21] and dramatizes the narrator's dependence on local knowledge.

It is true that Kirkland exposes pastoral conventions as inadequate for writing a western narrative, especially from a woman's viewpoint. Nevertheless, she explicitly refers to the pastoral tradition in European literature; what is more, she writes from within the conventions of the European pastoral, quoting Shakespeare, Bacon, and others, and drawing on a fund of cultural knowledge that she claims to share with her readers. This seeming indebtedness to European literary conventions has led Henry Nash Smith to conclude that Kirkland failed to find an adequate form for her western materials. Lacking a coherent literary tradition embodying egalitarian assumptions, the only form available to her, he argues, was the sentimental novel, permeated by the assumptions underlying the class structure of English society.[22] However, the European pastoral upon whose conventions Kirkland draws—she writes about "mistresses and maids," "fair hostesses," and "masters" of "mansions" in the woods—implies its own critique: the romantic cult of pastoral simplicity, in its scenario of reversed social hierarchies, playfully critiques social conventions as artificial and constraining. The reader anticipates the (temporary) reversal of social hierarchies as well as the figure of an innocent hero as part of its conventions; the self-mockery of the city dweller as an innocent in the "wilderness" serves to expose the artificiality of urban life.[23]

Yet even if Kirkland does dramatize her narrator's interaction with frontier settlers in terms of a pastoral scenario in which rough and humble peasants share their food and bed with the cultured metropolitan, she also shatters one of its conventions: the masking of relations of power and of economic dependencies. Kirkland's travelers pay a high price for the hospitality of the backwoods settlers. Her travelers and settlers do not interact on equal terms in a romance of reciprocity: while the settlers draw on republican assumptions of equality, the eastern newcomer expects relations of service and dependency: Mrs. Clavers' first problem related to dwelling on the frontier is "procuring a domestic" (38).

Although the eastern woman's expectations are frustrated, her basic assumptions about social hierarchies, presumably shared with her readers, remain in place. Western people's belief in social equality is mocked as pretentious (39). The eastern woman's apparent acceptance of this egalitarianism occurs on the same level—as a theatrical act.

> You may say any thing you like of the country or its inhabitants: but beware how you raise a suspicion that you despise the homely habits of those around you. . . . It would be in vain to pretend that this state of society can ever be agreeable to those who have been accustomed to the more rational arrangements of the older world . . . I must insist, that a greasy cook-maid, or a redolent stable-boy, can never be, to my thinking, an agreeable table companion. (52–53)

In Mrs. Clavers, Kirkland has constructed the subject of a newly emerging middle-class in the "woods." Her narrator defines herself in opposition to the laboring class of settlers (significantly represented as shunning labor for others), valuing industriousness, but veiling her own implication in the western commercial enterprise: Mr. and Mrs. Clavers stand in opposition to greedy land speculators, forming a new class between the farmers and a moneyed elite. It is significant that the nature of Mr. Clavers' business, which repeatedly takes him away from home, is never revealed. (William Kirkland had ventured his capital in the founding and promotion of the new settlement of Pinckney.)

Distanced from the materialistic and utilitarian spirit of the egalitarian frontiersmen and -women, the middle-class family has at the center of its value system the home, an appreciation for domestic comfort, taste, and beauty, and the woman who defines herself through the domestic chores she does not do: washing, cleaning, or performing domestic labor for others. The narrator represents herself in opposition to the women who are expected to perform these tasks for her, mocking the frontierswomen's pretensions to a concept of womanhood they cannot represent. Eccentric and unruly, these women smoke and spit, drink their tea from the spout of their tea pots, and dress in outlandish costumes. Nonetheless, the narrator must depend on the frontierswomen to initiate her into the secret laws of frontier life. The focus of the narrative soon shifts from travel to dwelling and personal exchange, home and the establishment of private space. Annette Kolodny has identified this type of emplotment as typical in women's western narratives, arguing that women writers, avoiding male assertions of a rediscovered Eden, "claimed the frontiers as a potential sanctuary for an idealized domesticity."[24]

Mary Pratt finds the same privileging of the indoor world, of the house and the private room, in travel narratives of European women in South America in the 1820s and 1830s, and relates this not to differing spheres of interest or expertise but to gendered modes of constituting knowledge and subjectivity. If the men's task was "to collect and possess everything else, these women travelers sought first and foremost to collect and possess themselves. Their territorial claim was to private space, a personal, room-sized empire." But it is also important to consider that, like Flora Tristan and Maria Graham in South America, Kirkland's narrator emerges from her home to explore her world in circular expeditions.[25] Her account is not restricted to her own domestic sphere but includes the customs and manners of her neighbors. She acquires local knowledge through personal interactions revolving around her own or others' homes—interactions marked by differentials of power and authority. Mary Pratt identifies this type of exploratory activity with the social reformism of urban middle-class women in the early nineteenth century, which as another branch of the civilizing mission "might be said to constitute a form of female imperial intervention in the contact zone."[26]

In contrast with what Pratt calls the "seeing-man" or the statistical observer, Kirkland's narrator, like her female contemporaries in

South America, avoids specialized languages anchored in expertise and seeks knowledge interactively, in participatory fashion. And yet, as Pratt observes, even as women affirm "non-industrial and feminocentric values," some also affirm European privilege. The same contradictory affirmation of class privilege occurs in Kirkland's text. On the one hand, Kirkland's narrator assumes a common bond of sisterhood between all women on the frontier; on the other, middle-class domesticity becomes a signal of class distinction and an instrument of social order. Despite social differences, women interact in relations of reciprocity, since they are dependent on each other's help: "What can be more absurd than a feeling of proud distinction, where a stray spark of fire, a sudden illness, or a day's contre-temps, may throw you entirely upon the kindness of your humblest neighbour?" In fact, middle-class women may be the most dependent of all: "And what would become of me, if in revenge for my declining her invitations to tea this afternoon, she should decline coming to do my washing on Monday?" (65).

Regardless of class, women on the frontier seem to have shared a common feeling of deprivation and exclusion from the freedom enjoyed by men. Kirkland implies that the absence of a domestic ideal on the frontier renders women powerless by denying them cultural influence, a suggestion which rests, of course, on the assumption that the middle-class ideal of domesticity does empower women. As she aims to show in *Forest Life,* equality may have been realized on the level of government and state, but within the frontier family, the patriarchal autocrat still rules uncontested, and the rhetoric of egalitarianism is nothing *but* rhetoric (123).

In both books, Kirkland's narrator speaks from the position of the doubly marginalized. Not only is she, in a patriarchal frontier culture, marginalized as a woman, but she is also cast as a member of a class that values culture and education in a world that privileges political and economic advancement. Kirkland's critique thus has not only a gendered but also a class-based edge, since the (marginalized) discourse of middle-class femininity reinforces middle-class assertions of authority. Despite her pretensions to powerlessness, the narrator of *A New Home* represents herself as instrumental in establishing middle-class values by introducing standards of domesticity among her neighbors. Assuming a voice of authority based on the superior cultural values she claims to share with her readers, she draws them into complicity, insisting that "those who find these inconveniences most annoying while all is new and strange to them, will by the exertion of a little patience and ingenuity, discover ways and means of getting aside of what is most unpleasant, in the habits of their neighbours: and the silent influence of example is daily effecting much towards reformation in many particulars." The values she shares with her readers, defined as neatness, propriety, and "that delicate forebearance of the least encroachment upon the rights or the enjoyments of others, which is the essence of true elegance of manner," only have to be "seen and understood to be admired and imitated" (53).

Those who "set forth in their own manners and habits, all that is kind, forbearing, true, lovely, and of good report" will find before long that "their neighbours have taste enough to love what is so charming, even though they see it exemplified by one who sits all day in a carpeted parlor, teaches her own children instead of sending them to the district school, hates 'the breath of garlic eaters,' and—oh fell climax!—knows nothing at all of soap-making" (53). This exemplary woman also stands apart from her neighbors through her love for flowers and gardening, occupations that nineteenth-century society considered part of the code of "true womanhood" but which these utilitarian neighbors regard as useless, since they value tasks in terms of "moneyed value" (80).[27] The appreciation of beauty and of nature, Kirkland suggests, is neither universal nor specifically gendered, but conditioned by a particular kind of education open to all classes. Nevertheless, Kirkland's representation of "indigenous" and new settlers obscures unequal relations of economic power and cultural authority between the two groups. Although the commercial middle-class helps to draw settlers into a new, capitalist market economy, Kirkland represents these relations—in the manner of an anti-conquest—as an opposition between materialistic western settlers (both men and women) and powerless, idealistic Easterners.

In Kirkland's portrayal of a western community's development, domesticity and the position assigned to women within its ideology—as preservers of tradition and as paragons of moral and spiritual values—are instrumental in asserting middle-class values against the materialistic, egalitarian claims of western "natives," quintessential specimens of the Jacksonian common man. Against her claims of a common sisterhood, the narrator depicts frontierswomen as odd individuals whose egalitarian assumptions are part of their eccentric behavior. By seeking to contain them in visions of social order, the ideal of domesticity reveals itself as the quest for the domestication of the disorderly frontierswoman.

Nonetheless, it is important that Kirkland's narrator also defines herself in opposition to another class of settlers, "refined" people of faded wealth, unused to labor, deluded by impractical visions of life in the woods, who—unlike the narrator—assume an air of unveiled superiority over their frontier neighbors (76). Thus the narrator's own positioning changes, halfway into the book, from the role of a traveler and outsider, safely rooted in the customs and manners of her eastern cultural background, to that of a seasoned dweller who now initiates other, especially "refined" women into the secret laws of frontier life. Sandra Zagarell suggests that the resulting juxtaposition of eastern and western codes of language and behavior constitutes "a major mode of cultural critique,"[28] arguing for a reconsideration of Kirkland as a sophisticated cultural critic whose outspoken satire makes A New Home unique among published works by antebellum American women.[29] In this context, Kirkland's work seems to contradict the prevalent middle-class ideology of "true womanhood," whose tenets of piety, purity, submissiveness, and domesticity are basically incompatible with satirical expression. However, as feminist historians and literary critics have shown, this ideology of domesticity did not restrict all women exclusively to the home, nor did it doom all women's writing to conventionality.[30]

Historian Nancy Cott has pointed to the peculiar and paradoxical conjunction in American history between the appearance of a cult of domesticity and the emergence of an activist feminism: American feminism, she shows, depended to a significant degree on the ideology of domesticity as a means of developing a sense of the collective importance of women and of their shared destiny.[31] Women were thus impelled to participate in crusades outside the home, using the sphere assigned to them to assert political influence in reforming American society (see chapter 5). In terms of gender conventions, Kirkland's narrative is thus unique as part of a genre basically incompatible with cultural conventions of womanhood, yet typical for nineteenth-century women's writing in the way it draws on and manipulates cultural configurations of domesticity and femininity.

In terms of class and hegemony, Kirkland's text shows that the authority of middle-class women, which historians have called "domestic feminism," rested on distinctions of class and race as much as on the difference of gender: working-class women and women of color were constitutive of the establishment of white middle-class women's claims to social authority, "whether as charitable objects or as domestic servants."[32] Recently, women's historians have called for a multicultural framework that questions the universality of the "true woman/separate spheres/woman's culture triad," and that can account for differences and power relations between women.[33] Read within these frameworks, Kirkland's *New Home* emerges as a text ambiguously positioned between cultural affirmation and cultural critique.

Women Writers and the Social Construction of Nature

In *The Land Before Her,* Annette Kolodny has argued that the most immediate impact of Kirkland's success was not that it introduced an element of realism to the literary depiction of the American West, but that it made the West available for literary treatment by women. Until the publication of *A New Home,* women writers living in the West had not used it as subject matter. After the book's enthusiastic reception, "Margaret Fuller felt encouraged to compose *A Summer on the Lakes* (1844) to stand beside Charles Fenno Hoffman's *A Winter in the West* (1835). And Eliza Farnham, befriended and encouraged by Kirkland in New York, was emboldened thereby to let her own experience of *Life in Prairie Land* (1846) compete with Washington Irving's *A Tour on the Prairies* (1835) for some share of the public's attention" (157–58). However, neither Farnham nor Fuller followed Kirkland's lead as pioneer realist but instead applied themselves to the task of reinventing the prairie West as nature. Kirkland had focused on the West as a social space, but Farnham and Fuller—like many of their male contemporaries—repastoralized it, either in images of natural abundance and agrarian civilization or as controlled wilderness. Nonetheless, this natural space is still constructed as a social space, a landscape onto which, as Kolodny has shown, domestic and familial fantasies are projected.

In *Life in Prairie Land* (1846), Eliza Farnham remembers the West as "a strong and generous parent, whose arms are spread to extend protection, happiness, and life to throngs who seek them from other and less friendly climes." In this magnificent, free, and beautiful country, all differences of "character, education, and prejudice" are resolved harmoniously, and artificial distinctions lose much of their force (iii–iv). As Kolodny has observed, Farnham projects a familial, rather than sexual, paradigm upon the land by creating the "fantasy of a landscape that might reconstitute some prior domestic community," a fantasy that, although it emphasized the spiritually uplifting impact of western nature, was "not religious but domestic."[34]

Ironically, Farnham's narrative immediately contradicts the promised loss of social distinctions in the paradisiacal West. Her account, which details her narrator's journeys to and in Illinois, her experience as homemaker in a prairie town, and her "studies" of western people, customs, and manners, is in fact framed by a man-made crisis: the economic crisis of 1837 brought about by western materialism and speculation. As in Kirkland's text, Farnham's observations of Illinois settlers and western nature are interlinked with the narrator's self-representation as a cultured participant-observer.

The narrative is compartmentalized into two modes of discourse: a serious, sentimental mode that relates to nature in terms of a universalist aesthetic experience, and a comic mode, often highlighting the eccentricity of Illinois "suckers," used to relate the narrator's adventures and experiences. The text builds its authority on the language of sentiment and the felt experience of a female recorder who defines herself in opposition to the disagreeable conditions she finds during the journey and in Illinois, some of which were "sufficient to have put to flight the sentimentality of a legion of school-misses" (22).

In her interaction with her sister, an early Illinois pioneer, the narrator presents herself as an unconventional woman who privileges the pleasures of discovery in the outdoors above the conventions of feminine behavior. Thus she wears neither gloves, sunbonnet, nor veil for fear of losing sight of "a leaf, or rock, or anything either curious or beautiful, for the sake of saving a shade of brown on my complexion" (55). Her sister's household provides an example of domesticity without domestics, where the men may enjoy more freedom of movement, but the women are not bound to their home and are able to explore their surroundings on visits to neighbors: "The equestrian of the prairies enjoys the largest liberty which falls to the lot of mortals. . . . Physical freedom is nowhere more perfect" (60). The housekeeping and farm routines in the "Prairie Lodge" are secondary; in the foreground is the West as the natural realm of social and physical freedom. Like many of her contemporaries, Farnham thus associates nature, in the tradition of romanticism, with freedom. The distinguishing feature of her text, however, is that this freedom is claimed equally for women— although not all enjoy it to the same degree.

In promoting the West to her readers, Farnham draws the link between the "superiority" of the (western) American climate and American democracy, which had become standard by the 1840s. Not even Thoreau could avoid the comparison when he argued that the American climate and geography will make "our understanding more comprehensive and broader, like our plains,—our intellect generally on a grander scale." In 1834, Daniel Drake had claimed that the "extended limits of the WEST, and the broad navigable rivers which traverse it in every direction, exert on the mind that expanding influence, which comes from the contemplation of vast natural objects," and James Hall suggested that the "majestic features of their country swelled" the ideas of western pioneers.[35]

Although Farnham's narrator projects memories of an eastern childhood and home onto the western landscape, her West is foremost a "young world" (71) in which history begins anew, a land that elicits mankind's buried energies (91). As if anticipating Willa Cather's novels, Farnham's scenario involves a land that empowers people not only to transform the land but also to realize their spiritual selves. Power is spiritualized, dissociated from human material action: "What are nations and empires the most potent, to the existence of which mind is conscious? The mightiest events of earth sink into insignificance before its own exulting sense of being. It asks no power but that which it can achieve for itself. . . . What are such reachings of the mind but a lengthening of the bonds

by which it is allied to Omnipotence?" (203–4). This spiritualization of nature keeps history and politics at bay and works in the
service of self-exaltation and self-transcendence, creating a self-
reliant, seemingly genderless American subject.

However, this philosophical discourse on nature, which echoes
American romantic thought, is somehow at odds with a personal
account that focuses on the narrator's interaction with the Illinois
settlers. The ideal West—an ennobling nature that safeguards the
narrator's physical freedom—clashes with an actual West that
never realizes its potential. Although Farnham's narrator finds
models of frontier housewives in the backwoods, and aims to convince readers that the "inherent virtues of cleanliness, order, and
self-respect are often more manifest in a simple than in a complicated style of living" (69), she nonetheless dramatizes the clash
between her own and the western settlers' values in terms of differing standards of comfort, cleanliness, and privacy: "Let the reader
figure to himself, then, the dirty house, the dirtier man, the dirtiest
woman, and the most dirtiest children . . . and the writer sitting in
the midst clad all in white of the most unsullied purity, and he will
have some faint conception of my debut in 'Sucker life'" (119). In
contrast to Kirkland's narrator, who humorously mocks herself and
anticipates her accommodation (although on her own terms) to life
in the woods, Farnham's narrator's revulsion for her hosts' culin-
ary habits and living arrangements is never undermined, but established as part of her femininity.

On the boat to Illinois she had cast herself, in a conversation
with a western farmer who had just "taken" a wife, as a supporter
of women's rights, denouncing the man's view of marriage as a
business instead of as a "moral contract" (39). Enraged at his rude
treatment of his wife, she attempts to speak on behalf of his victim,
assuming that there "is too much of the true woman in her for this
brute . . . an absolute waste of some of the fairest materials that
compose human nature to throw her away with this selfish animal" (41–42). Yet her feelings of solidarity based on the assumption of a universal sisterhood are soon exhausted: "There was no
hope for her but to settle into her slavery" (42). In the same way, her
filthy and disorderly westerner is not a true woman but "the mere
physical material of a woman, put together in a somewhat excep-
tionable style, and sadly soiled" (138). Far from being helpless

victims of poverty, one of these western women even presents a "perfect picture of self-satisfaction" in her filth (67).

In historical studies on western women, Farnham is often referred to as a feminist,[36] but her representations of western women show how her feminism is located less in an assumed sympathy for the other women than in the representation of the narrating self as an unconventional individual straining the bounds of domesticity. Thus, in describing her first homemaking experience in the West, she focuses on her "exploits"—overcoming the constraining aspects of housekeeping—as well as on the excursions that exemplify the potential for women's physical freedom: "Armed with thick shoes and provided with a basket each . . . without our riding dresses, that we may not be cumbered with them when we reach the wood—away we go, free as the winds. North, south, east, or west, the way is equally open. The wild Indian, mounted on his hunting horse, has scarcely a larger liberty than we" (173).

The philosophical discourse on nature, although personalized and located in an embodied, gendered self, nevertheless de-historicizes the West. When the narrator's sister Mary tells the story of her westward move, the reader witnesses how she "plunged" with her companions into dark forests and "emerged upon the great prairie," picturing herself as surrounded by a new creation (236). Kolodny has read Mary's narrative as a revision of the Adamic frontier story that introduces a frontier couple stripped of their innocence.[37] However, although it rewrites the frontier myth in terms of gender, the story nonetheless reinforces the colonialist fantasy of an empty and uninhabited land. Mary imagines the landscape as untouched and "unseen of any eye, save His who made it!"—a contradiction in itself, since she is the one who sees but denies seeing, interpreting the act as a human violation of sacred nature. Tribal people—the invasion of whose habitat she denies by configuring it as a new creation—only exist as traces on the land: "Then as we crossed the narrow, deep-worn trail of the dark people who had traversed it so long before us, I thought how much emotion had dwelt here." Further legitimating white invasion, she displaces guilt onto the native inhabitants: "In imagination, I could still see files of dark warriors stealing silently along, unmindful of the flowers and the bright skies, the gay birds and the happy creatures who reveled in the rich world of vegetation around them; intent only upon the fierce butchery to which they were marching" (237).

In addition, westward expansion is naturalized by general statements on the inevitable course of white settlement. The "western farmer" embodies the restlessness and freedom destroyed by the "thrifty growing estates of his Yankee neighbors," a freedom that has "fled to the untenanted plains beyond, and thither he must follow it." Not a builder, he "must be ever moving, ever in the van of civilization, pressing hard upon the Indian" (200). Like a later figure, the cowboy, he "journeys on, always toward the setting sun, for he knows that freedom such as he seeks had retreated thither." But it seems impossible to imagine him without social ties; the westward movement, although located in an iconic "he," is engendered as a movement of families. The women of this class share the men's love of freedom: "They love the anticipation of making a new home on the brow of the remote wilderness, and living there, with half the careless ease of the Indian and more than his happiness. Their minds exult in the boldness and freedom of those enterprises which demand little practical detail" (329). Nevertheless, it is men who are imagined as the first pioneers in a gender-neutral landscape (402).

What is more, this discourse of history—focusing on the conquest and taming of a wilderness but figuring the process as an innocent, harmonious coexistence—can only exist apart from the rest of the narrative, which foregrounds and depends on the discourse on nature, represented as an already contained middle landscape between wilderness and culture. Indigenous inhabitants are not only dislocated from their habitat—the "untenanted plains"—but are also moved out of history: the course of history is embodied in the western farmer.

Still, the narrator admits that the story of the Indian "is a melancholy one. I have often pondered upon it, with a sympathy that would not be hushed by the voice of reason; though it proclaimed that they had fulfilled their mission and must pass away." Negotiating between sympathy and manifest destiny, the narrator thus joins the chorus of voices that, as Lee Mitchell has shown, expressed ambivalence about the human cost of American westward progress in the nineteenth century. Ultimately, however, national destiny proves to be stronger than personal sympathy, and nature and reason are equally invoked to legitimize white westward expansion. Thus the voice of reason proclaims that a "fair land abounding in all that would contribute to the highest condition of civilized life, was the lawful estate of civilized man; and when he came to claim it, it was not the office of the savage to dispute his right." In the end, the narrator mourns not the fate of the Indian but the "indecent, the fraudulent precipitancy with which it was consummated by our selfishness. We had room and time enough to have waited more patiently, while Nature was finishing in her own way the plan she had begun" (345–46). By relegating responsibility for the fate of tribal people to the plan of "Nature" rather than to human action and accountability, the female vision of westward expansion reveals itself as another, more sentimental version of the anti-conquest.[38]

When traveling over the western prairies in 1840, Eliza Steele likewise envisions them as a new world. Although A Summer Journey in the West foregrounds the West as social space, a world of flourishing, prospering new towns and villages, her references to the scientific discourse of natural history—which configures western nature as a theater of natural forces, empty of human presence—emphasize that the region is simultaneously the realm of nature. This discourse of science is, however, accessible only by being linked to a theological narrative that represents nature as God's ongoing creation.

Steele's text points to the conjunction of religious and scientific discourses in the legitimation of westward expansion: "Why should we stop at second causes in considering the origin of prairies? . . . The Almighty mind . . . in his wisdom, foresaw the time would come, when the exhausted soil, and crumbling institutions, and crowded homes of the old world, would require a new field for its overgrown population, and held this world perdu beneath the ocean caves until the fitting moment." When its hour had come, this world "arose fresh and blossoming from the sea. . . . Now is not that a pretty theory?" (137). Steele presents her views playfully as a "pretty theory" and not as uncontested truth; neither does her religious belief contradict what offers itself to her as scientific knowledge. Rather, the discourse of natural history is continuously invoked in order to support religious and aesthetic beliefs. This confirms Barbara Novak's description of how, in the first half of the nineteenth century, science, art, and religion came to be regarded as parallel, mutually reinforcing modes of knowledge: "Nature's truth as revealed by art, could be further validated by the disclosures of science, which revealed God's purposes and aided the reading of His natural text. At mid-century, landscape attitudes were firmly based on this unity of faith, art, and science."[39]

In her reading of scientific explanations as proof of providential creation (137), Steele is obviously attracted to this conjunction. Like Farnham, she invokes a scenario of natural history and law that deflects responsibility for tribal decline away from white Americans. In this drama, "the Indian tribes were admitted into the new born world" when the mastodon's career was over, and whatever interest one may take in their fate, and however one may pity them, "we must all agree they have misused their gift. Their talent was hid, the fields were untilled, the stores of marbles and metals, and materials choice and rare, which were placed there that man might rear him a comfortable habitation, and lordly temples for his God, remained unknown in their secret deposites [sic]." The Indian, consequently, "was doomed to share the fate of the mammoth" (138).

One of the most explicit female versions of what Mary Pratt has termed the anti-conquest was formulated by another woman travel writer of the 1840s, Margaret Fuller. It has become almost a commonplace to quote Fuller's confident intention "to woo the mighty meaning of the scene, perhaps to foresee the law by which a new order, a new poetry, is to be evoked from this chaos" (21) as the most significant passage of *Summer on the Lakes* (1844). The writer describes herself as coming to the West "prepared for the distaste I must experience at its mushroom growth," but she has not come "with stupid narrowness to distrust or defame." Neither will she "confound ugliness with beauty, discord with harmony, and laud and be contented with all I meet, when it conflicts with my best desires and tastes" (21). She has come as a poet, to capture the "moods" of nature, to render visible what only a poet can see and express in terms of feeling and sympathy. Despite her focus on "seeing," however, Fuller attempts to avoid representation and the "prospects" of the travel narrative. Instead of presenting images held in her narrator's gaze, she abstracts most views into emotion and feeling.

Revisiting the topoi of travel in 1830s America—one of them Niagara Falls—Fuller brings with her the images, notions, and expectations created by the books she had read, at the same time invoking the fascination of original discovery. Thinking "only of comparing the effect on my mind with what I had read and heard" (9), the Niagara fails to impress her in the way she had thought it would: "Happy were the first discoverers of Niagara, those who could come unawares upon this view and upon that, whose feelings were entirely their own" (10). Only for a moment did she feel the sublime terror of an uncontained wilderness: "I realized the identity of that mood of nature in which these waters were poured down with such absorbing force, with that in which the Indian was shaped on the same soil. For continually upon my mind came, unsought and unwelcome, images, such as never haunted it before, of naked savages stealing behind me with uplifted tomahawks" (4–5).

Although at Niagara Fuller felt unnerved by "the weight of a perpetual creation" (3), on the Great Lakes she was able to appreciate the meeting of land and water as "a new creation" which "takes place beneath the eye" (13). In contrast, those who have come to live in this land, emigrants from New England, do not realize its aesthetic potential. Bringing with them "their habits of calculation," they regard the new scene as "a prospect, not of the unfolding nobler energies, but of more ease and larger accumulation" (14). Like many of her contemporaries, including Eliza Farnham, Fuller distinguishes between an ideal West, represented as nature, and an actual West, figured as a provincial, anti-intellectual, materialist social space.[40] This recurring juxtaposition of visions of a nonviolating relation with nature and the projection of a destructive propensity and responsibility onto western American emigrants is one of the patterns that define Fuller's female version of the anti-conquest. It enables her to create an innocent romantic subject claiming no transformative potential.

Nevertheless, Fuller appears to have been aware of the contradictory potential of transformation contained in the gendered aesthetic appropriation of the West as feminized nature: she seems to refuse to represent. She actually avoids describing the island of Mackinaw when she writes: "All looked mellow there; man seemed to have worked in harmony with Nature instead of rudely invading her, as in most Western towns. It seemed possible, on that spot, to lead a life of serenity and cheerfulness" (14–15 n). Her own (non)representation of the scenery is consciously nonappropriative, nonviolent, and non-erotic. Nature representation ideally implies a reciprocal act of seeing and being seen: "But he who has gone to sleep in childish ease on her lap . . . seeking there comfort with full trust as from a mother, will see all a mother's beauty in the look she bends upon him" (20).

Kolodny, who has drawn on psychoanalysis in her study of Fuller's text, has related these passages to Fuller's biography and sees them as the writer's attempt to recover her mother's garden.[41] These passages might also express Fuller's conviction that the ideal representation of the West requires relational, nonappropriative paradigms. The eye is important, yet not the sole provider of sensory experience, and it is embodied in a narrator who draws attention to her own physical presence: "But after I had ridden out, and seen the flowers, and observed the sun set with a calmness seen only in the prairies, and the cattle winding slowly to their homes . . . I began to love, because I began to know the scene, and shrank no longer from 'the encircling vastness' " (26). Here Fuller has not only pastoralized the prairies, but she has also avoided "naturalizing" a scene, as do many travel narratives, by erasing connotations of human habitation or blotting out the signs of human presence. Moreover, she draws attention to the way the experience of beauty and nature is culturally constructed: "It is always thus with the new form of life; we must learn to look at it by its own standard. At first, no doubt, my accustomed eye kept saying, if the mind did not, What! no distant mountains? What! no valleys?" (26).

In an excursion of a few weeks, the narrator and her female companion move in a landscape filled with signs of human presence. Along the road they encounter towns and houses, and they enjoy the hospitality of private families. Nevertheless, the land has to be imagined, almost obligatorily, as untouched nature: "We traversed the blooming plain, unmarked by any road, only the friendly track of wheels which bent, not broke, the grass" (30). And despite constant references to an aggressive, business-minded population, this West is still, at least in terms of its natural environment, part of nature's nation, an emblem for an ideal America: "I do believe Rome and Florence are suburbs compared to this capital of Nature's art" (40).

Fuller repeatedly draws attention to architecture and material culture as expressions of human relationships with nature. The house of an Englishman "seemed like a nest in the grass, so thoroughly were the buildings and all the objects of human care harmonized with what was natural" (29). In contrast, the American settlers' habitations express their owners' indifference in "the slovenliness of the dwelling, and the rude way in which objects around it were treated, when so little care would have presented a charming whole" (34).[42] Only the indigenous inhabitants of the country, who have left nothing but "traces" on the land, can be imagined as "the rightful lords of a beauty they forbore to deform" (34–35). Ironically, the prairie that impresses travelers as a landscape sculptured by an artistic natural force is actually an Indian creation, shaped by burning and human action.[43]

That the white settlers, whose progress is "Gothic, not Roman," will "obliterate the natural expression of the country" cannot be helped: "This is inevitable, fatal; we must not complain, but look forward to a good result" (35). The only way these contradictions of the West as untouched Nature and as natural abundance securing economic well-being can be reconciled is in somewhat naive utopian images of pastoralism, invoked in the service of social reform and progress: "I know not when the mere local habitation has seemed to me to afford so fair a chance of happiness as this . . . with a very little money, a ducal estate may be purchased, and by a very little more, and moderate labor, a family be maintained upon it with raiment, food, and shelter" (44). Like Farnham, Fuller weaves impersonal fantasies of social peace and personal dreams into an image of social and natural harmony: "To me, too, used to the feelings which haunt a society of struggling men, it was delightful to look upon a scene where Nature still wore her motherly smile, and seemed to promise room, not only for those favored or cursed with the qualities best adapting for the strifes of competition, but for the delicate, the thoughtful, even the indolent or eccentric" (45).

Margaret Fuller presented her narrative as a consciously selective account of travel. Ignoring certain conventions of the genre associated with the official status of many male travelers, she was not particularly anxious "to give the geography of the scene, inasmuch as it seemed to me no route, nor series of stations, but a garden interspersed with cottages, groves, and flowery lawns. . . . I had no guide-book, kept no diary, do not know how many miles we travelled each day, nor how many in all. What I got from the journey was the poetic impression of the country at large; it is all I have aimed to communicate" (50).

However, other conventions associated with western travel appear to have been unavoidable. After her return to Chicago, the narrative even becomes a tract on the necessity of political leadership in "this magnificent State" of Illinois (54). It is as if this narrative inevitably had to be compartmentalized into one discourse on nature and another on society/culture, each demanding a different narrative voice—one of the innocent female traveler expressing critique from the margin; the other voice that of the detached observer, seemingly objective, coming from nowhere, and assuming a position of cultural authority. Within the discourse on the future of the West, on the planning and designing of social space, the foreign immigrants who had heretofore played picturesque roles as exotic peasants become "rude foreigners," unable to govern the affairs of the new state. The discourse on nature shuns images of control, yet the political discourse emphasizes the "liberty of law, not license" (55). In her chapter on Wisconsin, Fuller even assumes the style of a guidebook writer, declaring herself pleased with urban growth, and improving the country with an economic vision she had heretofore shunned. No other discourse would have been appropriate for her stay in Wisconsin (which had attracted Kirkland's mobbish settlers)—it was "not the same world" as the one in which she had traveled before. It is only on the island of Mackinaw that she appears to have found her personal voice again, picturing herself in personal interaction with Indian women and men.

Anna Jameson's *Winter Studies and Summer Rambles* (1838) seems to have been an important reference text for Fuller, and the two women's itineraries and narrative themes are similar in many respects. Like Fuller, Jameson explicitly defends the "tone of personal feeling" pervading her account (vii). She also distances herself from objectivist discourses, arguing that for her, "no facts, merely as facts, are in the slightest degree interesting, except as they lead to some truth. I must combine them, and in the combination seek or find a result, before such facts excite either my curiosity or attention" (276). Thus she resists the idea (expressed in the nationalist rhetoric on America) "that our good and bad qualities, our virtues and our vices, depend more on the influence of climate, than the pride of civilised humanity would be willing to allow," instead preferring to believe in the necessity of moral strength in defending "the integrity of our own individual being" (28).

What is at stake in the new Canadian society, or rather, what is created in Jameson's text, is a female imperial self that can only possess itself but cannot be possessed: "I never can bring myself to admire a social system, in which the honour, rights, or happiness of any individual, though the meanest, is made to yield to a supposed future or general good." Women, she argues, have a special reason to protest against this principle of individual submission to the common good: "We are told openly by moralists and politicians, that it is for the general good of society, nay, an absolute necessity, that one-fifth part of our sex should be condemned as the legitimate prey of the other, predoomed to die in reprobation, in the streets, in hospitals, that the virtue of the rest may be preserved, and the pride and the passions of men both gratified" (112). No, she exclaims, "there is no salvation for women but in ourselves: in self-knowledge, self-reliance, self-respect, and in mutual help and pity" (118). What is constructed here is the female, autonomous subject of romantic individualism.

While the social and ideological configurations of Canada and America may differ,[44] the tropes representing Canada and America as nature are similar: woods and forests, lakes and prairies, silence and solitude, a new land in which history begins with the entrance of the white man or woman on the scene. Thus for Jameson, the Canadian wilderness is either "woods and waters" or a forest (2: 113–4). On her journey over the Great Lakes, Jameson, like Fuller, fancies herself "alone in a new-born world" (3:163). And in the solitude of the Canadian forest she perceives nature, in a similar way as Farnham's Mary, "in her first freshness and innocence, as she came from the hand of her Maker, and before she had been sighed upon by humanity—defiled at once and sanctified by the contact" (3:320).

Jameson is just as aware as Fuller of the contradictory implications of nature representation. As in Fuller's and many other women's narratives, the reader is reminded everywhere that her flights of fancy are anchored in the contained, safe space of a boat or a wagon. Thus Jameson may draw on adventurous modes when she writes that she "plunged at once into the deep forest" (2:228), but like Kirkland, she is unable to assume this adventurous mode except for the purpose of subverting it ironically: "Yes, I can well conceive what the exulting and joyous life of the hunter may be, roaming at large and independent through these boundless forests; but believe me, that to be dragged along in a heavy cart through their impervious shades . . . is quite another thing" (2:231–32).

Fuller's and Jameson's conflicted engagements with the conventions of nature representation are related to their critiques of American views of nature as a resource and an economic prospect—something hardly new in American literature. Lee Mitchell has revealed how, beginning in the 1820s, Americans became increasingly apprehensive about the devastation accompanying their activities of empire building, and many expressed their concern about massive alterations of the American landscape by attempting to preserve it in words, oil, and photographs.[45] Nevertheless, especially Fuller's refusal to fix the western landscape into visual images suggests that she attempted to revise the pastoral paradigm itself. Annette Kolodny and Susan Rosowski have read *Summer on the Lakes* as an attempt to engender the American pastoral, and Rosowski has argued that Fuller gives the conventions of transcendentalism an engendered slant.[46] Although I feel that Fuller's critique goes beyond the issue of gender, I agree that her ecocritical perspective can be identified as part of a tradition established in women's western travel narratives.

Assuming the voices of observers and commentators from the margin, women travelers criticized the destruction of the American forest and projected destructive behavior particularly on the iconic "he," the male western settler. Kirkland, in her *Forest Life,* describes "clearing" as the western settler's "daily thought and nightly dream; and so literally does he act upon his guiding idea, that not one tree, not so much as a bush, of natural growth, must be suffered to cumber the ground, or he fancies his work incomplete. The very notion of advancement of civilization, of prosperity, seems inseparably connected with the total extirpation of the forest" (43). Jameson was similarly irritated at the view of black, charred tree stumps, and she anticipates Thoreau when she argues that a Canadian settler "hates a tree, regards it as his natural enemy, as something to be destroyed, eradicated, annihilated by all and any means. The idea of the useful or ornamental is seldom associated here even with the most magnificent timber trees" (96). But neither of these women writers bemoans the destruction of an American wilderness. Rather, they see the aesthetic ideal of a middle landscape betrayed by the felling of trees or by the nonaesthetic disorder imposed on the American landscape. Instead of the primitivist admiration for untouched wilderness often found in their male contemporaries' narratives, women's texts present constructions of nature that explicitly envision the imprint of human society and order—and which, notwithstanding their engendering of the pastoral tradition, still are part of and contribute to the cultural practice of keeping at bay the guilt connected with the history of expansion and expropriation.

Kirkland and Fuller viewed the West as a mismanaged country, inviting scenarios of leadership and power. Likewise, Jameson repeatedly exults in "signs of progress and prosperity" (2:145) and imagines future vistas of "towns and cities, fields of waving grain, green lawns and villas, and churches and temples turret-crowned" in the present "boundless sea of forest" (2:171–72). She admits to beholding "in progressive civilisation progressive happiness, progressive approximation to nature and to nature's God" (2:172–73). Like Fuller, Farnham, and Steele, Jameson resorted to a divine law in order to reconcile apparently irreconcilable opposites, thus drawing on the same cultural discourses as her American counterparts, who invoked a manifest white American destiny. But then, as Jameson's text suggests, women must have a special stake in the idea of a "progressive civilization," which promises the improvement of women's social and political status.

Finally, in their postures of disinterested femininity, many of these women writers of the 1830s and 1840s obscured their narrators' (as well as their own) involvement in the economic pursuits they criticized: Kirkland and Farnham (as well as their narrators) were indirectly involved in the business of speculation as the wives of men who had capital interests in the founding and development of frontier towns. Frances Trollope never mentioned her own failed attempts, in 1827, to profit by the construction of a department store in Cincinnati, and by a venture into a western museum.[47] Moreover, all of these women's texts located themselves in a period of economic crisis and stagnation, often associated with the business of speculation. This picture of arrested growth, set against utopian images of agrarian bliss, not only reflects the sense of crisis connected with the country's future but may even have produced and reinforced a sense of the crucial importance of the nation's westward expansion beyond the Mississippi.

Gender and Race: Configurations of the Other

I suggested in the introduction that domestic and social configurations projected upon western landscapes and people—whether the cultural ideal of domesticity informing Kirkland's narrative or the less narrowly domestic, familial paradigms in Fuller's and Farnham's texts—should be read not only as female countervisions to male fantasies of conquest and appropriation but as complements to them. In the context of a national narrative of westward expansion, the ideals of domesticity and nature as social space may function, in a culturally problematic sense, as images of control set against the social and cultural disorder of the contact zone of the American West.

Images of control also appear in connection with female writers' discussions of western womanhood. Kirkland called women "the grumblers in Michigan," many of whom had made sacrifices for which they were not prepared. Almost every woman travel writer makes similar observations on western women, representing them as captives in their log cabins, but most American women's travel narratives combine these observations with lectures on the need for change in women's education. What emerges from these lectures is the program of a new womanhood—white American womanhood in a new, feminized American culture. Formulations of this new womanhood occur especially at a nexus in the texts, where the female narrators' visions of physical and intellectual expansion clash with images of discontented frontierswomen.

After drawing ideal images of social life on the prairies, Fuller admits to a great drawback, which is "the unfitness of the women for their lot." With all the disadvantages of western life, which she saw as weighing heavier on women than on men, women had fewer resources for pleasure. The problem, Fuller believed, lay in women's education: "Their culture has too generally been that given to women to make them the 'ornaments of society.' " Fuller's ideal western woman does not dance but she draws; instead of learning French, she should learn "the language of flowers," and have "strength of body, dexterity, simple tastes" (46). "To a girl really skilled to make home beautiful and comfortable, with bodily strength to enjoy plenty of exercise," she advises, "the woods, the streams, a few studies, music, and the sincere and familiar intercourse . . . would afford happiness enough" (47). What is demanded is not fashionable European imitation, but a new, more natural American elegance; however, Fuller's reduction of women's lives to a domestic ideal—"to make home beautiful and comfortable"—is ultimately at odds with what the narrator herself represents.

Farnham, who cast herself as the embodiment of a new womanhood combining outdoor exercise and the enjoyment of nature with domesticity, warned that the West held promise only for those who, like her, "delight in the perfection and beauty of the natural" (vi). Those unable to adapt to the conditions of life in the West should never think of emigrating, especially the "ladies" who are "so unfortunate as to have had their minds thoroughly distorted from all true and natural modes of action by an artificial and pernicious course of education, or the influence of a false social position." These may be the ones who will always dislike the country, "who endure the self-denial it imposes without enjoying any of the freedom it confers; who suffer the loss of artificial luxuries, but never appreciate what is offered in exchange for them" (v).

These ideas, which emphasize freedom and a more natural womanhood adapted to the West while simultaneously addressing the need for female self-control and self-denial, are repeated in many women's western travel narratives. Steele's reference to the education of "wives for the west" (179) in Benjamin Godfrey's Monticello Female Seminary reveals that the issue was a central concern for male educators as well. Women educated at the seminary, Steele claims, "saw how much better it was they should come prepared for these duties, and quite able to perform them, instead of wearing themselves out, and pining away over tasks, which, by being new, appear much more arduous than they are in reality" (178). Steele adopts the vocabulary of control that we usually associate with patriarchal authority when she declares that even ladies "bred in idleness . . . were soon . . . broken in, and sing as merrily over their wash tubs, as the other pupils" (179).

Although Jameson shared the view that many women were ill-prepared for life on the frontiers, she clearly rejected the vocabulary of control associated with women's education. Like her contemporaries, she attacked the English concept of womanhood that defined woman solely in relation to man, leaving her unfit for "the active out-of-door life in which she must share and sympathise, and the in-door occupations which in England are considered servile" (2:153). What Jameson envisioned was not an education of women for the Canadian West, but education for women. Exposing the language of power used in the context of women's education, she wrote: "I have heard (and seen) it laid down as a principle, that the purpose—one purpose at least—of education is to fit us for the circumstances in which we are likely to be placed. I deny it absolutely" (155). Education, she says, has "a far higher object . . . to develope [sic], to their fullest extent, the capacities of every kind with which the God who made us has endowed us. Then we shall be fitted for all circumstances, or know how to fit circumstances to ourselves. Fit us for circumstances! Base and mechanical! Why not set up at once a 'fabrique d'education,' and educate us by steam?" (156).

The rhetoric of domesticity in the service of visions of control, which Jameson has exposed here, becomes even more pronounced when considering gender and race issues in women's western narratives. Female travel writers of the 1830s and 1840s made their journeys in an inhabited, increasingly populated West that had been opened to white settlement through treaties and wars with Indian tribes. By 1825, the removal of Indian tribes had been decided upon as a definite policy. After the last efforts of tribal resistance in the Black Hawk War, tribe after tribe succumbed to white pressure until by 1837, nearly all of the "Old Northwest" was held by the United States.[48]

As Lucy Maddox has shown in her book *Removals,* the "Indian question"—that is, the question of whether Indians and whites could inhabit the same territory—was unavoidable in the first half of the nineteenth century and had to be confronted by anyone concerned with American history and culture. Whether or not an

American writer during this period wanted to address the question, it was almost impossible not to touch upon it in some way, and according to Maddox, the tacit assumption that there were no more Indians in mid-nineteenth-century America is a significant blind spot in most readings of nineteenth-century American literature. "We have experimented," she notes critically, "with identifying the master narratives of the nineteenth century as attempts to give discursive authority to the myths of patriarchy, of imperialism, of white racism. . . . And yet, we still haven't taken very seriously the presence of the Indians as a crucial factor in the shaping of any of these forms of American mythology."[49]

The possibility of personal encounters with Native Americans figures as a critical point in some women's accounts. When Steele traveled over the Great Lakes to Michigan and Illinois in 1840, she undertook a touristic journey along an established route. She is almost obsessed with staying within the confines of the space assigned to the traveler, particularly the female traveler, making this very clear in her comments on Jameson's travel narrative: "The scenery has been prettily described by an author of talent, Mrs. Jameson; but, as much pleased as I was with her book, I must regret she came here under such circumstances." These circumstances were not only that Jameson strayed from the path, but that she undertook this allegedly as a single woman—which gives her exploits a somewhat frivolous touch and causes Steele to warn her correspondent "against errors to which the very witchery of her genius would blind you. However passionate a desire you may entertain for the picturesque, I hope you may never leave the protection of your friends and wander in search of it alone" (112). The West may be safe for travel, but is it safe for women without male protection? And is it respectable for women to travel in the West, where they could meet Indians?

The West thus also became a symbolic space for the discussion of issues of race and gender. To be sure, in many women's travel and settlement narratives, the land seems emptied of its native inhabitants. Native Americans were replaced in Kirkland's text by new natives who invite scenarios of control and who are seen to exhibit the same traits stereotypically assigned to Native Americans: the first white settlers, uneducated and often from rural backgrounds, live in dirt and shun labor. Another category of "natives" is formed by women: the discontented, often unruly grumblers who have to be educated or "broken" for the West.

I have also noted that Native Americans appear in Farnham's and Steele's narratives within discourses of natural history as sad but necessary victims of a historical process seen to be culminating in civilization. Whether they are perceived as victims of a natural law formulated by science or a divine law formulated by religion—combined in the American rhetoric of manifest destiny as the laws of "progress" and "mission"—they are either absent as agents of history or are held accountable for their own fate on the grounds of being non-agents of civilization. Although the discourse of natural history seems only partially accessible to these women writers—only Steele makes explicit references to scientific works of natural history, and none of the writers can assume the role of the naturalist—it appears, nonetheless, in a more personalized, poetic, or religious form, in most women's narratives as a discourse on nature which relegates human agency to a marginal position.

If Native Americans ever appear within this discourse, they are naturalized as traces on the land or romanticized as an integral part of untouched nature. Thus Fuller exclaims in *Summer on the Lakes,* "How happy the Indians must have been here! It is not long since they were driven away, and the ground, above and below, is full of their traces" (39). Significantly, these traces are manufactured products of human industry, but Fuller links them to the landscape as if they were part of it instead. Interestingly, after Fuller encounters real tribal people on the island of Mackinaw, she describes them as despoilers of nature, who "left behind, on all the shore, the blemishes of their stay,—old rags, dried boughs, fragments of food, the marks of their fires. Nature likes to cover up and gloss over spots and scars, but it would take her some time to restore that beach to the state it was in before they came" (111). Fuller's reproachful look at the Indians of her day is similar to that of Thoreau, who exclaimed, "What a coarse and imperfect use Indians and hunters make of nature! No wonder that their race is so soon exterminated."[50]

By classicizing Indians of the past and distinguishing them from the Indians of the present, Fuller effectively distanced and resituated them, as Lucy Maddox has formulated it, "in a thoroughly aestheticized, spiritualized, and exoticized past." Like Thoreau, she thus denied the need to face the political and humanitarian questions raised by the current condition of Native Americans.[51] By privileging the artist's aesthetic consciousness as the sole arbiter of the Indian situation, she also silenced any commentary on the problematic history of conquest and dispossession. Similarly, Farnham invoked the Indian as a metaphor for physical freedom in nature when she compared herself, as a female equestrian, to the "wild Indian, mounted on his hunting horse," who "has scarcely a larger liberty than we."[52]

But this is only one generalized level on which Native Americans are represented in women's travel and settlement narratives. In some texts, the reader also witnesses personal encounters with Native Americans. Even in Kirkland's *A New Home,* Native Americans move in and out of the narrative on its fringes, bringing in wild berries and game to trade for money and clothing (81). The way these encounters are framed and represented, how the female narrative subject relates to this contact, and on whose terms these contacts are made are important aspects that generate meaning especially in Steele's, Fuller's, and Jameson's texts.

While Fuller imagined "savages" of the past lurking behind her at Niagara Falls, Steele's narrative reveals how Native Americans were incorporated into the tourist economy as manufacturers of souvenirs; she mentions a "shop for the sale of Indian curiosities and canes" (55). At another curiosity shop, the travelers add to their "stock of Indian bags and moccasins" (61–62). Interestingly, only native women participate in this economy of exchange; they "embroider beautifully, with beads and stained porcupine quills, upon birch bark and deer skin. These they dispose of at the shops, and to strangers at the Hotels" (62). Steele's account confirms Barbara Babcock's argument that Native American women and the things they make "become valued items of exchange, cultural brokers, and agents of change precisely because they embody a synchronic essentialism." The simultaneous rhetorical glorification in women's travel narratives of the exotic and the domestic in the imaging of Indian women may be explained, according to Babcock, as "something of a bourgeois dream of an alternative redemptive life, as well as an imagistic transformation of an unmanageable native into a manageable one."[53]

Although women's western narratives display the cultural and historical distancing that moved Native Americans out of American time, they still establish the contemporary Indian presence as an important element of the tourist experience. On Steele's journey to Niagara, a Native American woman brought the train to a stop by crossing the tracks, heedless of the engineer's bell and whistle: "the haughty princess scorned to fly before her country's foe" (53). Later, looking out from the boat at the Canadian shore, the narrator spots an Indian village and declares herself "delighted to behold a veritable Indian lodge, and to see real Indians, instead of those half civilized beings I had met at Niagara" (95–96). That these "real" Indians live in a village with a missionary church at its center does not seem incongruous but is actually an important part of the pictured scene, which is safely contained and thus can be admired and romanticized from a safe distance. What enhances the scene is that the people wear clothing that can be identified as "Indian": "Their mantles of cloth or blanket stuff, trimmed with gay colors, were gracefully thrown around them, and their ornamental leggins or moccasins glittered as they walked. How dignified is the tread of an Indian! we remarked as we passed the island" (96).

Fuller's personal encounters with Native Americans on Mackinaw Island are equally framed and distanced by the tourist situation. She had prepared herself by reading the available literature on her subject, and the way she describes her literary reading anticipates the way she read and represented her own encounters with Native Americans.[54] Thus it is important to read not only the description in which she glories in Mackinaw Island's untouched beauty, but also the passage that follows: "Some richly dressed Indians came down to *show themselves.* Their dresses were of blue broadcloth, with splendid leggings and knee-ties. On their heads were crimson scarfs adorned with beads and falling on one shoulder, their hair long and looking cleanly. Near were one or two wild figures clad in the common white blankets" (15 n, emphasis added).

The occasion of her visit is that "a large representation from the Chippewa and Ottawa tribes are here to receive their annual payments from the American government" (78). From Jameson's and Steele's narratives, we gather that far from being an idyllic island where, as Fuller insisted earlier, "Man seemed to have worked in harmony with Nature instead of rudely invading her," Mackinaw is actually a fortified town as well as an Indian mission and agency with a conflict-laden history. Although the presence of the tribes is circumscribed by their status as conquered nations, Fuller describes the situation as if she were a visitor in Indian country, interacting with her Indian "neighbors" and observing them among their "lodges." They are naturalized as part of the landscape: their "wild forms adorned it, as looking so at home in it" (81), although it is clear that they are definitely not at home, but displaced from their homes. Steele's description sums up the relations between tribal people and visitors on the island: "We visited some of the shops and laid up a store of Indian articles, which are made by these poor people and sold here" (110).

Fuller's first view of "these picturesque groups" is framed by a window; from her hotel room, she watches new arrivals set up their temporary dwellings (81–82). The domestic and the exotic are equally part of the setting, which is familiarized as a gypsy scene that would have inspired Walter Scott. The people held in Fuller's gaze, both men and women, are not silent but talk a great deal among each other. Although the narrator can neither hear nor understand them, she purports to have "a good guess at the meaning of their discourse," since they talk "with much variety of gesture" (82). But her encounters are not limited to observations from a distance, and she soon describes herself walking and sitting among them, holding communication with the women by signs.

At one point, the Indian women even participate, at least momentarily, as agents in this cultural interaction. Significantly, this encounter revolves around cultural objects. At first it seems to be governed by rules made by the narrator. She pictures the Chippewa women crowding around her, "to inspect little things I had to show them." At the center of interest are two objects defining their wearer as a white woman: a locket and a sun-shade. Her umbrella, she speculates, is probably of special interest to the women because it signals "the most luxurious superfluity a person can possess, and therefore a badge of great wealth." But her nonverbal exchange with a young Chippewa woman one morning hints at the possibility that the cultural encounter had been organized along the tribal women's, not Fuller's, rules all along: the woman borrows Fuller's sun-shade and holds it over her baby's head, a gesture which Fuller interprets as meaning to tell her: "You carry a thing that is only fit for a baby" (86). The white woman, who had seemed so much in control, has become the object of critical scrutiny.

Later, Fuller draws attention to how other white women perceived her interaction with the Chippewas. Mentioning the "hatred felt by the white man for the Indian," she adds, "with white women it seems to amount to disgust, to loathing. How I could endure the dirt, the peculiar smell, of the Indians, and their dwellings, was a great marvel in the eyes of my lady acquaintance; indeed, I wonder why they did not quite give me up, as they certainly looked on me with great distaste for it" (88). By entering into personal contact with tribal people, Fuller suggests, she transgressed the boundaries of her feminine world. The power of the gaze she had felt while framing her encounters with tribal women dissolves as a mere illusion of power, since it always seems to fall back on the woman who gazes. Consequently, she assumes again a detached, authoritative pose, lecturing on Native Americans and Indian policy in a generalizing way.

Fuller briefly raises the possibility of intermarriage as "the only true and profound means of civilization" but then abandons the idea, since it is apparently contradicted by nature, which "seems, like all else, to declare that this race is fated to perish. Those of mixed blood fade early, and are not generally a fine race" (96). There is no possibility of survival for tribal people—except in the realm of art: "ere they depart, I wish there might be some masterly attempt to reproduce, in art or literature, what is proper to them,—a kind of grandeur which few of the every-day crowd have hearts to feel, yet which ought to leave in the world its monuments, to inspire the thought of genius through all ages" (96–97). Here Fuller joins painters of landscapes and Native Americans like Thomas Cole and George Catlin, as well as naturalists like Louis Agassiz, in the reinvention of tribal cultures as archaeological objects, as prehistoric artifacts and "monuments."

With their extinction perceived as inevitable, tribal people became "a collection of skulls" for preservation in a museum while they were still very much alive and surviving as people on the margins of white culture: "We hope there will be a national institute, containing all the remains of the Indians, all that has been preserved by official intercourse at Washington, Catlin's collection, and a picture-gallery as complete as can be made, with a collection of skulls from all parts of the country" (100). Regardless of how she may have been "moved by the thought of their wrongs and speedy extinction" (101), Fuller did not want to write sentimentally about them: Native Americans had to be recognized and appropriated as original subjects for an American literature and history.

Jameson's travel book exhibits the same mixture of personal narrative and normalizing discourse full of generalized statements. Like Fuller, Jameson sees no possibility for Indian survival. What is required to solve the "Indian problem," she argues, is the impossible: cultural difference, which is naturalized in physical terms, is an insurmountable obstacle. Changing the Indians would mean to "overcome a certain physical organisation to which labour and constraint and confinement appear to be fatal" (274), or, in other words, to eradicate nature: Native Americans are moved out of history into the realm of nature, unchangeable but free.

On the island of Mackinaw, Jameson encounters "beings quite distinct from any Indians I had yet seen, [who] realised all my ideas of the wild and lordly savage" (29–30). Native Americans are represented simultaneously in terms of the exotic and the domestic, seen as part of their natural surroundings and in the context of family life (33). Like Fuller, Jameson views them through a window. Jameson's window-scene, however, reverses the relations of power involved in seeing and being seen. What I call the "darkening-of-the-window" scene is so often repeated in women's western narratives that it assumes the status of a topos. Sitting in her room, the narrator finds her windows suddenly darkened, "and looking up, I beheld a crowd of faces, dusky, painted, wild, grotesque— with flashing eyes and white teeth, staring in upon me" (42). Again the white woman finds herself the object of the exotic other's gaze.

Like Fuller, Jameson entered on repeated and lengthy discussions of the status of tribal women, and it is possibly her comments on the domestic power of Native American women that Margaret Fuller slightly discredited a few years later. "I should doubt, from all I see and hear," Jameson wrote, "that the Indian squaw is an absolute slave, drudge, and non-entity in the community, which [sic] she has been described. She is despotic in her lodge, and everything it contains is hers; even of the game her husband kills, she has the uncontrolled disposal" (75). Jameson seems to have found it strategically important—because of the light it may have thrown on her own femininity?—to assert the respectable femininity of the Native American women around her: "Generally, the squaws around me give me the impression of exceeding feminine delicacy and modesty, and of the most submissive gentleness," although, as she adds, female chiefs are "not unknown in Indian history" (78).

Despite these sympathetic portrayals, Jameson's own feminine delicacy is the main barrier to a more intimate relation with tribal people. She has to leave the room in which a treaty council is under way, because "I must needs confess it to you—I cannot overcome one disagreeable obstacle to a near communion with these people" (143). This obstacle is the people's "odour," a subject on which successive generations of women travel writers dwell with untiring repetitiveness. Nonetheless, she concedes that "a woman of very delicate and fastidious habits must learn to endure some very disagreeable things, or she had best stay at home" (144). Neither should she regard another aspect of Indian life, that is, the alleged absence of (male) clothing during a dance performance, as an affront to her feminine modesty. At least this is what Jameson suggests with characteristic feminine delicacy: "Of their style of clothing, I say nothing—for, as it is wisely said, nothing can come of nothing" (145). One could speculate that these expressions of feminine modesty achieve just the opposite of their purported effect. Instead of drawing the gaze modestly away, comments like Jameson's, repeated in a number of women's narratives, explicitly focus attention on the naked, exotic male body, titillating rather than quieting the voyeuristic impulse.

Sensationalism also guides, although in a different way, Jameson's description of an Indian dance, in which the attention is drawn to the suffering of the female spectator: "The whole exhibition was of that finished barbarism, that it was at least complete in its way, and for a time I looked on with curiosity and interest. But that innate loathing which dwells within me for all that is discordant and deformed, rendered it anything but pleasant to witness. It grated horribly upon all my perceptions" (147). When she addresses, in a more general way, the Indian question, Native Americans are normalized as natural men living in harmony with nature, but the personal narrative envisions them as practitioners of an unnatural dance. They become abnormal as soon as they are seen practicing their own culture.

A few paragraphs later, the narrator shifts again to the erotic gaze, looking at the well-formed male bodies of those who, ironically, had participated earlier in a deforming practice. As if in an aside, she mentions that "the figures of most of the men were superb; more agile and elegant, however, than muscular—more fitted for the chase than for labour, with small and well formed hands and feet" (148). One warrior in particular is even described as "a fine creature . . . like a blood horse or the Apollo" (149).

Jameson's representations of the Chippewa need to be seen in relation to the writer's self-representation. Her simultaneous presentation of them as harmless and as members of a warrior culture in need of rehabilitation is an important strategy for establishing the authority and respectability of the woman who describes them. Jameson appears intent on wiping a particular stain from the image of Indian warriors. Although later western narratives by women—especially those written by the wives of frontier army officers, such as Elizabeth Custer—reinforce the conventions of the captivity narrative by drawing attention to the rape of white women by Indian men, Jameson writes against the captivity script by claiming that "outrage against the chastity of women is absolutely unknown" (193). While these contradictory statements may be partially explained by regional and historical circumstance—Indian-white wars assume a different cultural centrality in the United States and in Canada, not to mention the increasing occurrence of military confrontations in the United States after the Civil War—they can also be related to the contexts in which these disparate statements are made. Jameson's account is obviously concerned with asserting the respectable femininity of the narrator in a situation that might be termed compromising by nineteenth-century standards of feminine propriety, thus the repeated references to the narrator's feminine delicacy. It is strategically important for her to clear the people with whom she interacts (as a single white female) of any taint of savagery.

Whereas Indian men appear as bodies in some women's narratives, Indian women mainly serve as metaphors for the discussion of women's rights. Fuller's narrator, after focusing on the women's appearance—"invariably coarse and ugly" (82)—enters on lengthy speculations on the status of tribal women, which are similar to those undertaken a few years earlier by her predecessor. Jameson had ventured the argument that "the woman among these Indians holds her true natural position relatively to the state of the man and the state of society; and this cannot be said of all societies" (300). Her explanation not only revises the stereotype of the lazy Indian hunter and the industrious Indian woman, but also casts a critical shadow on gender relations in Euro-American society: "When it is said . . . that the men do nothing but hunt all day, while the women are engaged in perpetual toil, I suppose this suggests to civilised readers the idea of a party of gentlemen at Melton, or a turn-out of Mr. Meynell's hounds;—or at most a deer-stalking excursion to the Highlands—a holiday affair; while the women, poor souls! must sit at home and sew, and spin, and cook victuals" (300–301).

Jameson repeatedly uses the non-white woman as a tool for her critical statements on women's status in white society. But in her attempt to rehabilitate the Indian woman, she is still unusually sensitive to the burden of history, a sensitivity that seems to wane progressively as the nineteenth century moves on. Thus she does not view Indian women detached from their colonial history but argues that Indian women's social status reflects historical changes in tribal economies: white contact and the subsequent introduction of new objects produced tribal economic dependence instead of self-sufficiency and also effected changes in the gendered division of labor (309).

The gist of Jameson's argument is that "the true importance and real dignity of woman is everywhere, in savage and civilised communities, regulated by her capacity of being useful; or, in other words, that her condition is decided by the share she takes in providing her own subsistence and the well-being of society as a productive labourer" (311–12). Where a woman is "idle and useless by privilege of sex, a divinity and an idol, a victim or a toy," she asks, "is not her position quite as lamentable, as false, as injurious to herself and all social progress, as where she is the drudge, slave, and possession of the man?" (312).

Fuller takes up the issues addressed by Jameson, but she gives them a different slant. Observations on women in Indian society help her to sort out the distinctions between women's domestic and socioeconomic power. "Notwithstanding the homage paid to women, and the consequence allowed them in some cases," Fuller argues, "it is impossible to look upon the Indian women without feeling that they do occupy a lower place than women among the nations of European civilization" (85). After earlier demanding that one must learn to look at every "new form of life . . . by its own standard" (26), Fuller now sets Native American women in the context of white women's concerns. They are judged, as if entirely knowable, by the standards of a white feminism that uses non-white women as foils and tools for its argument, either by assuming insurmountable cultural differences or by establishing a common bond of sisterhood. Thus Fuller discredits Jameson's argument—coming from Native American women themselves—that tribal women have great power at home, suggesting that this power "is good for nothing, unless the woman be wise to use it aright. Has the Indian, has the white woman, as noble a feeling of life and its uses, as religious a self-respect, as worthy a field of thought and action, as man? If not, the white woman, the Indian woman, occupies a position inferior to that of man" (87–88).

Some scholars have suggested that Fuller's *Summer on the Lakes* was her preparation for writing *Woman in the Nineteenth Century* (1845), in which she argues for female equality. Indeed, the representations of frontierswomen shut up in their log cabins and of Indian women at the mercy of their husbands seem to have been instrumental in the development of her position.[55] Her discussion focuses on the contradiction between women's domestic power and their socioeconomic dependence and thus formulates issues addressed, in a possibly less radical form, in women's domestic novels of the time.

The subject recurs with more or less emphasis in the western travel narratives of subsequent generations of women. One may even speculate that the theme of Native American women's status formed an integral part of women's travel narratives that helped to introduce, and often mask, feminist discussions about women's rights. The intensity with which the subject is discussed also suggests that it served as a rhetorical tool for opponents and supporters of women's rights alike.

All of the women writers discussed above, by exploring the geographies of class, race, and culture in their published writings about the western frontiers, may have staked out the territories of women's western writing for the women who followed. Their strategies of authorization, the instrumentalization of the theme of Indian women's status for their own purposes, their visions of female anti-conquests, and the way representations of western landscapes and people are intrinsically tied to the problematics of female self-representation recur in many subsequent western accounts written by women. And yet, different women on ever new and different frontiers continually had to face the challenge of writing about the West anew, confronting their own restrictions and creative possibilities in the various genres that were available to them. The next group of women writers, the diarists of the overland trails, struggled with experience, language, and representation in a way that, despite many similarities, distinguishes their western accounts from those of the highly literate women writing about the prairie West, who participated publicly in a national discussion on westward expansion.

Women on the Overland Trails

Before Caroline Kirkland wrote her first book, *A New Home,* Eliza Farnham had already found her prairie Eden blighted by the economic crisis of 1837. The same sense of crisis informed Kirkland's second book, *Forest Life,* published in 1842. Depression and unemployment had reached the Mississippi Valley, and settlers were beginning to feel crowded, as the moving population on the margins of Kirkland and Farnham's books attests. By 1839, there were at least ten "Oregon Societies" in the Mississippi Valley, and by 1840, people were looking to the Oregon and California territories as a new land of hope. The trip could even be made by families, as proved by the "first white women" to make the journey, Narcissa Prentiss Whitman and Eliza Hart Spalding, who were part of a missionary group that traveled to Oregon in 1836. In May 1839, Thomas Farnham left Independence, Missouri, as captain of the Oregon Dragoons, a group of nineteen young adventurers, upon whose ensign Eliza Farnham had embroidered "Oregon or the Grave." Once in Oregon, Farnham sponsored a petition asking the United States to annex the territory. His travel books about the Pacific region, together with the letters, reports, journals, and diaries of early visitors to Alta California in the Spanish and Mexican periods—such as James Ohio Pattie's *Personal Narrative* (1831)— shaped the image of the Pacific region as a promising but mismanaged country, and invited national intervention schemes. With the arrival in 1841 of the Bidwell party, the first emigrants to arrive overland across the Sierras, emigrant settler families began to fill up the lower Sacramento Valley.

In November 1841, the first larger California-bound group—

thirty-two men, the eighteen-year-old Nancy Kelsey, and her infant—had reached the San Joaquin Valley after a journey of trials.
In 1843, a thousand pioneers would begin the long journey west on
the trail John Charles Frémont's party was mapping. Most were
headed for Oregon, but a few were drawn to the still-mysterious
California.[1] As Kevin Starr has shown, California had been seized
by Euro-Americans imaginatively long before the United States
acquired the territory by conquest. An emigrant guide of 1845—the
year before the United States declared war on Mexico—emptied
the Pacific region of its Indian and Hispanic inhabitants, inviting
visions of a time when "those wild forests, trackless plains, untrodden valleys, and the unbounded ocean, will present one grand
scene of continuous improvements, universal enterprise, and un-
paralleled commerce." By the last days of Mexican rule, Americans had represented California to themselves as a luxuriant country awaiting correction and exploitation.[2]

As women's travel narratives about the "West" east of the Mississippi reveal, emigration further westward was viewed with ambivalence.[3] But while Margaret Fuller found her West on the island
of Mackinaw, the first exodus to Oregon had already begun, triggering a mass migration of unprecedented dimensions. Between 1841
and 1866, an estimated 350,000 men, women, and children undertook the overland journey to the Pacific territories. Neither the
perishing of the Donner party in the winter of 1846–47 nor the
1847 Cayuse Indian rebellion and subsequent killing of the Oregon
missionaries Marcus and Narcissa Whitman deterred emigrants.
When finally, in 1848, gold was discovered near Sacramento, there
was no staying of the tide.[4]

Women's participation in this mass migration is described in
men's and women's journals, diaries, letters, and reminiscences
focusing on the overland journey. As women writing domestic
novels explored female resistance against emigration to the Far
West,[5] female emigrants filled thousands of pages with accounts of
their westward journeys. Lillian Schlissel and others have noted
that no other event of the century except the Civil War evoked as
many personal accounts as the overland trails. Men, women, and
even children kept diaries and felt that for this one moment in
time, they were making history. This awareness is reflected in the
large number of personal accounts and the way diaries were kept:

everything that happened on the road seems to have acquired significance. Overland diaries were a special, semipublic kind of diary, often published in county newspapers or sent to relatives who intended to make the same journey.[6] This explains the sense of audience and the informative quality of many journals, which note the condition of the roads, the distances traveled, and where to find water and grass. These diaries were, as Schlissel writes, a kind of family history, "handed down through generations, to be viewed not as an individual's story, but as the history of a family's growth and course through time" (11). However, Schlissel's assumption that men and women knew "they were engaged in nothing less than extending American possession of the continent from ocean to ocean" (10) needs further analysis.

Scholars of the overland trails have noted that most pioneers went West in hopes of personal gain and self-improvement. Although the questions of why women went West, and how their position may have been changed by this journey and the new life in the West, have received contradictory answers in studies of westering women, women's historians generally find that women emigrants shared the men's economic concerns and optimism associated with pioneering.[7] In contrast, Schlissel writes that "however powerful the attempt to revise history, the period of the Overland Trail migration (1840–60) produces overwhelming evidence that women did not greet the idea of going West with enthusiasm, but rather that they worked out a painful negotiation with historical imperatives and personal necessity" (155). Arguing against studies that assert essential similarities between men's and women's diaries of the overland trails,[8] she finds "distinctions so profound as to raise the question whether women did not ultimately perceive the westward trek differently." Women, Schlissel claims, "did not always see the venture in the clear light of the expectation of success" (14).

Neither did they represent Native Americans in the same way as men. For many women, the real enemies of their journey were disease and accident, and they carefully noted the cost of the westward movement in human life (15). As men were carefully counting the miles traveled, women meticulously registered the number of graves they passed.[9] "In the very commonplace of their observations, the women bring us a new vision of the overland experience," Schlissel argues. "In reading their diaries we come closer to understanding how historical drama translates into human experience. Through the eyes of women we begin to see history as the stuff of daily struggle" (16).

Although I basically agree with Schlissel's comments on the special emphases in women's diaries, I would suggest that what male and female diarists shared as a common problem is not the translation of historical drama into human experience, but the translation of human experience into writing, and that men and women solved the problem in different, gendered ways that reflect differences in men's and women's access to discourses of westward expansion and empire building.

Stephen Fender has drawn attention to the phenomenon that although American writers projected their program for a new realism in American letters onto the West, the writing of the Far West turned out to be extremely formal, "more heavily plotted, than any of the more settled regions of the continent."[10] The forty-niners, he argues, were not only unaccustomed to writing but also had to cope with "the fear, the physical strain and the cultural agoraphobia of traversing an unplotted wilderness." What is more, they were uncertain of their role: they were neither explorers, natural scientists, nor pioneers. For the most part, they were not even emigrants; the majority of forty-niners went without their families "in circumstances bearing some (at least) striking resemblances to a holiday. Yet they were on business, or professed to be—the business of speculating for gold to free themselves and their families from the drudgery they left behind" (12). As the chief sign of this strain, Fender identifies in men's diaries a double style, a "fissure within a single narrative between descriptive templates held up, as it were, to the landscape." As soon as the descriptive project failed, "they subsided into the rhetoric of scientific description, the nomenclature of animals, plants and minerals, the statistics of altitude, temperature, latitude and longitude. The rhetoric, not the primary fact of science" (13).

In contrast with men's journals of the California trail, Fender finds in women's diaries "the more secure discourse of dependent or contingent members of a family unit, in which the anxieties of western travel were somewhat naturalized by the familial setting" (14). Indeed, when reading women's diaries of the trail, the westward movement emerges as a mass migration of families; women were part of the journey either because their fathers, husbands, and brothers had determined to go, or because they had participated in the decision-making process and wanted their families to move west.[11] While some of the male forty-niners "learned to write plainly (or unlearned how to write pretensiously)," Fender suggests, the women who went west with their families around the time of the gold rush appear to have possessed this skill almost from the beginning (88). Women's journals, he seems to imply, somehow escaped the force of rhetoric that acted so strongly in and on men's diaries of the overland journey. He links this to three differences between men's and women's writings: the supportive rather than active role assigned to women, their position within the family unit as emigrants rather than adventurers, and the different books men and women were supposed to have read (88–89).

As I will show, all of these factors need critical reconsideration. Although gender-role expectations did affect women's writing, writers did not wholly succumb to them. Moreover, female writers did occasionally assume the adventurous and objectivist poses associated with men's writing, but with different results. Lastly, women on the overland trails did not read only pious or domestic literature but were also familiar with the narratives and reports of western exploration.[12] Consequently, their accounts seem to be drawn in different directions.

Female diarists engaged with the discourses of westward expansion and empire building in ways that were complicated by discourses of femininity and by women's restricted access to positions of authority anchored in knowledge and expertise. Although some of the retrospectively written accounts superimposed narrative designs upon the journey, women's representations of western landscapes and people were basically inconsistent, insecure, and shifting, revealing the writers' struggles to make sense of what they saw and experienced.

Looking Back over the Years

When Catherine Haun recounted her 1849 journey to California years later for her daughter, she superimposed on her narrative a design of adventurous enterprise: "Early in January in 1849 we first thought of emigrating to California. It was a period of National hard times and we being financially involved in our business interests near Clinton, Iowa, longed to go to the new El Dorado and 'pick up' gold enough with which to return and pay off our debts." She had also undertaken the journey to improve her health, "for even in those days an out-door-life was advocated as a cure" for consumption. The Hauns had been married for a few months, and the California trail thus appealed to them as a "romantic wedding tour" (166).

For the most part, however, Haun's narrative is a general description of the composition of the wagon train, the practical details of the organization of a "trail government," and the everyday rhythm of travel and work on the trail. The wagon train emerges as a social unit organized less as a community than as a business enterprise; the goal is not permanent emigration but making money. The travelers had even filled the wagons with merchandise they hoped to sell "at fabulous prices when we should arrive in the 'land of gold.' The theory of this was good but the practice—well, we never got the goods across the first mountain" (167).

Train participants were chosen according to their experience and self-reliance, and those who seemed inexperienced and in need of help were deemed objectionable, since they could impede the speed of the train. Women and children were objectionable for the same reason, but they actually "exerted a good influence, as the men did not take such risks with Indians and thereby avoided conflict; were more alert about the care of the teams and seldom had accidents; more attention was paid to cleanliness and sanitation and, lastly but not of less importance, the meals were more regular and better cooked thus preventing much sickness and there was less waste of food" (171). Interwoven with such general description is the narrator's self-representation as a feminine but capable woman who, like all the other women in the train, was expected to perform "strenuous and altogether unladylike labor" (179), but who is intent on convincing her reader/listener that she has not lost her femininity. Gender distinctions are continually made in this originally oral account focusing on the different occupations of the men and "the womenfolk" (180).

In the 1880s, when Sarah Royce described her experience as a forty-niner, she superimposed a different narrative design upon her account. Unlike Haun's recollections, Royce's experiences are organized into a pattern of redemption through faith, which is closely linked to the circumstances that led to the telling of Royce's story. More than thirty years after her trip west, Sarah Royce reconstructed the journey for her son, the philosopher Josiah Royce, with the aid of her diary. The emphasis she placed on her mystical experience on the westward trek and her continued faith, which her son had made the object of scientific inquiry, may be read as evidence that "she is not merely narrating but is arguing with her philosopher son"[13] and enacting a dialogue between religious and scientific modes of knowledge and authority. This context may also account for the fact that in Royce's narrative the discourse of femininity is less foregrounded than in Haun's.

The accounts are similar, however, in how the women describe the West: both configure the territory before them in terms of obstacles to be overcome. Like Haun, Royce represents the western journey as a series of hard facts in the form of almost impassable roads, accidents, cattle stampedes, and dangerous river crossings. Tribal people are perceived as a source of anxiety, impeding and endangering the travelers' progress by stealing and begging. In the mornings, the travelers often find themselves without their comforters—frightening evidence that Indians had been there during the night (176). Although at first Haun eyes the Indians with curiosity and even admires "a bit of remarkable maternal discipline" (174), the "bucks" and "prairie redmen" are nonetheless generalized as insistent beggars, who at mealtime "disgustingly stood around and solicited food. They seldom molested us, however, but it was a case of the Indian, as well as the poor, 'Ye have always with ye'" (175).

Under these circumstances, the terrain along the Platte River assumes an alienating and frightening character. The travelers encounter a "desolate, rough country" devoid of beauty and "mighty full of crowching, treacherous Indians" (177). Native Americans are represented as unruly, spiteful, and shrewd obstacles whose actions seem guided by the single purpose of terrifying the emigrants, who are innocently passing through. Both western space and people are imagined as alienating, satanic nature: "We saw nothing living but Indians, lizards and snakes. Trying, indeed, to feminine nerves. Surely Inferno can be no more horrible in formation. . . . The demen needed only horns and cloven feet to complete the soul stirring picture!" (178).

Sarah Royce voices the same contempt when she describes the travelers being "annoyed by begging and pilfering Indians, male and female," who have to be kept at a distance, "in their proper place." In her narrative, the term "Indian country" denotes, in a similar way as in Haun's text, a country inhabited by but not possessed by Indians. One episode is telling in this respect. West of the Missouri, the travelers are stopped by a group of Indians who "had gathered to demand the payment of a certain sum per head for every emigrant passing through this part of the country, which they claimed as their own." The narrator is a detached observer who describes the reaction of the male travelers from a distance, but with apparent agreement: "The men of our company after consultation, resolved that the demand was unreasonable! that the country we were traveling over belonged to the United States, and that these red men had no right to stop us" (13). The men refuse to pay and move on, ready to use their firearms. Although this scene is described through the eyes of a female observer who is not involved in the decision-making process, there is no critique from the distance but rather an indirect affirmation of colonialist assumptions, including the belief that the country is indisputably part of United States territory.[14]

Although the land is not configured as inhabited space, it is nonetheless familiar as a series of landmarks described and named by such earlier travelers as John Charles Frémont, whose report the Royces had taken with them as a guide (3). Royce seems to have reacted to both the personal narrative of aesthetic experience and the scientific descriptions in this report. She describes Independence Rock rather meticulously as "a bare mass of rock, without vegetation, rising directly from the flat, sandy land bordering the river, and detached entirely from any other elevation. Its general outline is round, though somewhat irregular; and at a distance one might fancy it an enormous elephant kneeling down." This plain picture of a landmark already described in scientific terms by a previous explorer seems commonplace, but, significantly, it is followed by an account of Sarah's ascent of the rock, which she found "not too rash an undertaking. Another woman of our company joined me. One or two of her boys climbed with us, and . . . I took my little Mary. Of course I had to lift her from one projection to another most of the way; but we went leisurely, and her delight on reaching the top, our short rest there and the view we enjoyed, fully paid for the labor" (25). As Fender has noted, this description of the leisurely ascent by women and children discredits male explorers' and travelers' accounts in which the climb appears as a minor feat of exploration.[15]

For Sarah Royce, the Continental Divide forms the symbolic boundary between her old and her new life. She is tempted to mark the spot where she crosses into her frontier, not as an explorer giving testimony to a feat of conquest, but in the manner of a priestess performing a secret religious ritual. Moreover, this crossing of a symbolic boundary inspires her to look back instead of forward, dwelling on the pain of separation (26–27). Finally, Royce's western landscape is a space of communication with her God, emptied of everything but the divine presence, manifest to the true believer in signs that must be read and interpreted. In the Nevada desert, the travelers are stopped by "savages"—Central Basin tribes commonly called Digger Indians[16]—who were "importunate in demanding various things, acted with the air of victors . . . pressed close to the wagon, and looked in, with boisterous exclamations and impertinent gestures" (37). Although the travelers manage to escape a warlike confrontation by rushing ahead with an exhibition of confidence and firearms, Royce's narrative suggests that they were able to surmount all obstacles only by way of divine intervention. The desert is not, as in Haun's narrative, an alienating realm of evil, but the space in which the narrator is closest to the presence of her God.

Royce's mystical experience is clearly related to her sex: "Only a woman who has been alone upon a desert with her helpless child can have any adequate idea of my experience for the next hour of two. But that consciousness of an unseen Presence still sustained me" (45). Royce heightens the effect of this description by picturing herself, repeatedly, "all alone on the barren waste." While walking ahead of the wagons, she not only sees the biblical Hagar in this wilderness, "walking wearily away from her fainting child among the dried up bushes," but she also imagines herself as the biblical outcast woman in the desert (49).

The authority of religious experience is repeatedly invoked in

Royce's account and is, in addition, exclusively related to the female situation: none of the other travelers (all men) are seen to undergo a similar experience. It is also significant in this context that Royce does not represent herself in active work situations but rather underscores her narrative presence as a passive observer. Whereas the men receive strength and confidence by doing and acting, a "lone woman's" source of strength can only be spiritual. This narrative's focus is spiritual survival, which incidentally masks the guilt of trespassing. Its most powerful signals are the image of a desolate landscape empty of human habitation, an emphasis on human loneliness, the representation of indigenous inhabitants as tactical obstacles in whose (non-)actions the divine presence manifests its power, and the Madonna-like figure of a "lone woman" with her helpless infant.

In both Haun's and Royce's narratives, the western territory to be traversed is an extremely unsafe terrain that, as seen in Royce's representation of tribal people who have to be kept "in their place," invites scenarios of human control while simultaneously transferring agency to the divine presence. However, it is important to remember that both narratives were written decades after the events, at a time when the West could be imagined, in most of its parts, as a "safe" terrain already incorporated into the federal domain. On the other hand, as the history of Indian resistance shows, the West was a culturally contested territory for most of the second half of the nineteenth century—symbolized by the powerful impact on American culture of Custer's defeat in 1876. Both visions of the contemporary West may have indirectly inscribed themselves into these retrospective narratives.

Although Haun and Royce may have avoided appropriative designs relating to the western landscape, they nevertheless apply a language of colonial relations to the description of their encounters with native peoples—encounters between groups with conflicting interests. Yet the land is perceived in terms of a foreign country to be traversed. Their accounts, written or recorded in the 1880s, still exhibit an ambivalence toward the western territory that distances them from the rhetoric found, for example, in Frémont's discovery narrative. They present the terrain at the same time as an inhabited foreign country, a territory inviting control, and as a space in which the Christian God's—or, in Haun's case, the devil's—presence manifests itself. But they also configure it as a space that rejects and alienates the white woman, who, unlike the official explorer, makes no personal claim on the territory.

These women's travel accounts thus exhibit the sense of boundedness that Bruce Greenfield identifies in discovery narratives of the early nineteenth century. Referring to John Juricek's study of the usage of the "frontier" term, he claims that until about the mid-nineteenth century, most Americans saw their settled country as bordering not on emptiness, but on other countries, that is, Indian country. This contradicts, of course, Turner's conception of the frontier as lying "at the hither edge of free land," representing the "outer edge of the wave" of advancing white American settlers.[17]

By the time of Frémont's account of his 1842 expedition to the Rocky Mountains, discovery narratives had developed a different rhetoric, presenting the western lands not as inhabited countries but as "basically empty, politically unmodified spaces" (72). Women's overland diaries, whether written during the journey or many years later, still reflect earlier conceptions of the western lands as an inhabited Indian country, but they also begin to empty western landscapes by projecting aesthetic designs upon them or by appropriating them as realms for spiritual regeneration. In general, however, women diarists seem to have tread on insecure ground both as travelers and as writers. This is exemplified by the problems of representation that surface in their accounts.

Trying to Make Sense of It All

As Stephen Fender has noted, women diarists of the overland trail, who were generally given to few flights of rhetoric, became formulaic in response to particularly severe pressures, especially at the outset of the journey, when the anxiety of leaving home and friends tended to outweigh the sense of security provided by the family unit.[18] For example, Lydia Allen Rudd opens her diary rather formulaically on May 6, 1852: "Left the Missouri river for our long journey across the wild uncultivated plains and uninhabited except by the red man." She continues with a panoramic sweep over the landscape, but her gaze rests not so much on what lies ahead as on what is left behind. Tearing herself away, the narrator sets out on the journey in the pose of an adventuress doing her duty: "But with good courage and not one sigh of regret I mounted my pony (whose name by the way is Samy) and rode slowly on" (188).

The same year, Mary Stuart Bailey starts out with the words: "Left our hitherto happy home in Sylvania amid the tears and parting kisses of dear friends, many of whom were endeared to me by their kindness shown to me when I was a stranger in a strange land, when sickness and death visited our small family & removed our darling, our only child in a moment, as it were" (49). Like Rudd, she sets the stage for the journey by looking back and tearing herself away, but soon she records how easily she adapts to the new circumstances of outdoor life (54). A few days later the twenty-two-year-old Vermont native proudly reports another "first": "Slept in the tent for the first time. I was Yankee enough to protect myself by pinning up my blankets over my head. I am quite at home in my tent" (55). After a month on the road, she expresses enjoyment of outdoor life: "We enjoy ourselves better as we get used to this way of traveling & living out of doors. We have good appetites and plenty to eat although we sit down & eat like Indians" (66).

At one point Bailey even seems to mock the cultural tendency to reserve adventurous enterprise to men: "Forded the Green River. Had to raise our wagons but did not get into the water although we were somewhat frightened. Do not know as there was much danger, but the men say the women must always be frightened" (73). In another passage, the men themselves are the object of descriptive mockery: "It was really amusing to see the men stand in the river to wash. They all acted so awkward" (61). As a matter of fact, in many women's accounts, men do not always conform to the self-image they present in their own narratives. Instead of being hardy pioneers and manly, enterprising adventurers, the men are often not only careless but also unreliable and fearful when their courage is in demand.[19] Moreover, women were not always impressed with men's reasoning and decision-making abilities and with their capability to protect the women and children. Lucy Rutledge Cooke, pointing to her well-armed husband, joked dryly: "Hope he won't hurt himself" (85). Mary Rockwood Powers' journal exposed her husband's inability to cope with the stress and responsibilities connected with the journey. At a time when travelers were urged to join larger wagon trains for safety, he insisted on self-reliance and independence, which under the circumstances bordered on irrationality. At a climactic moment, Powers confides to her journal that she felt "at the mercy of a mad man" (29).

Most women's diaries of the year 1852 convey the impression that the overland journey was a mass movement. Bailey describes the road as stirring with people: "It does not seem as though we are out of the world to see so many people. More stir than you would see in a goodly city" (59). In her first letter home, Cooke writes to her sister: "But oh, I fear we shall have a terrible time, for there seems to be thousands going" (10). Although travelers still call California the "Golden Land," many of the female diarists are more attracted to Oregon, which had, from the beginning, been promoted as a farming country. Lydia Rudd, on her way to Oregon, cannot even imagine going to California, describing five men on their way there as "some of the persevering kind I think wanting to go to California more than I do" (190).

Emigration to Oregon was probably more alluring to her because married women could stake claims of their own there: under the Oregon Donation Act of 1850, both husbands and wives were entitled to enter claims. One can imagine that the "demand for brides sky-rocketed in the Oregon Territory," where, as Frances Fuller Victor shows with unveiled cynicism in one of her stories, the marriage market could take bizarre and rather misogynist forms.[20] Rudd's goal of personal economic independence becomes clear when her journal ends, after her arrival in Oregon, on a note of resignation: "I expect that we shall not make a claim after all our trouble in getting here on purpose for one I shall have to be poor and dependent on a man my life time" (197). Like many female travelers, especially those going to California, she had anticipated a temporary stay of a few years, during which she wanted to save enough money to return to "the States."[21]

By 1852, one of the main dangers faced by the emigrant trains was sickness. News of gold had become intertwined with reports of disease: emigrants carried measles, typhoid, smallpox, and cholera, which they also spread among the indigenous population. Both Bailey and Rudd repeatedly note that they feel sick, and both report sickness among fellow travelers. Rudd's diary has repeated references to graves and illness. This daily preoccupation with sickness and death also explains why Rudd hardly takes note of the landscape she is passing through. Lillian Schlissel speculates that "the detailed pattern-making, the recounting of trivial daily tasks that one finds in the women's diaries was the necessary counter-balance in a life pitted against catastrophe." She reads the almost obsessive tabulation of the number of graves in some women's journals as suggestions of female rebellion against the journey.[22]

Many women draw attention to their own health, either men-tioning that they feel sick—which, as Schlissel suggests, often serves as a coded reference to pregnancy—or noting their physical well-being. Harriet Sherrill Ward, a fifty-year-old Vermont native who was attracted to California by enthusiastic letters from her son, presents herself as rejuvenated by the overland journey. After several moves in a westward direction, from Ohio to Wisconsin, in 1853 she went overland with her husband and a sixteen-year-old daughter, and she wrote a diary of her journey, having promised to send it back to the rest of the family—some of her children re-mained in Iowa—at the journey's end. She records her observations and personal experiences, often humorously drawing attention to herself as a comic figure: "I think you might possibly have been somewhat amused to have witnessed the transit of the ladies and children of our party," who took off their stockings and boots dur-ing a river crossing. Recounting her ride over the mountains on a man's saddle, Ward explains half humorously, half apologetically, that there "remained no alternative for me but to assume a posi-tion not altogether compatible with the delicacy of an American lady."[23] Traveling through Iowa, she expresses the conviction that "I can bear the winds and the rains as well as the youngest of our party" (33), and in Nebraska she finds that she can walk "three or four miles without fatigue, and Father and I both can read without spectacles" (72). Once she even jumps on her horse's back "with-out a saddle and rode off triumphantly. You will think I am re-juvenating and indeed I am, for I thought the day past when I could run, jump and walk as I do now!" (91).[24]

One reason why some parts of women's journeys are narrated as rejuvenating sightseeing tours may be that some landmarks were already familiar to travelers who had read about or had seen paint-ings of them: "We are now in sight of Laramie Peak," Lucy Cooke writes humorously, "but failed to see the buffaloes that are in that picture at Mrs. Telfair's in Davenport, but perhaps that Indian killed them" (46). And Ward, upon seeing the Mississippi, "at once recognized one of Catlin's beautiful views" of the river (24). Even in Rudd's diary, some passages—significantly those describing, as in Royce's narrative, the rock formations along the Platte—break through the gloomy tabulation of graves: "At noon we stoped about a fourth of a mile from devils gate I went out to see this wonder and it surpassed anything that ever I saw in my life The sweet water river passes through a gap or gate as it is called of the rocky mountains it has made a channel about two rods in width through the solid rock a quarter of a mile in length the rocks are perpendicular and in places overhanging to the height of more than two hundred feet." She even uses the language of adventurous enterprise when she records that she "got out to prospect a little found a few strawberries" (192).

Bailey tries to make sense of strange natural phenomena by attempting a protoscientific description that nonetheless always leads to rather homely comparisons: "One mass of rocks all worn into every fantastic shape. In the deep ravines were large trees. I noticed a stone that resembled a bust of an old lady sitting alone. She looked as though she felt lonely" (62–63). Like Eliza Steele, Bailey is not unfamiliar with natural-history discourse and attempts to use it to explain the formation of the landscape: "In all this region the country in many places has the appearance of being the bed of a vast lake or stream. In many places the earth mingled with rocks are left in shapes of buildings or cupulows [sic]" (74).

The Oregon missionary Mary Richardson Walker also seems versed in the vocabulary of natural history, which during the nineteenth century had become a popular hobby as well as a scientific endeavor, and which played an important part in the curriculum of female seminaries where women's interests in nature were smoothly integrated with broad-based gender-role expectations.[25] Walker was especially interested in minerals and commented repeatedly on the geological nature of rocks and soil, describing Independence Rock in 1838 in meticulous detail.[26] Harriet Ward even casts herself as a prospector, mentioning that she had passed "an extensive Iron ore bed which would, I think, yield sufficient Iron to built [sic] a railroad to California" (83). Once, after she had discovered "something seeming at first sight to be wood which had been in the hands of a carpenter, but found upon examination to be rock of some kind," she expresses a desire for a scientific knowledge implicitly inaccessible to her: "Oh, how I wished for knowledge! . . . Being no geologist, I was obliged to wonder and admire and leave it thus. Some thought it a petrifaction of wood, but if so whose hands have been employed here?"(106).

Women diarists thus adopt, at least tentatively, the language of natural history, which implicitly displaces indigenous inhabitants from the territory and denies them a history of their own by privileging the history of natural forces. Yet there is no single unifying pattern in these diaries. At times the journey resembles a tourist excursion, but at other times it is an excruciating and toilsome pilgrimage with a doubtful destination. Consequently, descriptions of western lands and people are never consistent but repeatedly shift between presenting the West as Indian country—unattractive, foreign, and alienating—and claiming it materially and aesthetically for white Americans.

Upon crossing into Nebraska, Ward declares the country erroneously as "inhabited only by Indians" (44), finding it "a miserable, unpleasant place indeed, [which] can never be inhabited except by the red men of the forest" (57). It is an interesting irony to assume that the "red men of the forest" should be the only ones adapted to this treeless land: "It requires the pen of the poet or the pencil of the painter to portray its beauties, but it should remain sacred to the redmen of the forest, for there is little to induce the white man to wrest it from them, in consequence of the scarcity of timber" (44). The longer she travels, however, the more attractive and suitable the country gets for settlement "by a civilized race of beings" (70).

Although Ward may draw attention to the travelers' alienation from the land by picturing them as pilgrims in "a lone wilderness," a few paragraphs later she may mention the presence of indigenous inhabitants, romanticizing them as pastoral figures in an appealing landscape: "I could not longer wonder that the Indian and the Gypsy should become attached to this wild free life, where the beauties of nature are continually spread out before them" (151). The narrative mode Ward most often resorts to is that of personal aesthetic experience described in religious terms. Devil's Gate is "one of the most gloriously magnificent spectacles upon which my eyes have ever delighted to dwell," a sight that makes her cry and exclaim in humble admiration: "Oh how readily does the heart turn in contemplation of such scenes from nature up to nature's God!" (90–91). In the Rocky Mountains she sees a scenery "sublime and glorious beyond description." Despite a patriotic overtone—"Switzerland cannot boast a sight more glorious"—her language is decidedly nonappropriative. Standing on the top of a mountain, feeling momentarily transported to "the Summit of dear old Snake mountain," she avoids the panoramic sweep of what Mary Pratt calls the "monarch-of-all-I-survey" topos,[27] instead emphasizing the humbling effect of the sublime scene: "And oh! how small, how insignificantly small is man, with all his boasted knowledge, in the scale of being!" (115).

Sarah Raymond Herndon, standing on the summit of a mountain, records the same experience of humbling, losing, even offering herself. On Bear Mountain she feels "that God is here in his might, majesty, power and glory. I feel His nearness now, and as I gaze from these dizzy heights upon the country spread out beneath my feet, I am lost in admiration, the scene is so grand, so magnificent, that I forget my own vanity and nothingness. I feel that I am standing upon an altar raised by Nature's grateful hand up to Nature's God, and that I could offer myself a willing sacrifice" (228).

Women seem to resist the panoramic sweep of possession especially on account of their access to what Rob Wilson has called the "Christianized sublime." They were writing from within a Protestant tradition that links "the 'rapt contemplation' of nature . . . to the contemplation of God." Rooted in issues of aesthetic theory that since the eighteenth century have been popularized in travel literature, the sublime as an unmasterable excess of beauty that marks the limits of representation has stood at the center of discussions of art and representation also in America, where the "newness" and vastness of the continent challenged the powers of representation: "If the enlightenment sublime had represented the unrepresentable," Wilson wrote, "imagining the vastness of nature . . . as the subject's innermost ground," the American sublime internalized national claims by establishing this vastness as the American self's inalienable ground.[28]

The issue of representation surfacing in these women's travel diaries is certainly not exclusively a personal or particularly feminine problem but is part of a cultural convention. Women's rhetorical practice of humbling themselves in view of the vastness and incomprehensibility of western sights is related to a cultural discourse on American nature—in religious and secular prose, poetry, and art—which builds upon the tensions between powerlessness and empowerment, representation and the unrepresentable. The reduction of the self to (seeming) insignificance before the spectacle of American nature is constitutive of the American sublime. However, if the sublime in so many male American writers' works functions as a trope of self-authentication and self-empowerment,[29] female overland diarists essentially avoid this scenario of self-making, engendering the sublime as a trope of exaltation through prostration, worship, and sacrifice.

Of course, these professions of powerlessness often had another, very plausible source. If these emigrant women, like Margaret Fuller, avoid the description of grand scenes, they do so with a difference. While Fuller avoids it with full intent, as part of her aesthetic program, the female overland travelers give up the task of description on account of a felt lack: not having learned how to write, they feel untalented and incapable of representing. Ward, for example, declares herself unable to picture the mountain scenery before her: "Had I been gifted with the pencil of a Catlin I would have presented you with sketches today of wild mountain scenery . . . but as nature has withheld the gift I can only say it was grand and magnificent beyond the power of words to describe" (84). Yet, despite their lamentations and disclaimers, one begins to understand that women diarists did not deem it necessary to provide accurate descriptions: those who could be persuaded to follow would see these western sights for themselves. What seems to have been more important to them was the record of a unique experience; once these ephemeral moments of extreme hardship and pleasure were written down, they would never be forgotten.

This may also account for the fact that many women diarists represent themselves as being in the landscape instead of describing the landscape itself. The instances in which they look at themselves from a distance and embody themselves, often in a comic pose of self-mockery, are also the moments in which they create themselves as subjects, approaching the strategy of self-empowerment that informs male versions of the American sublime. However, these women's acts of self-creation occur not in confrontation with an awe-inspiring landscape of vastness and grandeur, but in relation to the activities of wandering, rambling, acting, and being *in* a landscape.

Some women diarists also became detached observers of the whole emigrant enterprise. Ward assumed the stance of a reporter of the overland journey, pondering its meaning and purpose. Especially on the last leg of the journey, she tires of the "wildness and strangeness of the works of nature" (140) and wonders whether California is worth all this hardship and toil: "We have passed the entire summer in this wild, wandering way, toiling onward day after day . . . towards that far off land where thousands have gone before us to die of disappointment, and perhaps no better fate awaits many of us. I often look about me and wonder who, of all the numerous throng by whom we are daily surrounded, are to be favorites of Dame Fortune: but the anxiety of all seems to be to reach our anticipated goal, and when reached I presume our anxieties will only take a new form" (142).

Counterpointing her personal narrative, which emphasizes the sharpening of sensibilities, are repeated observations on the desensitizing effects of the journey. The travelers become indifferent to danger and too accustomed to witnessing death and suffering: "We have passed several emigrant's graves. How soon the mind becomes familiarized to things which at first strike us so unpleasantly" (54). This numbing effect is manifest even on the surface-level of language: "We have passed several emigrant graves today. The wild flowers are beautiful and the prickly pear grows luxuriantly here" (61).

Overall, it seems that women had more difficulties describing what they saw than with narrating what happened on the journey. This also applies to women's representations of encounters with Native Americans. One of the images haunting Haun's narrative was the fear of a "massacre," culminating in the capture, torture, and rape of white women by "savage" Indians: "After the possible massacre had been accomplished their booty would have been our money, clothing, food, and traveling paraphernalia—and worse still those of our women who had been unfortunate enough to have escaped death" (178). Many women, especially in their reminiscences, record similar anxieties and fears connected with Native Americans, instilled in them by popular narratives of captivity and constantly reignited by rumors of Indian attacks.

Some women, however, also point to the deflation of their fears and to changes in their attitudes towards Indians. In her reminiscence of her trip to California in 1849, Luzena Wilson dwells self-mockingly on the fear of Native Americans she had upon starting her journey: "I had read and heard whole volumes of their bloody deeds, the massacre of harmless white men, torturing helpless women, carrying away captive innocent babes. I felt my children the most precious in the wide world, and I lived in an agony of dread that first night." The Indians were "friendly, of course, . . . but I, in the most tragi-comic manner, sheltered my babies with my own body, and felt imaginary arrows pierce my flesh a hundred times during the night."[30]

Margaret Frink reports a similar deflation of exaggerated fears when the expected hostile relations with Native Americans turn out to be friendly relations of trade. Her encounter with Sioux women is represented as a reciprocal interaction in which the native women "were much pleased to see the 'white squaw' in our party, as they called me," while the white woman offers material objects in exchange for food. It is quite obvious that the travelers had equipped themselves beforehand with certain objects, "trinkets" of minor value to white Americans but deemed valuable to Native Americans.[31]

Lillian Schlissel has noted that by 1852–53 the westward movement was "now not only a major demographic surge, but also a monumental movement of capital and of goods."[32] The overland trail had become a commercial road on which trappers and Indians ran ferries, bridges, and supply stations, and demanded fees for their services. Lydia Rudd, who had envisioned herself traveling "across the wild uncultivated plains, . . . uninhabited except by the redman," describes almost commonplace reciprocal relations of barter for food and clothing between travelers and Indians. On the last leg of the journey, she presents her personal trading with the Indians of the Great Basin with an unveiled sense of achievement: "Some of the snake indians came to our camp this morning I swaped some hard bread with them for some good berries. . . . I traded an apron today for a pair of moccasins of the indians. . . . bought a salmon fish of an indian today weighing seven or eight pounds gave him an old shirt some bread and a sewing needle" (192–93).

In Rudd's diary, the bartering relations between travelers and Indians seem to have been based on reciprocity, but the first Indians whom Bailey meets appear to have been in a less favorable position. Bartering with Indians is less commonplace in her diary, which is more reminiscent of Haun's and Royce's descriptions of nonreciprocal encounters perceived as molestations. Like Royce, Bailey finds the Indians' begging for food annoying (56–57). However, her account of the travelers' encounters with Indians resembles Rudd's in the way she adds descriptive details without commenting, a mode of reporting that tends to soften, even subvert, the narrator's pose of superiority.[33]

Native Americans seem to have puzzled both diarists. As if external appearance could provide a clue, both Rudd and Bailey focus almost obsessively on Indian dress and appearance, which seem to function as indications of both native poverty (or well-being) and native morals (or their absence). But the narrators are still uncertain of the meaning of their observations. At the beginning of Bailey's journey, one Indian who "brought a paper stating that the tribe were in a very destitute condition" is described as "nearly naked," while the next day they pass "any quantities of Indians, some dressed in robes & others not dressed at all scarcely" (56). It is as if Indians could be solely comprehended by way of their dress, as if here lay a clue to their identity, their difference from the travelers, their sameness. After the travelers pass a deserted Indian village, an Indian they take for a Sioux "was dressed in good style & his horse had a nice blanket also" (57). Passing a French blacksmith's shop, Bailey observes his Indian wife, "a squaw of the Siox [sic] tribe," sitting at the door of the log hut, "well drest, robed in a scarlet blanket. She looked rather sober but well. Another squaw on horse back chasing a drove of horses & mules, half dressed" (64–65). Reading these passages, one gets the impression that Bailey is struggling to come to terms with the meaning of what she sees: probably she had not expected an Indian woman, married to a rough "squawman," looking "well." The sight of a "half dressed" Indian cowgirl probably insulted her feminine modesty and challenged her own conceptions of woman's sphere and woman's work.

Like Lydia Rudd, Bailey seems to have been unable to make generalized statements about Indians, still trying to make sense of the variety of appearances and lifestyles she observes.[34] Near the Laramie Mountains they pass an "Indian village. They have a great many horses & also some cattle & mules. A Frenchman lives with them, too. They were well dressed with blankets trimmed." Significantly, the people "were all out running after sheep & took not the least notice of us" (66). The country they traverse is clearly inhabited, although references to the Frenchman seem to signal that tribal life is unfavorably changed. Bailey reports of a visit to "our neighbors the Indians," noting it as "a great curiosity to see so many at home. They are very indolent but healthy looking, hardy & capable of enduring fatigue. I would think there were 200, from an old blind woman to a little baby not more than 4 days old, all sorts & sizes" (67).

As in men's official surveys, every detail seems to be relevant: "A trader lives with them. He will not let them sell a pony without his consent. One old man had been to Washington. They all wear rings on their wrists & on every finger. Some of the children were white enough to belong to any white family." It is obviously significant to Bailey that a white man lives with Indians, just as it is significant that the Indians appear healthy. Had she expected something different? Indians do not seem to conform to preconceived ideas: they have been in contact with white American culture (one of them had been to Washington) and some of them are even the same color as the travelers themselves. But it seems that in the manner of Margaret Fuller and other earlier travelers, Bailey disapproves of the ways in which Indian-white contact takes place. Indians are taken advantage of, presumably by the white trader living among them: "My heart aches to think of their extreme ignorance & as many white men & Christians as pass them without thinking of doing them good" (67).

Bailey is evidently disconcerted by a Danish man, who "frankly told us that he had an Indian wife. He bought her while he staid here for a pony & two blankets. I was somewhat shocked to think of such a loose state of morals. He said it is nothing more than Yankee men do" (68). Again one wonders what shocks her more: the interracial sexual relationship, the businesslike way in which the man describes it, or his comparison with white American marriage customs? Catherine Haun declares herself equally disgusted with a "renegade" man "who having lived for years among the Indians had forgotten his native language and dressing and eating as they did, his long unkept hair and uncouth appearance was loathsome in the extreme; it being hard to distinguish him from his brother Indians" (182). That Haun should express disgust at his unkempt appearance should not surprise us. However, what seems most abhorrent to her is the renegade's loss of manliness and of distinctive ethnic traits. Compared to his life, she suggests, Indian life is rather noble (182). Sarah Raymond is just as explicit: "There are three wigwams within sight of our camp. Sam and Hillhouse went hunting to-day. On their way back they stopped at the wigwams and found them occupied by white men with squaws for wives. Ugh!" (207).

Glenda Riley has noted that female overland diarists seemed especially obsessed with a need to chronicle every French trader who had an Indian wife and halfbreed children, while men seemed less concerned about intermarriage and polygamy. Indeed, as seen above, most women reacted with dismay, even disgust, to these domestic arrangements. Although Riley speculates that women were more tolerant of intermarriage, since "the female value system permitted relatively easy adjustment to the concept of intermarriage,"[35] I would argue that women's narratives of the overland trail suggest rather the opposite. Even if the western journey obviously destabilized many of their ideas of social and racial order, the specter of miscegenation and polygamy remained the biggest threat to their conceptions of white womanhood, a threat that they distanced with gestures of dismay. Their negative stance on intermarriage also shows how, in a context of expansion, the regulation of sexual relations may figure prominently in the construction of social and racial hierarchies.[36]

Interestingly, female overland travelers' views of miscegenation contrast sharply with the attitudes found in earlier women's novels and poetry. As many scholars have observed, the marriages between white women and Indian men in the works of Catharine Maria Sedgwick and Lydia Maria Child seem to suggest "terms for an alternative, female, frontier fantasy" which point to less hostile attitudes toward miscegenation among women writers than among their male contemporaries. Others interpret the occurrence of intermarriage in these works less as a comment on miscegenation itself than as a fictional strategy supporting the writers' argument for the value of social reform. In order to merge issues of gender and race, Lucy Maddox suggests, these writers only experiment with "moving their Indian characters, for a short time, into the privileged domain of the white woman."[37] These comparative observations should not only alert us to the variety of women's attitudes, whether based on generational differences or differences of class and education, but also to the different discursive demands of fiction and the travel diary.

As adamant as most women diarists of the overland trails seem about their views of intermarriage, some women's views of Indian-white relations did change. Cooke describes the Sioux as "a noble-looking tribe . . . so well dressed: such gay trappings on them and their ponies, and the beautiful beaded work they wear" (46). Ward portrays people of the same tribe as "a fine, intelligent looking race" who are "friendly to the whites," yet "not to be trusted" (77).

The authority invoked by Ward, and elsewhere by many of her contemporaries, is phrenology, a nineteenth-century medical theory assuming that people are entirely knowable in their characteristics, or faculties, from the shape and bumps of their skulls: "I noticed a young squaw with an infant whose head would, I thought, be a fine study for a phrenologist for I certainly never saw a finer development of brain in an infant's head. The evil propensities were very small indeed, while benevolence, reverence and conscientiousness were very large and its intellectual faculties uncommonly developed. I would like much to see the effect of education upon the child. Some of them were fantastically dressed and they certainly have intelligent countenances" (78–79).

The passage shows how ideas of the civilizing mission—assigned to women as a cultural responsibility—may be mediated, even in women's texts, by a scientific, or protoscientific, discourse. Moreover, Ward's strategy of self-representation, mingled with an attempted objective description of the Indian other, indicates how discourses of femininity complicate women's access to an imperial voice. Generalizing statements may stand side by side with a personal narrative that devalues objectivist claims. Thus, when Ward draws attention to her own person, picturing herself writing amidst Native Americans, she simultaneously subverts and reinforces the conventions of imperial rhetoric by underscoring the harmlessness, and thus the manageability, of the Indian other: "they appear perfectly harmless and you would be surprised to see me writing so quietly in the wagon alone . . . with a great, wild looking Indian leaning his elbow on the wagon beside me, but I have no single fear except that they may frighten the horses" (78). Although Ward, by drawing attention to herself, avoids holding the other in her gaze, she still fashions herself as the innocent heroine of an anti-conquest.

Nevertheless, one should not underestimate the pervasive tendency in these women's narratives to deflate the image of courageous pioneers facing warlike Indians and to draw attention instead to the daily interactions between travelers and inhabitants. Although women, like men, are implicated in a discourse that stereotypes native peoples, denies them culture and individuality, and thus marginalizes their claim to the land, women's access to objectivist discourses of appropriation is often subverted by personal narratives that focus on cultural interactions. Women diarists of the overland trails seem to have had an insecure hold on imperial claims, often fashioning decidedly nonappropriative relations with their surroundings and creating self-conscious feminine selves guided and constrained by the ideas of gendered behavior. All these elements are especially pronounced in the travel diary of Susan Magoffin, which enters into a dialogue with a male text and which will be discussed separately.

Of course, as Mary Pratt and others have noted, the essentializing power of colonial discourses is impervious until those who are seen are also listened to. Personal narratives in general, whether by men or women, contain more Indian voices than we assume. Almost tucked away in women's texts, in between the condescending generalizations and the wide-eyed wondering, Native Americans appear as individuals and agents whose voices are heard, who are playing their own jokes on emigrants (and especially emigrant women),[38] and who have developed their own style of cultural mix in language, behavior, dress, and work in reaction to the emigrant wave.

The record of friendly interaction should not, however, deceive us about the very real climate of violence shaping Indian-white relations on the overland trails by the mid-1850s, when tribal people began to realize how their lifeways and subsistence were being endangered and destroyed by the masses of people traversing their homelands. Emigrants had become an increasing threat to both their cultural and economic survival, and the Indian attacks that Haun and other women travelers had always feared began to materialize more often. In response to emigrants' increasing fear of Indian "scares," a growing presence of army contingents was deployed with orders to police and control the frontiers. Perhaps this can explain the phenomenon that unlike earlier travelers who had struggled with their impressions of Native Americans, women travelers of the 1860s began reacting—at times almost violently—to a romantic, literary image of the Indian.

After a time-delay of two decades, James Fenimore Cooper's "noble savages" were being challenged in the same way that Caroline Kirkland had satirized, in her sophisticated manner, male romantic conventions of describing the West. When Sarah Raymond Herndon first encountered an Indian on her 1865 journey to Montana, "he did not even grunt. He was very disappointing as the 'Noble Red Man' we read about. He wore an old ragged federal suit, cap and all. There were no feathers, beads nor blankets. He was not black like a negro, more of a brown, and a different shade from the mulatto. He was ugly as sin" (73).

Hostile Indian-white relations, competition over land and resources, and very real signs of Indian poverty—in many narratives disguised as a state of degradation—conspire in the unmaking of "the noble red man," and also shape women's narratives of their experiences in the frontier army (see chapter 3). Before discussing these accounts, however, I will focus on a diary that stands between the western narratives of the literate women who wrote about the prairies, and the overland diarists who crossed the continent on their way to the Pacific. This diary of a young woman on the Santa Fe Trail at the time of the Mexican-American War introduces the Southwest as the third region to appear in women's western narratives of the time, and thus also provides a link to the subsequent accounts of women in the frontier army.

Susan Magoffin on the Santa Fe Trail

When Susan Shelby Magoffin, the daughter of a well-to-do Kentucky family, accompanied her husband down the Santa Fe Trail into Mexico in June 1846, she was eighteen years old. She had been married to the Santa Fe trader Samuel Magoffin for less than eight months, and she went on the journey for "adventure and sight-seeings" as well as for health reasons: she was expecting her first child (73). Magoffin traveled in style in a traders' caravan—the avant-garde of economic colonialism—at a time when Mexican territory was in the process of being claimed by the United States. When the Magoffin wagon train began its journey in June 1846, President Polk had already declared war on Mexico, and thus the Magoffins were traveling as members of an invading force. At the same time, they were subject to shifting power relations, never sure about the "natives," who could be potential friends or enemies, victorious or vanquished.

At the outset, Magoffin casts herself as a tourist traveling for health and pleasure, aloof from the economic and political circumstances and purposes of the journey. The longer the journey lasts, however, the more she has to face its political implications. She also positions her account, at least at the beginning of her journey/narrative, in relation to a male text, repeatedly referring to Josiah Gregg's The Commerce of the Prairies (1844), a copy of which, as Howard Lamar has suggested, she not only owned but had apparently learned by heart: "Until she and her husband reached Bent's Fort, in fact, the diary clearly resembles Gregg's chapters dealing with life on the trail, the major difference being that Mrs. Magoffin traveled in what was, for the Santa Fe Trail, extraordinary luxury."[39] However, even if she had Gregg's book in mind as a model for her own narrative, it is significant to understand how this model was adopted and modified.

First of all, I want to suggest that Susan Magoffin's adoption of a public narrative is unstable; at certain critical points in the journey, the adventurous mode provided by Gregg's account is dropped and replaced by a personal mode of religious introspection. At the beginning of her story, the narrator fashions herself as an adventurer and pleasure seeker in the manner assumed by Gregg. His traveler, however, in a narrative mixture of adventure and enterprise, had invoked an official authority as the representative of his nation and as an advance scout for American trade and capital, an authority which Magoffin cannot and does not assume. On his way to Independence, Missouri, Gregg's narrator had cast his observing eye over the country, configuring it as a land inviting mastery and appropriation, a land full of promise yet mismanaged by the current possessors, the Indian tribes. The traveler's improving vision sees a stream "bordered by the most fertile bottoms and beautiful upland prairies, well adapted to cultivation." Unexploited nature does not fit aesthetic standards. Moreover, this vision is objectified as one representative for all travelers: "All who have traversed these delightful regions look forward with anxiety to the day when the Indian title to the land shall be extinguished and flourishing white settlements dispel the gloom which at present prevails over this uninhabited region" (31).

Further on, in Mexico, the landscape is an inhospitable desert. But again this is not traced to natural factors but to human neglect. Everything points to the country's need for improvement (151). Gregg's vision draws on what Mary Pratt has termed a "negative esthetic of neglect," which legitimized European interventionism.[40] Like the Euro-American travelers of the 1820s in South America, the American travelers in the Southwest of the 1830s and 1840s could no longer cast themselves as discoverers of a primal world. Spanish America, inhabited and full of the evidence of a long cultural history, demanded new rhetorical practices and had to be invented as backward and neglected, in need of American cultivation and exploitation. What held this reinvention of Spanish America together was the language of the civilizing mission, "with which North Europeans produce other peoples (for themselves) as 'natives,' reductive, incomplete beings suffering from the inability to have become what Europeans already are, or to have made themselves into what Europeans intend them to be."[41]

Henry Nash Smith saw Gregg as the first writer to move toward a revision of the myth of the Great American Desert and to draw attention to the potential of New Mexico for American settlement and economic development. What Smith neglected to mention, however, was that the revision of the myth inherently legitimized the political appropriation and economic exploitation of a foreign country, an appropriation formulated as a civilizing mission extending the blessings of freedom to "benighted" Mexicans and Indians.[42] The "discovery" of the American Southwest was, as William Goetzmann has emphasized, essentially a rediscovery of a region that for nearly three centuries had been the scene of spectacular feats of discovery by small parties of Spanish conquistadores and missionaries.[43]

Magoffin's travel diary differs significantly from Gregg's narrative in that it lacks this negative aesthetic of neglect. Moreover, in contrast to Gregg's traveler, who often hides his presence behind the authority of the improving vision, Magoffin's narrator-traveler is present in the landscape as a female rambler, toiler, rider, and collector of specimens, who playfully undermines her own claims to authority. Her relation to the landscape is decidedly nonappropriative, mediated in terms of personal aesthetic experience. Instead of seeing the landscape as a resource—trees as timber, prairies as future fields or as hunting grounds—she sees it as a playground, even a field for innocent study.

Magoffin presents herself as a rambler, more a naturalist than an explorer, contemplating, collecting specimens, naming and collecting flowers—not for scientific purposes but as curiosities. She is a tourist on a pleasure tour, disclaiming any hold on the land. Yet she is also an actuary of the road, recording the "hard facts" of traveling—the weather, road conditions, grass, water, distances— and looking out from her traveling carriage to watch the inhabitants from behind her veil. Unlike Gregg's tenderfoot traveler who becomes a man on the trail but retains his claim to innocence, Magoffin's traveler loses her innocence and must grow up to face her responsibilities. At first, however, she can still cherish the aura of irresponsibility and innocence.

From the beginning, Magoffin's journal is authorized by the unusual nature of a female travel experience: "My journal tells a story tonight different from what it has ever done before" (1). It even bears a title: "Travels in Mexico Commencing June, 1846. El Diario de Doña Susanita Magoffin." Traveling with a maid and servants, Magoffin is unencumbered by any duties and clearly enjoys the novelty of physical exercise in the outdoors as well as the romance of homemaking in a traveling home on the plains. "It is the life of a wandering princess, mine" (11–12), she writes, and she describes her new life in romantic formulaic terms as a pastoral contrast to a confining settled life (10).

Magoffin's journey also provides an escape from female domestic confinement, and she subsequently creates her persona as a woman who tests the boundaries of her feminine sphere. Climbing up steep hills or down river banks in order to pick flowers, to catch a picturesque view, or to inscribe her name on a rock, she casts herself as a reckless adventuress. "Women are venturesome creatures!" she exclaims (27), after she has contemplated her future as an overland emigrant: "If I live through all this—and I think from all appearances now I shall come off the winner—I shall be fit for one of the Oregon pioneers" (23).

The heroic mode implies its own parody, however: Magoffin faces mock-trials by stepping on snakes—who show more fear than the woman—and she assumes a mock-heroic pose, playing with the image of the helpless, fearful woman. Although the danger of an impending war increases daily—she reports army movements for the protection of the Santa Fe traders from increasing Indian hostilities—the dangers of the journey are played down through comparisons with Gregg's account: "And we also had a rattle-snake fracas. There were not hundreds killed tho', as Mr. Gregg had to do to keep his animals from suffering, but some two or three were killed in the road by our carriage driver, and these were quite enough to make me sick" (50). Like Kirkland, Magoffin deflates male hyperbole while playfully undermining her own narrative authority.

In the manner of the Victorian explorer who put himself on a promontory in order to survey the land and to paint it verbally for his home audience, Magoffin also aestheticizes the landscape by representing it as a painting. But it is a painting that is alive: "The scenery is truly magnificent. At one view we have sketched before us lofty hills entirely destitute of shrubbery; at their base gurgled along in quiet solitude a pearly [sic] stream laving the feet of giant trees that looked down with scorn upon the diminutive creature man" (19). In contrast with male narratives of discovery in which, as Pratt has shown, the aesthetic pleasure of the sight constitutes the whole value and significance of the explorer's journey, and in which a relation of mastery is predicated between the seer and the seen,[44] the value and significance of Magoffin's journey lie in the possibilities it offers for a representation of the female self. More-over, any mastery assumed by the narrator over the landscape is immediately subverted by a mock-heroic pose. Like her female contemporaries on the overland trails, she resists the imperial sweep of promontory scenes, declaring herself unable to represent, self-conscious about her limited artistic power, and leaving the task to the "genius of an artist" (83) and the "artists pencil" (19).

In contrast to Gregg's New Mexico landscape, which is emptied of human presence, Magoffin's land is inhabited. Although her descriptions follow the conventions of the picturesque, her observations of natural phenomena are embedded in insights about indigenous cultural practices and social relations (76). Her promontories contain human beings. At times, she even seems to challenge the "monarch-of-all-I-survey" trope of the discovery narrative. Her view from a height does not unveil the scene lying before her; rather, both natural scenery and human beings deliberately hide themselves from the observer (81).

This female narrator assumes various roles: the innocent child bride in love with her protective husband, the traveling princess, the staunch Oregon pioneer, and the brave Amazonian warrior testing the boundaries of female behavior. She is also the mistress of her servants, holding a position of authority by way of class privilege. Her husband even assigns her the role of train leader during his absence, a role in which she wields authority over Mexican men: "I rode on and with as much dignity as I am capable of commanding, which upon a pinch is not a little in my own opinion, selected a camping ground, and ordered the Mexican servants about in broken Spanish" (87). Later, in Mexico, she is both the trader's wife, standing her ground in business relations with customers, and the homemaker, conducting herself as a genteel lady and a resourceful helpmate.

Most of the other roles Magoffin assumes are accompanied by humorous self-distancing: the narrator is an actor, playing roles, at times standing beside herself and laughing at her own picture (28). Neither the pose of the fearful lady nor that of the adventuress is taken seriously. Nevertheless, in situations of danger, where self-distancing is inappropriate, the journal becomes a confessor. Then the mock-heroic adventurous mode is at least temporarily replaced by a serious mode of religious introspection, a language foregrounding faith, self-denial, self-castigation, and submission, which is diametrically opposed to the narrative of adventure and calls into question her breach of the boundaries of her feminine sphere. The narrative position becomes unstable, oscillating between narrative modes and reflecting the shifting demands of the diary form.

The first part of the narrative already contains references to sickness, especially in the aftermath of a carriage wreck and the collapse of her tent. At Bent's Fort, Magoffin is checked by a French doctor, an excellent physician, "especially in female cases" (53), who advises her to travel to Europe rather than along the Santa Fe Trail. She should never have consented to take the trip on the plains, she ruminates, "had it not been with that view and a hope that it would prove beneficial; but so far my hopes have been blasted, for I am rather going down hill than up. . . . But cease my rebellious heart! How prone human nature is to grumble and to think his lot harder than any one of his fellow creatures" (64). After a few days of silence, she reveals to her diary that she has had a miscarriage: "The mysteries of a new world have been shown to me last Thursday! In a few short months I should have been a happy mother and made the heart of a father glad, but the ruling hand of a mighty Providence has interposed and by an abortion deprived us of the hope, the fond hope of mortals!" (67).

What seems to disconcert her beyond her personal pain is that while she had lost a child, an Indian woman in the room below had given birth "to a fine healthy baby, about the same time, and in half an hour after she went to the River and bathed herself and it, and this she has continued each day since." Watching the other woman, she finds it "truly astonishing to see what customs will do. No doubt many ladies in civilized life are ruined by too careful treatments during child-birth, for this custom of the hethen [sic] is not known to be disadvantageous, but it is a 'hethenish custom'" (68). For this brief moment, she stands apart from her own culture, whose claims to authority over women's bodies are destabilized by the difference between the white woman's sickness and the native woman's health. At the same time, she begins to distance herself from her husband's journey and its economic purpose, in which she had been implicated. Thus she meditates on "the follies and wickedness of man" who strives for "wealth, honour and fame to the ruining of his soul, and loosing the brighter crown in higher realms" (69).

This indirect self-castigation, however, is temporary. The journey continues, and Magoffin is forced to build new strength for the dangers ahead: "In that case, if danger were near, I should be obliged to buckle on my pistols and turn warrior myself, rather a touch above me, at Amazonianism!" Considering the pain of losing her child, it is almost unbelievable how she can quip about her sorrowful experience of "confinement" by writing herself into the role of a captivity heroine: "There is a little romance attached to my life: taken prisoner, for we were compelled by the soldiers to come here, confined in a Fort, and when I left there had to fight my own way through blood thirsty Indians, before reaching a place of any safety" (70). The journey demands most of her attention again, and she is now crossing the frontier into a foreign country, although like the women on the trails to California, she is gazing back rather than looking forward (72).

Discourses of femininity are foregrounded in the first part of the account, but colonial discourses soon enter the narrative in Magoffin's descriptions of the people she sees and meets on her journey. As in women's overland diaries, Indians represent dangerous obstacles to the traveler, calling forth the horrors of a possible captivity. At the same time, the danger adds spice to the journey, which enhances the female traveler's courage and boldness (18, 40–41). In the Hispanic villages they pass, she finds herself the center of attention and even feels molested by "the constant stare of these wild looking strangers." Discourses of femininity now guide her representation of the villagers who challenge her feminine sense of modesty and morality: "It is truly shocking to my modesty to pass such places with gentlemen. The women slap about with their arms and necks bare, perhaps their bosoms exposed (and they are none of the prettiest or whitest) if they are about to cross the little creek that is near all the villages, regardless of those about them, they pull their dresses, which in the first place but little more than cover their calves." Magoffin also finds it "repulsive to see the children running about perfectly naked, or if they have on a chimese it is in such ribbands it had better be off at once. I am constrained to keep my veil drawn closely over my face all the time to protect my blushes" (95). Seeing for Magoffin becomes a passive act of suffering. But seeing is nevertheless reciprocal. Drawing her veil, the symbol of white femininity, over her face not only protects her from the "constant stare of 'the natives,'" but also affords her "a screen from whence to beholding my schrutinizing [sic] spectators, and while I carried on a conversation with Mr. Houk on the outside respecting them" (92).

After arriving in Santa Fe, Magoffin quietly settles into the rhythm of the town, adapting to Mexican life as a homemaker in a place where she once "would have thought it folly to think of visiting." Still, she feels compelled to cast her entry into the town as an event that is outstanding on account of her sex and nationality: "I have entered the city in a year that will always be remembered by my countrymen; and under the 'Star-spangled banner' too, the first American lady, who has come under such auspices, and some of our company seem disposed to make me the first under any circumstances that ever crossed the Plains" (102–3).[45] Although she relativizes the claim of being the "first American lady" as a term conferred upon her by others, she still positions her journey within the history of conquest. She sees herself standing at the center of attention, picturing herself promenading over the plaza and "of course attracting the attention of all idle bystanders— my bonnet being an equal object of wonder with the white woman that wore it" (134).

As the wife of a trader, she finds herself empowered by her economic and social standing, priding herself on her ability to organize, to manage, and to order the activities of others in her roles as mistress of a household and of a business. Used to having servants around her, she sees the world hierarchically ordered and finds her worldview confirmed by the social stratification in Santa Fe society. She had shunned the poor Mexican villagers on her journey, but in Santa Fe she becomes friends with upper-class Mexican families, especially with those who had welcomed a connection with the United States, either as a state or as a territory, believing that American civil institutions and capital could bring progress.[46] After the discomfort she had felt when stared at by the simple Mexican villagers, she now enjoys the attention of the American soldiers and the Mexican ricos, with whom she is delighted: "What a polite people these Mexicans are, altho' they are looked upon as a half barbarous set by the generality of people" (130).

As Magoffin describes herself in interaction and conversation with her Mexican hosts and guests, their voices are increasingly heard, giving advice, expressing opinions, affirming their presence: "What an inquisitive, quick people they are. . . . They examine my work if I am engaged in any when they are in, and in an instant can tell me how it is done, though perhaps 'tis the first of the kind they have ever seen" (115). Mexican women, to her amusement, draw her into their feminine confidence by giving her advice on how to "manage" her man. Yet she also stands in a mistress-servant relation to many Mexicans who serve her, and whose pleasant submissiveness she praises (111).

When Magoffin finally leaves Santa Fe, she is again the center of attention: "The women stand around with their faces awfully painted, some with red which shines like greese [sic], and others are daubed over with flour-paste. The men stand off with crossed arms, and all look with as much wonder as if they were not people themselves" (150). The experience repeats itself when the travelers pass a Pueblo village where the people "are around the tent peeping in at me and expressing their opinions. It is a novel sight for them" (151). Her representation of the exotic other thus contains a curiously inverted version of the touristic gaze—it is the white woman who is cast as the object of curiosity and wonder, the center of the Pueblo gaze, while she herself professes indifference and denies seeing those who gaze at her.

Magoffin also enters into trading relations with women on the trail—relations of barter between people with wholly different perceptions of value: the caravan trades empty bottles instead of money for goods, to the satisfaction of the native women and the amusement of the Magoffins (153–54). Bartering mainly revolves around food—the lack of which renders the travelers most dependent and vulnerable—and Magoffin repeatedly records that native women presented her with tortillas, which she now enjoys wholeheartedly (154). She also describes herself in conversation with native women who come to visit her in her tent, talking "of all family concerns from the children down to the dogs" (160).

Thus, although Magoffin assumes an imperial voice by fixing Mexican and Indian people into an iconic "they" or "she"—"like the rest of her kind she is curious, and loves to talk" (163)—the discourse of femininity, drawing on ideas of female solidarity, nevertheless undermines colonialist demarcations between "us" and "them." Furthermore, the positioning of the female narrator as an object of curiosity, subjected to the gaze of the other, blurs the clear distinctions and distributions of power contained in the imperial rhetoric of othering: the way she is singled out by the native gaze simultaneously empowers her and makes her vulnerable. By drawing attention to herself as an object, Magoffin paradoxically undermines and confirms her position within the sex-gender system. She is simultaneously writing herself as the center of her narrative and opening herself to the gaze, which is interestingly gendered: the native gaze is perceived as mainly female. Describing herself from the outside, through the eyes of others, she at the same time submits to the gaze and heightens her own sense of value.

On the other hand, Magoffin also increasingly records military and political events in connection with the American occupation of California and New Mexico, which has led to historians' acknowledgment of the diary as a valuable source in the study of the Mexican-American War.[47] Magoffin's own views of political events are developed in a dialogue with American and Mexican voices. At first, General Kearny's occupation of Santa Fe is not seen as an act of conquest but an attempt to liberate the Mexican people from tyranny (103). At a Mexican American dinner, she notes that "the people toast to the union of Mexico and the U.S." (135). Soon the political events dominate the journal, and "movements of the army as we hear it is all I can find to write about these days" (179).

When the travelers are held up at San Gabriel, Magoffin records being sick and anxious from the constant danger of being murdered or taken prisoner, and her language becomes increasingly religious: "I have not prayed with sufficient fervour to have my weak faith strengthened. . . . I have joined in merry and useless conversation. I have spent time foolishly that should have been spent in doing good" (171). At the same time, she attempts to mute her horror and fear by invoking a sense of adventure: "This is truly exciting times! I doubt if my honoured Grandmother ever saw or heard of more to excite, in the War she was [the War of 1812], than I have here. The Indians are all around us; coming into the soldiers' camp and driving off their stock, and killing the men in attendance of them" (180). When news of revolts against Americans at Santa Fe and Taos reach them, Magoffin writes, "It is a perfect revolution there" (191).

In the midst of these entries on outbreaks and revolts, Magoffin develops a position of her own, which is relativistic in the way it tentatively breaks up the monolithic category of the other: "My knowledge of these people has been extended very much in one day. There are among them some of the greatest villains, smooth-faced assassins in the world and some good people too" (192–93). Magoffin seems to have found it increasingly difficult to take sides in the Mexican-American conflict, as evidenced by her lack of comment on the following criticism of the U.S. government, voiced by the Magoffins' Mexican host Don Ygnacio. An admirer of George Washington, Don Ygnacio "says the course Mr. Polk is per-suing in regard to this war, is entirely against the principals of Washington, which were to remain at home, encouraging all home improvements, to defend our rights there against the incroach-ments of others, and never to invade the territory of an other na-tion" (211). Magoffin refuses to take sides: "Never could I wish harm to or exult over the other party, if I were able I would have all peace" (216).

Magoffin's diary shows how nationalist rhetoric may be compli-cated by discourses of gender. Although her patriotic statements recurrently contrast with her concern for and interest in Mexican people, lifestyles, and affairs, they do not necessarily exclude each other. The positioning of this female narrator within an expansion-ist discourse is essentially unstable, oscillating between national loyalty and the privileging of personal relations. It is these fissures in some women's western narratives that contain a cultural cri-tique which shatters the complacent, self-contained pose of the anti-conquest.

part 2

Army Women, Tourists, and Mythmakers, 1860–1890

As the overland diaries have shown, throughout the 1850s a steady stream of white travelers flowed westward, with gold and silver as well as the promise of land inviting immigration and stimulating agriculture, commerce, transportation, and finally industry. By 1860, settlers beyond the ninety-fifth meridian had multiplied more than threefold.[1] Texas, California, and Oregon had become states, and nearly all the rest of the land west of the Missouri River had been organized into territories. The Civil War hardly slowed the pace of the westward movement, and as population grew and spread, so did the transportation and communication networks. By 1869, the transcontinental railroad was completed, connecting the Far West with the East and providing the nation with a new, technologically shaped image of the process of westward expansion.[2]

The railroad not only opened the Far West to tourism but was also instrumental in the rise of the cattle business. Interest in ranching and other uses of natural resources brought a new quality to explorations of the West, which earlier had served the function of map making preceding settlement.[3] Moreover, as Alan Trachtenberg points out, the events stimulated by the railroads in the 1870s and 1880s revealed "not an agrarian but an industrial capitalist scenario. Penetrating the West with government encouragement, the railroad and the telegraph opened the vast spaces to production." Richard Slotkin registers a similar change in the meaning of the term "frontier." After the Civil War, he claims, the emphasis shifted from a political to an economic interpretation of American history.[4] The first decades after the Civil War were also characterized by Indian wars erupting all over the West, which confronted

America with the need to solve its Indian problem like never before.

As Patricia Limerick has noted, the capacity to deal simultaneously with multiple points of view may well be one of the most important skills necessary for the writing of Western history.[5] The same is true for an analysis of women's western writings in the second half of the nineteenth century. Urban and agricultural frontiers, mining and Indian frontiers develop and continue to exist simultaneously in the American West, overlapping, determining, contesting, and complementing one another. The U.S. Army may have fought violent battles with Indians in one area, but another area may have developed into a romantic spot on the map of fashionable tourist sightseeing, or into a prosperous mining or agricultural region. Women's writings on the West reflect this simultaneity of frontiers, which impedes the construction of clear-cut chronologies.

Since the 1850s, women had accompanied their husbands in the frontier army, had served as army laundresses, and had traveled West as "camp followers." The latter group seldom left written records of their experiences, but women married to army officers contributed a wealth of letters, diaries, and personal narratives to the literature on the western military frontier. However, with the exception of Teresa Viele's *Following the Drum* (1858), Josephine Clifford's stories in the *Overland Monthly,* and Margaret Carrington's *Ab-Sa-Ra-Ka* (1868), few army women's narratives saw publication before the end of the Indian wars in the 1880s.

Elizabeth Custer, the widow of General Armstrong Custer, who perished with his whole cavalry unit in the famous battle on the Little Bighorn, seems to have taken the lead in 1885 with the publication of her *'Boots and Saddles,'* followed by two sequels in 1887 and 1890. The popularity of Custer's books, together with an increased interest in American history and especially the history of American pioneering, may have stimulated other women to present their reminiscences of army life to the public.

The sheer number of women's army reminiscences published— and reviewed in major eastern periodicals—from the 1890s through the 1910s indicates that they must have been highly visible on the literary market. The 1890s saw the publication of reminiscences by Lydia Spencer Lane (1893), Frances A. Boyd (1894), and Mrs. D. B.

Dyer (1896), followed by those of Ellen Biddle (1907), Martha Summerhayes (1908), Frances Roe (1909), Frances Carrington (1910),
and Alice Baldwin (1929). (Many of these works have recently been
reprinted owing to the resurgence in the past two decades of interest in western women.) What often seems to have made these reminiscences possible, however, is not the women's own stories but
those of their more or less famous husbands. For example, Margaret
and Frances Carrington's books are informed by the purpose of defending the actions of Colonel Henry Carrington in connection with
the Fetterman Massacre of 1866. Elizabeth Custer also directed her
literary efforts to the defense of her husband's memory and reputation, and so did Jessie Benton Frémont, who in reaction to troubled
family finances took up the pen in the 1870s and 1880s to reminisce
about her life with the "Pathfinder" John Charles Frémont.

While some women were accompanying their husbands to the
Indian frontier, others were still moving along the overland trails
to new homes, permanent or temporary, in the newly opened western territories. By 1869 the Union Pacific Railroad had reached San
Francisco, but many people still traveled in covered wagons like
their predecessors. From the 1870s through the 1890s, Carrie Adell
Strahorn accompanied her husband on his explorations of the
West for railroad routes and settlement possibilities, sharing the
hardships and excitement of travel through "unexplored" territory. By the 1870s, eastern and European women also "did" the
West as tourists; the journey between Chicago and the Pacific
could be comfortably undertaken by rail, and traveling the West for
health and pleasure became a fashionable luxury. Colorado and
California became new El Dorados, this time sought by tourists.
San Francisco and Denver developed into cosmopolitan centers.

Sara Lippincott, alias Grace Greenwood, traveled to Colorado
and California in 1871, followed by Helen Hunt Jackson in 1872,
and in 1873 by the Englishwoman Isabella Bird, who took a side
trip from San Francisco to Colorado on her tour around the world.
All of these women who wrote about their travel experiences as
tourists either were established writers or sought to establish themselves, through their travel accounts, as writers within an eastern
or European literary or journalistic culture. Lippincott, Hunt, and
Bird wrote serial travel letters for New York, Boston, and London
magazines, and they later collected their travel narratives in books.

Laura W. Johnson's narrative of a tour to Indian country in 1874–75 was first published serially in *Lippincott's Magazine* in 1875, and then in 1889 as *Eight Hundred Miles in an Ambulance,* indicating that already in the mid-1870s, tourists were seeking ever new places, and even Indian reservations had acquired a certain exotic attraction.

Other women writers located themselves within the newly emerging regional publishing markets centering around San Francisco's numerous magazines and periodicals, and they contributed columns, travel narratives, and stories to the *Golden Era* or the *Overland Monthly.* Some women, like Caroline Churchill, edited periodicals and published and distributed their work by themselves.[6] By the 1880s, a regional interest in the pioneer past had developed, giving rise to the writing of pioneer histories and reminiscences of overland travel and early frontier life in the Far West, among them the previously discussed reminiscences of Sarah Royce, Catharine Haun, and Sarah Raymond Herndon.[7]

By then, America had rediscovered the Southwest as a place of romantic and historic interest. Women writers like Josephine Clifford, Helen Hunt Jackson, and Gertrude Atherton became important creators of a California myth anchored in the romanticization of the Hispanic past and of Indian missions in the Southwest. The West had become a vocation not only for women writers but also for women who were increasingly making their mark in male-dominated realms as historians, natural scientists, and anthropologists. Other women created professions for themselves as missionaries and teachers on Indian reservations. Women's writings about the West, whether they were published in the nineteenth century or appeared in the form of reminiscences in the early decades of the twentieth, reflect this diversity of women's interests in the West.

chapter 3

Women and the Rhetoric of Indian War

In 1846, General Stephen Kearny promised Hispanic New Mexicans protection from Navajos and Apaches, who since Spanish times had regularly raided Hispanic and Pueblo settlements. The promise was repeated as the U.S. Army made its move westward. Indeed, as Robert Utley observes, "the promise to eliminate the Indian menace to white settlement was implicit in the nation's westward expansion to the Pacific."[1] Government officials, who had begun to recognize the need for an Indian policy after the annexation of the northern Mexican borderlands in 1846, focused on three major objectives that acquisition of the new territories imposed on federal Indian policy: the military protection of citizens threatened by Indians; the extinction of Indian title to lands coveted, needed, or claimed by whites; and the development of policies to integrate Indians into the American nation, now that removal to a previously envisioned permanent Indian frontier seemed no longer possible.[2]

Frontier military needs had been partly addressed in 1846 when Congress authorized a string of guardian forts along the Oregon Trail—and the creation of a special unit to garrison them. The army at first followed a defensive strategy, acting as a policing force, but soon began mounting offensive campaigns. Both Congress and the executive branch failed to appreciate the additional demands on the poorly staffed frontier army, which had to deal with unfamiliar geography—vast distances, climatic extremes, and scarce food, water, and fuel—and an elusive foe, mounted and adapted to the environment, and engaging in an unorthodox guerilla warfare.[3]

Treaties remained the main mechanism for extinguishing Indian title and defining all other relations between the United States and a tribe, but by the 1850s the idea of the reservation had become official policy, with a goal of "concentrating the Indians on small, well-defined tracts of land, protecting them from white contamination, teaching them to become self-sufficient farmers, and conferring on them the blessings of white Christian civilization."[4] Although western settlers and politicians habitually blocked the reservation policy, protesting against giving Indians any lands that might hold agricultural or mineral potential, by 1860 the reservation had become the cornerstone of federal Indian policy.

The history of the Indian frontier for the next half-century, Utley argues, was to be largely the record of Indian resistance, not so much to white intrusion but to the reservation system (63). By the end of the Civil War, the Five Civilized Tribes[5] in Indian Territory were internally divided, and the Navajo had been herded, after Kit Carson's scorched-earth campaign, into the concentration camp—like reservation of Bosque Redondo. With offensives being mounted against the tribes on the northern and southern Plains, it appeared that the generals and western politicians had made Indian policy overwhelmingly a military policy (93).

But there were also other voices to be heard. In 1864, the nation momentarily heaped outrage on the military, condemning Colonel Chivington's massacre of a sleeping Cheyenne village at Colorado's Sand Creek, which became a "never-to-be-forgotten symbol of what was wrong with United States treatment of Indians."[6] Army offensives against the Plains tribes in 1865 ended in complete failure and were beginning to severely discredit a purely military solution to the Indian problem. That same year, new congressional enactments marked the first tentative steps toward a different kind of Indian policy, a peace policy that favored "conquest by kindness."[7]

Over the next several years, Indian policy would be characterized by ambivalence and indecision between the rifle and the peace pipe. What is more, military men invoked the rhetoric of the civilizing mission as the only means to ensure Indian survival, which suggests that the alleged rift between militarists and philanthropists was not as absolute as it seems, but that military and philanthropic discourses actually complemented each other. Americans, whether military officials or reformers, Easterners or Westerners, had learned to put the blame for Indian wars on other groups: reformers blamed the military, Easterners blamed Westerners and vice versa, and military men blamed the American government, sentimental Easterners, and land-grabbing Westerners, casting themselves as innocents caught in between.[8]

Despite negotiations of peace treaties, wars flared up almost everywhere in the West in the 1860s and 1870s. In 1868, General Ulysses S. Grant, anticipating his election as the next U.S. president, told reporters that settlers and emigrants had to be protected even if it meant the extermination of every Indian tribe. Nevertheless, Grant's Indian policy during his administration (1869–76) would be known as "Grant's Peace Policy." The president sought advice and recommendations from church groups, and the reservations were staffed with members of the Christian denominations.[9] However, as Utley argues, Grant's peace policy was not consciously crafted as an instrument of radical change but was prompted by a combination of forces. One of these forces emerged after peace sentiment crystallized into organized lobbying activity. Major religious denominations launched attempts to influence Indian policy and formed humanitarian organizations for the "protection and elevation of the Indians."[10] It is in this area of humanitarian reform, as discussed in chapter 5, that women made their influence known and heard in the 1880s and 1890s.

Although the most conspicuous feature of Grant's Indian policy was its focus on peaceful means, the administration still looked to the army to play a central role. Many tribes resisted the concentration and civilization programs at the heart of the Peace Policy. By the end of Grant's second term in 1876, the peace between Indians and whites had turned out to be largely illusory, not least as a consequence of Custer's Last Stand on the Little Bighorn, the shattering news of which reached the nation during its centennial celebrations.

Thus the era of the so-called peace policy ironically featured some of the most violent warfare in the history of Indian-white relations. With a goal of placing all Indians on reservations—where they could be kept away from the settlements and travel routes and where they could be ultimately "Americanized"—the policy drew bitter resistance from Indians who soon realized that reservation life meant the loss of their land, livelihood, and distinct cultural identity. Virtually every military battle after the Civil War, Utley argues, was fought to force Indians onto newly created reservations or to make them go back to reservations from which they had fled (164).

From one standpoint, it is important to take this political and ideological framework into account as a context for women's narratives of life in the army, since it affected not only the lives of the men at the expanding network of western army posts, but also those of the women who accompanied them, often with their children. The very fact of women's presence, although not acknowledged in army regulations, indicates that the army did not envision large-scale military confrontations with Indians in the West, and that the Indian frontier was regarded as safe enough for families. General William Tecumseh Sherman had even encouraged officers' wives to accompany their husbands and "to take with them all needed comforts for a pleasant garrison life in the newly opened country, where all would be healthful, with pleasant service and absolute peace."[11] By the 1870s, army posts had even become vacationing spots for hunter-sportsmen and unmarried young women.[12]

Federal policy, however, can only provide a marginal framework for the study of women's western narratives and women's relation to political rhetoric. As Patricia Limerick has warned, overplaying the significance of federal policy in the writing of western history may be tempting, but following its chronology actually leads away from the complexities of cultural interaction.[13] As a matter of fact, one would be hard put to follow the chronology of federal Indian policy in women's western narratives. Nevertheless, it is important to define the way women locate their texts within the discursive frameworks provided by Indian policy discussions and by public discourses that manipulated the distinctions between war and peace, Indian extermination and civilization, and liberal humanism and social control in the context of westward expansion.

Women's Narratives of Army Life

In 1866, an infantry regiment under Colonel Carrington was sent to build forts on the Bozeman Trail and protect the emigration to the gold fields in Montana.[14] Three women who participated in the march would leave written records of their lives in the army: Margaret Carrington, Elizabeth Burt, and Frances Grummond (who, after the death of Margaret in 1870, would become the second Mrs. Carrington). At Fort Kearny, General Sherman had suggested that the "ladies of the expedition" keep a daily journal of events. Elizabeth Burt had already kept a journal for quite some time, and Margaret Carrington apparently took up the suggestion then and there.[15]

Margaret Carrington's account stands out from other women's army reminiscences not only because of its textual status—it is not a memoir written many years after the fact—but also because of its impersonal, factual style. Avoiding the first-person singular, Carrington intended to present nothing further "than to express the facts so recorded just as they were impressed upon the judgment or fancy" (xix). The narrator's purpose is to describe "our life and the exact history of the first year of the military occupation of Absaraka" and to provide guidance for those undertaking their first visit to "Absaraka, Home of the Crows" (xx).

Like Frances Carrington's reminiscence, which was published in 1910, Margaret Carrington's journal centers on the character of her husband Henry Carrington and on the so-called "Fetterman Massacre" in 1866, where Frances's first husband George Grummond lost his life.[16] The Fetterman Massacre had propelled the possibility of an Indian war into national prominence and intensified the debate over Indian policy. Supporters of a peace policy were now clearly in the ascendant, and military operations were under serious public scrutiny.[17] Margaret Carrington's book was thus more than the personal account of an army officer's wife, because it impressed eastern readers with the seriousness of Indian resistance against white expansion.

This is the context in which the appearance of Margaret Carrington's *Ab-Sa-Ra-Ka* should be located. Henry Carrington, although not found culpable by the investigation, never received the opportunity to publish his own official report of the Fetterman battle, and John McDermott even suggests that the book was Carrington's own vehicle for apologia. Although it is difficult to surmise how much he contributed to his wife's account, McDermott assumes that he assisted in the writing.[18] The story surrounding the two Carrington books thus illustrates the problematics of female authorship and the degree to which women's narratives of the army frontier were implicated in military politics. This poses the question not so much of the authenticity of women's narratives, but of authority and power within these texts.

In her books, Elizabeth Custer undertook a similar defense of her husband's reputation. George Armstrong Custer, the "boy-general" who at age twenty-three had been promoted to the rank of brigadier general—the youngest man to hold that rank prior to World War II— had always been a controversial figure, known for his impulsivity and eccentricity.[19] To be sure, Elizabeth Custer does not openly participate in the debate over the events leading to "Custer's Last Stand," claiming in *'Boots and Saddles'* that she had little opportunity to know much of official matters because they were not discussed at home (114–15). Instead, she provides an indirect commentary by focusing on her dead husband's character and portraying him as a gallant and loving husband; a disciplined, responsible, and popular officer; and, significantly, a "sincere friend of the reservation Indian" (187). Later, Custer's widow did participate in the controversy over her husband's military actions, and she began to monitor articles about him and urge others to defend him, manipulating as much as she could the public memory of his military exploits.[20] Even in her first book, she had laid the foundation for a Custer myth that would be perpetuated in historical works, popular literature, and art.

Although there is always the danger of overestimating her public influence,[21] it is important to consider the curious relation between Elizabeth Custer's public activities and the feminine professions in her books of noninvolvement in the public arena. The purpose of her first book, as stated in its preface, was explicitly nonpolitical: "Very little has been written regarding the domestic life of an army family, and yet I cannot believe that it is without interest; for the innumerable questions that are asked about our occupations, amusements, and mode of housekeeping lead me to hope that the actual answer to these queries contained in this little story will be acceptable" (xxix). Custer's focus on the personal and what she calls the "domestic" seems to have led the way for other women's reminiscences of frontier life in the late nineteenth century.

Reviews of Custer's books by her contemporaries not only reveal how positively they were received by an eastern public but also illustrate the influence of gender ideology in the critical reading of her works. A reviewer of the book traces the charm of the "unpretentious little book . . . to the writer's entire self-forgetfulness, her unusual absorption in another, her singular lack of self-consciousness."[22] The book also has merit as an autobiography: "If it reveals to us the man of whom the author is constantly thinking, it also reveals, though quite unconsciously, the woman who shared and illumined his life with the glory of a perfect and utterly unselfish devotion" (813). Thus Custer's book is not read as a personal account of Indian war, but as an illustration of a military man's character and personality, putting it in the class of books whose charm is almost wholly independent of "the importance or unimportance of their themes" (814).[23]

Lydia Spencer Lane, who had "joined the army" in the 1850s, makes similar claims of noninvolvement in discussions of military politics. Although she describes herself as a member of the army who loved everything connected with it, at the same time she remains aloof, avoiding "squabbles and political discussions, which I detested, and of which I knew nothing whatever" (130). Compared to other women who "spoke of 'our regiment' and 'our troop' (or company), as if they had command," she found she was "far behind the times, believing, as I always had, that the less a woman knew of military affairs, and what went on in garrison, the better for all" (162). Unlike Margaret Carrington, who affected objectivity in her impersonal style, Lane wrote in a personal mode that emphasizes female suffering and a marginal feminine vision. As will be seen, this marginal voice can nevertheless become an important medium for a colonialist discourse and the mentality of Indian-hating, which as Dawn Lander has argued, has been stereotypically attributed to women in American literature and history.[24]

In contrast to the narratives of Custer and the Carringtons, Lane's text does not focus on her husband. It is not authorized by the story of a famous and controversial man but by the everyday experience of western pioneering, which seems to have drawn increased public interest in the 1890s. Lane underscores this in her last chapter: "My experience was that of hundreds of other women, many of whom are far more capable than I of telling the story; but few, if any, have done it, and only the younger ones, with no knowledge of ante-bellum days" (192). Addressing the army women of the 1890s, her narrative focuses on the hardships, deprivations, and compensations of a representative woman's life in the old army before the arrival of the railroad. As officer-writer Charles King's review suggests, Lane's book also was enlisted in contemporary discussions about women's rights and their movement into the public sphere: her story "of danger and privation, unflinchingly met, is one that American women ought to read and be prouder than ever of their queendom."[25]

Some women still felt compelled to write their stories within the framework of men's military heroism. Like the Carringtons and Custer, Frances Boyd framed her story of army life within her husband's story, and Alice Baldwin's memoirs evolved as an appendix to her husband's autobiography (which she had helped him to begin but which was never finished).[26]

Other women's writings cannot be subsumed under the story of military men, drawing their appeal from the special nature of a woman's western experience. When Frances Roe published *Army Letters from an Officer's Wife* in 1909, they were not authorized by a man's story but by the special authenticity and realism of a woman's account, as opposed to the "flowery" style associated with sentimental writing on the West. Sentimentality is also absent from Ellen Biddle's (1907) and Martha Summerhayes' (1908) reminiscences of army life, which are informed by realistic revisioning and even disillusionment. Army life reveals itself, in the words of Summerhayes, as "glittering misery" (7). More than earlier texts, Summerhayes' narrative focuses on gender and the critique of gender conventions. Her husband is relegated to a secondary position and at times receives unusually negative critical attention. But most women's accounts of life in the army remain, at least allegedly, within the framework of women's writing by emphasizing their personal and private nature and placing themselves within the context of a family audience and history.

With some exceptions, most of these women wrote their memoirs of the Old West at a time, between the 1890s and the 1910s, when Americans were developing a deeply ambivalent attitude toward America's pioneering past. On one hand, Americans looked to the West for a myth of unity and a usable past, attributing almost all that was desirable in American life and character to the effects of the pioneering experience, and seeking to retain what they considered the picturesque glamour and glory of the Old West.[27] Frederick Jackson Turner and Theodore Roosevelt were among the ardent supporters of the belief that the frontier had been the most significant force in shaping national institutions and character. They were convinced that it was necessary for Americans to appreciate the frontier past in order to reconcile the contradictions of American democracy in the 1890s, and they believed that the long-anticipated crisis of closure connected to the end of the frontier was now at hand. Their rediscovery of the frontier was thus not simply a look back, but a look ahead.[28] On the other hand, especially in the first decades of the new century, American intellectuals sought to renounce the American pioneering experience as a useless past, attacking it as a source of American cultural and intellectual deficiencies, as "the scapegoat for all that was wrong with contemporary America."[29]

By the 1890s, the West had also emerged in the popular consciousness as the "Wild West," a terrain of danger, adventure, and violence that appealed to Easterners as an image of contrast to urban society. In dime novels, the West in its wildness retained older associations with freedom, escape from social restraint, closeness to nature, and this image persisted, "especially as a protopopulist image of opposition."[30] By the end of the century, however, when eastern corporations had virtually accomplished their control of western enterprises, the image of the West and of the western hero had shifted.

When the Western solidified into the form that would remain the staple of twentieth-century popular culture, it appeared as a fable of conservative values, a cultural equivalent to incorporation—a development already complete in Owen Wister's *The Virginian* (1902), where the implicit egalitarianism of earlier western narratives is turned into an explicit ruling-class vision, preoccupied with order and patriarchal dominance.[31] Women's memoirs of army life thus appeared at a time when the frontier was rediscovered as the last repository of American values and virtues, a rediscovery that was accompanied by a rhetorical remasculinization of American culture as well as a pronounced emphasis on empire.

According to T. J. Jackson Lears, by the end of the nineteenth century, "antimodern" sentiments had spread among the educated and affluent on both sides of the Atlantic, sentiments which found their expression in the recoil from an "overcivilized" modern existence to more intense forms of physical or spiritual experience, supposedly embodied in medieval or Oriental cultures as well as in the martial ideal—the idea of war as the promise of social and personal regeneration. This belief reemerged in the 1880s as an antidote to overcivilization, which may also be interpreted as a backlash against what many perceived as the "feminization" of northeastern culture.[32]

Militarism, which served as cultural revitalization, transformation, and protest, was expressed in the promotion of a masculinist "literature of action," in stricter child socialization through athletics and military drill, the revival of capital punishment, and the yearning for a scientifically sanctioned racial identity in a society where all identities seemed in dissolution. It was also reflected in Theodore Roosevelt's cult of strenuosity, which reasserted the virtues of self-improvement and self-control.[33] This preoccupation with the militaristic, of course, was also related to U.S. expansionist activities overseas.[34]

Women wrote about their experiences of hardship in the frontier West at a time when people had largely escaped from physical pain, were insulated from danger and discomfort, and felt that their lives had become too soft, too civilized.[35] Scholars have identified the emergence of the western genre around the turn of the century as a popular version of high culture's yearnings for the authentic and the strenuous life. John Cawelti has shown how a formulaic Western developed as a new genre, distinct from earlier literary and subliterary traditions, and encoding a particularly masculine definition of human worth as well as a particular definition of American history and society.[36]

Jane Tompkins has emphasized the correspondence between the emergence of the Western and women's "invasion of the public sphere" after 1880, asserting that the true subject of the western narrative is the male fear of losing patriarchal control. The Western, Tompkins argues, needs to be understood as part of a remasculinization of cultural territory, countering the inwardness, spirituality, and domesticity of the dominant (female) sentimental literature with a rough and tumble, secular, man-centered world, in which the focus is on physical pain and endurance, a preoccupation with death, and the desire to dominate the western environment as well as to merge with it.[37] Although I find most of Tompkins's reasoning convincing, I disagree with one particular premise of her argument. Defining the popular Western as an answer to the domestic novel and as a male attempt to silence and deauthorize the voice of evangelical-reform Christianity in women's domestic novels, Tompkins excludes women as authors of the western genre, assuming two separate traditions of men's and women's writing. My study obviously questions Tompkins's restriction of women's writing to the genre of the domestic novel.[38]

In short, the fact that reminiscences of women in the West, and particularly of women in the frontier army, had come to be popular at exactly the time when the Western emerged as a genre may be explained by a whole series of extrabiographical factors connected with an increased interest in the American West. Women's texts may have related to the same historical issues as those of male writers, although they may have done this to a different end. Of course, by the end of the century, most of the "army women" had reached an age at which reminiscing and writing memoirs became appropriate. Moreover, many writers, after the death of a husband, lived on meager, if any, army pensions, and writing became a source of income. Nevertheless, without a receptive reading public, none of these women could have published their accounts. That these narratives appeared in such a condensed fashion, roughly between the 1880s and the 1910s, must be explained by both the women's life cycles and the special needs of the times. Just as the frontier itself, the "Old Army" had become a thing of the past, and women who had experienced both became authorities on a bygone era and life. But how did they locate themselves within a climate of cultural revitalization that seems to have been so highly charged with gender symbolism?

Given my earlier observations on the discursive constraints surrounding the production and reception of women's army narratives, it may not come as a surprise that these texts seem to focus on the domestic, everyday aspects of army life rather than on military politics and warfare. After all, women's army narratives were those of dependents, not soldiers. Moreover, most of the women who left records of their army life were officers' wives, a group of predominantly eastern middle- to upper-class women who located themselves within discourses of womanhood and domesticity, and who saw it fit to show that their lives centered around husbands, home, and family.

Women's army narratives are thus often interpreted as tending to concentrate mainly on details of home and garrison life, and on the problems of making a home and raising a family under new, and often difficult, conditions.[39] Indeed, women described their quarters and furnishings as well as their efforts to transform unattractive housing into homes, recalled details of camp life and travel during the frequent marches from one garrison post to the next, and talked about getting used to the routine of constant moves. They recorded their problems with servants, child care, and clothing, as well as with the scarcity of food items beyond the habitual beef and hardtack, such as eggs, fruit, and vegetables.

Many women who began army life as young brides were inexperienced as homemakers. They described, often with humorous self-mockery, their sometimes comic, sometimes desperate efforts at housekeeping, which were made more difficult by primitive conditions.[40] Like other female overland travelers, many had accompanied their husbands to western posts despite pregnancies; consequently, the anxieties and concerns surrounding childbirth and childrearing under primitive conditions were special concerns that kept many women, both in real life and in their narratives, within the bounds of their homes and families. Also like their predecessors on the overland trails, they remain silent on sexuality, family planning, and unwanted pregnancies. Most do not even reveal their pregnancies—except in coded references to their health—until they mention, almost in an aside and in a somewhat impersonal manner, the birth of a child.

These women's frontier narratives seldom consciously record transgressions of prescribed feminine behavior. Instead, their narrative personae present themselves within the boundaries of matrimony and genteel respectability. Significantly, many female writers of army narratives feel compelled to legitimize their journey west with the army. Elizabeth Burt, for instance, informs her readers that "he [Andrew Burt] and I had discussed the matter and agreed that wherever order took him, baby and I would go too, if at all possible" (20). Most narratives start with the couple's marriage, with hardly a hint of the preceding courtship, and it is almost a convention for the writers to point to the fierce resistance of their families to this decision.

A frequent issue for critical comment is the fact that although women were encouraged to join their husbands in the army, regulations provided nothing for wives or children, not even mentioning their existence. Women had to travel in ambulances and to restrict their baggage to a minimum. "It seemed very strange to me," Custer wrote, "that with all the value that is set on the presence of the women of an officer's family at the frontier posts, the book of army regulations makes no provision for them, but in fact ignores them entirely!" (105–6). Boyd notes that many women "rebelled at being considered mere camp followers," maintaining that it is "a recognized fact that woman's presence—as wife—alone prevents demoralization" (136). Roe legitimizes her own decision to accompany her husband by arguing that it is at dreadful places like dilapidated army posts that "the plucky army wife is needed. Her very presence has often a refining and restraining influence over the entire garrison. . . . No one can as quickly grasp the possibilities of comfort in quarters like these, or as bravely busy herself to fix them up" (81).

In their emphasis on the hardships of army life, these narratives also underscore what women shared with men. They experienced exhausting marches over unknown terrain, often in danger of being attacked by Indians; they suffered from the extremes of climate and had to cope with insects and reptiles; and they shared with the men their inadequate diets, poor health facilities, low salaries, and the monotony and isolation of garrison life. Many women, like Lane, were actually "roughing it" on the marches and travels, while others like Custer, who were cared for by servants, described a more leisurely experience. But they also wrote about the special attractions of army life for women, especially at large posts where garrison life could present an alternative to the isolated, home-centered life of the middle-class nuclear family, with possibilities for social entertainment and companionship beyond the confines of the home. Some even adopted a military style of dress featuring military buttons and cavalry-style hats.

Although women did not participate in the Indian campaigns, their lives, like those of all women involved in war, were intimately affected by the fighting. Women had to face the threat of an

Indian attack and even came under fire themselves. The outcome of battles mattered to women as much as they did to men: either victory or loss could change their lives, although they may not have been as physically threatened as the men. Instead, women were often condemned to inactivity, although Custer reports that they once stayed at the garrison without any substantial protection, left to worry not only about their husbands' fates but also their own.[41]

Often implied in the telling of war experiences is the danger of captivity and the threat of sexual violation, which doubtless added to the persistent popularity of captivity narratives, still appearing and avidly read in the 1880s.[42] Lydia Lane describes the imagined dangers from Kiowa, Comanche, and Apache raiders on a journey from New Mexico to Texas in 1859:

> Woe to the hapless party that fell into the devilish hands of a band of Indians! Men were generally put to death by slow torture, but they were allowed to live long enough to witness the atrocities practiced on their wives and children, such things as only fiends could devise. Babies had their brains dashed out before the eyes of father and mother, powerless to help them. Lucky would the latter have been, had they treated her the same way; but what she was forced to endure would have wrung tears from anything but an Indian. Do you wonder at our dread of them? (73–74)

Like their female contemporaries on the overland trails, some women suggest that the fear of capture was inspired by men's warnings and by culturally created images of Indian warfare. Conditioned by stories of Indian atrocities and captivity, their fears of Indian attacks—often increased by their own helplessness and dependence on men's protection—were worsened by husbands and friends who handed them pistols or revolvers with orders to shoot themselves and their children to escape captivity or a fate "worse than death."[43] Alice Baldwin even parodies the stereotype of the hysterical woman in the face of an Indian attack: "I had read and heard that women had hysteria and swooned and were bathed in tears in times of danger. I felt that I was not at all romantic, because in the midst of my solitude I bethought me of eating a piece of pie—which I did!" Nonetheless, after the attack was over, she had "a sort of relapse, and wept and sobbed and went into hysterics" (67). On the whole, however, for both men and women, life in the army was characterized less by dramatic warfare than by unspectacular routine and monotony.[44]

The conditions of frontier travel and life often threatened established patterns of "ladylike" behavior, requiring a modification of standards of cleanliness, dress, and propriety. Women's enjoyment of outdoor physical exercise and the experience of "roughing it" seem to have demanded a counteracting strategy that underscored that women still remained ladies, even though they might, in adapting to the necessities of western travel and life, transgress the boundaries of circumscribed gendered behavior. For example, Burt tells her readers that rather than giving up her delightful rides, she substituted her long waterproof cape for a skirt: "To ride then in a divided skirt and astride as is the custom of the present day, was unheard of" (16).[45] On the other hand, women's narratives underscore the transformative aspects of their western experience in terms of their increasing indifference to conventions of dress and appearance: both Lane and Custer present themselves as sensible but feminine dressers who have become indifferent to fashion.

The frameworks of women's narratives of army life suggest that constraints on these texts were not only working through discourses of femininity but also through a discourse of loyalty to the army, not as an institution but as a way of life that actually authorized and made these texts possible. As a result, readers will find no pacifist questioning of army operations in the West, but rather a defense of individual military men and of the service rendered by both men and women in the frontier army. Officers' wives, like their husbands, fill their letters, diaries, and memoirs with defenses of army activities.[46] Elizabeth Custer, for example, created in the figure of her husband the prototype of the innocent who stands between his duty and his humanitarian sympathies for the Indians he kills.

Women's published narratives of army life generally paint a positive picture of both military society and garrison life, but as Judy Lensink's discussion of a western woman's diary entries on the Civil War has suggested, the relation between women and war is more complex.[47] Also, women's detachment from military affairs can assume a subversive as well as supportive nature.

One of these contradictory undercurrents in women's narratives, which negotiates between protest and conformity and which may subvert openly affirmed stances of loyalty and detachment, is the rhetoric of self-denial and self-control. In her impersonal style, Margaret Carrington points to the lessons learned by women in the army as a painful but salutary exercise in domesticity and submission: "Woman had a choice field in Absaraka for the exercise of many industrial pursuits, and fortunate were those who in earlier days had been advised that other rooms than the parlor have their use, and other fingering than that of the piano must be employed in roasting and boiling, in frying and broiling, in baking and stewing." Reminding us of Steele's women who needed to be "broken" for the West, Carrington claims that army life on the plains is a good school for women, who learn to tackle constant setbacks and adapt to the conditions they find (174).

This common emphasis on self-control and self-denial reminds us of the focus on the control of women in women's western narratives of the 1830s and 1840s. Although self-control may seem to entail the suppression of behavior culturally construed as appropriately feminine—particularly the expression of sentiment and emotion—it was also part of the ideal of femininity codified in the "cult of true womanhood" described by Barbara Welter, which is based on self-denial as well as physical and mental endurance.[48] The emphasis on self-control also provides a link between women's western narratives and the concurrent emergence of the western genre, which has been described as documenting the shift in American society "from a culture of punishment to one of discipline."[49]

The painful lesson of self-denial and submission particularly informs Custer's *'Boots and Saddles.'* After surviving a winter blizzard, she tries unsuccessfully to suppress her tears and is reminded by her husband "that he would not like anyone to know that I had lost my pluck" (16). On the march to Dakota, she is so disheartened that she can hardly suppress her tears: "It was an unmistakable fit of sulks, and I was in the valley of humiliation next morning, for I knew well how difficult it is to have ladies on the march, and how many obstacles the general had surmounted to arrange for my coming." Her part consisted in "drilling myself to be as little trouble as I could. I had really learned, by many a self-inflicted lesson, never to be too cold or too hot, and rarely allowed a thought of hunger if we were where no supplies could be had." It was a long struggle, she remembers, and she "wished to be so little trouble that everyone would be unconscious of my presence, so far as being an inconvenience was concerned" (35). Custer's emphasis on her battle to maintain self-control during the march to Dakota is especially significant because this journey was not her first test of endurance: she had experienced strenuous marches before and had already lived in various army garrisons in Kansas and Kentucky. She could have called herself a "seasoned" army wife.[50] Instead, she chose to emphasize the lesson of self-control, a decision that underscores the functional centrality of this element of feminine self-representation in her account.

Custer's focus on self-control and self-denial seems to have been a model for other westering women's accounts.[51] The lesson runs as a common leitmotif through most women's personal narratives of army life, which present themselves as female autobiographies shaped by an emphasis on the gendered, culturally prescribed education of the female subject, a subject who achieves growth through repression and control. Of course, as Boyd suggests, this is not necessarily a particularly feminine lesson to be learned, since it is shared by every soldier who "had to make the best he could of life where the fundamental lesson to be learned is simply that of strict obedience to authority, whatever of discipline, self-denial, or hardness it involves" (107). For men, however, the internalized morality of self-control, which scholars have identified as the basis of modern Protestant culture, is linked to the virtue of autonomous achievement, a virtue that women could not claim in the same way as men.[52]

In contrast to published memoirs, women's private letters, such as those of Alice Baldwin, reveal the conflicts and negotiations accompanying this repression of self-interest. Alice Blackwood had graduated from the Albion Female Seminary in Michigan before she married Frank Baldwin in 1867 and accompanied him to forts in Kansas and New Mexico. Her memoirs present a woman who had come to terms with her role as an officer's wife, but her letters reveal how much she suffered from and rebelled against her passive, secondary role. Discontent with her confinement to the private sphere, she dreamed of writing for publication, singing in public, and actively promoting her husband's advancement in the army. Instead, while he served on campaigns against Indians, she lived in boardinghouses in Kansas or at her family's home in Michigan. In her letters to her husband, Baldwin expressed her frustration with her unfulfilled life and also revealed the problematic side of army marriages that suffered from frequent separations.[53]

It is, of course, understandable that women omit from their published memoirs these private tensions and difficulties with their feminine roles and instead cast themselves as adaptive and willing army wives. In the process of describing the everyday subjects to which many of the women restrict themselves, however, they reveal possibly more than they intended to, including the dynamics of power within the social microcosm of the army garrison, and also between the army garrison and the western world "outside" that it was supposed to control and police.

Some accounts of army life, for instance those written in the 1860s by Margaret Carrington, Eveline Alexander, and Sarah Canfield,[54] were not even directly concerned with the domestic. These texts—some of them private diaries—also show the range of authorial strategies available to women. Carrington invoked the official authority of the military mission, following the conventions of the male travel narrative, and Sarah Canfield and Eveline Alexander adopted the stances of the student of Indian life and the tourist and adventurer. What is striking about most army women's narratives, however, is that they obscure the army's mission and represent the West, as did their predecessors on the overland trails, as an extremely insecure terrain where American culture and politics have a tenuous hold.

Insecure Terrains: Mapping the Geographies of Gender, Race, and Culture

Margaret Carrington's *Ab-Sa-Ra-Ka* engages in the conflict over the Black Hills country by establishing white claims and de-legitimizing Sioux rights over the territory. At stake is not just the Bozeman Trail as a thoroughfare to the gold mines, but the whole country through which the trail leads, which still has to be recognized as a land of promise, boasting "exhaustless game resources" and an unsurpassed "production of wild fruits, grasses, and cereals; while its natural scenery, made up of snowy crests, pine-clad slopes and summits, crystal waters, and luxuriant vales, certainly has no rival in our great sisterhood of States" (13–14). In this country, the army serves as an advance guard of civilization.

The expedition of 1866 at the center of the two Carrington books forced the Sioux "to accept the challenge of the white man for the future possession of their stolen dwelling-place" (15). The impersonal mode of narrative invokes the official authority of the military mission, an authority that still needs to be asserted for an eastern American public. The military task is even cast as a humanitarian mission, reflecting the strong alliance of military and philanthropic discourses that at that time dominated the rhetoric of Indian war. Thus the encounter with a proud Cheyenne chief is described as an occasion "when all idea of the red man as the mere wild beast to be slaughtered, quickly vanished in a prompt sympathy with his condition, and no less inspired an earnest purpose, so far as possible, to harmonize the intrusion upon his grand hunting domain with his best possible well-being in the future" (116).

Carrington's narrative is informed by the intention of educating her countrymen about Indian-white relations in the West, and moving them to military action against the Sioux. Unlike other women's accounts of army life, typically held together by the narrative mode of personal experience, Carrington follows the conventions of the (male) travel narrative and narrative of exploration, compartmentalizing her material into separate chapters. The narrator, writing as a collective "we," assumes an authority based on knowledge seldom claimed by nineteenth-century women. As a collective "we," she is even involved in the planning and execution of the expedition, which implies reading the reports of earlier explorations.[55] All participants in the enterprise form a collective entity suffering common hardships. At strategic points, the reactions of the "ladies of the expedition" receive a special mention, serving either to defend the commanding officer's decisions or to emphasize the sacrificial nature of frontier army service. The women's agreement with the officers' decisions and opinions is repeatedly underscored (125).

Carrington's account impresses her readers with the powerlessness and the special needs of the frontier army in a situation that, contrary to public opinion in the East, was characterized not by peace but by war. It formulates a critique of an indecisive official

Indian policy and the sacrifice of a frontier army, which on account of its numbers was inadequate to fulfill its task, and which included as dependents the women and children who had been led to believe that the country was safe. It thus also establishes an image of the frontier officer as a marginal figure of limited cultural power, at the mercy of both powerful western Indians and eastern politicians.

As Carrington's narrative shows, in the 1860s the American claim to some parts of the western territory, although legally and politically authorized, still had to be practically established against Indian nations. This political and historical complexity of westward expansion is seldom openly addressed in reminiscences of women's army life and pioneering, but it surfaces in the way women mask the army's operations and in the insecure hold women have in this West, which can only sporadically be safely claimed as reassuring nature. This complexity also surfaces in descriptions of personal encounters with Hispanic and Indian people, which seem to revolve predominantly around children, Indian dances, the distribution of annuities, and the daily interaction between Indian "visitors" and white women in and around their houses in the army garrison. The focus on Indian appearance and dress as well as a racialist aesthetics remain important strategies of representing the Indian other.

Many women's narratives, whether journals or reminiscences, configure the western frontier as a foreign Indian country, strange and alienating, in which the white woman has no place, but the narrators seldom openly address the contradiction implied by the U.S. Army's presence on this frontier. Lydia Lane's retrospective account is similar to other women's narratives of army life in the way she glosses over the reasons for her husband's constant moves from one Southwest garrison post to the next. Between 1854 and 1870, she accompanied her husband on each of his assignments, never staying more than six months at any one post, yet the army units move as if propelled by an invisible force. In Texas, Lane travels through a country which is in turn inhabited and emptied of human presence, and which is perceived as a foreign country, at times fascinating, at times alienating. Indians are formulaically grouped with plants and animals. Further on, in New Mexico, travel takes her along a line of army forts, frontier settlements, and houses. Only gradually does the country emerge as an inhabited land with a distinctive, foreign, and exotic Hispanic culture that has a life of its own and which is positively acknowledged in its difference, timelessness, and absence of change, but which is also at times derogatorily reduced to exotic quaintness, meaninglessness, and even arrogance.[56]

At the time of Lydia Lane's marriage in 1854, the Southwest had been part of the United States for less than a decade. Outside of Hispanic settlements along the Rio Grande, New Mexico and west Texas were still thinly populated, with only a small fraction of Anglo-Americans who had come to the Southwest as merchants, investors, or government officials. Since Spanish times, the Kiowa, Comanche, and Apache had raided Texas settlements. In New Mexico, which then still included Arizona, Indian-white relations during the 1850s were also largely characterized by military operations. For three centuries, nomadic tribes—Ute, Apache, and Navajo—had waged sporadic war on Spanish, Mexican, and then American settlements. In the 1850s, the army thus had two goals: to protect travel on the Overland and Santa Fe Trails and to end Indian raids southward into Texas and Mexico. In the 1860s, however, the army's goal was to force Indians onto newly created reservations or to make them go back to the reservations from which they had fled.[57]

Many women writers in their reminiscences of army life tend to avoid discussing these power relations by focusing on the representation of western nature and on the personal experience of outdoor life. Like women on the overland trail, army women on the move enjoyed what they term their "gypsy life" once they acquired the routine of moving. Still, their pleasure is often linked to landscapes that remind them of familiar eastern countryscapes, full of grass, budding trees, and flowers. Elizabeth Burt enjoys such a landscape even more with the added thrill of outdoor life (30). After arriving at Fort Bridger in Utah Territory, she is pleased that there are no Indians in the vicinity, "except occasional bands of Shoshones passing through on hunting trips. Thus fortunately we were relieved of fear of our red brethren, and at liberty to ride about the country in safety." She could therefore enjoy horseback rides, which gave her intense pleasure, and the greater part of her time was spent "in the bracing, open air, giving us health and good spirits" (67).

However, the feminine enjoyment of nature cannot be separated from Indian-white relations and is always intricately linked to the state of intercultural affairs. Indian presence is not as easily blotted out in visions of an empty, inviting land as in many male narratives of discovery and conquest. Nevertheless, in Burt's narrative a different process of obfuscation occurs, either through the narrator's lack of knowledge or as a conscious act of historical interpretation: the country is represented as pacified, without any traces of previous conflict. Actually, however, Fort Bridger had been converted from a trading post into a military fort in the course of the "Mormon War," which was fought in the autumn of 1857 to force Brigham Young's private Mormon state of Deseret into accepting the power of federal authority.[58] Neither had the years before Burt's arrival in 1866 been peaceful, although the diarist maintains that the Shoshoni, who visited the post while passing through on hunting trips and who brought buffalo robes, beaver, and otter skins to trade, had "always been friendly to the white people owing to the fine control which their Chief Washakie exercised over them" (84).

In fact, the Shoshoni had suffered tremendously from the inroads that white overland travel had made into their homeland, and they were destitute by the mid-1850s.[59] Although Washakie's band may have been peaceful, other Shoshoni bands had attacked emigrant trains. During the Civil War, the "California Column" under Carleton and Connor had crossed the Southwest in order to garrison and protect the central overland route, California's precarious link with the East. In January 1863, Connor and his men attacked the village of Shoshoni Chief Bear Hunter, killing the chief and more than two hundred of his people. In the remaining war years, the army led similar operations against Indians of Utah, Nevada, and Idaho. In 1861, Fort Bridger had been established as an Indian agency. In 1863, treaty negotiations were held with the Eastern Shoshoni, which meant the cession of land and the establishment of a reservation. The army presence at the fort was thus rooted in the need for control of the Shoshoni, who were not, as Burt suggests, freely passing through, but actually in the process of losing their autonomy as a people.[60]

Other women's landscape descriptions are similarly tied to a friendly or hostile Indian presence—a phenomenon that would support the argument that the liberation of the white woman in terms of space and physical expansion is correlative to the pacification of Native Americans: women's freedom in the West is more often than not related to the policed environment of army garrisons and Indian agencies.[61] Even friendly Indian-white relations were always in danger of getting out of control, and one could speculate on whether women's statements on the link between Indian presence and the enjoyment of western nature can be construed as invitations for white interventionist schemes. This seems to be the case in Margaret Carrington's narrative, in which comments on western nature and the prevention of feminine enjoyment of nature reinforce the interventionist message. Carrington pictures the women at Fort Phil Kearny enjoying horseback rides in the surrounding country, yet this enjoyment of Wyoming nature is curtailed by the presence of hostile "savages": "Everything in nature is so beautiful, and the climate is so restoring and healthful, that one could look upon such frontier life with something like complacency were it not for these savages" (198).

Some women found the enjoyment of nature at western army posts essentially restricted to men. Ellen Biddle emphasizes that women's lives at army posts in general were monotonous, while the men "could swing a gun over their shoulders and go hunting" (89). In contrast, many other women at army posts recorded their own "hunting experiences" in diaries and memoirs, pointing to the realization of the new femininity envisioned earlier by Margaret Fuller. Burt and Canfield enjoyed fishing, and Lane witnessed the exciting spectacle of a buffalo hunt. In her journal of 1870, Annie Gibson Roberts describes how women were caught in the excitement of the chase and the hunt, and even notes that she shot one buffalo, "brought him on his knees and then to his death" (29).

When Frances Marie Antoinette Roe recorded her experiences as a young bride in the frontier army, she especially focused on her enjoyment of physical exercise in the outdoors—of riding, fishing, and hunting. The series of letters to a female friend revolves less around everyday army life than adventures and unusual events: more or less fearful personal encounters with Indians, the excitement of a buffalo hunt, hairbreadth escapes from sand storms and blizzards, the antics of her pets and horses, and her own achievements as a rider and outdoorswoman as well as a homemaker. In reference to other women who cannot seem to adapt to western military life, Roe advises: "If they would take brisk rides on spirited horses in this wonderful air, and learn to shoot all sorts of guns in all sorts of positions, they would soon discover that a frontier post can furnish plenty of excitement. At least, I have found that it can" (42).

In one of her initial letters from Colorado Territory in 1871, Roe writes of her first fearful encounter with a group of Utes, who were preparing themselves for war with their enemies, the Cheyenne. During a visit to a little village store with two other women, she receives her first introduction to the "noble red man," which shatters her romantic ideas of Indians:

> . . . almost all my life—I have wanted to see with my very own eyes an Indian—a real noble red man—dressed in beautiful skins embroidered with beads, and on his head long, waving feathers. Well, I have seen . . . a number of Indians—but they were not Red Jackets, neither were they noble red men. They were simply, and only, painted, dirty, and nauseous-smelling savages! Mrs. Phillips says that Indians are all alike—that when you have seen one you have seen all. And she must know, for she has lived on the frontier a long time, and has seen many Indians of many tribes. (10)

The Indian men had stormed into the store and pushed the women aside "with such impatient force that we both fell over on the counter. The others passed on just the same, however, and if we had fallen to the floor, I presume they would have stepped over us, and otherwise been oblivious to our existence" (11). The two women were actually prisoners, "penned in with all those savages, who were evidently in an ugly mood, with quantities of ammunition within their reach, and only two white men to protect us" (12).

Only two years before this encounter, the entire Ute nation had been on the warpath, "and one must have much faith in Indians to believe that their 'change of heart' has been so complete that these Utes have learned to love the white man in so short a time." Like many of her female contemporaries, Roe points to the fragile balance of Indian-white relations: "No! There was hatred in their eyes, as they approached us in that store, and there was restrained murder in the hand that pushed Mrs. Phillips and me over" (13). This alleged propensity to kill is underscored by the Indian men's "hideous" appearance and their "odor." The next day, the narrator's suspicions are confirmed when she hears of the battle between the Utes and the Cheyenne: "You can see how treacherous these Indians are, and how very far from noble is their method of warfare! They are so disappointing, too—so wholly unlike Cooper's red men" (14). As in women's narratives of the overland trail in the 1860s, the "noble savage" image is revised by especially targeting Cooper's fictional Indians.

The move to their new post in 1872 takes Roe even farther into Indian country. At Camp Supply, they are surrounded by Indians who, hostile to the army presence, seriously curtail the army women's riding pleasures and range of movement. Although they continue their rides, they must be escorted by a soldier. These precautions are taken after the women encounter an Apache who had chased them back to the post, apparently enjoying their fright: "as we drew in our panting horses that hideous savage rode up in front of us and circled twice around us, his pony going like a whirlwind. . . . He said 'How' with a fiendish grin that showed how thoroughly he was enjoying our frightened faces, and then turned his fast little beast back to the sunflower road" (72). The Apache obviously enjoyed playing the same joke on white women as the Sioux men who had given overland travelers like Lorena Hays such a fright.[62]

Women's narratives of army life largely avoid representing western lands as empty and inviting spaces for the taking. Army garrisons are vulnerable to attack by Indians who dispute the army's presence in their territory, and army operations appear as fruitless and inglorious searches for an elusive Indian foe, or as policing duties on a lawless white frontier. If women configure this West as a space of personal freedom and physical expansion, it is, nevertheless, still a culturally contested terrain in which the U.S. military presence has a precarious hold, never quite able to guarantee the white woman's safety. Women's narratives thus also display an indirect concern with territorial control as the prerequisite for their adaptation to western life. Margaret Carrington had even played out and invited interventionist fantasies of controlling Indian territory by way of a benign and humanitarian military mission of pacification, linking the mission to white women's safety. Elizabeth Custer's *'Boots and Saddles'* reveals a similar preoccupation with the image of a benevolent military mission of control in Indian territory. At the same time, the military's inevitable failure, symbolized in Custer's Last Stand, hangs over the narrative like the sword of Damocles.

Six years after the treaty of Fort Laramie, in which the southwest quarter of Dakota Territory, including most of the Black Hills, was set aside for the exclusive use of the Sioux, peace on the northern plains had still not been established. In 1873, the Northern Pacific Railroad began to move illegally across the reservation, protected by the Seventh Cavalry regiment as a part of the Stanley Expedition, which surveyed the railroad route. In 1874, the same regiment under George Armstrong Custer explored the Black Hills. The expedition consisted of 1200 men, 110 wagons, 60 scouts, and a number of miners, photographers, and newspapermen—and Custer's reports of "gold at the roots of the grass" became a significant factor in causing the rush of miners into the region. The expedition triggered the fierce resistance of the Sioux and other northern plains tribes against white encroachment on their territory, and led to Custer's defeat at the Little Bighorn in 1876, which has held the public imagination captive ever since.

On the whole, although many women comment on the shocking news of the "Custer Massacre," they seldom endow it with a special meaning. The event is wholly ignored in the memoirs of Lane, Boyd, Biddle, and Summerhayes, which deal mainly with the Southwest. Although some women wrote histories surrounding the Custer defeat,[63] the only text framed by Custer's Last Stand is, of course, Elizabeth Custer's *'Boots and Saddles.'*

Richard Slotkin has defined the conflict over the Black Hills as one of the most important organizing metaphors in the American public ideology, and as the core of a post–Civil War myth of a new, and final, frontier. Central to this myth is the figure of the military aristocrat, part of a government of military gentlemen making the world safe for white ladies, while the disorderly frontier democracy becomes peopled with roughneck men and sluttish women. In the eastern press, George Armstrong Custer was glorified as the incarnation of the heroic, self-restrained, virile, and tough-minded American at the center of a new paternalism, yet for others he was a pompous, self-centered, and immature individual who rashly sacrificed his men on the altar of his own ambitions.

The "Last Stand" legend was to become the central fable of the industrial or "revised" post–Civil War myth of the frontier, which Slotkin says offered a vision of "how the different races and classes that divided American society might restore their 'harmony,' through the sanctified and regenerative act of violence."[64] What Slotkin has not emphasized enough, however, is that this image of a virile, controlled Custer is partly the product of a woman, "Libbie" Custer, who in all her attempts to manipulate the public memory of her husband was especially intent on refuting the impression of an uncontrolled, rash, and immature young man.

Although Custer stresses, in her books, her personal resistance against military campaigns, she simultaneously becomes a decided apologist for the presence of the army on the western frontiers. She describes how the regiment, upon its arrival in Dakota Territory, is welcomed with joy by the frontierspeople, who "felt the sensation of possession when they knew that these troops had come to open the country and protect those more adventurous spirits who were already finding that a place into which the railroad ran was too far east for them" (24). The army is an avant-garde of white settlement and the handmaid of adventurous pioneers. But it also enters territory assigned to and claimed by Indian tribes.

When the cavalry marches through the reservation of the Sioux, what initially appears in Custer's account as a friendly and harmless visit of the soldiers to a Sioux village is understood by the Indians as an occupation. Two Bears "demanded, in behalf of the tribe, payment for the use of the ground on which we were encamped, and also for the grass consumed, even though it was too short to get more than an occasional tuft. He ended, as they all do, with a request for food. The general in reply vaguely referred them to the Great Father in payment for the use of their land but presented them with a beef in return for their hospitality" (48).

Describing how she follows her husband into a Sioux tepee, Custer casts herself as a fearful woman, stressing the Indian men's protests against her presence: "I crept tremblingly in after the general, not entirely quieted by his keeping my hand in his . . . as I sat on the buffalo robe beside him. . . . I knew how resolute the Indians were in never admitting one of their own women to council, and their curious eyes and forbidding expressions toward me did not add to my comfort." The focus on Indian patriarchy serves to stress both the military officer's gallantry and the white lady's elevated social position. Meaning is centered in the presence of the white woman, who shrinks from the grotesque, carnivalesque spectacle, so seemingly out of control: "there was something unearthly in appearance; their painted faces, grunts and grins of serious mirth as they wheeled around the tepee, made me shiver. How relieved I felt when the final pipe was smoked and the good-by said! The curious eyes of the squaws, who stood in the vicinity of the lodge, followed us, as they watched me clinging to the general's arm while we disappeared" (37).

Unlike Roe and Alexander, Custer describes herself as a passive, fearful lady who enjoys neither fishing nor shooting and consequently feels helpless in situations of danger. Her pose of feminine noninvolvement, however, is deceptive in light of her critical stance toward Indian resistance to government control, blaming them for their own and the environment's decline (44). Perhaps, though, her general emphasis on her helplessness is strategically necessary in order to enhance her husband's heroic aura. One can assume that Custer was perfectly aware of the controversies surrounding her husband's action in the Black Hills, which some Easterners had denigrated as an invasion of Indian land. Thus she chose to describe it instead as a romantic feat of exploration in new lands, recording his descriptions "of the charm of traveling over ground no white feet had ever before touched" (158).

Custer's characterization of her husband as an adventurous explorer, virile frontiersman in buckskin, and paternal leader of the regiment is only one side of Custer, however; the other side is the boy, "so like a woman, who can scarcely exist without encouragement" (147). Armstrong and Elizabeth Custer are thus not only the "general" and his "lady," but embody the complementary figures of the boy-father and the girl-mother. Although at home he may play boyish pranks, in his relations with Indians the general is the benign paternalist. In her account of a military court action in which two Sioux are on trial for the alleged murder of two white men, Custer emphasizes her husband's "patience with Indians."

Again she throws a broadside at Sioux patriarchy when she describes their reaction to the presence of white women and enhances the white military gentleman's superiority: "a few of us were tucked away on the lounge, with injunctions not to move or whisper, for my husband treated these Indians with as much consideration as if they had been crowned heads. The Indians turned a surprised, rather scornful glance into the 'ladies' gallery,' for their women were always kept in the background" (175).

All of Custer's books systematically deflect criticism from her husband's various military actions, subtly answering those who decried his dealings with his subordinates and Indians. Her self-representation, which builds on the figure of the fearful lady who emulates her husband's self-control, is thus an intricate part of her message. In *Following the Guidon* (1890) she adopts the additional strategy of defending her husband's campaigns against Indians by drawing attention to his success in rescuing white women from Cheyenne captivity, and by praising the army's contribution to civilizing the West (2).

In her memoirs, Katherine Garrett Gibson credits Elizabeth Custer with linking women's army life and empire building. Quoting Custer, Gibson writes:

> . . . we army women feel that we are especially privileged, because we are making history, with our men, by keeping the home fires burning while the soldiers are guarding the railroad engineers and surveyors against the Indians as . . . they are building the railroads straight across the continent until the oceans meet, which will open up the country to civilization. Then the products of the Western grain . . . will be conveyed to the Eastern and foreign markets. Mining properties will be developed, scientific farmers from all over the world will seek this virgin soil. Yes, my dear, we are the pioneer army women, and we're proud of it.[65]

Gibson also listens to Custer's tales about prowling "all up and down Oklahoma, Kansas, Nebraska, and Dakota, chasing Indians," and she realizes that these adventurous tales were a way to conceal the women's fears for their husbands. She repeats Custer's argument that army campaigns started with the violation of white women, when "the Indians, growing bolder, began to carry off young white women" (119).

Not all women relate to the rhetoric of Indian war in such an unambiguous manner as Custer. In fact, women's emphasis on their personal experiences often allows for ambivalent attitudes, especially toward the history of Indian dispossession. Frances Carrington, for instance, rehabilitates the Sioux whom her predecessor Margaret had condemned so wholeheartedly, describing them as people "who would fight to the death for home and native land, with spirit akin to that of the American soldier of our early history, and who could say that their spirit was not commendable and to be respected?" (45). Teresa Viele, who had painted a grim record of Comanche atrocities and suggested extermination "as the only remedy against this scourge," also adds a more personal note: "My ideas of these savages were acquired from the Texans and Mexicans, of course not from actual contact; yet I cannot refrain from some feelings of sympathy for a people, who are driven from their rightful possessions, and can see, in their ignorance, many excuses for their tiger-like ferocity and bitter hatred of those who they feel have wronged them so sorely" (123–24). The specter of the Indians' loss of home and property does not fail to grip the sympathy of this woman who otherwise pays lip service to American expansionism. In these narratives, the Indians' resistance against the loss of home becomes an integral part of the historiography of westward expansion, reinforcing the general impression of the West as a fiercely contested space. The sympathy for the wronged Indians, however, is only expressed in reference to an Indian land that is already pacified and wrested from Indian control.

Elizabeth Burt expresses similar sympathies in her memoirs when she asks whether the Sioux who sympathized with Red Cloud's protest against the invasion of their hunting grounds could be blamed "for objecting to their lands being taken from them?" (54). She also comments with understanding on the abandonment of the Bozeman Trail in 1868, which had temporarily raised doubts about the fundamental rights of white Americans to Indian land (170). Such recognition of Indian resistance contradicts representations of the West as an empty land for the taking. Moreover, Burt expresses doubts about the moral legitimacy of a military mission that supports not only an invasion of Indian lands by white people motivated by material interests, but also the construction of a railroad of doubtful necessity. Recalling the conflict over the railroad,

Burt writes that the Indians "were bitterly opposed to the building of another railroad across their hunting grounds and were determined to fight its construction. But what mattered the Indian rights or wishes as long as the white man wanted the road!" (182).

Inside Looking Out: Indian War, Commercialism, and Private Space

Women in their published reminiscences may have aligned themselves, at least on the surface of their texts, with military views of westward expansion and Indian wars, but their private letters reveal, not surprisingly, more conflicted interpretations of the army presence in the West.

Caroline Frey Winne, in her letters from Sidney Barracks and Fort McPherson, Nebraska, to her family in New York State between 1874 and 1878, is rather outspoken about the military campaigns in the area. Winne's West is a place of exile in a desolate country, surrounded by a godless frontier society almost at her doorstep, and the only diversion is the Indians: "There are lots of Indians in town returning from their hunt which has been very unsuccessful, and besides the Utes stole about 250 of their best ponies. They are the most horrible looking creatures I ever saw." Personal contact and interaction occur around the store: "Mrs. Monahan and I went to one of the little stores the other day and there were about half dozen of those noble savages dressed in buffalo skins and red blankets with beads and feathers & all sorts of tin ornaments" (6–7). Like Frances Roe, she expresses horror at the painted and armed Indians—probably Oglala men, women, and children—and "should have turned and run home, but Mrs. Monahan has lived so much in New Mexico and Arizona, she has lost all fear of them. So she answered their 'How,' which is more of a grunt than a spoken word. But I tell you I was glad to get out." The same afternoon, while she is standing on her porch, some Sioux pass by: "I stood my ground to see what they would do, in mortal fear that they would all want to shake hands, but they passed by" (7).

Although Winne shrinks from the men's touch, the Sioux are apparently interesting to her from another perspective, since she tells her brother: "This is not a good time to get things of them.

The squaws have been employed in tanning skins instead of fancy work. Parties coming from the reservations have the things we want to get." These efforts to acquire Indian items for her family dominate her letters to her brother, who seems to have brought together a "museum" to which the Winnes are asked to add some Indian objects. Her husband tries to get the pipe of Old Man Afraid of His Horses, and she herself expresses interest in acquiring an earring worn by Sitting Bull, who "looked first fondly at his food, then at me and said to tell the lady he would study about them." Although she did not get the earring, a large hoop, she got the pendant, "really a great curiosity as being worn by the great Chief Sitting Bull too" (9–10).

At times, Winne's brother seems to have been less interested in the news from the West than in the Indian artifacts to be had (30). Ironically, as Indians all over the West were being forced by the military to abandon their lifeways and cultural traditions, the American public was demanding traditional Indian craft objects, which had become commodities isolated from their cultural context. Significantly, it was Indian women who answered this demand and supplied an Indian crafts market with the valued objects, entering the market economy through middlemen.

To Winne, the Sioux are both exotic curiosities and an annoyance: "The garrison is full of Indians today, squaws with their papooses on their backs & children of all sizes and colors. Yellow faced ones in green blankets & red ones in blue blankets & robes. They stand around on the piazzas and stare in the windows" (7). As in Jameson's account, a "darkening-of-the-window" scene carries the meaning of Winne's description, which signals the Indian invasion of the white woman's private space. Her contempt for them seems relentless: "The Indians have all taken their departure much to my delight. It was not pleasant to say the least. To look up and find your windows darkened by 'Lo' and his brothers & wives & children. Their dirty painted faces pressed close to the glass. They are poor miserable creatures. It would be a great mercy to them if they could all freeze to death, as many of them have this winter" (8).

In February 1875, Winne reports that her husband reads aloud to her "a very interesting book, 'Primative Cultures.' We are very much interested in it." But she does not seem to draw any connection between Edward Tylor's "interesting" book, which argued that culture existed among all men, in however "primitive" a form,[66] and the less interesting Indians, whose departure she does not deplore: "At first they were a novelty to me and it amused me to watch them, but they are a very uninteresting race, and a great nuisance hanging about a post. They are dreadfully dirty" (11).

She is now more preoccupied with critically following the activities of the new commander, Crook (20). To her the whole campaign "seems no more nor less than fearful wrong & willful murder to me. . . . I wish Genl. Crook had been left quietly in Arizona" (22). Mentioning the news of Crook's Battle on the Rosebud—a prelude to the disaster on the Little Big Horn a few days later—Winne declares her satisfaction that they will not celebrate the 4th of July, "for I am not over enthusiastic on the subject of this glorious country. I think it's a great fraud. The man who has the most money and can find place and position gets them. Money and political influence govern this glorious 'free' country. There is too much wire pulling" (23). The news of Custer's debacle reaches them on July 16: "The Custer massacre is too dreadful to think of, particularly as it was caused so uselessly by his own folly & disobedience of orders" (24). A few days later she is even more explicit: "this dreadful Custer massacre has cast a gloom over everything and makes us constantly dread a repetition of it. Custer's own foolhardiness and vanity & well known love of display & notoriety was the sole & only cause of this horrible affair and of the sorrow brought into hundreds of homes. All who speak of it say only this" (24).

Crook's "Starvation March," in which the soldiers in pursuit of the victors at the Little Big Horn were reduced to eating horseflesh, receives the brunt of her anger: "And for all this suffering Sherman and Sheridan are alone to blame. Sheridan, drunk all the time in Chicago in his fine house, says there are troops enough, and Sherman, on his general's pay in Washington, never having fought an Indian & knowing nothing at all about them, practically upholds him." However, Winne's critique is not directed at the army's Indian campaigns, but at the army's hierarchy and its willingness to sacrifice its soldiers: "This summer's work and blundering is a burning shame & disgrace to our country, if our country can be disgraced anymore. It seems as though the limit had been reached" (25). As in Carrington's narrative, the frontier army is described as under siege, sacrificed by incompetent government officials. But Winne's private critique is harsher, targeting not only the military hierarchy but her whole country, which has been disgraced by scandals and incompetence.

Criticism of military operations as well as the connection between Indian war and commercialism also surfaces in the letters of Emily McCorkle FitzGerald, written from army posts in Alaska and Idaho to her mother in Philadelphia between 1874 and 1878. Again, these letters record an experience of exile and a look at the West from the self-contained world of the home and family. In May 1874, FitzGerald's husband—an army doctor, like Winne—received orders to report to the Military Department of the Columbia with headquarters at Fort Vancouver, a department which included Alaska, purchased by the United States from Russia in 1867 and administered by the army. The FitzGeralds, their fifteen-month-old daughter Bess, and their fifteen-year-old black nursemaid Mary left New York on a steamer bound for Panama, crossed the Isthmus of Panama by rail, and sailed up the Pacific coast to San Francisco, where they found they were ordered to Sitka, Alaska.

At the time of the journey, the twenty-four-year-old Emily Fitz-Gerald was four months pregnant, and her first letters to her mother focus on her anxieties about her pregnancy and their unsettled state of affairs. Her main concern is "to be settled in a home of our own with some home comforts around us" (10). FitzGerald is not headed "west" but "home." The possibility of being ordered to Alaska comes as a shock, which is, however, quickly rationalized: "Don't be horrified. We are going to Sitka! I thought at first it was doleful, but we find the worst part is its isolation . . . it is a good place for children. They always thrive there. Then there is going to be a much more pleasant garrison there than ever before" (23).

In these private letters, FitzGerald reaches out to her mother for communication, advice, nurturing, and help, while at the same time establishing herself as a grown, capable woman with a family of her own. Her writing revolves around her home and children, the family's health and economic worries, and the difficulty of finding domestic help. Writing is necessary to establish and maintain close ties over a long distance, to preserve a shared sense of values, and to enable FitzGerald to re-create domestic life after the model of her familiar world: it is her mother who sends her the objects needed to reproduce an American home in Alaska. These letters from the frontier reveal how women's presence, through their culturally assigned emphasis on materially re-creating domesticity on the frontier, reinforced the American hold on "new" territories.[67]

After a year in Alaska, FitzGerald still does not feel at home there: "I want to go East again so much, but I dread the long, long journey. I don't think I was made for an army woman. I don't like change and travelling" (105). There is no distinct sense of Alaska yet; it is an alien place beyond, against which she sets the security of her comfortable home and her close-knit family, but which nevertheless intrudes upon her private world. FitzGerald's letters record events as they happen. The writing is done in fragments, interrupted by a crying child or the steamer coming in, which means new letters from home and also forces her to close her letters in haste. Her children receive most of her attention, but increasingly her black nanny Mary emerges as a character in her letters: still a child herself, "real noisy and rough," she is impatient and cross with FitzGerald's daughter and begins to resist her employers' authority and control, rebelling against her position of domestic servant, and longing to move up in society and become a "lady."

In time, FitzGerald begins observing life in Alaska, registering the natural sights of the country—very often seen through her husband's eyes—and, like Winne, sending exotic artifacts home to her family. Her letters accompany Tlingit baskets, carved knives and forks, dolls, and furs, while her mother in turn sends her much-needed articles such as sewing materials, clothes, and gifts for the children. Occasionally her limited vision is expanded by walks with her husband and by social contacts with other officers' wives, but in general, native and Russian[68] life exists outside of the garrisoned army post, beyond her world, and is confusing and often alienating. Her first descriptions of Sitka rely on the accounts of her husband, who has already explored his surroundings. Later, after her first walk with her husband, she appreciates the beauty of her environment, which is connected to its "newness" and unfamiliarity (44). In a letter to her aunt, she even assumes the pose of the guidebook writer, hinting at the future possibilities of the country (99).

The army post is an American enclave that shuts out and controls indigenous life around it: "There is a dirty little town scattered around the post full of Russians. Then, off to one side, is the Indian village. The Indians are not allowed in the garrison until after nine in the morning and are obliged to go out the gate again at three." To Emily, these Indians are "the most horrible, disgusting, dirty hideous set I ever saw. Their faces are all painted and they have rings through their noses and chins" (42–43). The difference between "Russians" and "Indians" and the complexities of cultural interaction seem inaccessible to FitzGerald, whose perspective appears, so to speak, always framed and filtered through the windows of her home. It is possibly also shaped by the rules regulating the interaction between military officials and the populations they are assigned to control.

Only Mary rebels against rules that govern social and racial interaction in the fort. She violates not only the cultural boundaries of the post by playing with Russian and Indian children, but also her employers' sense of propriety by flirting with the soldiers. Mary's moral and sexual integrity as defined by her employers is actually one of the issues around which the conflict between Emily and Mary ensues: "There is no place for her to go and no one here but soldiers and bad Russian women, more than two-thirds are prostitutes" (90).[69]

On one of her walks within the confines of the fort, FitzGerald encounters a group of Indians: "Such wretches! They are the most horrible looking things you can imagine. They crouch down in a corner somewhere or on some steps. . . . Their faces are painted every way imaginable. . . . The women all have rings in their noses and their lower lips pierced with a silver pin. . . . They all go barefooted over the ice and snow and the children that are too young to hold blankets around them are almost entirely naked" (83). Again we have a female observer who casts herself as a passive sufferer assailed by the horror of sights and sounds without meaning (87).

FitzGerald also describes the trader's store, full of furs and Indian curiosities, which are both interesting and hideous: "I wish you could have been behind the counter with me. If you could have stood the awful Indian smell, you would have been interested in the medley of things—furs, skins, feather, Indian dollies, Indian rattles, Indian carvings of all sorts and painted all colors (hideous things), little dollie hats (about the neatest thing there), and lots of table mats made like the baskets" (85). FitzGerald's letters, like those written by Winne from Nebraska, reveal the commodification of indigenous artifacts yet obscure the economic rationale for the military presence in Alaska, which is to control the seal-fur trade.

In fact, in these letters, the military presence is only indirectly rationalized. FitzGerald's representation of Alaska natives—the Coastal Tlingit—is shaped by her fear and disgust; her subjective impressions suggest that violent propensities exist under the indigenous surface. In order to observe a "pow-wow" from a safe distance, the narrator climbs on some rocks to peek over the stockade, watching the people "in their bright colored blankets, all jumping around, talking and gesticulating in a violent manner. They all had spears and every now and then would fire off guns. I am awfully afraid of the Indians" (94). Although at times she adopts an impersonal, descriptive mode, fixing the Tlingit in a timeless ethnographic present, her personal presence always shines through her "chapter on Indians." Her knowledge is located and circumscribed by the boundaries of her world, which are defined by men: "The village is a wretched looking place. I have not been in it yet because Doctor says it is too dirty, but I have looked over the stockade" (106). Most of her "Indian" knowledge is based on second-hand reports, since she herself has no opportunity—and obviously no desire—to observe Indian life any closer.

Like some diarists of the overland trails, FitzGerald collects fragments of knowledge, still trying to make sense of them. She seems most interested in burial rituals and in the custom of slavery. She is convinced, however, that "the old Eastern Indians with their Great Spirit and happy hunting grounds had a much more exalted idea of the hereafter than these do. These tribes don't seem to have much of an idea of religion of any sort" (107–8). This distinction between the "old Eastern Indians" and Alaskan tribes is telling: while the Eastern tribes—extinct, removed, and relegated to the world of legend—can be claimed as the heroes of an American antiquity, northwestern Indian groups, alive and still retaining their alienating difference, cannot be incorporated into American history. They are simply a "fearfully dishonest set and think it is a credit to them to be able to thieve successfully" (108).

As noted earlier, women's reminiscences of army life rarely touch upon firsthand experience of war. Indian war exists on the margins of most narratives as a series of isolated attacks and of Indian campaigns that separate wives and husbands. But FitzGerald's letters from Lapwai in Idaho Territory, where the family is ordered in 1876, provide an unusually close look at Indian war from a woman's perspective. At the new post, she is confronted with the possibility of an Indian war after the Nez Perce refuse to give up their claim to the Wallowa valley. On July 2, 1876, FitzGerald expresses a special interest in the Sioux campaign in the Dakotas, "as we all have friends with the troops, and as we are surrounded by Indians here, we are all the more anxious that victory doesn't crown the Plains Warriors" (201). Men and women at the post fear that the regiment will have to join the campaign against the Sioux, and FitzGerald is among those who demand the use of force against the "hostiles" who "should be shown no quarter!" (201–2).

On July 16, FitzGerald shares with her mother the shock of the Custer defeat. Yet unlike Winne, she focuses her anger not on Custer but on those who defeated him: "Did you ever hear anything more terrible than the massacre of poor Custer and his command? This whole part of the country is excited about it, as indeed, judging from the papers, is the entire country. We wait for the news here most anxiously and hope the Indians will be shown no quarter." As outspoken as Winne, FitzGerald is relentless in her demand for military operations against Indians. Her views are colored by her own anxieties surrounding the possibility of her husband's going into battle: "War is dreadful anyway, but an Indian war is worst of all. They respect no code of warfare. . . . It is like fighting to exterminate wild animals, horrible beasts. I hope and pray this is the last Indian war. Don't let anybody talk of peace until the Indians are taught a lessen [sic] and, if not exterminated, so weakened they will never molest and butcher again. These Sioux Indians will give trouble as long as they exist, no matter how we treat them, 'for 'tis their nature to' " (204).

In September 1876, she reports that "Indian trouble" is brewing after Chief Joseph's band of Nez Perce attempted to drive white settlers from their homeland in the Wallowa valley. In her next letter, she notes that the Indian peace commissioners are being sent to Lapwai "to treat with the dissatisfied Nez Perces who made the trouble. I wish they would kill them all (the Indians—not the Commissioners)" (207). From that point on, "Indian trouble" floats in and out of her letters. In times of impending crisis, she seeks solace in religion, but religion had lost its authority in American culture. It had been challenged and replaced by scientific authority in the wake of Charles Darwin's and Herbert Spencer's widely popularized work on evolution, leaving her without anything to believe (212–13).

In November 1876, FitzGerald gives her mother an account of the treaty negotiations between the Nez Perce and the Indian commissioners. She had watched the "wild Indians . . . coming in," thinking of "the horrible Indians and my two little babies left up at the Fort," imagining all kinds of murders and massacres. Professing disinterest in the proceedings, she is drawn to the council by others and by the promise of a spectacle. Joseph's band had already arrived, "horrible, dirty looking things all rolled up in blankets and robes." On the other side of the building she witnesses the "Treaty Indians," wearing shirts, pants, and coats or jackets. Meaning is carried by appearance and dress. Interestingly, FitzGerald distinguishes between the assimilated and "wild" Nez Perce in terms of skin color. Many of the assimilated Indians "looked like colored people," while the "wild" Indians "were very Indian looking, indeed. Such ferocious headdresses you never saw" (220). She also notices the bright colors of the Indian women's dresses and robes. But aside from these visual impressions, FitzGerald's observations on the council are limited: overpowered by the "Indian smell" in the building, she leaves before negotiations begin.

While another council is under way, she repeatedly plays down her fears, writing that "we fuss over our dinners and clothes, etc., as if it was the most usual thing in the world to have trouble with the Indians. Oh, how I hate them. I wish they could be exterminated, but without bloodshed among our poor soldiers" (249). Some days later, she reports that the Indians "have begun their devilish work. . . . The Indians have . . . attacked an emigrant train killing all. They broke one poor woman's legs, and she saw them kill her husband and brother" (259–60).

War has no clean chronology here but exists in a repetitive series of climactic and anticlimactic events. FitzGerald's letter of June 15, written in fragments in the morning, afternoon, and later at night, captures the reality of war with gripping immediacy and expressive clarity. At first she writes simply: "Mrs. Boyle and I have just been sitting looking at each other in horror" (260). We gradually realize that a war is beginning as the letter is being composed. FitzGerald's letters written during the next days reflect her confusion, and they capture the crowding of her senses following the news of battles fought only fifty miles away. More than half of the command is dead or missing. Women have to console the widows as well as lodge and feed the troops passing through the post. In these hours of anxiety and extreme stress, the writer directs her anger not at the Indians but at a government that sacrifices the lives of soldiers. Like Carrington and Winne, FitzGerald targets a peace policy that has neglected to expand the army force needed in an Indian war. To her aunt she writes: "You ask about the Indians. They are devils, and I will not feel easy again until we are safely out of the country they claim as theirs" (264).

FitzGerald's letters suggest that although she openly endorses the use of military force against Indians and calls for their extermination, the western country is not worth the fight and sacrifice of white soldiers' lives. Her alternatives are not, as in the jargon of Indian policy, extermination or "conquest by kindness," but extermination or abandonment of the country. Like many women following their husbands in the frontier army, FitzGerald never views the West as a potential home for herself but instead distances herself from western settlement and white populations in the West.

News of Nez Perce women assisting their men in warfare confuses her sense of gender distinctions: "Mamma, I wish I could talk to you this morning instead of writing. One of the things I meant to tell you yesterday was the active part the Indian squaws take in these fights our soldiers have had. They follow along after the men, holding fresh horses and bringing water right in the midst of all the commotion. . . . See what an advantage that is to them" (273). Could she have been suggesting that the enforced passivity of white women was a disadvantage to the U.S. army? Concentration on the rhythms of everyday life is impossible: "There are lots of things I want to speak about connected with the children and things you mention in your letters, but to save my life, I can't think of them when I sit down to write. My head is full of Indians. It was very warm yesterday, and I baked a cake and churned my butter on a table on my back porch, and I kept one eye and one ear up the ravine watching for Indians all the time" (277).

The next day she gratefully notes that Joseph may give up. Interestingly this is attributed to the dissatisfaction of the Nez Perce women: "The squaws are wanting to know who it was among their men that took the responsibility upon themselves of getting into this war with the Whites. They have lost their homes, their food, their stock, etc." (278). But instead of the war ending, it starts anew for FitzGerald when her husband is ordered into the field. Lonely and anxious about her husband, she also feels uncomfortable about Indian prisoners held at the fort: "They are horrid looking things, and I wish they would send them away." However, when the prisoners are actually transferred to Vancouver, she cannot help but feel compassion: "The squaws seemed to feel awfully about being taken away. Some of them moaned and groaned over it at a great rate. I did feel sort of sorry for them, as parts of their families were still up here. One poor woman moaned and cried and really looked distressed" (288).

This passage is revealing in the way that the compassion felt for the women has to be legitimized and accounted for, as if it had come as a surprise. The women "seemed to feel awfully," and FitzGerald felt "sort of sorry" for them; one woman "really looked distressed." What appears to dawn on her, and what does not seem to be self-evident at all, is that Indians can be described as human beings with human feelings. The racialist rhetoric that assigns tribal people to an inferior stage on the scale of human evolution, although it categorizes them as instinctual and "natural," excludes them from the "higher" faculties associated with morality, love, motherhood, and family loyalty. As unthinkable and shocking as this may sound, it is important to face the implications of this dehumanizing and naturalizing process, which seems to have been so deeply ingrained in the minds of nineteenth-century men and women that the realization of Indian humanity comes as a surprise.

This apparently widespread belief in Indians' lack of emotion, which observers inferred from their stoic appearance, is addressed by the Colville Indian writer Mourning Dove in her autobiography and in an article in which she described her goals as a writer: "It is all wrong, this saying that Indians do not feel as deeply as whites. We do feel, and by and by some of us are going to be able to make our feelings appreciated, and then will the true Indian character be revealed."[70]

In September 1877, the campaign against the Nez Perce came to an end, and the FitzGeralds were ordered to a peaceful post in Boise, Idaho, where Emily's letters record a completely different life, filled with social responsibilities and community activities.

Female Powerlessness and the Domestication of the Indian Man

In 1875, two officers' wives who later became writers met at Ehrenberg, a detached post in the Arizona desert. One of them was Martha Summerhayes, whose husband was stationed at the post, and the other was Ellen McGowan Biddle, who was on her way to Fort Whipple, Arizona. Summerhayes does not mention Biddle in her *Vanished Arizona,* but Biddle remembers "Lieutenant and Mrs. Jack Summerhays," who lived "entirely isolated from the world . . . with only one other white man." She especially remembers her surprise when a very tall, thin Indian, entirely naked except for a piece of cotton about the loins, came in the dining room to serve the dinner, "which he did quite well" (150).

Biddle had also been shocked while traveling into Arizona along the Colorado River by the sight of Chemehuevi Indians on the banks of the river. She found the men "entirely naked except a piece of cotton which they wore about the loins, and hanging down both front and back; the women wore skirts reaching to the knee; made of leaves; leaving the breasts and legs bare; both men and squaws wore their hair long; they were very dark, tall and most brutal in the expression of their faces" (147–48). With such description, Biddle casts herself as the innocent and passive female subject who is assailed by the "brutal" sights she has to endure. Seeing is conceived as a passive act.

At Fort Whipple, she had a young Apache living with them as a valet. The description of her domestic life with the young man again centers on fear and helplessness. Tall and slender, "not very dark, with quite a good expression of countenance," he follows her around the house to express his affection for her. However, she instructs him "that he must not enter any room where I was without permission, and although he seemed docile and fond of us I was never quite at ease when alone with him." She teaches him to read, yet he seems discontented and depressed, and they "let him go for three months," hoping that "he would find how hard the life was and would be glad to get back and be more content" (182). Instead, he "reverts" to his "Indianness" and wears a blanket around his shoulders, leading Biddle to express the skeptical view shared by most other officers' wives regarding the possibility of Indian assimilation: "He was just as much Indian as the others, who had never lived in a house or been with civilised people. . . . Since then I have never thought the plan of sending Indian boys to the schools in the East to educate them, and then allow them to go back to their reservations, a good one. There are too many generations of Indians back of them, and the few years of civilisation are soon forgotten" (183).[71]

Biddle's interaction with the young man is based on the hierarchies of race and class, which are complicated by gender hierarchies. Although she is his employer, she is unable to "domesticate" him and assume power over him; his offers of friendship and affection are conceived as invasions of her privacy and violations of a taboo, and possibly as a sexual threat. The hierarchies of gender reverse the hierarchies of race, which can only be reinstated and upheld by de-sexing and domesticating the Indian man, a common strategy in many women's western narratives. Of course, this deflation of the stereotype of the sexually threatening Indian man—so much a part of the captivity tradition—must also be related to the fact that these narratives were written for children and family.

The difference between Indian and white attitudes toward the naked body often leads to misunderstandings, which women comment on by hinting at their feminine modesty and respectability. At Fort Robinson, a Sioux man, "the largest Indian I had ever seen," had brought Biddle some moccasins to trade for a pair of her husband's old trousers: "He had a large piece of cotton cloth wrapped round and round him, extending far below the waist, and I thought he had on a pair of old trousers. He had not had the clothes I gave him in his hands a moment when he gave the cloth wrapped round him a jerk, throwing the whole thing off; and there he stood naked, save for the clout he wore, and on each leg, tied just above the knee, were pieces of an old pair of trousers, which he also pulled off." Biddle was "considerable startled," but before running off to call her husband, she "could not help remarking how very small his legs were, nothing but muscle and very thin, while his body was that of a giant" (226).

Ella Bird Dumont records a similar incident in her memoir of life in Texas. Alone with two women at a ranch house, she sees Indian men approaching who apparently want to trade clothing for groceries. Some of the Indians, Dumont explains, wear clothing "given them by the government of which they used but little, preferring to wear buckskin instead." Since the women's stock of groceries is low, they cannot accommodate the Indians' wishes, and one of their guests wants to trade his clothing for Dumont's gun, an intention the women are slow to understand: "I did not understand him and did not make any reply, so he began laying off his clothes one by one. He was taking off his shirt when Mrs. Jones and I looked at each other in helpless dismay. It was useless for us to offer any protest as to our right, for the poor fellow was dead to anything in the line of etiquette" (28).

Martha Summerhayes' description of her entrance into Arizona along the Colorado in 1874 contrasts significantly with Biddle's account. Whereas Biddle emphasized her shock at the Chemehuevis' nakedness, Summerhayes describes the same people in terms of aesthetic pleasure: "Sometimes the low trees and brushwood on the banks parted, and a young squaw would peer out at us. This was a little diversion, and picturesque besides. They wore very short skirts made of stripped bark, and as they held back the branches of the low willows, and looked at us with curiosity, they made pictures so pretty that I have never forgotten them." Summerhayes' description is almost erotic, focusing on the Indian women's bodies: "We had no kodaks then, but even if we had had them, they could not have reproduced the fine copper color of those bare shoulders and arms, the soft wood colors of the short bark skirts, the gleam of the sun upon their blue-black hair, and the turquoise color of the wide bead-bands which encircled their arms" (41).

What surfaces as an important pattern in Summerhayes' narrative is the problem of agency. Her account is informed by the narrator's resistance against the hardships of life in the West. Her efforts at accommodation and transculturation are specifically gendered in that they are linked to a sense of female powerlessness. Significantly, her husband plays an inglorious role in her ultimately unsuccessful accommodation process: he is a source of stress by attempting to retain her in her culturally assigned role as a white woman in the West, who upholds the standards of white domesticity and secures white men's well-being on the frontier. When she rebels against the conditions under which she is forced to play the traditional role of housekeeper, she is told to be reasonable, and she submits to her husband's wishes, but not without trying to legitimize her submission: "Having been brought up in an old-time community, where women deferred to their husbands in everything, I yielded" (14).

Like other women in the army, Summerhayes was constantly on the move, following her husband on his various assignments. One of their homes was in Ehrenberg, Arizona, where Summerhayes and Biddle met in 1875. Summerhayes soon realizes that Ehrenberg, which she described earlier as an "unfriendly, dirty, and Heaven-forsaken place, inhabited by a poor class of Mexicans and half-breeds" (42), is "no fit place for a woman" (139). Her desire to simplify her life by becoming "Mexicanized" in dress and lifestyle is countered by her husband's conservative standards of womanhood: "I yielded to the prejudices of my conservative partner, and sweltered during the day in high-necked and long-sleeved white dresses, kept up the table in American fashion, ate American food in so far as we could get it, and all at the expense of strength." Left alone with her male Indian helper and her Mexican nurse, she often wishes she had "no silver, no table linen, no china, and could revert to the primitive customs of my neighbors!" (146).

Summerhayes' narrative suggests that at least in some cases, the standards of American culture were not so much internalized by women as they were imposed upon them by men who showed less cultural flexibility. The quintessential script of American culture is reversed: while the man clings to the comforts of material civilization, it is the woman who yearns for transculturation and rebels against the ideological task of upholding the standards of white American culture on the frontier. On the other hand, Summerhayes cannot deny her own complicity: "How often I said to my husband, 'If we must live in this wretched place, let's give up civilization and live as the Mexicans do! They are the only happy beings around here.' . . . But we seemed never to be able to free ourselves from the fetters of civilization, and so I struggled on" (169). One exception to this rule is her morning bath with her Mexican laundress, who like the other Mexican women is "spotlessly clean, modest and gentle." Invited to share in the women's bath in the river at daybreak, the narrator "was only too glad to avail myself of her invitation, and so, like Pharoah's [sic] daughter of old, I went with my gentle handmaiden every morning to the river bank" (148).

Compared to the Mexican American women to whose lifestyle Summerhayes feels attracted, the Indians of Ehrenberg appear mainly as marginal, thieving people idling around the village and the village store and keeping the narrator from venturing beyond the enclosure around her house: "One never felt sure what one was to meet, and although by this time I tolerated about everything that I had been taught to think wicked and immoral, still, in Ehrenberg, the limit was reached, in the sights I saw on the village streets, too bold and too rude to be described in these pages" (165). Again, there is an exception to this generalization: the male Indian helper whom Biddle had mentioned in her account. Summerhayes' first encounter with "Charley" differs significantly from the one described by Biddle: "I saw before me a handsome naked Cocopah Indian, who wore a belt and a gee-string. . . . His face was smiling and friendly and I knew I should like him" (136). She mentions that the man astonishes their guests when he waits on them at table, "for he wore nothing but his gee-string, and although it was an every-day matter to us, it rather took their breath away" (150).

The narrator denies any attempts at "domesticating" her male servant, declaring instead her aesthetic pleasure in the man's body: "Tall, and well-made, with clean-cut limbs and features, fine smooth copper-colored skin, handsome face, heavy black hair done up in pompadour fashion and plastered with Colorado mud, which was baked white in the sun, a small feather at the crown of his head, wide turquoise bracelets upon his upper arm, and a knife at his waist—this was my Charley, my half-tame Cocopah, my man about the place, my butler in fact, for Charley understood how to open a bottle of Cocomonga gracefully, and to keep the glasses filled" (150).

This description is reminiscent of the exotic realm of colonialism usually associated only with plantations in Asia, Africa, and South America. And in this realm of colonialism, aesthetics can never be innocent. As Stephen Greenblatt has pointed out, aesthetic recodings of the "savage" can be read as attempts at neutralization and distancing, as strategies of containment.[72] Barbara Babcock argues that all colonial discourse "entails the objectification and aestheticization of the dominated, and . . . in the business of commodifying the Other, racist and sexist gestures frequently compound each other." The "ethnographic pastoral" is just as much a part of the discursive maintenance of inequality as racialist discourses that deny equality.[73]

A domesticated, "half-tame" native man with a pompadour who wheeled the Summerhayes' baby along the river banks in a percolator must certainly have been an incongruous sight in Ehrenberg: "There sat the fair-haired, six-months-old boy, with but one linen garment on, no cap, no stockings—and this wild man of the desert, his knife gleaming at his waist, and his gee-string floating out behind, wheeling and pushing the carriage along the sandy roads" (151). To be sure, Summerhayes' Indian butler did not stand alone; a host of white men were also performing domestic tasks. Bowen, the family's "striker,"[74] takes the women of the company "under his wing, as it were" (52). Soldiers, Summerhayes notes, often "displayed remarkable ability in the way of cooking, in some cases, in fact, more than in the way of soldiering. . . . I often thought the family life . . . appealed to the domestic instinct, so strong in some men's natures." They "performed uncomplainingly for me services usually rendered by women" (78–79).

On the other hand, Summerhayes begins to share the feeling of regimental prestige that "held officers and men together" (88), and she watches a battle "like a man" (93). This reversal of conventional gender roles is observed by many women travelers and settlers in the Far West. Although their narratives do not dispute the existence of rugged individuals, they nevertheless draw attention to the domestic side of the men living in a West where women are still scarce in numbers.

In Summerhayes' text, the aestheticization of Indian men functions as a strategy of distancing and disempowerment, creating a
marked tension with discourses of female powerlessness and lack
of agency. The rhetorical feminization of the exotic other thus not
only marks the male gaze. Rather, it is apparently also deployed by
women writers in the service of their own empowerment. Another
strategy connected to the rhetorical disempowerment of Indian
men is the recurring imaging of Indian male dress as a form of
effeminate cross-dressing. Lydia Lane's description of an Indian
man's costume in 1860s Kansas presents the wearer as a strange
and rather ridiculous spectacle: "A regular dandy honored us one
day, and this is what he wore: an army officer's coat, well but-
toned up, an old sword dangling from a leather belt, a soldier's cap,
and moccasins; no sign of trousers nor leg-covering had he, and
he seemed utterly unconscious of the absence of those garments
deemed so essential in the presence of ladies and polite society. He
bore himself with becoming dignity, no doubt being perfectly satisfied with his appearance" (133).

This matter of appearance is one of the important strategies of
meaning-making in women's narratives. The recurrent description
of Indian men's dress in women's western narratives, perceived as
dandyish and slightly effeminate, seems to reflect women's attempts to make sense of gender roles in Indian tribes and to neu-
tralize unsettling images of Indian power. Eveline Alexander's representation of Indians is a case in point. In Colorado Territory, she
had reported meeting "a couple of Utah Indians . . . a 'buck' and a
'squaw' whose costume exceeded anything I have seen yet. . . . She
was dressed like the buck in doeskin and one thing and another,
and as she rode astride her horse it was hard to define her sex" (79).
This impression of gender confusion is repeated in Sara Lippincott's western travel narrative (see chapter 4), and Teresa Viele
records that the Carese Indian women "looked more like men than
women," combining this remark with comments on their lack of
maternal show of affection (203–4).

Women's representational strategies point to how, as Marianna
Torgovnick has suggested, "the rhetoric of control and domination
over others often exists alongside (behind) a rhetoric of more obscure desires: of sexual desires or fears, of class, or religious, or
national, or racial anxieties, of confusion or outright self-loathing.

Not just outer-directed, Western discourse on the primitive is also inner-directed—salving secret wounds, masking the controller's fear of losing control and power."[75] The way women represent Indian men to themselves and their readers forms a part not only of a rhetoric of control, but also of a rhetoric of desire in women's narratives—women's desire to attain control and power over their own lives.

This interpretation of female representational strategies cannot serve, of course, as an excuse for women's implication in colonialist rhetoric, but it is a reminder of how colonialist conventions—the feminization of the exotic other—are deployed by women in the service of their own empowerment. Nevertheless, women's narratives of personal encounters with Indian men and women also potentially disrupt their visions of control (of self and others) by representing Indians as speakers, commentators, and actors who assert power over their own lives. An analysis of these personal interactions as rhetorical scenes is helpful in understanding how the presence of women (and women's writing) affected power relations between Indians and whites and helped to establish American culture in an environment where Indians either rejected or were forced to emulate white notions of civilization.

White Women among Indians: Interactions and Interventions

In 1858, at a fort in New Mexico, Lydia Lane noted the presence of Mescalero Apaches, who "were in camp that winter near the post, and came and went as they pleased, walking into our houses and sitting on our porches without the least hesitation" (65). Interactions between the white woman and the Indians take place within the seemingly uncontrolled environment of the reservation and the military agency, and at times carry a humorous note. Thus one day Lane finds a young Mescalero in front of their quarters with a child's colored picture-book in his hands, "chuckling and muttering with great delight. Coming closer, I saw he was holding it upside down, and turned it for him. He was much pleased and surprised when he was able to understand the pictures, and laughed and talked quietly to himself. I do not suppose he had ever seen a book before" (66).

Like so many other women, Lane also records a "darkening-of-the-window" scene in which the white woman is the powerless object of curiosity, exposed to Indian scrutiny: "I never could become accustomed to the Indians staring at me through the window when I was sewing or reading. Often while sitting beside it a shadow would come between me and the light, and on looking up I would find two or three hideous creatures, with noses painted every color flattened against the glass. I would move away at once, out of range of their wondering eyes. I could not endure to be watched so curiously." But whenever the Mescaleros overstep their boundaries by entering her quarters and invading her privacy, she "did not use much ceremony in putting them out and locking the door behind them" (66).

Lane, again like many other women, does not define the context of these interactions, but later in the account she describes the distribution of annuities, one of the events most written about in women's army narratives. Ironically, this spectacle of distribution casts the female spectator as a potential victim of violence. Lane records with horror how, when the butcher knives were brought out, "deep guttural sounds from the men and screams of delight from the women were heard on all sides. I felt as if we were going to be scalped, and I am sure the recipients of these treasures would not have been at all averse to trying them, bright, new, and sharp, on us, if it could have been done with safety to themselves" (67). Although this personalized description of the event doubtless reinforces, through a language of female sensationalism, racist conceptions of Indians as savages bound by animalist instincts, women's observations of the potential violence involved in treaty councils and the distribution of annuities may actually capture the complexity and precarious tensions characterizing Indian-white relations better than bureaucratic, official descriptions, which emphasize the controlled nature of these events and tend to exaggerate their peaceful quality to prove the success of the official act.

Summerhayes also includes an annuity scene in her account. At Camp Apache in 1875, she had found White Mountain Apaches "under surveillance of the Government, and guarded by a strong garrison of cavalry and infantry." Within this policed environment, the distribution of rations becomes a spectacle that the officers' wives witness in the absence of other amusement. The narrator records how she "used to walk up and down between the lines, with the other women, and the squaws looked at our clothes and chuckled, and made some of their inarticulate remarks to each other. The bucks looked admiringly at the white women, especially at the cavalry beauty, Mrs. Montgomery" (82). Again the relations consist in looking, surveying, admiring, and registering appearances such as the "extraordinary good looks" of one of the Apache leaders.

In view of the unequal power relations that make one people prisoners of war while the other assumes the role of warden, it is understandable that there is no trust between the peoples. Although the Apaches were "quiet at that time," Summerhayes never felt "any confidence in them and was, on the whole, rather afraid of them." But this fear is restricted to the Apache men: "The squaws were shy, and seldom came near the officers' quarters" (83). Summerhayes notes that young lieutenants attempted to flirt with the Apache girls, but that the latter apparently "cared more for men of their own race" (84).

Summerhayes is a primitivist in that she privileges what she perceives as original Indianness, especially in the way of dress. This Indianness is also marked by closeness to nature, and natural instincts expressed in sexual terms. When she sees older Apache women "with horribly disfigured faces" and learns that they had been punished for being unfaithful to their husbands, she sympathizes with the women's free expression of their sexuality: "Poor creatures, they had my pity, for they were only children of Nature, after all, living close to the earth, close to the pulse of their mother. But this sort of punishment seemed to be the expression of the cruel and revengeful nature of the Apache" (84). This configuration of the Indian woman as freely expressing her sexuality, although restrained by (male) prohibitive practices, is unusual in women's reminiscences of army life, in which allusions to sexuality usually suggest Indian women's immoral behavior or are typically restricted to male Indian sexuality as a threat to white women's purity. This is doubly surprising given the purported family context of the account.

Indian women are associated with nature also in a different context, that is, their apparently uncomplicated practices of childbirth. Like Susan Magoffin, Lane discovers that for Apache women, childbirth is not accompanied by the period of confinement customary among white women. Finding an Indian woman sitting on the ground by their house, she notices that "leaning against her was a board, on which was strapped a new-born baby, which we learned afterwards was about two hours old! The woman intimated she was hungry and we gave her food, when she picked up her baby and walked three miles to camp. Before we saw her, she and her baby had taken a swim in the little river that flowed close by. . . ." (66). What is obscured by or unknown to the white narrators, however, are the often very strict taboos and sets of rules surrounding pregnancy and childbirth in tribal societies.[76]

If applied to Apache men, of course, this image of unrestrained physicality takes on a threatening quality, especially in the context of the Apaches practicing their religion. For Summerhayes, watching an Apache dance is a terrifying experience. The length and the colorful nature of many women's descriptions of Indian dances, however, suggests that this terror is linked to a fascination that can seldom be admitted. Thus Summerhayes not only describes "hordes of wild Apaches" darting about, shocking in their nakedness, but also notes the entrancing impact of the scene (91). But the female spectator cannot bear the tensions transported by the sights and sounds, which take on a threatening quality. As in so many other women's accounts, seeing becomes a passive act entailing suffering and torture. Detachment is impossible, and the spectator is involved as a potential victim of aggression and violence: "Suddenly the shouts became warwhoops, the demons brandished their knives madly, and nodded their branching horns; the tomtoms were beaten with a dreadful din, and terror seized my heart. What if they be treacherous, and had lured our small party down into this ravine for an ambush!" (91).

Elizabeth Custer describes an Arikara dance performed by the scouts living near Fort Lincoln, a "Strong Heart Dance" in preparation for a peace negotiation with their enemies, the Sioux. For the white men and women of the garrison, the dance is a spectacle that provides diversion in their monotonous existence. Custer suggests that women were excluded not only from Indian councils but also from the dance, since they "were not permitted to come near the charmed circle in front of the fire." The male dancers were naked, "except for the customary covering over their loins," and their faces were "hideous, being painted in all colors." (108). Her focus is on the visual impression of the dance: "All the dancers rotated around together for a time, their bodies always bent, and they howled as they moved. In the shadowy gloom, only momentarily made brilliant by the flashes of light from the fire, these grotesque, crouching figures were wild enough for gnomes." The dance is a spectacle of sight and sound, grotesque and without meaning to the white spectator. Meaning is produced not in the dance, but in the connection drawn between race and aesthetics. Only white blood can create an aesthetically pleasing body: "Only occasionally, where there was a large mixture of white blood, did we see a well-developed figure. The legs and arms of Indians are almost invariably thin. None of them ever do any manual labor to produce muscle, and their bones are decidedly conspicuous" (109). When the white women "left the unearthly music, the gloom, and the barbaric sights, and breathed pure air again, it seemed as if we had escaped from pandemonium" (111).

A few days later, the Arikara women came to give a dance exclusively for the white women: "It is an unusual occurrence, for the women rarely take part in any but the most menial services." Custer registers that much of the "finery we had seen at the genuine war dance was borrowed from the warriors for this occasion" (111). The women's dance, in accord with what Custer thinks she knows about Indian women's status, is not genuine, but a mere imitation with "borrowed" paraphernalia. Compared with that of the men, she suggests, it is a sham, performed for fraudulent purposes: "When the women stopped their circumvolutions for want of breath, we appeared on the porch and made signs of thanks. They received them with placid self-satisfaction, but the more substantial recognition of the general's thanks, in the shape of a beef, they acknowledged more warmly" (112).

Relations between Indian and white women often center around their children, but although it may seem that this could lead to friendships forged beyond the boundaries of race, women's narratives often tell a different story.[77] At times, power relations between white and Indian women revolved around the issue of children, as the politics of Indian transformation and education implemented by white women amply attest (see chapter 5). Boyd records how, in an Indian camp, she "found" a "beautiful dark-eyed baby boy," whom she dresses and bathes—without his mother's consent. Boyd is actually surprised at the mother's reaction. Her action, she writes, had "evidently caused his mother to decide that I had sinister designs upon her prize, for on my subsequent visits no trace of the baby could ever be found. Had his sex been different, I probably could have obtained complete possession; but boys are highly prized among the Indians" (65). The white woman, denying the Indian woman the feelings and prerogatives of motherhood which she exclusively claims for herself, competes with her over the care of her children. This isolated scene provides a glimpse of the way American authority would be established over the most private realms of Indian lives in missionary projects and government programs meant to "civilize" and transform Indian culture.

Most of the time, however, interactions revolving around children were more one-sided. Boyd's interest in the Paiute child is unusual in army women's reminiscences, since most women emphasize the interest in white babies. Boyd herself describes how the bathing of her own baby created a sensation among Indian women, who would "crowd about and indulge in ecstasies over the little white baby whose ablutions were a source of constant and serious wonderment. This can be well understood when one remembers that Indians rarely, if ever, use water other than for drinking purposes." Significantly, as a young mother she now claims the prerogative she had denied an Indian mother at Camp Halleck: "I never permitted any of them to touch baby, being afraid to do so" (150).

Elizabeth Burt's personal encounters with Indians center in a similar way around her infant. Although she is in constant fear of Indians stealing her baby, she does allow her daughter to be held by a Crow chief's wife, "[a]s she seemed dressed in clean garments" (121). Later she is visited by Crow women who are especially anxious to see the baby, "the first and only white baby ever at Fort C. F. Smith." However, she is reluctant to let all the women come in the house and hold the child, "as their reputation for cleanliness was not of unquestionable nature; but they were all in gala attire and looked as if their skins had been scrubbed with soap and water." The women also wish to see the interior of the house, as well as Burt's dresses. The white woman apparently respects their curiosity "to see the clothing and modes of living so different from their own" (155), yet she does not comment on the outcome of the visit. Neither is the inquisitive interest reciprocal. Burt denies any curiosity as to Crow women's mode of living and has no desire to test their cooking.

Burt's relations with Indian men at the fort were of a more fearful nature, especially when three Indians slip into her room, discussing her baby daughter (158). As a consequence, Indians were forbidden to enter the post without permission. A similar repercussion follows an Indian attack on a group of women gathering flowers near the fort. Running for their lives, the women make it back to the fort, and henceforth their walks are restricted to within a few feet of the gate of the stockade. In consequence of the raid, Burt explains, all except Crow, Snake, and Nez Perce Indians were considered hostile (161).

In letters to her mother, Emily FitzGerald's descriptions of her encounters with Tlingit women resemble those found in Burt's memoir. Personal contact occurs within the policed confines of the garrison, mainly around white women's houses, and revolves around food and children. Native women come to FitzGerald's back door every day to sell venison, birds, fish, and berries. One woman frightens her by speaking to her little daughter: "She saw her and came back and said, 'Your papoose?' I said, 'Yes.' She pointed out the gate to a little Indian baby off on the grass and said, 'My papoose.' She came again this morning with some birds to sell and again noticed Bess. Just a little while ago she appeared again with the paint washed off her face and, with her, the baby also washed. Evidently she was bringing her papoose to see mine." But it seems impossible to have the two children play together. Instead they look at each other, separated by a window: "She sat on the backsteps and Bess looked out the window and appeared very much delighted" (43). This encounter is again one-sided, obviously initiated by the Tlingit woman. Although FitzGerald's letters reveal the garrison's dependence on the food provided by native men and women, she apparently did not appreciate the reciprocity of the situation.

Summerhayes tells a rather striking story about the care for her newborn baby shown by Apache women. Although the boy's birth had been an important event that had drawn men from all around who came to congratulate the father and admire the boy, the mother is left "inexperienced and helpless, alone in bed" (97–98). On the seventh day after the baby's birth, a delegation of Indian women pays her a formal visit. They bring some finely woven baskets, "and a beautiful pappoose-basket or cradle, such as they carry their own babies in. This was made of the lightest wood, and covered with the finest skin of fawn, tanned with birch bark by their own hands, and embroidered in blue beads; it was their best work" (100–101).

Summerhayes seems to have realized the ritual quality of the offering and describes a sense of mutual understanding among women across the borders of race and culture: "I admired it, and tried to express to them my thanks. These squaws took my baby (he was lying beside me on the bed), then, cooing and chuckling, they looked about the room, until they found a small pillow, which they laid into the basket-cradle, then put my baby in, drew the flaps together, and laced him into it; then stood it up, and laid it down, and laughed again in their gentle manner, and finally soothed him to sleep. I was quite touched by the friendliness of it all" (101).

Relations between Alice Baldwin and Navajo women at Fort Wingate in 1868 revolved around dress and lifestyle. When some Navajo women express interest in the way Baldwin arranges her hair, she gives in to the request of one woman to fix hers in a similar manner. The next morning, the Navajo woman brings with her several of her companions, and "each and every one was treated likewise. Each assisted in adorning the other, and such an array of giggling, crimpheaded squaws had never before been seen in all the history of Fort Wingate. Feminine vanity and tastes are much the same the world over, no matter what the race or color" (79).

Later, in 1877, Baldwin visits an encampment of Crow Indians in Montana and walks among the tents of the women: "They were filled with wonder as to my attire, and urged by their innocent, and I must confess, feminine curiosity, I consented to undress and let them see for themselves. They crowded around me. Crinoline and corsets they marveled at, but did not admire" (99–100). Through an interpreter, they tell her that they cannot understand how she is able to wear so many clothes, fearing that she must suffer from heat and exhaustion—a critique of the encumbering dress that was also expressed by white female dress reformers in the service of women's rights. Baldwin describes the voices of the women around her as "naturally soft and melodious," and as she sat or stood among them, "listening to their chatter and laughter, and no doubt passing uncomplimentary comments about me, I felt that it all meant sincerity, which does not always prevail in a cultured and fashionable society" (100).

Ellen Biddle's encounters with Indian women take place under less friendly circumstances. In her account of her stay in Colorado Territory, the native population is a fickle factor in the safety of white army women who undertake a brave visit to a camp of Southern Cheyennes: "we thought we would not be afraid going with officers and men, but when we got there and saw those terrible looking creatures, with such brutal faces, I felt far from comfortable. The older women were most repulsive in appearance, their faces were full of deep lines, showing the hardships they must have endured." The encounter with Cheyenne women is physical and again centers, although in a more negative manner, around the white women's dress and hair: "they put their hands on us and felt my cheeks and hair and insisted upon my taking it down for them to see, but I was afraid as several of the Indians were climbing up on our ambulance wheels begging Kate, my niece, for the feathers in her hat, which she gave them, also a string of amber beads, with which they were delighted; in return they gave her a pair of broad silver bracelets, very well engraved with Indian characters" (116). Although the incident was probably perceived by the Cheyenne women as a case of reciprocal exchange, Biddle's account suggests that the white women saw it as a molestation of their private sphere.

It is amazing how women's "darkening-the-window" scenes resemble each other, forming one of the tropes of women's western narratives. Sarah Canfield describes her window scene in almost the same words as Lane and Frances Carrington, as a "cloud" passing: "One day as I sat working a pair of slippers with bright wool yarn what seemed to be a cloud passed. I looked up to find two squaws with their faces against the window pane. I held it up for them to see. the[y] laughed and chatted to each other" (215). Canfield's experience is rendered without the usual implication that being stared at through the window is experienced as a form of molestation and invasion of a woman's privacy, but windows in all of these narratives signify both a conception of the private home and the possibility of its violation. Women sit in their houses, as on a stage, presenting idyllic self-portraits of American middle-class domesticity to Indians for possible emulation. Yet in contrast to women's domestic novels, in which the look through the window often reinforces the exemplariness of the family scene, the act of seeing from the outside has turned into a voyeuristic act that parodies and destroys the illusion of middle-class privacy.

Especially in Custer's and Roe's narratives, Indian men's alleged lack of respect for women serves as a subtle evidence of the barbaric state of Indian societies. In Burt's memoir, this issue leads to an expression of female solidarity across the boundaries of race. At Fort Bridger, relations with the Shoshoni are friendly, although the diarist cannot suppress her criticism of Indian men's apparent disregard for women. At a dinner the Burts give for Chief Washakie, she is impressed with his good manners, except in one respect: "Women are such very inferior creatures in the estimation of an Indian that Kate and I engrossed little of their attention" (85). Although she describes him as "a man born to command, having strength and dignity, endurance, and a countenance expressive of fine character and determination" (she even compares his features to those of Henry Ward Beecher), she is critical of the power and authority Washakie is said to wield over the women of the tribe.

Still, Chief Washakie escapes Burt's general condemnation of Indian men. "My first impression of domestic life among the Indians," she writes, "was intensely disagreeable and prejudiced me greatly against the lordly chiefs. I saw one of them walking in front of a squaw, whose back was bent under a heavy sack of something, probably flour, while he, with his tall strong body wrapped in a gayly colored blanket, carried nothing but a stick" (89). Women repeatedly express this critique in their western narratives, interpreting the special division of labor in most Indian tribes as oppressive and sexist, and missing the cultural rationales for certain customs and practices.

The Colville Indian writer Mourning Dove attempts to set things straight in her own autobiographical writings: "Women and children followed the packhorses, and the men rode ahead to watch for game animals and also to protect us from grizzly bears. In the days of tribal wars, this order of march was necessary for the safety of the family, and it may have been the origin of the custom of an

Indian man walking a few steps in advance of the women and others. This frequently amuses whites, but some of their own customs seem just as odd or foolish to the oldtime Indians."[78]

Since Burt, like most of her contemporaries, misunderstood this practice, which also implies that women carry heavy loads, she becomes an advocate of women's rights by default: "The brute!" she exclaims. "How I wished for a good strong soldier to knock him down but no one was there but my sister and myself. When I poured out my tale of outrage to my husband he said that if the Indian had been treated as I wished trouble would undoubtedly have resulted with the tribe; that the squaws were accustomed to this kind of treatment and my indignation was wasted" (89). While her husband connects the "primitive" character of the male Shoshoni to the violence against women by implying that it exists as a natural part of their tribal life, Burt refuses to accept the nature of tribal power relations. Her reaction shows that power relations are, despite the apparently friendly surface, always in a precarious balance, easily tipped by white women's actions.

What Burt ignores in her outrage at Indian men is white men's abuse of Indian women. Her denial of racist and sexist oppression is a case of what Laura Donaldson has called the displacement "down the chain of signifiers from their appropriate sources and onto their historical victims."[79] By projecting violence against women onto Indian men, Burt absolves white men of their own responsibility for colonialist violence.[80] Thus the representation of the Indian woman as a drudge and slave does not stand alone as simply a misrepresentation of the reality of Indian women's lives that underestimates women's power in some tribal societies. Rather, together with the aestheticization of Indian men and with their representation as effeminate dandies, it forms part of a strategy to disempower Indian men by representing them as lazy slavemasters who are not "man enough" to provide and care for their wives, and to deny both Indian men and women the ability to manage their own lives. Interestingly, women's critiques of the division of labor in Indian society do not extend to the class- and race-based divisions of women's work in nineteenth-century American society, where minority women were invariably assigned to the positions of white women's domestic servants.

Nevertheless, the description of personal encounters between white women and Native Americans often disrupts these strategies of disempowerment. In some women's accounts, both Indian men and women thus emerge, at least momentarily, as speakers, commentators, and actors with power over their own—as well as white men's and women's—lives.

chapter 4

Touring and Mapping the West

With few exceptions, the stories of women traveling with the army were largely untold until the 1880s. While they were encountering a hostile frontier full of military conflicts over contested territories, other women were writing accounts of travel on a new touristic western frontier, embracing the American West as a cornerstone for professional writing careers. Those who had come to live in the West found professional opportunities, albeit limited, in the emerging regional publishing cultures, engendering regional traditions in their travel narratives, journalistic writing, and fiction. The following chapter discusses these women's western narratives of the 1870s and 1880s, charting the emergence of western writing as a female vocation during that period, and tracing not only the various discourses that inform women's western writing of the time but also the ways in which these writings created and shaped cultural configurations of the West.

The preceding chapter revolved around the thematic center of the army frontier, bringing together texts of the 1860s and 1870s as well as reminiscences written around the turn of the century. The following chapter is organized by a more historicist concern with the relation between women's writing and cultural discourses on the West during a certain time period. Although my initial focus will be on the touristic frontier, my main interest concerns the various ways that women charted and mapped the West as a discursive terrain in their writings of the 1870s and 1880s. What becomes clear in studying these narratives is that not only are there common breaks and fissures, but also networks, or nodes, of allusions and tropes that seem to weave together what appear to be disparate women's narratives about the West.

After completion of the transcontinental railroad in 1869 had opened the West to tourists, overland travel became a fashionable luxury. New western resorts and hotels sprang up along the railroad routes and catered to those who could afford to travel the West for health and pleasure. By the early 1880s, packaged excursion parties such as the Raymond tours were organized, which ensured that travelers were effectively insulated from the world outside: they rode in luxurious Pullman cars and stayed at resorts that often were self-contained cities owned by railroad companies. California and Colorado became the new El Dorados of the affluent eastern and European, especially British, tourists, health seekers, and investors—at a time when the frontier army was still fighting bitter battles with Indian tribes in various other parts of the West. What tourists expected was, as one traveler put it, "Eastern life in a Western environment," and western communities, eager to attract the eastern investor, tried to present promising pictures of respectability and growth.[1]

In his study of the tourist in western America, Earl Pomeroy makes the point that both tourists and the Westerners who aimed to attract them presented the West for a long time in terms of eastern or European conventions. This applied to the facilities expected by and offered to tourists as well as to the representations of western nature in travel writing of the 1870s and 1880s. In the West, Pomeroy suggests, "there was hardly a mountain, a seaside cove, or an eruption of foul-tasting water that did not nourish ambitions for another Manitou or Pasadena, and that did not wait for a fairy godmother railroad president to conjure up another New England hotel." The tourist never traveled innocently through the West. Rather, each tourist "changes the West when he looks at it . . . because Westerners change the West into what they think he wants it to be or, with less commercial intent, even change themselves into what they think he is."[2] What these travelers sought, according to Pomeroy, was "in fact, not the West . . . but rather Italy, and the older part of the Old World" (32). Conventions of classical and European history, literature, and art were superimposed on the western scenery, while the Indian and Hispanic past was erased, until around the turn of the century, it gained an ornamental status as background material enhancing the appeal of the West for tourists.

Pomeroy suggests that Americans' inconsistent attitudes toward other living American cultures and their remains may be explained by the fact that nineteenth-century American standards of taste were "insecure and much in flux" and that nature had to meet the test of the approved criteria of romantic and sentimental European art and literature (43). However, the Europeanization of the western landscape also masked a flight not only from American history but from the American present: it was part of the denial of the process of Indian dispossession, which was going on with unprecedented force in the 1870s and 1880s.

As much as travelers may have tried to conform western nature to pastoral conventions, both western nature and history resisted their efforts. There were still real dangers and hardships to be distanced and controlled. Therefore, the nature that the western tourist professed to admire "must not be too natural, or too close to the history of the long struggle of Americans across a continent" (70). In sum, the post–Civil War tourist seemed "to demand of the American West that it correspond closely to standards that were Eastern rather than Western, and generally feminine rather than masculine" (73).

As this quote shows, Pomeroy's study formulates interesting ideas about the gender coding of the touristic frontier. The most significant characteristics of the Pullman tourist who participated in the Raymond tours, and wintered or summered in the fashionable resorts of California or Colorado, were that "he" was not only wealthy, but preponderantly female. This subject of "feminine" mass travel, looking at the West in terms of its correspondence to eastern standards, is contrasted with a different kind of traveler, the "masculine" subject discovering a wilder West. This traveler "represented a kind of outpost of masculinity in a feminine jurisdiction, and tried to meet the West on its own terms" (73).

Instead of analyzing the function of these concepts of femininity and masculinity as cultural constructs, Pomeroy speaks from a position within the discourse, pitting feminine mass travel against the individualist, masculinist West of sportsmen like Theodore Roosevelt. The nationalist mood that developed in the 1890s, and which found its expression in Roosevelt's politics and writing, is thus explained as a "natural" reaction to "the pallid dilettantism of the years following the great orgasm [sic] of Civil War, which had sought out cheap effeminized European substitutes for authentic goods in art, literature, and architecture, as well as in vacation travel" (110). Associating preciosity and artificiality with the feminine, yet defining the search for the authentic as a masculine activity, Pomeroy fails to acknowledge the ideological framework of a cultural rhetoric that used gender symbolism as part of its message. Nevertheless, his quote of a Colorado miner's letter of 1860 hints at the discursive constraints that may have worked on both men's and women's writing when dealing with the West: "I know it is often thought that it is nothing but a sickly affection to appear charmed at the beauty of a landscape and that all raptures at a view of nature in mountain, foliage, or stream, should be left for romantic misses or lackadaisical young masculines, while sober practical men have other matters far more important to attend to, and should move straight on, noticing only what brings the almighty dollar" (102). The constraints on men's writing, resulting from discourses of masculinity, may have been just as strong, although possibly differently negotiated, as the discourses of femininity that influenced women's writing.

Traveling Ladies

In the first issue of the *Overland Monthly,* published in San Francisco in July 1868, the center of discussion was not the western travel account but American accounts of European travel. Claiming that "the days of sentimental journeying are over," editor Bret Harte declared that the "dear, old book of travel, with its conscientious desire to instruct, its guidebook directness, its dreadful distances, and more dreadful dates; its feeble moralizing, its poetical quotations from Moore, Byron and Rogers . . . is a thing of the past. Sentimental musings on foreign scenes are just now restricted to the private diaries of young and impressible ladies, and clergymen with the affections of the bronchial tubes, whose hearts and mucous membranes are equally susceptible" (101): in sum, Americans have lost "the romance of foreign travel." Proof of this conclusion were Californians abroad—Ross Browne, Mark Twain, and others—who were parodying the "dear, old book of travel."

After the Civil War, it had become fashionable and almost a convention for American writers to visit England and "the Continent," and to send back voluminous letters to the numerous periodicals in New York and Boston. Yet by the end of the 1860s, it had also become customary to poke fun at the wonders of the Old World. In 1869, Mark Twain's *Innocents Abroad* appeared simultaneously in the San Francisco *Alta California* and the *New York Tribune.* It was possibly his combination of the travel book and the burlesque that the editor of the *Overland* had anticipated as a positive contrast to the "sentimental journeyings" of "young and impressible ladies."

In view of this assumed competition between obviously gendered versions of travel, one must wonder whether Harte was thinking of such female travel writers as Sara Jane Lippincott and Helen Hunt (Jackson), who wrote, respectively, as "Grace Greenwood" and "H.H." Neither of them was very "impressible" nor particularly young at the time of their European journeyings. Lippincott, a poet and journalist for, among others, the *Ladies' Home Journal,* the abolitionist *National Era,* and the *New York Times,* as well as a writer and editor of children's stories, was the author of the widely read *Greenwood Leaves* (1850). She had recorded her European tour in *Haps and Mishaps of a Tour in Europe* (1854), which anticipated Twain's satirical account by more than a decade, mixing "sentiment and gush, American chauvinism, and some of the dry Yankee wit later to be fully developed in Twain's *The Innocents Abroad.*"[3] As a journalist and lecturer, she spoke out strongly in support of abolition, women's rights, prison reform, and against capital punishment.

Helen Hunt, after the loss of her husband and two sons, started writing in the 1860s. She made her first European tour in 1868 and wrote sketches, letters, and poems for magazines with family audiences. In 1870, she published her first book of poetry, followed in 1872 by her first collection of prose, *Bits of Travel.* Both Hunt and Lippincott undertook a journey to the West in the early 1870s and wrote serial travel letters for the eastern press, which they later collected in books. Lippincott's western travel letters, written between July 1871 and November 1872, appeared in the *New York Times* and were republished as *New Life in New Lands* in 1873. Hunt left for the West in May 1872 and wrote travel letters for the *New York Independent*, which together with other essays were assembled in 1878 into the volume *Bits of Travel at Home.*

Both Hunt and Lippincott wrote as single women travelers and, in contrast to the writers of army reminiscences, self-authorized their travels as well as their writings. Together with a growing number of female regional writers such as Sarah Orne Jewett, Rose Terry Cooke, and Mary Wilkins Freeman, Lippincott and Hunt were visible and established in eastern periodical culture. The reception of their work, however, points to the rather rigid gender segregation that existed in the publishing culture of the mid-nineteenth century,[4] and indicates the constraints working on these writers through the conflicting discourses of femininity and feminism. One of Helen Hunt Jackson's biographers points out that early reviewers of her work almost without exception referred to her sex, "comparing her work not to writing in general but to that of other women." American publishers and readers had separated female and male writing so distinctly "that both in form and subject matter expectations were clear."[5] As Rosemary Whitaker argues, readers expected women's separateness to be most obvious in the expression of their emotions and in their focus on the spiritual: "readers expected that women, in expressing appreciation for all things maternal and domestic, would pay homage to God and His handiwork, nature, as sources of inspiration and solace" (8–9). For a long time, Hunt remained "H.H.," signaling with her denial of female authorship a potentially hostile attitude toward women writers. Only in her later works, *A Century of Dishonor* (1881), a bitter indictment of America's dealings with Native Americans, and *Ramona* (1884), a novel in which she aimed to draw attention to the plight of the California Mission Indians, did she sign her name openly.[6]

Ironically, a contemporary review of Helen Hunt Jackson's western travel letters contradicts Whitaker's definition of the expectations associated with women's travel writing. The review demonstrates that even though women were expected to wax rapturous over God's nature, they were also easily criticized for expressing too much sentiment: "The little book is so full of raptures over all

manner of wild flowers, over sunsets and mountains, and is generally so intense . . . that many readers will probably feel cloyed
before they have gone half through it, and will sigh for some soberer
narrative." Are not the raptures over the scenery, the reviewer asks,
"what we first skip in the letters from our friends who are abroad?"
By her "enthusiasm over wild flowers and clouds," the reviewer
suggests, the writer has severely limited her audience.[7]

Sara A. Hubbard's obituary on the occasion of Jackson's death
in 1885 could not be more telling of the problematic status of
the woman writer in American culture. The discourse on gender
forms an intrinsic part of this writer's acknowledgment of Jackson's achievements. "Her genius was a secondary power," Hubbard wrote. "Her femininity surpassed it in overmastering charm.
Had her purely intellectual qualities, strong and brilliant though
they were, been encased in a man's brain and shaped and toned by
masculine moods and feelings, they would never have secured the
distinction they gave her." It was "her sweet and gracious womanhood," her "single spontaneous impulse, with a poet's and a woman's self-forgetfulness and abandon," that distinguished her. But
when she took up the cause of Indian policy reform in *A Century of
Dishonor,* her "very enthusiasm . . . neutralized her efforts. A judi-
cial matter-of-fact mind is needed to deal fairly and effectively
with the subject of our relations with the Indians. Helen Hunt's
exuberant fancy and passionate feeling were of splendid service in
the realms of poesy and fiction, but proved the worst hindrances
when she tried to work in the domain of fact."[8] By taking up a
political cause with the passion and emotion associated with feminine writing, Hubbard suggests, Jackson overstepped the boundaries of her female sphere and was inevitably doomed to fail.

Obviously, "feminine" and "masculine" views of the West were
linked to gendered domains of writing circumscribed in terms of
both subject matter and style. But as shown in the preceding chapters, women's western writings can never be fully reduced to the
constraints that work on writers through discourses of femininity.
Rather, attention should also be directed to the ways women writers negotiate these constraints in the genre of western travel writing, which is so highly charged with the authorization of expansion and conquest, and with the production of knowledge and the
assumption of power.

Both Hunt's and Lippincott's travel letters are characterized by a paradoxical combination of sensitivity and feminine reserve on the one hand, and almost violent derision of western people on the other. But whereas Hunt exhibits, in the manner of many eastern and European travel writers, a distaste for rough western frontier settlements, Lippincott becomes a booster for a new West of growing and prospering urban communities.

Lippincott's travel route led her from Chicago through Colorado, Utah, and Nevada, to San Francisco, and to the Yosemite Valley, a route that was almost canonical by the early 1870s. What she focused on was not a wild West, but a new West characterized by growth and prosperity. What she first encountered was not boom but bust, not increase but decrease, but what she saw and described was mainly change, economic enterprise, growth, prosperity, respectability, and breathtaking engineering feats—the image that frontier communities themselves wanted to present in order to attract immigration and capital. The "old West" is now a story that can be told, safely, from a distance of time. With Indian wars still flaring up all over the West, however, the Indian presence could not yet be so easily distanced. Thus "a lot of dirty, lazy, greasy-looking Indians and squaws"[9] on a freight train are an unwelcome sight reminding the traveler of the unsolved Indian problem.

Lippincott's journey to the West was not yet the packaged tour of later years, but she did have an itinerary. The author was already well-known in both the East and West, and she was armed with letters of recommendation and invitation. Her travel letters convey the sense of a network of cultured hosts all over the West, into which the tourist is integrated. Lippincott apparently also took advantage of the practice of railroad companies to give special rates to or invite journalists, artists, and writers, who would then be the best promoters for western railroad travel.

Many of Lippincott's hosts were railroad or mining officials who welcomed their guests into their homes and invited them on excursions to western sights, among which were less the wonders of nature than the wonders of engineering and industrial labor. Consequently, western travel writing, whether by women or men, was involved in a network of patronage. Men, however, could undertake (and finance) their western travels in a professional or official capacity—with their travel writing a by-product of their work—

whereas women often had no other choice than to pay for their travel by writing about it. Another possibility for women to finance their travels was to give talks about women's rights along the way,[10] making women writers potentially subject to different forms of patronage than their male counterparts.

Lippincott's travel narrative is part of a tradition of individualistic travel that preceded the great influx of fashionable tourists. The narrator thus warns all her readers "ambitious of having an experience like mine,—a wild, galloping drive like Phaeton's, without the responsibility and the peril," to lose no time in making their journey to the West (291). Lippincott is not yet a Raymond tourist, but she travels "over well-traveled paths." Her traveling persona is a cultured woman who, although she has "always at heart the woman question, and preaching everywhere the gospel of equal wages for equal labor" (23), emphasizes that she stays within the bounds of her sphere. She presents her travel letters, within conventions of feminine apologia, as deficient "in matter of philosophic thought and valuable statistics," as "only rock-crystals of fancy and sentiment" (vi). But these boundaries are themselves the object of humorous jest, as when she pretends to be shocked by female circus artists who are "plunging heels over head out of their sphere" (43).

Although Lippincott locates herself within a tradition of feminine writing, this tradition does not necessarily entail feminine standards of nature representation but rather their parody—which brings her closer to the satire of the masculinist western "Sagebrush School" than to the "feminine" standards of the Raymond tourist described by Pomeroy. The representation of western nature in terms of the picturesque and the sublime is even critically commented upon as a commercially effective convention, especially profitable in the genre of landscape painting. Watching a thunderstorm in the Rocky Mountains, the narrator notes with comic irreverence how the spectacle approaches "as near the real thing as nature can get to Bierstadt," mockingly suggesting that nature imitates the art of the "great painter of twenty-thousand-dollar pictures" (98).

As in most western travel accounts of the time, railroad travel is a theme by itself; to comment on accommodations, food, and fellow travelers had become a convention.[11] Lippincott goes beyond convention, though, and also hints ironically at the escapist nature of western travel, noting that the tourist could comfortably remember that "the Westfield disaster, the great New York riot, and the iniquities of the Tammany Ring, wild stories of frontier life, of Indian massacres, of murder and robberies and lynchings . . . were a great way off, or a great while ago" (53). It appears that Lippincott can only address the painful aspects of westward expansion and its politics through the filter of burlesque and allegory. In a witty aside on Indian war and Grant's peace policy, she asks for respect of the rights of the prairie dogs, through whose "colonies" the railroad passes: "When our wise and goodly men of the Indian Commission have settled our little border difficulties,—have made the amende honorable to the Ogalialla Sioux, and restitution to the Arapahoes for all their robberies, and soothed the lacerated feelings of the Apache, they will perhaps turn their philanthropic efforts toward righting the wrongs of these canine colonists of the prairies" (37).

Because the Modoc War of 1872 had touched off a nationwide attack on Grant's peace policy,[12] any contemporary reader would have understood the harsh edge of Lippincott's wit, which vents itself repeatedly with disparaging remarks on Indians and on Grant's administration. Some mountain groups in Colorado, she writes—the Chief, Squaw, and Papoose—represent "the only dignified 'noble savages' and really 'friendly Indians' I have yet seen, and the only ones not likely to move on" (97). At the Colorado State Fair, this conviction is confirmed. Like Burt, Custer, and others, Lippincott disqualifies the "noble savage" by pointing to his alleged lack of regard and respect for women. Like Eveline Alexander, she notes the absence of distinction between male and female Ute dress. Instead of reacting with confusion, as Alexander did, Lippincott takes issue with this apparent want of gender distinction and turns it against the Indian man, who now appears emasculated and disempowered: "The Ute is of a squat figure and of a broad, blank countenance. It is difficult to tell the mounted braves from the wild belles who gallop through the streets with them; for alike they wear rouge and ear-rings, part their back-hair, and ride astride" (119). This type of "equality," which could have served to make a feminist point about Indian women, is satirically discredited. Thus the narrator, with her "advanced ideas on the woman question," expresses herself "gratified to see that the noble red woman so nearly resembles the stern lord whose burdens and blows she bears; that her countenance is marked, equally with his, by that lofty stoicism and quick sensibility, that princely pride and native modesty, that keen-eyed sagacity and childlike trustfulness, that matchless subtlety and fearless honesty, that iron resolve and plastic gentleness, which we read of in the pleasing romances of Cooper and the Peace Commissioners" (119–20).

Satire becomes a filter for racialist discourse. Gazing out from her lodging in Virginia City, she sees "more Chinese than I had before beheld, and more Indians." The latter, she is "happy to say, are to a considerable degree accepting the situation, and becoming civilized and Christianized. When sorely pinched the noble red man will bow his proud neck over the saw-horse to earn his daily tobacco and whiskey, and allow his squaw to earn their bread and potatoes by washing" (175–76). Although Lippincott's representation of Indian women is formulated in ironic reference to the rhetoric of women's rights, her critique of Indian patriarchy detracts from both white patriarchy and white colonialism. By turning the lens on Indian women's complicity in their own victimization, she effectively prevents the critical identification of white and Indian women's common oppression and deflects attention away from the relations of unequal power between whites and Indians. The language of women's rights thus reinforces essentializing discourses of race, keeping white and non-white women at a distance.

Whether writing about Colorado, California, or the Nevada desert, Lippincott shaped and was part of a tradition that, as Kevin Starr has noted, defined what the West was and what it should be. The literary tourism of writers like Bayard Taylor, Horace Greeley, Charles Nordhoff, and Sara Lippincott helped to create a California myth that almost exclusively centered on nature. It was "an act of observation, selection, and judgment in which they described what California was and should be. Universally they agreed that it should mean the authentication and liberation of man through nature, since nature in California was such an overwhelming fact; hence indifference to and abuse of landscape and wildlife took on for them the significance of an especially distressing problem."[13]

The elements of the California myth were also part of the frontier myth, and they were at work all along the canonical itinerary of the touristic frontier, which included Colorado, Nevada, and California. Thus Lippincott sought to fit her description of Colorado mining into her idealistic view of Colorado as a recreational paradise, which has to remain agricultural rather than being marred by the ravages of industrial mining. At Clear Creek Canyon, the natural beauty of a stream is seen sacrificed and transformed by gulch-mining, a "fearful transformation" full of "violence and cruelty and remorselessness" (73). Mining itself is less than romantic: it is a "slavish business," which necessitates not only hard work, but also capital.

However, the destruction of nature and the oppressive labor can be reconciled and redeemed in an image of honest enterprise that suggests control and restraint. Instead of lawless, rowdy miners, Lippincott presents well-disciplined "brave miners" and "heroic women," many of whom are well educated, "the bravest humanity of the age,—the vanguard of civilization and honorable enterprise" (81). Her miners are gentlemen, sober and law-abiding, who shun drinking and gambling and reflect their college background, ensuring a homogeneous and orderly society, to the exclusion of the poorer and less educated classes (127–28).

While Lippincott presents Colorado as the realm of honest enterprise paired with luxurious recreation, the cornerstone of her representation of California is nature. Catching her first glimpse of it after crossing the Sierras is "almost like witnessing a creation." Mediterranean similes abound: California reminds her of Italy, and San Francisco is compared to Genoa. Yet there is "nothing of the Italian dolce far niente" about this California coast. On the contrary, "it is perpetual excitement, and prompts to supernatural bodily activity. There is 'a spirit in my feet' that will not let me rest. I cannot see enough of this picturesque land. I cannot drink in enough of the quickening sunshine, and the balmy, healing air of this strange new summer, of this vast new sea" (192). California also seems to demand a new language, less witty and satiric, less journalistic, more personal and poetic, a narrative mode that draws attention to the narrator who "might, in fact, believe myself young again, to all intents and purposes" (193).

Indian-white relations are harmoniously incorporated into this inviting scenario of a rejuvenating and benign nature. On the ranch of General Bidwell—actually a *ranchería,* which is the Californian equivalent of an Indian reservation—the narrator finds a land-scape "peculiarly Italian in its character," and she spots a group of "picturesquely dressed women" who catch her fancy: "Large and straight, and free in their movements, they reminded me at once of Italian peasant women. Yet they are native Indians, commonly called Diggers. They are employed in the mill, and work well. They live in a little village, or rancheria, on the estate. General Bidwell gladly employs both men and women, who are able and willing to work, and supports the old and infirm—some sixty of them—who were on the land when he came here" (233). Anticipating Jessie Benton Frémont, Lippincott's California version of the plantation myth transforms a history of violence and disinheritance into an image of beneficent paternalism.[14]

It is in the representation of Yosemite Valley, however, that Lippincott and other literary tourists formulated the most typical version of the California myth. As Starr points out, "Yosemite Valley . . . was destined to become one of the primary symbols of California, a fixed factor of identity for all those who sought a specifically Californian aesthetic." Celebrated in the landscape paintings of Albert Bierstadt and Thomas Moran, Yosemite became "the high shrine of California pilgrimage." Throughout the 1860s and 1870s, tourists came to Yosemite in ever-growing numbers, and in May 1871, even Ralph Waldo Emerson was among the visitors. "So standard became descriptions of the Valley in tourist literature," Starr notes, that one writer excused himself from writing about it on the ground that he could not possibly say anything new: "Cumulative, from literary accounts, from paintings and photographs, from reports of all sorts, Yosemite began to assume a primary significance in the minds of Californians. Here was the one adequate symbol for all that California promised: beauty, grandeur, expansiveness, a sense of power, and a sense—this in the geological history—of titanic preparation for an assured and magnificent future."[15]

Both Lippincott's and Hunt's travel narratives point to the special nature of a trip to Yosemite for women. There, they suggest, women travelers have to rough it and experience the outdoors in a way that demands deviations from feminine standards of dress and behavior. It is this thrill of deviation that women's narratives of the outdoors thrive on—and capitalize on—in the 1870s. Consequently, they focus on the hardships and discomforts of the trip, the dust and the physical exertions.[16] This emphasis is particularly significant in view of the fact that in 1872, the year they visited Yosemite, Lippincott was forty-nine and Hunt was forty-one years of age. Lippincott warns all mere lovers of pleasure, "all bon vivants, all dainty and dandiacal people, all aged, timid, and feeble people, all people without a disciplined imagination," to keep away from the valley: "The entire trip will prove to all such a disappointment and a drag, weariness, and hardship, and the valley itself a great hollow mockery of wild, vague extravagant hopes,—the biggest man-trap in the world." But to men and women "of simple minds, to healthy, happy natures, to brave and reverential souls, in sound unpampered bodies," she would advise a trip to Yosemite "for the crowning joy of years of pleasant travel" (305).

Lippincott thus defines the ideal California traveler in contrast to the fashionable Raymond tourist. She dwells with self-parodic humor on the trip's requirements for women, who discover that in the absence of side-saddles they have to take to the Mexican saddle, and ride *en cavalier:* "So, with a tear for the modest traditions of our sex, and a shudder at the thought of the figures we should present, we four brave women accepted the situation, and, for the nonce, rode as woman used to ride in her happy, heroic days, before Satan, for her entanglement and enslavement, invented trained skirts, corsets, and side-saddles" (313). After a few days they come to the conclusion "that this style of riding is the safest, easiest, and therefore the most sensible, for long mountain expeditions, and for steep, rough, and narrow trails. If Nature intended woman to ride horseback at all, she doubtless intended it should be after this fashion, otherwise we should have been a sort of land variety of the mermaid" (314).

For this narrator, Yosemite Valley is the realm of a feminized, benign nature, and she revels in the "novel and wild and primitive and delightful" (315). She is convinced that "here was Nature's last, most cunning hiding-place for her utmost sublimities, her rarest splendors. . . . It was but a little strip of smiling earth to look down on, after all; but ah! the stupendousness of the surroundings!" (321). Her Yosemite reminds us of Fuller's Mackinaw Island and Niagara Falls. Lippincott is inspired with awe and "thrilled by fantastic terrors. . . . Somehow you feel that Nature has not done with this place yet. Such a grand, abandoned workshop invites her to return" (325–26). Just as Fuller had described how her nerves were shaken at Niagara, Lippincott finds it impossible to concentrate on her writing in the valley: "You are for a time mentally unnerved; but you feel that in your powerlessness you are gaining power; in your silence, more abundant expression" (328). In the end, Lippincott, like Fuller, resists visual description altogether, resorting to the record of sensual impressions.

Lippincott was able to distance herself from the earlier Yosemite narratives of female travelers such as Therese Yelverton and Olive Logan because she had as her guide John Muir, who showed her sights "not set down in the Yelverton chronicles," and taught her facts "which not even the most careful student of Olive Logan has come at" (334).[17] Using the same strategy that male travel writers applied to distance themselves from female travelers, she describes her experience as more authentic, intense, and physical. John Muir himself had derided the "blank, fleshly apathy" of women visitors to Yosemite in the face of nature: "They climb sprawlingly to their saddles like overgrown frogs pulling themselves up a streambank through the bent sedges, ride up the valley with about as much emotion as the horses they ride upon, and comfortable when they have 'done it all,' and long for the safety and flatness of their proper homes." He rejoiced that most of them floated "slowly about the bottom of the valley as a harmless scum, collecting in hotel and saloon eddies, leaving the rocks and falls eloquent as ever . . . with imperishable beauty and greatness."[18]

Apparently Lippincott had not stayed at the bottom of the valley but had followed Muir to Tenaya Falls and the Porcupine Creek cascades, creeping up and sliding down boulders, and crossing streams on logs and slippery stones. To behold Tenaya Falls, "a shy, secluded little savage," demanded hardship and toil and represented a minor feat of discovery: "To look at her face, you must fight your way through brake and brier, as the fairy Prince fought his way to . . . Sleeping Beauty. You have to face the perils of poison-oak, tumbles and bruises, torn clothes, wet feet and scratched faces" (358). The narrator thus playfully fashions herself as a male-discoverer figure in relation to a feminized nature. But instead of simply following the conventions of casting Nature as feminine, she plays with its metaphorical possibilities in a practical, almost

trivial manner, reminding us of the homely similes of female overland travelers.

On the ride out of the Yosemite, Lippincott meets the incoming
stage, among whom she recognizes " 'H.H.' and 'Susan Coolidge,'
the *Independent's* delightful contributors, travelling quite inde-
pendently, like the brave women they are. They were going into the
Yosemite, looking singularly bright, fresh, and neat. I wonder how
they came out!" (370). Helen Hunt Jackson recorded her trip to
Yosemite as an adventurous experience full of toil and hardship,
primitive accommodations, and trying food. Although their ever-
solicitous guide John Murphy took care to lead the women on safe
trails and to not tire them, "H.H." records persuading him to guide
her out of the valley along an unfinished trail miles from the usual
tourist haunts. Like Lippincott, she could thus distance herself
from the "regular tourist," and instead cast herself as an adventuress. Still, she concludes that the masculinist conventions of the
adventurous discovery narrative, which bases its claims on the
arrogance of naming, are equally unacceptable: "The words seem
singularly meaningless, face to face with the falls. How do men
dare to name things so confidently?" She even insists on calling
the valley by its Indian name, Ah-Wah-Ne. Yet, like Margaret Fuller, she privileges an ideal Indian past against the Indians she herself encounters, de-legitimizing their claim to the valley: "They
are descendants of Tenaya, no doubt; but Tenaya would scorn them
to-day."[19]

In the 1850s, the tribal inhabitants of Yosemite Valley had been
herded onto a reservation, but a group of Indians continued to live
there in camps after the valley's development by white people. The
men earned money by fishing and breaking horses, and some of the
women worked as laundresses and maids. In time, Indian women
even made their special mark on Yosemite tourism by giving dem-
onstrations of tribal artwork.[20] Neither Lippincott nor Hunt, who
registers Yosemite's Indian past as a romantic asset, acknowledges
any legitimate contemporary Indian presence in the valley. Instead, the discourse of natural history detracts from a history of
dispossession: for Lippincott, the valley is a "grand, abandoned
workshop," a theater of natural forces in which any trace of its
indigenous inhabitants is blotted out. Jean Bruce Washburn, the
"resident poetess" of Yosemite, drew the obvious connection by

rhyming "Ye gushing torrents—never to cease nor tire, / While meteors fall, or human tribes expire!"[21]

In Search of "the Real Thing": Touring the Reservation

In 1874–75, *Lippincott's Magazine* published Laura Winthrop Johnson's epistolary account of a journey to "some of the forts and Indian agencies of Wyoming Territory and beyond." The narrative was published posthumously in 1889 in one volume, *Eight Hundred Miles in an Ambulance.*[22] Johnson starts out with the following interpretation of American westward expansion: "The United States is the only country in the world that has its frontier in the middle. The Great American Desert . . . is now the true divide between the East and the West" (11). At the time Johnson was writing, America was gradually closing this frontier, a historic act that transformed the perception of space. Although the railroad had literally opened the frontier to travel, it metaphorically closed it in terms of dulling the travelers' senses: "Like a dream the desert glides by . . . and the Rockies that loomed before us are circumvented and flanked; we whirl through a wild canon, and they are left behind. Have we seen the desert, the mountains? No. It is but a glimpse,—a flat space blackened with prairie fires, a distant view of purple peaks. Few become intimate with this our wonderful frontier, and most people scorn it as an empty, useless, monotonous space, barren as the sea" (12–13).[23]

Johnson's text thus locates itself within the discussion over American expansion into what had been termed, since the western explorations of the early nineteenth century, the Great American Desert—considered uninhabitable for whites but an acceptable place to which the Indians could be removed. Johnson's text also fits within the framework of western nature tourism, which stresses the search of eastern urbanites for a more authentic, natural, and physical experience far from the artificialities of the city. This was an experience eastern tourists expected to find on the last western American frontiers.

Laura Johnson undertook her journey with a party of "twelve persons, including six ladies and three children," who start out with the promise "that we should see wonders, and should go where no white women had ever been before" (13–14). By this time, the area had been officially proclaimed pacified, and Johnson represents Indian reservations as destinations for exploratory touristic travel. By claiming that Indian land is safe for white women and children, Johnson reaffirms the establishment of white authority over Indian country, the scene of earlier Indian wars. In this context, the "first white woman" topos is a powerful tool in the establishment of white hegemony.[24] Ironically, shortly after Johnson's visit, peace in the area turned out to be an illusion in the aftermath of Custer's expedition into the Black Hills.

Johnson describes the terrain of the Sioux reservation as both a life-sustaining wilderness and, in orientalist terms, a barren but fascinating desert. The travelers find themselves "alone in the midst of one of the loneliest lands in the world. Sahara itself, that bugbear of childhood, could not be much more desert than this" (15). Like other women's narratives, Johnson's text stresses the novelty of camping out, which gives the travelers "a delicious sense of adventure, a first sip of the wine of the wilds" (20–21).

Around Fort Fetterman, the center of Margaret Carrington's book published six years earlier, the country "was still wilder and lonelier than that we had seen, and not a single habitation lay upon our route. All had been burnt by the Indians" (29). The overland trail to California, once the major travel route, is now "deserted for the railroad," and the stories of desperados like Jack Slade, of whom "you may read the history in Mark Twain's 'Roughing It,'" had already become legends associated with certain locales (32–33). On they go, into "a wilder country still, the Indian Territory itself, and to visit Red Cloud and Spotted Tail agencies, the names of which alone gave us a sense of adventure and of nearness to savage life" (46).

Added to the sense of adventure is the awareness that the travelers are "now no longer in the United States, but in the Indian country. No ladies have ever taken this journey before except the wives of the agents, who have been there but a few weeks." As in so many women's narratives of army life, Indian country is perceived as lying beyond the boundaries of the United States, with the Indians always potentially contesting the authority of the federal government (47). Nevertheless, Indian wars had already become stories of the past, to be told around the campfire. Listening to such stories, the travelers become "Desdemonas of the hour. We felt that though we were probably as safe as ever in our lives, yet there were possibilities that gave our position just enough spice of danger to be exciting" (53). Although Indians had been put on reservations, and the country was termed safe, danger still lurked because "an Indian is an inscrutable mystery, a wolf on two legs, and it is not easy to know what he may do" (55). The iconic Indian is knowable, represented in terms of nature, and yet, ironically, inscrutable.

At Red Cloud Agency the visitors are eager to see the Indian dance they had been promised. "Squaws" and children were already there, "dressed in their gayest blankets and embroideries" (57). The narrator reduces them to their appearance, as if something had to be proven by aesthetics: "Most of them had flat faces and flat noses; very few were in the least good-looking" (58–59). Soon the men come "dashing along in all their feathers and warpaint, an inconceivably wild, savage cavalcade" (59). It was, the narrator suggests, "a piece of real savage life."

Savagism had become a theatrical spectacle, at the same time fascinating and alienating, presented as on a stage for the benefit of the white visitors who look down from the agent's house upon "the barbaric crowd." The Indians' "weird song . . . had a measured cadence, but not the semblance of music," the dresses of the dancers were "varied and splendid," and the warbonnets that made "a tremendous show" were recognized by the visitors as part of their own commercial culture: the turbans "adorned with tall eagles' feathers in a crown, such as we see upon the wooden figures before cigar-shops" (60–62). With condescending amusement, Johnson registers the eccentric individuality of the male dancers' dress, emasculating them as "savage dandies." She singles one of them out as "the most grotesque horror of the whole," who "completed his charms with a great pair of blue goggles" (64). Such passages in Johnson's writing are reminiscent of the rhetorical strategies used in women's narratives of army life: the reduction of native people to appearance and dress, the aestheticization of the male Indian body, and the subsequent neutralization of the "savage" man's power—over both tribal land and white women.

Adding spice to the spectacle is the taste of danger: "These Indians were Sioux of the wildest kind, about as savage as any there are. Our lives were in their hands, and they were well mounted and well armed" (65). However, the travelers feel safe enough, "for they [the Sioux] are very prudent and never attack unless they are five to one. Besides, they have rations given them every ten days by government, and they don't quarrel much with their bread and butter. In fact, they are paupers, and we are all taxed to support them and the army, which is more than necessary as a police to keep them in order" (66).

Johnson makes no effort to hide the fact that the tourist spectacle itself is presented within the policed and controlled environment of an army garrison. Soldiers are seen coming into the gate, producing "quite a panic among the squaws and children" (66). Indians have become policed entertainers, giving bored Easterners a taste of "the real thing": "One might live a thousand years at the East and never see anything so wonderful as this dance; it is impossible to give a true idea of its life and color. It was the real thing, not a theatrical or Cooperesque imitation. All was new to us, and we were probably as new and strange to most of our entertainers" (66–67). After the dance, however, the roles of the white tourists and Indian entertainers are reversed. Then it is the Sioux who regard their white visitors as curiosities, crowding around them and plying them with "questions as to our ages, the relationships that existed between us, whose squaws the ladies were, and whose were the little blond-haired children" (67).

Part of the ritual of this tourist visit is the handing out of gifts from the trader's store, commodities produced in the East, such as beads "made especially for them in one place in Massachusetts" (68). Another part of the ritual seems to be the visit to Red Cloud's tent, where the ludicrous emptiness of this touristic encounter is revealed. The two parties have nothing to say to each other, and becoming bored, the white visitors, who think the Sioux will not understand them anyway, start singing the "Lord's songs in that strange land" and all the songs that come to their minds (75).

The next staged event was the Sun Dance, with the men looking "like demons, with little clothing and painted in the most grotesque manner" (77). Obviously the Sioux adapted the dance to the tourists'—and the government's—tastes and presented a bloodless version. One young man on foot, painted all over with yellow ochre, has "imitation wounds upon his breast and body." Like

Elizabeth Custer, Johnson draws an ethnocentric link between race and beauty, arguing that the man "was so handsome, statuesque, and graceful that it was impossible to believe he could be a full-blooded Indian. His profile was faultless, but his full face, a little flattened, showed Indian blood" (79). The actual ceremony was to be performed the next day, and Johnson considered it "not likely that we could have borne to see much of this, but we wished—some of us—to have a glimpse of the horror" (82). However, the schedule of the apparently well-organized tour demanded that they travel to the next agency.

Soon after, it becomes evident that the travelers had undertaken their tour in the midst of a potentially explosive situation. The threat of Indian resistance had been underestimated, and news reaches the travelers "that the Indians were in a bad humor, having heard some exaggerated accounts of General Custer's doings in the Black Hills, and had refused to allow any whites to see the last ceremonies of the Sun Dance" (91–92). Deciding to cut the tour short, the travelers spent a week "among the untrodden wilds of Laramie Peak" (99). Mediterranean similes abound for the benefit of the eastern reader; the landscape is compared to the Roman *campagna,* and in the mountains, a "Swiss scene" presents itself, "with the mill and huts for chalets." The next morning they see "a true Alpen-glow burning upon the summit of the peak" (99–104). The essence of the experience, however, transcends the conventions connected with European scenery. The travelers are roughing it, casting themselves as explorers in a new world: "No ladies have ever entered these canons before. . . . Ah! this is the wilderness, the real thing! These passes are untouched virgin soil, unspoiled by tourists and advertisements of hair dye" (106–7).

Like Lippincott, Johnson opposes commercialized nature tourism and claims a more authentic experience for herself. This outdoor life is attractive, "for it is real, and with all its drawbacks it is fascinating to many" (116). Significantly, Johnson refuses to comment on the Indian question, "as everybody at the East has an opinion ready formed upon the subject" (116). Her claim of noninvolvement places Johnson within the tradition of a touristic anticonquest, with the travelers presented as innocent, nonappropriative students and lovers of nature, whose views of the land have undergone a transformation. What had seemed wild at the beginning of the journey has become "tame . . . compared with its aspect five weeks ago, when it was our first taste of wild life!" (129).

As the narratives of Lippincott, Hunt, and Johnson show, women travelers drew on the same values that Pomeroy associates with masculinist writing on the West. Like their male contemporaries, they had a taste for the "wild," the "authentic," even the "savage" aspects of the western experience. But the "real" America is not exclusively located in wild natural spaces. Lippincott, especially, and Hunt remain present in their accounts as genteel white women who speak as representatives of a feminized, urban eastern culture. They also speak with a certain degree of authority that is not equally attainable for the women who began writing from within a western regional publishing culture.

Voices from the Far West: Engendering California and Oregon

In 1893, the Californian writer Ella Sterling Cummins presented a study of California literature on the occasion of the Columbian Exposition in Chicago. There she discussed the writers that were popular—and forgotten again—at certain periods in California history.[25] Her study was informed by a special interest in issues of power and popularity, and by a particular concern with the distinctions between men's and women's writing.

Cummins notes that women writers of the time were "gleaning right and left for all the stray sheaves that may have been overlooked," producing a literature that would make no special impact and would soon be forgotten. And this because women writers' work was being absorbed by the daily press, "in long columns of ephemeral writings suited to the hour, but without name or even initial to identify the writer" (366–67). Women's writing also tended to be dated and short-lived because many women had to write for a living, Cummins argued. Whereas men could earn a living in other professions, women who were dependent on their writing for a living were forced to grind out the stuff people wanted to read, burning themselves out in the process. Part of the problem lay "in the defective taste of the public," and in editors who, in order to keep the finger on the popular pulse, introduced special departments—theater, fashion, gossip, entertainment—given over exclusively to women. Thus, Cummins concludes, "we make a distinction right here between this writing to order, which is to fill this demand of the popular press, and the creative writing, which is born of a human soul who feels that she has a tale to tell—a tale she must tell whether the world will hear or not. She may give to the world a masterpiece . . . but which will not bring to her the bread to keep her alive" (368).

Cummins' observations on women's writing are particularly pertinent to the study of women's western writings in a regional publishing context. The story of California literature revolves around periodicals and newspapers rather than books, and it begins in the early 1850s with the *Golden Era.* This periodical, and later the *Overland Monthly,* founded in 1868, came to be identified more than any other medium with California and Californians. From its beginnings, the *Golden Era* had a high proportion of women contributors, to whom its founder and first editor, J. Macdonough Ford, attributed its demise: "Oh, yes! The *Golden Era* was a great paper, and, if the same policy had been continued, it would be a great paper to-day. But I will tell you where we made the mistake, and that was when we let the women write for it. Yes, they killed it—they literally killed it, with their namby-pamby schoolgirl trash."[26]

Nevertheless, Ina D. Coolbrith was acknowledged in the East as one of the best California poets, Ada Clare was heralded in the largest of type as the "Queen of Bohemia," and Florence Fane, under her own name of Frances Fuller Victor, became a historical researcher for Hubert Howe Bancroft and wrote stories that, Cummins claims, "where published in the *Overland* unsigned, were afterward copied in the East and Bret Harte's name appended as the author" (160). Another woman, writing as "Hagar," stands out distinctly on account of her "strong and vigorous" writing. Drawing the lance for women's equality, she soon aroused "a tempest among the male writers, who wrote replies of various kinds—impertinent, spiteful, and but one of them manly" (27–28). "The one woman," Cummins concludes belligerently, "who has a pen and a brain in this good old time is treated so discourteously by the men weaklings of the hour that she makes a dignified farewell and is heard no more. The *Golden Era* deserved to be killed by the effusive scribblers who were left. If it had realized the truth it would have shut its columns to the rest and given 'Hagar' full sway" (28).

This discussion of California literature illustrates once again how gender has shaped the way literature has been produced and received. In her critical assessment of women's status in California literature, Cummins implies that California demanded from its women writers a language different from that traditionally conceded to women; it had to be, like the style adopted by "Hagar," full of "power and strength" (12). In discussing the hegemonic struggle within California literature, Cummins, herself a novelist and writer of short stories, also defined the problematics of a regional literature and the difficulties facing women writers who wished to find a place within it. What came to be termed "local color" emerged as an overwhelmingly male domain represented by such writers of humor and travel as J. Ross Browne and the writers of the so-called Sagebrush School—Mark Twain, Dan De-Quille, and others.

As scholars have emphasized, California was a unique frontier that did not follow the historical pattern set by other frontiers. Franklin Walker described it as a "civilization created overnight, grown articulate enough in the days of its youth to speak while frontier conditions still existed." San Francisco, especially, "remained rough and grew sophisticated at the same time."[27] California also seems to have been quicker about its own commemoration in print than other western frontiers. Already in 1850, the same year California became a state, the California Society of Pioneers was founded. By the mid-1850s, publishing houses were popping up in San Francisco, Sacramento, and Los Angeles, and San Francisco boasted "that it published more books than did all the rest of the United States west [sic] of the Mississippi."[28]

The competition between men's and women's writing and the skeptical reception of Bret Harte's and Joaquin Miller's work in California, however, tell a more complex story. Although Walker defined the San Francisco frontier as demographically "male and young" and as "youth without women that welcomed adventure and new ways of doing things" (8–9), the strong presence of women as writers and mentors in the development of the city's literary culture—which he does not deny—has to be accounted for.

"Dame Shirley" Amelia Louise Clappe[29] taught the first public school in California and shaped the writing careers of Charles Warren Stoddard and others, and Bret Harte's emergence as a writer was assisted by Jessie Benton Frémont, who wielded a subtle influence over San Francisco culture through her salon.[30] Women writers had an important share in the literary productivity of California, encouraged by a receptive audience and a supportive publishing industry, although as Cummins' study suggests, powerful discourses of gender shaped both the production and reception of this literature and led to the division of labor between men and women writers.

Ida Rae Egli argues that the demise of California women writers in the 1880s began with the departure of such major male writers as Bret Harte, Joaquin Miller, and Mark Twain in the 1870s. While they went east or to Europe, most women writers remained in the state, "but after the golden years found few publishing opportunities and faced mainly conservative audiences not particularly interested in women's literature."[31] Moreover, Egli claims, Californians were soon overwhelmed by literature from New York and the eastern seaboard (xxii).

Although stories and poems by California writers still sold, "the collective spirit had been lost." With it, Egli argues, went "the promise of a women's literature that might have fully flowered had it been granted more time in its nurturing environment." The novels and collections of short stories and poetry that female writers had produced during the frontier period "slowly slipped further back on library shelves and were eventually sold at Friends of the Library sales for pennies." Of the fifteen women represented in Egli's anthology of California women's literature, seven died in poverty, and nearly all were unappreciated as writers in their lifetimes: They wrote "without 'rooms of their own,' often without even desks or tables" (xxii).

In 1896, Frances Fuller Victor, possibly stimulated by Cummins' study, again brought up the issue of the downfall of the *Golden Era,* reacting to the saying that women writers had killed it: "Now, there were 218 writers . . . who contributed to that paper, seventy-eight of whom were women, giving a preponder[a]nce of forty to the men's list."[32] The women, she argues, "if they did not make, certainly did not unmake the reputation of the *Golden Era.*

In fact, a large degree of the support received by that 'remarkable paper,' as Horace Greeley called it, was due to the bright things said by the women who wrote for it. The decline of the *Era*'s period in literature was due to new conditions. The men who had fostered it by their abilities had found wider and more remunerative fields, and the women likewise." The paper lost its popularity not on account of its women writers, but "because the world moves."[33]

What Egli overlooked, and what Victor saw very clearly, is that the "native Sagebrush literature" of California was exactly the type of regionalist genre being prescribed for the entire nation by eastern publishing and literary figures and was itself part of the development that Egli blamed for the "demise" of California literature—like the critics who, as Gerald Haslam has observed, "have been duped by the absurd, if hoary, belief that somehow eastern American experience is national, while everything else is 'only' regional."[34] Egli enlists this dubious distinction between "regional" and "mainstream" literature to defend regional literature as a kind of counterhegemonic resistance against incorporation into the national mainstream. What she also fails to define is what may have made California literature so special, except for its "collective spirit," and what exactly a flowering women's literature could have meant in this regional context. As it is, Egli locates early California women writers' difference in "a gentler, more malleable and somehow more cyclical and ongoing local heritage" (xxiii). If California, as Egli and Walker suggest, had become too provincial for its male writers, how did it seem to women writers, who from the beginning had been caught in a mixture of gender bias, provincialism, and cosmopolitan openness?

Frances Fuller Victor's career as a travel writer and historian illustrates the problems of authority and patronage encountered by western women writers who embraced the West as a vocation and who located themselves within western discourses that aimed to create a tradition and an identity for the region. Victor seems to have compartmentalized her writing into society columns and stories on the one hand, in which she addressed local concerns and women's issues, and historical work and accounts of travel in Washington and Oregon on the other hand, in which she suppressed discourses of femininity in favor of a promotional rhetoric. She had arrived in San Francisco with her husband, a naval engineer, in 1863 and soon started writing city editorials for the *San Francisco Evening Bulletin* and poems, short stories, and a weekly column for the *Golden Era,* signing herself "Florence Fane." She was thirty-six years old and already a published writer in the East. Together with her sister Metta, she had enjoyed some renown as a poet and novelist, writing several dime novels for the publishing house of Beadle and Adams in the 1850s. Between 1865 and her death in 1902, she wrote eleven books and a large number of articles about the life and history of the Pacific Northwest.

The society columns Victor wrote were far from being "namby-pamby schoolgirl trash." They were at times rather incisive essays of social criticism, even if rendered in a light style that invoked a feminine marginality and irresponsibility. She wrote scathingly about the tendency of pioneer gatherings to heap praise upon heroic pioneer men: "I have often wondered, when I have heard of the Pilgrim Fathers, where had been the Pilgrim Mothers. Was the zeal which inspired them to leave homes and kindred, for a shelter in the wilderness, less holy in them than in the Fathers? . . . Pilgrim Fathers, forsooth! These mutual admiration societies all on one side of the house do not recommend themselves to my admiration."[35] She also wrote about urban poverty, especially of working women, exposing the dark underside of the optimistic images of economic opportunities for women in California.[36]

In 1864, Victor followed her husband to Oregon, where she became a travel writer and historian. She set herself to the task of studying the people and the history of the Pacific Northwest, and trying to make a living after she and her husband separated in 1868.[37] In May 1865, Victor undertook the first of her numerous "voyage[s] of observation" to see Oregon and Washington Territory. In her travel sketches for San Francisco papers, she stressed her awareness of the anomalous position of the woman traveler who, by undertaking her journeys alone, leaves her proper sphere. She also expressed her skeptical distance from the romantic pioneer history promoted by the Oregon settlers themselves, which led her to relinquish a self-promoting, regionalist position in favor of the objectivist stance of the historian who aims to consider several sides of an event. Nevertheless, her main focus was on promoting the country for white settlement and agriculture, and on sharing her knowledge about the history of the discovery, exploration, and conquest of the Pacific Northwest. When she traveled along the Columbia River, Victor had "a copy of Irving's *Astoria* in my pocket, and some extracts of Lewis and Clark's *Journal* fresh in my mind."[38]

In view of the fact that Victor sought the financial support of the Oregon legislature for her historical work on the Pacific Northwest, it is not surprising that her writing reflects constraints connected with problems of authority and patronage. She had decided to write a handbook describing the land and resources of the Pacific Northwest, but these histories and travel narratives demanded a different kind of authority than her columns on San Francisco affairs. Instead of capitalizing on her feminine marginality in order to express social criticism, she needed an auctorial persona that could invoke a more central, official cultural authority.

In August 1869, Harte's *Overland Monthly* printed Victor's first historical article, which bore the title "Manifest Destiny in the West." It traced the history of American expansion into the Pacific Northwest along a series of historical coincidences and providences, as a result of chance and accident: "That remarkable succession of circumstances quoted oftentimes as 'Manifest Destiny,'" she opens her article, "is nowhere in history more wonderfully illustrated than in the rapid spread of Americanism from the eastern to the western shores of the North American continent." Aware of the rhetorical weight of her introduction, she retracts: "Does this opening sentence seem to smack of the national self-praise and confidence in our sacred mission as exemplars of all the highest virtues of republicanism and free institutions?" Conceding that belief in a manifest destiny "ought, indisputably, to inspire us with enthusiasm to fulfill it to the utmost," she contends that it was not of "that belief or that sentiment we were thinking when we took up the pen to utter our dogmatical first sentence." It is not a nationalist ideology she is concerned with but the historical evidence and, first of all, the human agents of "the march of empire in the Western hemisphere."[39]

The story of the discovery, occupation, and possession of the Pacific Northwest is less a story of national power plays in which republicanism carries away the victory than a game of fate with various individual players: political and social power is not determined by superior force but by favorable circumstances. In this game of fate, Victor suggests, the cards were simply not stacked in favor of the British, who seemed doomed to always arrive in second place. She also argues that it was not the fur trader "who first made Destiny manifest" but the missionary, who became "the avant courrier of commerce" (153). By linking the latter to commercial interests, she began her longstanding criticism of the Oregon missions, exposing their commercial rather than philanthropic motives and attacking the "romantic notions concerning the red men" in the very year that Grant's peace policy was being debated on a national scale.

In 1870, Victor published *The River of the West*,[40] a biography of mountain man Joe Meek, whom she had met during her travels in Oregon. As soon as Oregonians began reading the book, she found herself under attack for her critical observations about the Oregon missionaries. In her reply in the *Pacific Christian Advocate,* she defines her historical methods for the first time, asserting herself as a professional historian: "My course had been from the first, in gathering the material for my book, one of impartial hearing of all sides." Although she leaves it to the judgment of the public to believe Meek's mountain stories, she claims something more for the historical commentary interwoven with the narrative: "Having access to old files of papers—all the books previously written about the country and its history—private papers and public documents, it would be strange if, with a disposition to write the truth without fear and without favor, I had not arrived at something approximating to it."[41]

Victor's handbook on Oregon, which she began writing in 1865, was finally published in 1872 as *All Over Oregon and Washington,* a mixture of personal narrative and promotional tract written with a view "to aid immigrants in the selection of homes" and "to induce the very curious to come and see for themselves" (iv). It illustrates how a woman historian in search of a profession abandons a subjectivist personal narrative and suppresses discourses of femininity (and feminism) in the service of promotionalism. As in "Manifest Destiny in the West," she starts out with a historical narrative of discovery and possession. The "vast territory" is naturalized, "rich with every production of the earth" and yielding up "its illimitable wealth to distant generations" (12).

Writing implicitly against the violence of conquest, Victor casts her male discoverers and explorers as heroes of an innocent anti-conquest: "Men are apt to dwell with enthusiasm upon the pride of a conqueror; but, certainly, there must be that in the exultation of a discoverer, which is far more pure, elevated and happifying. To have secured, by patient research and energetic toil, in securing that which others secure by blood and devastation only, is justly a subject of self-congratulation, as it is also deserving of praise" (28). Apparently, though, Victor was uncomfortable with the pose of the historian, and she announces that "we shall proceed to the more congenial contemplation of the physical features which the country presents, touching lightly now and then upon its history, as tourists may" (34).

The traveler appears in the text as the woman who is out of place in a masculine territory, both as a woman traveling alone and as a female travel writer who authorizes her narrative by invoking her role as a quasi-official promoter and servant of the country. If discourses of femininity appear at all, they reinforce the promotional gist of her argument. Although outspoken on issues of gender in her newspaper columns, Victor skirts them as a travel writer. Neither does she address the issue of Indian dispossession other than from within the framework of the extinction/civilization argument. She is traveling through a country claimed and inhabited by white people, a country in which the indigenous inhabitants are nothing more than a ghostlike presence whose ruin, although lamented melancholically, is inevitable and necessary. The history of disinheritance is naturalized in a poetic formula: "The white race are to the red as sun to snow: as silently and surely the red men disappear, dissipated by the beams of civilization" (49).

From Victor's stance as a travel writer, everything in Oregon points to progress. Traces of the past had been effaced by flourishing commercial towns, and the hard-working Astorians, oriented toward business and material progress, had almost completely replaced the indigenous inhabitants. Like Anna Jameson before her, and like her contemporary Mary Hallock Foote, whose stories cast engineers as heroic figures,[42] Victor admires untouched nature, yet at the same time expresses a fascination with the possibilities of industrial technology, reconciling both into an image of naturalized power and energy: "The silent grandeur of the Columbia is to be made busy and vocal with the stir of human labor, and the shriek of 'resonant steam eagles' that speed from ocean to ocean, bearing the good-will of the nations of the world in bales of merchandise" (67). The traveler shares the Oregonians' visions of improvement: "the men of this period are not dreamers. Even in the sacredest haunts of Nature, they plot business, and talk railroad! We certainly thought railroad, as our eyes wandered over this beautiful, but isolated valley, and our imagination became busy with the future" (211–12).

At other times, however, the tourist and nature lover wins over the commercial developer. The removal of a natural dam "presents itself unfavorably to the mind of the worshiper at Nature's shrines— one of whose happiest emotions must ever spring from the thought, that it is impossible for Man ever to intermeddle with the eternal majesty of scenes like these" (80–81). But poetry is in general an inadequate mode of expression for the writer of a handbook. Thus a pretty village suggests "numerous quotations from the poets, who, we recollect with a sigh, are not, after all, very reliable real-estate agents" (233).

The historical travel narrative thus seems to have posed generic obstacles to Victor's accommodation of her feminism, which are probably related to problems of authority and patronage. It is only in her short stories that Victor engages with certain myths about Oregon pioneers and the position of women in the Pacific West. In her stories, she writes as an anthropologist of the early West, at times critically targeting the ideal of womanhood as established in California society, which hindered women from developing a voice and identity independent of men. Whereas in her travel narratives Victor adopts a rather monologic mode, asserting authority over her subjects, in her stories she adopts a more dialogic narrative. Many of her stories are framed as storytelling performances in which the narrator listens to somebody's history, and at times even participates in it or witnesses its unfolding.

Victor's story "The New Penelope" contradicts the idea that in early Oregon and California, women enjoyed particular respect and high esteem on account of their scarcity. Rather, she exposes this new society as deeply conservative, perpetuating the circumscription of women's lives by viewing marriage as the only reality for women and by condoning men's power over women in marital relationships. Moreover, she describes a society that always tries, but fails, to escape from its history.

History always catches up with Victor's western characters. The author's feminism surfaces in her narrator's dialogue with a pioneer woman whose story illustrates the problematic position of women in the Pacific West. Forced into marriage by public opinion—by men and women alike—although able to support herself, Mrs. Greyfield elicits the narrator's solidarity and anger. Victor seems to dissect not only the contradictions of women's position, but of gender ideology itself. When the narrator asks Mrs. Greyfield whether she thinks "that the enlargement of woman's sphere of work would have a tendency to elevate her moral influence," Victor has her character answer: "The way the subject presents itself to me, that it is degrading to have sex determine everything for us: our employments, our position in society, the obedience we owe to others, the influence we are permitted to exercise, all and everything to be dependent upon the delicate matter of a merely physical function."[43] The cult of true womanhood, which compensates women for their lack of socioeconomic and political power by assigning to them the sphere of moral influence, exposes itself as flawed and brittle.

In 1878, while Victor was doing research for her history of Oregon, Hubert Howe Bancroft offered her a position as an assistant in his library, where she wrote the *History of Oregon I* and *II,* published as part of the Bancroft *History* in 1886. The history series had begun with five volumes on the *Native Races,* published between 1874 and 1875. Victor resigned from the History Company in 1889, disgruntled with Bancroft's editorial practices and his claim to the authorship of her work. He had made it a policy that the work done in his library "is wholly mine. I do what I can myself, and pay for what I have done over that; but I father the whole of it and it goes out only under my name. All who work in the library do so simply as my assistants."[44] Apparently, however, Victor never resigned herself to relinquishing authorship. At the World's Columbian Exposition in Chicago in 1893, she presented four volumes that she had written for the Bancroft history series, with her name placed on the back of each book, publicly claiming authorship for the work she had done. With this symbolic act, she reclaimed what Bancroft had claimed to have "fathered."

Victor must have found it increasingly difficult to make a living as a freelance writer. Struggling to support herself, she began complaining about these adversities in her letters. Like other women writers of the 1870s and 1880s, she had adopted the West, so to speak, as a profession. But although her work had come to the attention of eastern historians through her participation in the historical controversy over the role played by the missionary Marcus Whitman in the immigration of 1843—a key event leading to U.S. jurisdiction over the Oregon Territory in 1848—she faced a basic problem as a woman historian. History had become institutionalized as an academic discipline in higher education, and it had developed its own media of communication in the form of the American Historical Association and its organ, the *American Historical Review*. Victor had access to neither; the process of professionalization and specialization, which also resulted in the evolution of specialized academic methodologies and discourses, had passed her by. Despite all her efforts to make herself heard in the historical controversies concerning westward expansion, it was academic historians who took up her subject with claims to scientific authority, at times not even acknowledging her as their source: "Now, when people are writing books and essays," she complained in 1900, "leaning to one side or the other, each new historian talks as if he had made an original discovery."[45]

Although the American Historical Association ultimately adopted Victor's arguments—that Marcus Whitman had been led by personal motives and ambitions to undertake his 1843 journey to the East, and that he had had only limited influence in starting the emigration of the same year—she realized with bitterness that "the gentlemen who spoke for it, every one of whom received his information directly or indirectly from me failed to mention that his 'attention had been called to it.' "[46] In an autobiographical sketch written late in her life, Victor noted that "while men, even men of no great intellectual or moral value to society, can create a constituency which will bring them profits of reputation, position, and hard cash by means of which women cannot or will not avail themselves, the woman of no matter how much industry, ability, or moral worth is not recognized because of her refusal to adopt certain of their methods, as well as on account of her inferiority from a political point of view."[47] In the end, her writing had only brought her "All work and no pay."[48]

Women Writers and the Creation of a California Myth

In March 1858, Jessie Benton Frémont boarded a steamer in New York with her husband, their three children, the son of a family friend, and four servants, to live for a few months on the family's estate in Bear Valley, California—Las Mariposas, a Mexican land grant, which was then a so-called floating grant with no set boundaries and held tenaciously by Indians. John Charles Frémont had purchased Las Mariposas in 1847. In January 1848, gold was discovered, and Frémont hired Sonoran miners to work his estate on shares. In the years that followed, mismanagement, legal suits, and the lack of definite boundaries handicapped development, and the land was soon overrun by prospectors and squatters. Finally, an official U.S. survey was made, and a patent granted in February 1856 for the property.[49] Due to questionable business practices and a national economic depression, Frémont gradually lost his fortune and slid into bankruptcy in the 1870s, and Jessie Benton Frémont took up writing professionally to help support the family, reminiscing about her stormy life with the so-called Pathfinder.

During her second stay in California between 1858 and 1861—the first had been in 1849—she had established herself as the patroness of an emerging San Francisco literary culture, offering her salon as a gathering place for intellectuals, and supporting writers like Bret Harte on the road to literary fame. In 1876, at the request of *Harper's New Monthly Magazine,* she started writing about her gold-rush experiences, which were published serially between 1877 and 1878. Her sketches were reissued in 1878 in book form as *A Year of American Travel,* which some people criticized for making a hero of her husband.[50] During the 1880s, she chronicled her days at Bear Valley in sketches for *Wide Awake,* a popular children's magazine. In 1890, the year after her husband's death, they were republished, together with other stories, in *Far West Sketches.*

Born in 1824, Jessie Benton grew up in luxurious surroundings in Washington, D.C., and St. Louis as the daughter of Senator Thomas Hart Benton. As Pamela Herr notes, she enjoyed an unusually broad education for a woman of her time, gaining knowledge in fields conventionally closed to her sex, including politics and the natural sciences. In 1841, she eloped with and married Second Lieutenant John Charles Frémont, then a member of the Army Topographical Corps. She spent the next fifteen years waiting for her husband to return from four expeditions to the western frontier, caring for a growing family, and collaborating with her husband—although the extent of her role is controversial—in writing the best-selling accounts of his western explorations, which earned him fame and made his scout, Kit Carson, a legend. In 1849, Jessie Frémont had sailed to California with her six-year-old daughter to join her husband at the height of the gold rush. In 1856, with "Frémont and Our Jessie" as a slogan of the antislavery North, she became, according to Pamela Herr, the first presidential candidate's wife to play an active part in a political campaign.[51]

By the time Frémont began writing her reminiscences, she was a well-known personality, but like Elizabeth Custer, she consistently authorized her writing through her husband's story and passed off her writing as mere scribbling, a hobby that happened to pay.[52] Also like Custer, she created in her life story the image of a benign patriarchal frontier elite, represented in the romantic story of "the Colonel" and his supportive "lady." While geologists and historians were establishing the antiquity of the desert Southwest, California became—or rather, remained—in Frémont's writing a "new" country possessing a Mediterranean charm. Kevin Starr even speculates that Jessie Frémont's cosmopolitanism colored her husband's earlier vision of California as an American Mediterranean. He also suggests that the Frémonts brought to California a spacious lifestyle "which expressed their sense of themselves as linked to the Spanish and French civilizations of the Creole South." Dressed in plantation white or as a Hispanic Californian, Frémont supervised the Sonorans who worked his mines, and the staff of Indians, blacks, and miscellaneous Europeans who serviced the estate.[53] What Starr seems to have overlooked, however, is that this patriarchal plantation image had been forged in Jessie Frémont's writings of the 1880s.

In her first letters from Bear Valley to a friend, Frémont struggles with her position as the mistress of a frontier estate.[54] Nevertheless, in subsequent letters she describes settling down contentedly to a domestic routine of gardening, entertaining, and teaching her children, with pleasant interruptions such as outdoor excursions and summer camps in the mountains. She also describes the interior of her house, whose velvet carpets, piano, bronze clocks, and marble-topped furniture must have been strikingly incongruous in the social and natural surroundings of "the valley." She asks for letters from home, wanting "such letters as I write you all 'I do & I am & we are.' You may put in a little politics but very little. I've cut the shop and taken to farming."[55] In the manner of Emily FitzGerald, she modestly leaves out her own wishes and needs, justifying her presence in California by pointing to the needs of her family. This discourse of feminine self-denial also informs Frémont's published sketches, in which she assumes an overly passive role as the frail, genteel lady in need of protection.[56]

In July 1858, she wrote about the outbreak of "regular border ruffian warfare" in the valley, explaining that thereafter her husband and the greater part of his men had to go to Mariposas "to be tried as rioters for taking up arms in self-defence & in defence of the property they were employed to work upon. Among the men on the other side are the most noted criminals of the country—one who has served two years in the penitentiary here" (69). The Frémont claim to the property is contested by men whom the narrator disqualifies as lawless criminals, and the events are worked into a story entitled "Besieged," in which the female narrator-protagonist assumes the role of the passively suffering innocent. Nevertheless, the narrative voice asserts its authority by dramatizing the conflict as one between lawless men of the working class, associated with foreigners and supported by representatives of the law, and Frémont, the innocent lawful property owner. According to Jessie Frémont, it was a case of Americans protecting their property against foreigners: "We had in California at this time a bad element of foreigners. It was believed the English authorities over the convict settlements of Australia did not 'take notice' of the shiploads of escaping convicts crowding into California. We had enough bad Americans, but they, being Americans, had not that long inheritance of want and crime known to older countries" (44).

The social geography of Bear Valley is mapped in terms of class and ethnicity; the "good" people on Frémont's land are pitted against "bad" outsiders. This community, whose social organization is configured like a plantation, confronts a group of invaders from Hornitas, "a place of evil fame just below our mountains—a gambling nest such as Bret Harte tells of—a place 'where everything that loathes the law' found congenial soil and flourished" (44–45). "The Colonel" appears as a benign paternal presence whose main activity is hoping that "above all by keeping away drink from them they would, as there were Americans among them, come to a better mind and see that violence would not ultimately profit them" (48).

Shirley Sargent explains, however, that many of the men of the Hornitas League were miners from other mining camps, not criminals, as Jessie Frémont claimed, and they were contesting Frémont's ownership of the mines they had developed.[57] What the narrator fails to reveal in her story is the problematic status of the Frémont claim and of California land claims in general. Instead, she describes the miners on Frémont land as disciplined, faithful citizen entrepreneurs, and as men who "at every risk and sacrifice, in those early days built what was best in America into the very foundations of this empire of California; not amusing to read of as the Bret Harte characters, but the men who had home traditions and guarded them, and handed them down broader and stronger from fiery trials" (57–58).

In another sketch, the narrator introduces herself as the mistress of a large estate with responsibilities to her neighbors in an Indian village, the immigrant and American settlers, and the women the Frémonts brought with them from "the States." The Frémonts' house, created after the "vision of a New York home," contrasts significantly with the dwelling of the Calhoun family, neglected and devoid of beauty. Poor whites from the South, they "were entirely useless but equally harmless people, neither bad nor good, nor any thing. Quite contented in their own way undisturbed by knowledge of any kind and satisfied with their idle life where a little gold-digging and hunting provided for all they knew of as comforts" (83–84). The narrator describes her role in maternalistic terms as bringing American tradition, manners, and taste to the valley. She also performs nursing work among the Calhoun children, victims of their mother's ignorance and their parents' disorderly life.

As in the narratives of women who wrote about army life, relations with Indians are characterized by interactions between the women revolving around white and native households: "Near by was a large Indian village, some hundreds, settled there. The young women from it came constantly to our house and sat about on the grass chatting together of us and laughing as they watched our doings with frank curiosity. We were their matinee" (84–85). In turn, the narrator's family visits the Indian villagers, watching the native women at work: "Their ways all had object and meaning—the sewing of squirrel skins together, the pounding of acorns into meal for bread, the basket weaving, and they were fairly clean and gay" (85).

The narrator enjoys giving them beads and food, and she invites them, together with her "American" neighbors, to her Christmas tree. Again the interaction is restricted to girls and women, who flock to the house expressing their amazement: "They had evidently some dim traditional memory from the old Missions and, liking and trusting us already, we were accepted by them as the same with the missionary priests, for the Cross was to them assurance of protection and good-will—not the usual ill-will of the whites" (85). The narrator's family, whose matriarch is also cast as the benign mother of her female Indian family, has replaced the Catholic padres.

In "Sierra Neighbors," these benign maternalist efforts to widen the circles "of gentle influences for peace and good-will" (87) extend into labor relations. The biggest difficulty for Frémont's narrator, as it was for Kirkland's narrator Mary Clavers, is to find a laundress. The white women in the valley "were too much at ease in this prospering mining community to fatigue themselves, which was good for them while it was trying for us" (100). Finally she finds a laundress, whose husband "was a surly creature, holding himself high above our two colored men because he was white; but not above living off his wife's work" (101).

Yet even as the narrator denounces the man's hierarchical thinking, she asserts her own superiority over Indian women: "I boldly utilized Indian girls from their village hard by" (102). Under the white woman's influence, differences of race seem to dissolve. The women "looked of a different race after they had seen the advantage of cleanliness, and learned to plait their thick hair in a club. Starch in their own calico skirts was the crowning touch of finery." This positive influence flowing through domestic channels is traced by the narrator to her southern plantation background and her ability to "make allowance for untutored people, as I knew them of all grades, from the carefully trained and refined house-servants to the common field hands; and knew that with them, as with us, they must have nature's stamp of intelligence and good-humor, without which any teaching and training is not much use" (103).

Just as the mission fathers "had taught weaving and cooking to the women, and simple agriculture and the care of flocks and herds to the men, and left in the fine mission building proof of their capacity as workmen," this plantation matriarch "experimented on these Indian women with advantage to them as well as to ourselves" (103). The narrator is convinced that women who weave compact baskets and gather heavy loads of acorns, berries, and mushrooms of their own accord, who are industrious and have "useful purpose & forethought in their occupations," could do more "when instructed, encouraged and rewarded" (105–6). But as much as she may acknowledge the Miwok women's work and talents, the learning experience is basically a one-way-street: while they learn from her household by watching, her household watches native women at work only for entertainment.

Frémont's Indian subjects are malleable and manageable in their feminine submissiveness, but their cultural traditions present an obstacle to the narrator's matriarchal power. She decries the Miwoks' apparent neglect of their old people, charitably intervening in favor of the latter. After giving warm clothes to an old woman, she found them worn by a young Indian man. When her entreaties to the young man failed to get a response, she "tried Prussian war-tactics and made their whole village responsible—no more presents to any one unless they all joined in keeping for the one we gave to what was his or hers." The white woman here acts as a culture bearer with an iron fist, enforcing in her own way the adoption of white American values, defined as the right to private property and the Christian law of sympathy: "And it worked about as well as our elaborate methods of securing justice. There is no protection for age and helplessness except among really Christian communities" (104).

This benign but interventionist maternalism is also extended to the other white families in the valley, a heterogeneous group within which relations are ordered according to established hierarchies of race and ethnicity. The "poor white" southern family concentrates their whole pride in the fact "that they were white: this, by the curious alchemy of ignorance and self-conceit, endowed them with complacent superiority. The swarthy, black-eyed, black-haired Italians they looked down upon with contempt because they were so dark, and because 'that Eye-talian worked like a nigger.' He worked a great deal harder" (107).

This hard-working Italian family escapes Frémont's Americanism, appealing to her Mediterranean sensibilities. Nevertheless, she freezes the family into a pastoral peasant image that by its essentializing power asserts American hegemony in the same way it does over indigenous people. Thus, when she first sees the young Italian woman "in her picturesque peasant dress," the narrator writes, "her own young beauty and the noble baby in her arms made a vision of artistic beauty, and Old World art-associations—a true peasant Mother and Child" (108).

Frémont's sketches represent California as a plantation presided over by a genteel matriarch and shaped by hierarchies of class, nationality, race, and gender. But hers was not the only female contribution to the creation of a California myth. In contrast to Frémont's vision of the American expansion into California as a benign act of intervention in the service of social progress and empire building, Josephine Clifford and Helen Hunt Jackson, delving deeper into California history, present a more ambivalent interpretation of the course of westward expansion. While Jackson wrote from within an eastern publishing market, attempting to shape the agenda of the federal government with respect to California Mission Indians, Clifford positioned herself within both the eastern and the western publishing cultures, engendering California and the Southwest in her sketches of army life and her stories of early California.[58]

Josephine Woempner Clifford (McCrackin) was among the women writers who contributed to the *Overland Monthly* regularly from its beginnings in 1869 into the 1890s. The daughter of a German baroness and a Prussian army officer, she was born in Prussia in 1839 and brought to America as a child in 1846. In 1864, she married an army officer and moved with him to Washington. Two years later, Lieutenant Clifford was assigned to the Southwest Territory, and Josephine accompanied him, traveling in the same column with Lydia Lane. Clifford's travels and experiences as an army wife in Arizona and New Mexico became the basis of her sketches of army life, which together with her short stories about California life were published in the *Overland Monthly* and other regional and national magazines. Her sketches and stories were collected in three volumes: *Overland Tales* (1877), *'Another Juanita' and Other Stories* (1893), and *'The Woman Who Lost Him' and Tales of the Army Frontier* (1913).[59]

Cheryl J. Foote has analyzed Clifford McCrackin's stories as autobiographical accounts providing insight into the lesser-known aspects of frontier military life—unhappy marriages and infidelity, alcoholism, and domestic violence: "unraveled, separated, and placed into a chronological order they lacked in publication (and with official military records as corroboration), these autobiographical sketches provide a remarkably intimate view of Clifford's marriage to an army officer and other details of her life at military posts throughout the Southwest." Foote reconstructs Clifford's story of physical and mental abuse at the hands of her alcoholic husband from her sketches and stories, which resulted in her escape from her husband in 1867 and her flight to San Francisco, where she became Bret Harte's editorial assistant and established herself as a writer. Not until the 1880s, however, when she learned of her husband's death and remarried, did she put into print her most terrifying experiences.[60]

In the context of this study, the autobiographical aspects of Clifford's sketches of army life are less important than her representations of California and the Far West. In many of her sketches and stories—a generic mixture of personal narrative and fiction in the manner pioneered by Caroline Kirkland—the Far West provides a refuge for female protagonists on the run from their pasts. Many of her stories also rewrite the romantic script of love and marriage by featuring unhappy endings. The southwestern army frontier is a land of contrasts; for the female protagonist of "A Lady in Camp," it is a place of exile, although a "tolerable" place and not "altogether a howling wilderness." The desert becomes a metaphor for her unfulfilled life "unfolding before her, lone, and drear, and barren; without change or relief, without verdure, or blossom, of goodly springs of crystal water; the arid desert—her life, dragging its slow length along; the frowning mountain—her duties, and the unavoidable tasks that life imposed upon her."[61]

As in other women's narratives of the army frontier, the Southwest is a contested territory, still largely in the hands of Indian tribes, a land at the same time desolate, violent, and beautiful, a varied country that surprises the narrator with unexpected beauty, yet weighs her down with its deathlike stillness and silence.[62] In these early sketches, Mexicans appear as dirty and lazy figures, while Indians are represented with the satirical humor of a Sara Lippincott and a Mark Twain: "It was by no means my first glimpse of the 'noble savage' that I got on the banks of the Colorado, or I might have been appalled at the sight of a dozen or two of barely-clothed, filthy-looking Indians, squatted in rows wherever the sun could burn hottest on their clay-covered heads. The specimens here seen were different from those that had come under my observation on the Plains."[63]

This broadside against the noble savage stereotype is already familiar from women's overland narratives of the 1860s and from army women's narratives. It is followed by a satirical commentary on missionary efforts to assimilate Indians by "civilizing" them through American dress: "That Indians can be civilized William Lloyd Garrison would not doubt, could he but see with what native grace these dusky belles wear their crinoline. Nor can they be accused of the extravagance of their white sisters in matters pertaining to toilet and dress; the crinoline (worn over the short petticoat, constituting their full and entire wardrobe, aside from it) apparently being the only article of luxury they indulge in, except paint —and whiskey, when they can get it" (304). This scathing representation of Yuma women is concluded by the equally familiar imaging of the Yuma men as emasculated dandies.

Indigenous inhabitants are fixed in their present degraded state, disconnected from human history: "the shimmer of romance and poetry one would willingly throw around them, is so rudely dispelled by the sight of these lank, dirty, half-nude creatures, with faces exhibiting no more intelligence than (perhaps not so much as) the faces of their lean dogs, or shaggy horses" (307). Moreover, like Lippincott, she deploys her representations of burlesque Indian figures in order to comment critically on Grant's peace policy and the missionary efforts of eastern reformers. Overall, there seems to be no room for female alliances with evangelical Christianity in women's public and private western narratives of the period.

Clifford's sketches of army life in the Southwest were written as personal narratives based on the authority of experience. Her stories of California, in contrast, seem to have demanded different rhetorical strategies, obeying the logic and laws of fiction. Reading some of her stories, we are suddenly confronted with a more critical interpretation of the westward course of white America. In "La Graciosa," Clifford focuses critically on the history of white conquest in California, presenting the region in the years after the Mexican-American War as a contact zone of Spanish and American cultures. Again, the protagonist is a woman escaping to California from an abusive marriage. The setting is a landscape that mirrors the character's emotional state. The story unfolds at the meeting point of Spanish and American cultures, at a time when American hegemony was being asserted over Spanish California through corrupt land-grabbing practices and environmental abuse. "La Graciosa," in dealing with American conquest, Spanish-American intermarriage, and intercultural exchange, thus antedates Helen Hunt Jackson's efforts to address the problems of America's expansionist past in her novel *Ramona* (which had been intended to draw attention to the plight of the California Mission Indians, but instead stimulated the romanticization of California's Hispanic past).[64]

"La Graciosa" focuses on the meeting and alliance between a gallant and wealthy Mexican landholder and a young American woman who has arrived on the train in widow's apparel to live with her sister after her husband's alleged death. The man's "Indian face," "native grace and demeanor," and "air of chivalrous gallantry" distinguish him positively from the "more cold-blooded, though, perhaps, more fluent-spoken, Saxon people surrounding him," most of them lower-class and uneducated.[65] The discursive terrain differs significantly from that of her army sketches: Indianness is now aestheticized and acquires a new symbolic significance. However, in the end, Clifford's deployment of race and skin color in her plot of romantic entanglement has the same effect as her rhetorical dehumanization of southwestern Indians in her army sketches: it ultimately leads to the erasure of the Indian presence.

From the outset, the issue of skin color is invested with symbolic meaning. When the narrator contrasts Nora Rutherford's fair skin and Don Pedro Lopez's olive skin, his hand looks dark beside hers. One of his servants seems to be "a full Indian, though hardly darker than his master" (16). The woman is charmed by the man's attention, and she accepts his efforts to lighten her gloomy mood by entertaining and courting her. As the story unfolds, however, it becomes clear that Nora is divorced, and that Don Pedro's attentions are not enough to "cover [her] past life and its miseries" (19). The Don's passion for her is not reciprocated by Nora, who shuns the man's touch but who accepts him as a suitor now that she is in need of male protection and financial support. His passion is answered by her more or less calculated accommodation.

The story is set at a time of increasing tensions between Mexican landholders and American newcomers. Don Pedro is still a wealthy landowner, but many of his compatriots "had parted with their broad acres, their countless herds, all too easily, to gratify their taste for lavish display and easy living, with its attendant cost under the new American regime; or had lost them through confiding . . . to the people whose thoughts were bent on securing, by usury and knaves' tricks, the possessions of the very men whose hospitable roof afforded them shelter" (17–18). Don Pedro's landholdings are immense, and he is in the process of buying a new ranch farther to the south, which "the Americans have not yet succeeded in cutting . . . up into building-lots and homestead blocks" (19). His sons also exhibit their father's chivalrous behavior, which "distinguished them favorably from the uncouth flippancy of some of their young American neighbors" (18). The latter are not congenial company for Nora and never appear personally in the story.

When Don Pedro invites Nora, her sister, and her brother-in-law to go south with him, it is tacitly understood that Nora's consent implies a commitment. The hospitality of Don Pedro's Hispanic friends is legendary, and the travelers are welcomed warmly everywhere (31). Nora's observations during the journey focus on the negative cultural and environmental consequences of the Ameri-

can conquest, which is described in mainly economic and aesthetic terms. At the old mission church of San Luis Obispo, Nora
finds a "group of fig-trees here and there, a palm-tree sadly out of
place, in a dirty, dusty yard, an agave standing stiff and reserved
among its upstart neighbors, the pea-vine and potato." The ornamental and beautiful has been replaced by the practical and material. Nora registers with dismay that even a "proud avenue of
olives, towering so high above all, has been cut up and laid out in
building-lots" (30).

Among the destructive inroads of American culture into California's ecology and material culture are the "obtrusive frame houses
of the fast-crowding American population" set up in the midst of
the mission garden at San Buenaventura. It makes her sad, she tells
Don Pedro, "to see the stately olives of a century's growth spread
their great branches over flimsy little shops; to see the neglected
vines trailing their unpruned lengths over rubbish-piled open lots,
which a paper placard announced 'for sale'" (38). She also points
silently "into a yard, where a half-grown palm-tree stood among
heaps of refuse cigar-ends and broken bottles. The house to which
the yard belonged was occupied as a bar-room, and one of its pa-
trons, a son of Old Erin, to all appearances, lay stretched near the
palm, sleeping off the fumes of the liquor imbibed at the bar" (30).

The invasion is not only preponderantly male, the story suggests, but also defined in ethnic terms. The Old World is represented by Irishmen, who are contrasted with another group associated with the Old World, the "true Castilians" who are "fair of skin,
hair lighter than Nora's tresses, and eyes blue as the sky." It is
among these Hispanos of "pure Castilian blood" that Nora will
eventually find her partner, more suitable than the dark, Indian,
creolized Don Pedro.[66] During their stay with one such Castilian
family, the net of narrative entanglement is woven: the young
daughter of the family pines away with unrequited love for Don
Pedro, while the young son, Manuel Del Gada, declares his love for
Nora. What distinguishes him, and what suggests him as a suitable
partner for Nora, is his whiteness: "Such clear blue eyes as he had!
All the sunshine of his native Spain seemed caught in them; and
his hand was so white! Nora's own could hardly vie with it" (32).

Nora becomes pensive, wondering "whether she had a right to
barter herself away, body and soul, truth and honor, perhaps, for

a grand home and a great deal of money" (38). In Los Angeles, events reach a climax: Manuel implores Nora to marry him, and she declares her love for Manuel, but at the same time, her former husband appears and blackmails her. Don Pedro, who "had often declared that seeing a divorced woman gave him the same shuddering sensation that was caused by looking upon a poisonous snake" (21), witnesses the scene of revelation. After he recognizes Nora's ex-husband as the murderer of a friend, he is fatally shot by the man, who escapes but then drowns during his flight.

With both her former husband and Don Pedro dead, there is only one obstacle left between Nora and Manuel: his impending poverty. In a truly romantic strike of the pen, Clifford removes the impediment by reinstalling Manuel into his heritage and reversing the process of Hispanic dispossession: "the report of an adverse decision from Washington on the Del Gada suit had been false" (51). The story's romantic ending, however, carries an ironic note. Both Nora and Manuel are not only romantic but calculating lovers: " 'But you would never have married me—a poor man,' he says, bantering. 'Nor would you have married me—a divorced woman,' she returns, demurely" (52).

By eliminating Don Pedro, Clifford removed not only an unloved suitor, but a dark one "tainted" by Indian blood, and she replaced him with a light-skinned suitor of "pure" Castilian blood, that is, of European descent. By reinstating the white Hispanic into his legacy and uniting him with an American woman, Clifford also reversed the historical process of Hispanic dispossession that she had traced in her story, and she configured a future California characterized by the selective possibility of Spanish-American unions on the basis of color and descent. This union, however, although represented as a romantic marriage, depends on the exclusion and extermination of the dark Indian presence.

The (Re-)Discovery of the Southwest

The differences in Clifford's representations of Hispanic and Indian claimants to the Far West anticipate the distinctions made in the memoirs of army women in the Southwest, who excluded Indians as an unwanted and troublesome presence while envisioning the possibility of temporary alliances and relations with Hispanic

Americans. Narratives of emigrant women on the southwestern trails to California draw similar distinctions. Whereas Indians are seen as a constant threat to settlers and emigrants passing through Texas, Mexicans provide emigrants with food. Harriet Bunyard, a young girl traveling through Texas in 1869, notes seeing a "very brilliantly lighted" house inhabited by a "White man with a Mexican wife," and records how Mexicans came to their camp, selling fruit, vegetables, and fish (224). They are described as "very nice looking people, white as anybody," whose house "looked so nice and clean inside" and who had "black Mexicans for servants" (227). The recurrence of references to skin color as well as to dress suggests how southwestern Hispanic people and cultures challenged overland travelers' simple black-and-white views of race and color.

Bunyard's representations of Indians differ significantly from her sympathetic curiosity about Mexican life. The Pima Indians of Arizona are described as "detestable. . . . All the men riding and the women walking and carrying all the load" (239). Maricopa Indians who bring the travelers melons and corn appear as "an ignorant, silly looking people." On the whole, the country is seen as "suited only for Indians to live in" (240). The forty-four-year-old Maria Shrode looks at the Pima Indians from the more indulging maternalist stance of the civilizing mission: "They are a friendly tribe and Uncle Sam is trying to teach them to work. O, what a field for a good missionary is here and good persevering teachers. Some of them only half clad and the little ones go entirely naked" (288).

In her sketches of army life, Josephine Clifford's representations of the Southwest and its people are based on the authority of personal aesthetic experience, which defined beauty in the landscape as the presence of flowers, grass, trees, water, and color. Other women travelers' conceptions of the beautiful land are linked to more practical considerations and often project an improving vision upon the southwestern country, with an appreciation of beauty resting on the land's suitability for agriculture and stock.[67] In these women's diaries, there is yet no discursive basis for the aesthetic appreciation of the southwestern landscape. If the country does not show the signs of fertility, it is a barren waste; the view of red soil and red rocks cannot inspire the journalists beyond the fact that the color indicates the soil's unsuitability for cultivation.[68]

Southwestern landscapes and people apparently challenge previous configurations of the West as a "new" and "fresh" country, for what women travelers see here is an "old" country, full of the signs of a long cultural history.

The contradiction between the Southwest as a romantic blank on which a new history can be inscribed and the Southwest as a land full of history also informs the travel narratives and sketches of another woman writer who made it her task to revise the image of the Southwest as a historical wasteland, but who ultimately failed to establish it as a land of culture and cultural history. At the end of January 1879, Susan E. Wallace arrived in the Southwest to join her husband, the newly appointed New Mexico Territorial Governor Lew Wallace, in Santa Fe. When Wallace had assumed his post a few months earlier, he had accepted the difficult task of restoring law and order in a territory shaken by corruption, murder, and theft during the so-called Lincoln County War—a war that would become the stuff of legend through the involvement of such outlaws as Billy "the Kid" Bonney. During her stay in New Mexico between January and October 1879, Susan Wallace saw her husband struggle with his task and at times accompanied him on his travels. On May 11, 1879, she wrote to her son Henry: "We should have another war with Old Mexico to make her take back New Mexico. I did not think anything could make me think well of Santa Fe, but this hideous spot [Fort Stanton, N.M.] does."

Because Billy the Kid was rumored to have threatened her husband's life, the Wallaces were forced to live behind closed shutters at night, leading Susan to conclude: "This way of living does not suit me; some men find an unaccountable fascination in the danger and outlawry of the frontier far beyond my understanding. Sweet home was never sweeter to my thought than now in this wilderness without the manna."[69] Susan Wallace never could get used to life in the territory and, pleading bad health, went back to Crawfordsville, Indiana, in October 1879.[70]

However, the travel sketches she started writing shortly after her arrival in Santa Fe for the *New York Tribune,* the *Independent,* and the *Atlantic Monthly* tell a different story. Her husband had been invited by the *Tribune* to contribute occasional letters, but he was too busy with his governorship and with the writing of his novel *Ben-Hur.* Instead, Susan Wallace took up the pen, exploring the

Southwest for its literary and historical potential and writing about visits to turquoise mines, abandoned and inhabited pueblos, and landmarks such as Canyon de Chelly and Inscription Rock. While her husband dealt in his writings with a distant country and a distant time, she devoted herself to the task of chronicling the romantic past of the American Southwest—significantly with a focus on prehistory and with hardly a reference to the troubled present of the territory. Her travel sketches were collected and re-published in 1888 as *The Land of the Pueblos.*[71]

Wallace came to the Southwest the same year that the first eth-nological expedition under the auspices of the newly formed Bu-reau of Ethnology of the Smithsonian Institution set out for the Zuni pueblo of New Mexico with James Stevenson in charge. He was accompanied by his wife, Matilda, who developed an interest in ethnological work and became an anthropologist in her own right.[72] This was also a time when tourists and curiosity seekers were engaging in a flourishing business with Indian artifacts. Even before the Civil War, the discovery of ancient ruins in the Americas had become, in the words of William H. Goetzmann, a "national cause" that stirred romantic interest in the mystery of America's antiquity.

The historian William Hickling Prescott had produced two monumental histories on the prehistoric cultures of the Americas, *History of the Conquest of Mexico* (1843) and *History of the Con-quest of Peru* (1847), which became longstanding best-sellers. In 1875, the discovery of Anasazi ruins in Chaco Canyon by Wil-liam H. Holmes and photographer William H. Jackson marked the beginning of a long series of rediscoveries of southwestern prehis-toric ruins, which led to the anthropological reconstruction of in-digenous life in the region. As Goetzmann points out, time was the central focus of the study of man during what he terms the "Second Great Age of Discovery." Darwin's and Spencer's evolutionist theo-ries merely accented the question that occupied peoples' minds: the question of man's origin, descent, and cultural development. Thus Lewis Henry Morgan, in his *Ancient Society* (1877), saw mankind progressing, at different paces in various parts of the globe, from "savagery" to "barbarism" and "civilization." Geo-graphical and ethnographical discoveries were now all seen from the vantage point of evolution and history.[73]

Wallace's *Land of the Pueblos* can be located within this context. Her interest in the Pueblos centered not so much on Pueblo culture as on what it meant for America, American history (and prehistory), and American literature. Her narrative is still preethnological in that it does not present a scientific but a novelistic mode of producing knowledge in the form of personal narratives and fictional stories. There is not yet the focus on the Pueblos' social and ceremonial organization, on kinship and marriage, or on witchcraft, all of which would later concern anthropologists. Rather, her interest lay in collecting tribal myths and tales, which are never presented as texts in their own right. Instead, they serve as illustrations of a quaint, primitive past that inevitably has to give way to white American civilization—a framework that was not as far from anthropological studies as one might think. Early American ethnological research undertook a mission not only of preserving relics but of providing a record of cultures that were disappearing; it seemed necessary to collect information about them that could facilitate the implementation of civilization programs.[74] The civilizing mission was thus part of the ethnological rhetoric.

Recalling Nathaniel Hawthorne's lament of "the lack of the poetic element in our dear native land, where there is no shadow, no mystery, no antiquity, no picturesque and gloomy wrong, nor anything but commonplace prosperity in broad and simple daylight," Wallace contradicts him by pointing to the American Southwest: "Here is every requisite of romance,—the enchantment of distance, the charm of the unknown,—and in shadowy mists of more than three hundred years, imagination may flower out in fancies rich and strange." In other words, the southwestern past can hold its own with the Puritan past of the Northeast (15). But although Wallace attempts to recover the cultural history of the Southwest in nationalistic terms—exclusively for North America and in opposition to Spanish America—the Spanish conquest retained the romantic aura that it had had since Prescott's *Conquest of Mexico.*

Unlike Helen Hunt Jackson, whose sympathetic treatment of the Hispanic past in *Ramona* contributed to the image of benign Spanish missions among docile and helpless Indians, Wallace focuses on the cruel, yet still fascinating and romantic, legacy of Spanish colonialism among American Indians, a legacy of greed and feverish dreams of gold as well as of a romantic passion for adventure. The Southwest is a forgotten land beyond time and history. "At last, at last," the narrator exclaims, "I am not of this time nor of this continent; but away, away across the sea, in the land of dreams and visions, 'renowned, romantic Spain'" (14).

Like her husband's *The Fair God,* which casts Indian Americans, in the form of the Aztec rulers, as the pharaohs of the New World,[75] Wallace's sketches depict the Southwest as the site of a prehistoric Indian kingdom. But she also aims to tear the veil from one of the pervasive myths about the Southwest, that of a highly developed prehistoric Aztec civilization that had peopled the land. The story, she claims, had been created by the Spanish conquerors, who covered their disappointment and legitimized their journeys by giving the area an alluring mystery. These erroneous ideas about the area's history were also held by travelers visiting prehistoric ruins, who "ascribe them to an extinct race and lost civilization, superior to any now extant here. They muse over Aztec glories faded, and temples fallen, in the spirit of the immortal antiquary, who saw in a ditch 'slightly marked' a Roman wall, surrounding the stately and crowded praetorium, with its all-conquering standards bearing the great name of Caesar" (26).

Wallace locates herself in opposition to the prehistoric craze and the fascination with antiquity that had struck her contemporaries. The target of her revisionism is clearly the emerging romanticization of the prehistoric Southwest by Americans who appropriate it as the site of an American Rome or Athens. She agrees with Oliver Wendell Holmes, whom she quotes as having said: "Whether the arrowheads are a hundred or a thousand years old who knows, who cares? There is no history to the red race, there is scarcely an individual in it. A few instincts on legs and holding a tomahawk;—there is the Indian of all time" (50). Research into prewhite American history, she suggests, can only come up with one result: history begins with the advent of Euro-American culture. The American continent does have an antiquity, but one inferior to that of the Old World, and one beyond history—beyond change, development, and progress. Instead of establishing the Pueblos as the proud descendants of an old civilization with a continuous cultural history, Wallace's narrator can only devalue Pueblo history as the story of primitive stagnation. At the same time, she

establishes the builders of abandoned pueblo ruins as the ancestors of the present-day Pueblos, an interpretation of Pueblo history
confirmed by twentieth-century scholarship, although with a different twist: while Wallace devalued the cultural achievements of
the prehistoric builders and their progeny, anthropologists have
established the complexity of prehistoric and Pueblo cultures.[76]

Like ethnologists and evangelical philanthropists of the time,
Wallace claims a common origin for European and Indian peoples,
a claim that supports the assimilation and incorporation of Indians
into American national life (see chapter 5). This claim of a common humanity reinforces an expansionist rhetoric that celebrates
the American march of empire across the continent: following
these "dead-and-gone tribes . . . our elder brethren" who leave no
memory, "we are moving forward in the resistless march, holding
in our hands messages appealing to futurity—messages addressed
to darkness, dropped into oblivion" (107).

Wallace's view of the Spanish conquest is marked by an anti-
Catholicism that stands in striking contrast to Jackson's sympathetic portrait of the achievements of the Spanish padres. Moreover, whereas Jackson emphasizes the helplessness and largely
voluntary submission of the California Indians, Wallace's chronicle of Spanish-Indian relations in New Mexico deals with the historic evidence of resistance and rebellion of the Pueblos against
their colonizers. These two interpretations of southwestern history, based on differences in regional history, must of course also
lead to different assessments of the American conquest of the
Southwest: in Clifford's "La Graciosa" and in Jackson's *Ramona,*
American occupation is indicted as a cruel conquest based on materialism and greed; Wallace's American occupation is the story
of the Pueblos' liberation from their Indian and Spanish oppres-
sors (36).

The subject Wallace chose as evidence for an American romance
is almost intractable, and her writing is riddled with contradictions. On one hand, the Pueblos are a declining people, victimized
by conquest and servitude during the Spanish period; on the other
hand, they are an extremely conservative people who, by building
an invisible wall around themselves against the inroads of both
Spanish and American cultures, have retained their traditions and
lifestyles against all odds. Wallace's sketches show once more that

theories of an indigenous American past, of the romantic shadows on the American land, have to battle with the actual contemporary presence of tribal nations claiming the American soil.

The Pueblos' conservatism leads Wallace to the contemporary discussion about Indian reform. In the East, she writes, there is a "popular superstition that the noble aboriginal soul disdains artifice, and is open as sunlight to the sweet influences of truth and straightforward testimony:—an illusion rising from the misty enchantments of distance." Speaking with the authority of experience, the author dispels this illusion: "Come among them, and you will soon learn to make allowance for every assertion; and as for vanity and self-love I have never seen any equal that of the children of nature debased by contact with the white men." She clearly satirizes the idea of "children of nature" debased by white contact: "They cannot be instructed, because they know everything, nor surprised, because their fathers had all wisdom before you were born" (37). Interactions with the Pueblo people reverse conventional hierarchies in white culture, leaving the white teacher without the power to teach: "We then gave it up. Like the Chinese they so closely resemble, nothing can be named which they did not have ages ago; and having so long possessed all knowledge, they steadily resist your efforts to show them their ignorance. They think themselves the envy of the civilized world." Among such a people, the white woman "soon learns to repress assumption of superiority or effort to impress the calm listener with your grammatical sentences" (38).

Studying the Pueblos, Wallace suggests in another sketch, may be a highly problematic enterprise for a female student on account of the Pueblos' exclusion of women from their cultural knowledge. She had once visited Tesuque, she writes, "with a view of gaining some knowledge of their primitive ceremonials" (263). She had wanted to visit the *estufa*[77] and is smilingly led to an empty, abandoned shrine: "The old arrow-maker was joking when he conducted us to the altar place; the shrine was abandoned, the sacred fire was dead, the secret temple with all its holy and guarded mysteries was laid open to women even!" (264–65). Within this framework of thought, which assumes the patriarchal exclusion of women from ceremonies, it is impossible for white women to study the sacred ceremonies of the Pueblos.

Nevertheless, the narrator still hopes to find authentic knowledge somewhere else, as far away as possible from the Catholic priest and the Protestant missionary (266). In Arizona, she travels to the villages of the Moqui (Hopi) and Papago (whose official name is now Tohono O'odham).[78] South of the Gila River, she finds the Maricopa and the Pima irrigating lands and raising two crops of corn a year. Wallace views the sexual division of labor that assigns farming to women—actually a source of women's economic and social power in many tribal societies—with dismay; and she reduces Pima women to a negative aesthetics, belying the romantic portrayals of Spanish explorers with their "Mongol cast of features— narrow button-hole eyes, almost no eye-brows, high cheek-bones, thick lips, tattooed chin" (222).

As in other women's contemporary accounts, aesthetics carry the full weight of meaning. At Tesuque, Wallace finds the "typical" young woman "without beauty of any sort . . . raw boned and high shouldered, inclining to fat; of an ashy sunburnt skin, flat face, high cheek bones, thick lips, mannish gait, harsh voice. She is nearly akin (if there's anything in likeness) to the Mongolian Ah Sin" (264). Gender (the mannish gait) and ethnic traits (the comparison with the Chinese) carry additional weight in this representation of the other woman held in the gaze of the female narrator.

At the same time, however, native women awaken the narrator's emancipatory zeal. Like Elizabeth Burt and others, she denounces the "noble red man" as a misogynist slave driver: "How I longed to hand that noble red man over to the mercies of a woman's rights convention. The husband may disfigure or insult the wife at pleasure, divorce her without form or ceremony by a mere separation, and she has no protection or appeal" (277). Although no girl is forced to marry against her will, the iconic Indian wife "never hears of protoplasm, equal suffrage, social science and the like. She often builds the wigwam after Romeo has cut the poles, always bears them on her shoulders in the march, plows the field with a crooked stick, raises the beans, hoes the corn, bakes the cakes, without a complaint" (279). As in the western narratives of Wallace's female contemporaries, this discourse of female oppression essentially deflects attention from colonial history. It obscures the problematic effects of white expansion and Indian-white relations on an agriculturalist people who supplied travelers and settlers with produce, but who increasingly suffered from the effects of white settlement.[79]

Southwestern Indians are romantic in their unchangeability only as long as they can be imagined as a pastoral people, and as long as their past and present can be cast in classical terms. Wallace's recourse to classicist and orientalist models underscores this attempt to pastoralize tribal claimants to the land. Orientalist conventions deterritorialize tribal people, neutralizing their hold on their southwestern homelands as well as on their cultural practices. One Indian man is represented as "a perfect mountain prince, erect and stately in his crown of green leaves, and striped Navajo blanket draping his shoulders, held in place by one symmetric hand. The noblest Roman wore his imperial mantle with no better grace" (49). Her Mexican driver is a denizen of the Old World; he "grew to man's estate under this fierce Syrian sun, sitting against the mud wall of a Syrian hut, has a soft Syrian face. No positive beauty (I have never seen out-door people except Arabs who have), but comely features, unchanging, melancholy eyes, and a gentle, passive voice, very winsome" (76). The landscape itself presents an orientalist picture, "desolate and forsaken as the wilderness of Engedi" (78).

What always confuses such peaceful images of oriental pastoralism and manageability are the ceremonial and religious practices of tribal people, which according to U.S. policy needed to be debased as meaningless, unaesthetic, and barbaric. Indian dances, as in other women's narratives, represent spectacles without meaning. The costumes of the dancers are admittedly picturesque, and the dance itself—"a yearly delight celebrated in the changeless fashion set before these people in the primeval years"—confirms the Pueblos' resistance against change. But the singing accompanying the dance "is a long-continued strain of unearthly howls and yells of the sort to drive one crazy, to make your flesh, aye, the very marrow of your bones creep. . . . The choral howling proceeded with the dire monotony of everything Indian" (54–55). Ultimately, the performance can only corroborate their image of cultural poverty and inferiority (57).

At the same time, Wallace presents the country as a white frontier that carries the seeds of its own destruction. The illusion of the desert as old and "Arabic" is now ironically dispelled by the discovery of waste left behind by the recent arrivals. Instead of valuables dropped by Haroun and Mohammed, the travelers find "a battered sardine-box, a sliver of wagon-tongue, the broken end of a saw . . . four greasy cards . . . two used-up paper collars, and an empty black bottle. Strong testimonials to the high superiority of our arts, and the refinements of our boasted civilization" (94). And, in the middle of nowhere, there appears the "Sweet Home Saloon," fringed by the "white tents of the vanguard of civilization—an army of laborers, working day and night on the railroad track. They will not march until they have broken the fascinating spell" (95). Adopting the by now well-known rhetoric of innocence, Wallace, like Frémont and Clifford, heaps the responsibility for destroying this paradise on an ethnically defined "army of laborers," on the "pick and shovels of Mike Brady and the O'Flannegans," who will "have put to flight the finer fancies of musing antiquary and dreaming pilgrim" by the time the narrator's letter reaches its audience (96).

The romance of the Southwest is necessarily short-lived. But the tourist, dreaming dreams and seeing visions, is an innocent, noninterventionist presence who has no share in the work of destruction performed by Irish laborers and the railroad. Wallace's history of the Southwest, which denies the destructive inroads of the earlier, military American conquest, essentially flees from history by putting the blame on European immigrants, participants in the late-nineteenth-century wave of immigration from the poorer regions of Europe. It is an ironic role for the wife of a man who came to New Mexico as a politician invested with the official power for change, the representative of the federal government aiming to prepare the territory of New Mexico for its future as a state of the Union.

Female Primitivism: Caroline Leighton at Puget Sound

The 1880s marked the appearance of a number of women's pioneering reminiscences in which the writers significantly focus less on their spiritual influence on raw western frontiers than on their achievements as enterprising, hard-working women who became businesswomen—not by choice, but out of the need to survive.[80] Women writing about California put a special emphasis on the state's business opportunities for women,[81] which can probably be related to Californians' general inclination to recast Bret Harte's rowdy as the entrepreneur of the Far West.

Kevin Starr has suggested that in the corporative 1880s and imperial 1890s, "the enterprising Pioneer became the assured Capitalist, the Darwinian man of brains and energy, a little flamboyant perhaps, but always purposeful, who had made the Gold Rush serve the constructive purposes of capital."[82] With Jessie Frémont's accounts of her travels and life, we also have a genteel voice giving expression to the matriarchal version of a patriarchal California plantation myth, which parallels Helen Hunt Jackson's influence as the founder of a California "mission myth." At the same time, memoirs of army women like Elizabeth Custer cast the military presence on the Indian frontier as an act of benign patriarchal intervention and engage critically with the rhetoric of Indian reform.

One woman's travel account of the 1880s deserves special attention within the context of this debate on Indian reform. Caroline Leighton's *Life at Puget Sound,* published the same year as Jackson's *Ramona,* was promoted by the well-known and influential voices of John Greenleaf Whittier, Wendell Phillips, and Thomas W. Higginson, the latter praising the volume as "the most delightful outdoor book produced in America for ten years. For the first time we see the great North-West through the eyes of a woman, thoroughly cultivated, thoroughly adventurous, and thoroughly humane." The abolitionist Wendell Phillips interestingly positions the book within philanthropic movements that address the situation of both Indians and Chinese in the West. He describes it as "full of life, deeply interesting, and with just that class of fact and suggestions of truth that cannot fail to help the Indian and the Chinese."

Curiously, however, Leighton's narrative resists the philanthropic rhetoric by foregrounding an ethnological interest in studying nature and native life in the Pacific Northwest before the arrival of the railroad, while at the same time promoting the country as a new center for tourist travel and white settlement. The book's publication even coincided with the completion of the Northern Pacific Railroad Company's main line in 1883, connecting

Minneapolis–St. Paul with the Puget Sound area. As one review of the book suggests, Leighton's narrative accomplished its promotional goal and was read by her contemporaries as an invitation to see what she had described.[83]

In her preface, Leighton offers the book as "selections from observations and experiences during a residence of sixteen years on the Pacific Coast," although it seems she never lives anywhere but is instead constantly on the move. The publishers' advertisement offers the information that Leighton accompanied her husband, who held a position in the U.S. Treasury Department.[84] Nevertheless, Leighton never foregrounds this personal family context and is rather reticent about revealing autobiographical details. Her husband appears in her narrative as "R-," her "travelling companion." Midway into the book, a baby appears out of nowhere as a third traveler. As a result of this distancing from the personal context of her travels (accompanying her husband on his official mission), Leighton authorizes her own travels as a project of her own, distinct from her husband's task.

After a tempestuous and adventurous sea voyage, during which they are even temporarily stranded on a reef, the two travelers arrive in Washington Territory in July 1865—the same year that Victor embarked on her travels through the same area. But while Victor described a land claimed and settled by white Americans, the Leightons are seen entering Indian country, still largely untouched and exotic (18–20). Significantly, Leighton never mentions, as Victor does, the existence of Indian reservations. Thus, when the couple goes on an "expedition" into the woods, the narrator enters the terrain with the awareness "that no white woman had ever crossed there" (27). Passing through the dark forest, she recalls "the Indian's dread of *skookums* (spirits)" in the deep woods: "To him, the mere flutter of a leaf had a meaning; the sighing of the wind was intelligible language. So many generations of Indians had crossed that trail, and so few white people, I felt as if some subtile [*sic*] aroma of Indian spirit must linger still about the place, and steal into our thoughts" (28–29). Leighton has entered a natural world in which the Indian presence is not erased but lingers on, in the white primitivist imagination, on the level of personal aesthetic experience.

However, Leighton's primitivist configuration of western nature does not exclude the contemporaneous Indian presence, which demands some readjustment of her angle of perception. When the couple is led by an Indian guide to his village, where he shows them his mother, she is at first described as "the exact representation of a sphinx,—an old gray creature lying on the sand, with the upper part of her body raised, and her lower limbs concealed by her blanket." The narrator expects to see the man run and embrace his mother, but instead "he walked coolly by, without giving her any greeting whatever; and she remained perfectly imperturbable, never stirred, and her expression did not change in the least." Leighton describes herself as "horror-stricken" at first, but then alters her position, coming to the conclusion "that she was a good, kind mother, only that it was their way to refrain from all appearance of emotion" (33–34).

The observation and study of Indian life are the main sources of Leighton's narrative, which records the couple's participation in the seasonal rhythm of Indian economic and ceremonial life. Her account of Indian customs and manners is informed by the quest for objective knowledge, but because she has hardly any previous ethnological knowledge to resort to, Leighton must draw her own conclusions. In contrast to other female narrators who aim to convey meaning by describing appearances and resorting to aesthetics, Leighton is interested in the meaning behind appearances. External semblances, she suggests, should not necessarily be trusted. The cultural/racial other cannot be known by way of his/her appearance, and she learns, as she later states, "never to judge any one by appearance or occupation" (105). This challenges the often undisputed visualism in women's narratives in which authority is located in what is seen.

Leighton's narrative is structured less on the movements of the travelers than on the rhythms of Indian life. The narrator watches a marriage ceremony and the celebration of spring (the "Red *Tamahnous*"), sees women gathering the kamas-root, and witnesses the "Black *Tamahnous*," during which the Indians call up all their hostility to the white invaders. In the manner of an ethnologist, she searches for patterns of meaning behind everything she sees and observes, as when she explains the tribal custom of remaining silent, that is, not telling stories, during the winter: "They sympathize too much with Nature to sing in the winter. Now the warm, soft air inspires them anew" (39).

Unlike other female travelers who expressed horror at tribal customs that involved painting faces and bodies, Leighton admits that she likes the Indians' body painting, "for in them it is quite a different thing from what it is in fashionable ladies. They do it to show how they feel, not commonly expressing their emotions in words" (42). She also points to the striking parallels between geological theories and Indian traditions about the origins of certain natural phenomena, identifying herself as a primitivist who privileges adolescent, precivilized "instinct" over adult scientific "reason" (51). Of course, in the context of colonial relations, this primitivism, which pits Indian wisdom against white science, works in the service of expansion by identifying tribal people with an early stage of human evolution, and by denying them change and development as individuals and as members of their cultures.

The works that Leighton refers to most are narratives of exploration and travel, geological textbooks, and Emerson's writings. In all of them she finds parallels to what she sees and experiences.[85] She exhibits a protoscientific interest in both her natural and her social surroundings, yet her observations are linked to a narrative persona who foregrounds the subjectivity of her personal impressions and draws on classical mythology in her representations of natural phenomena, as in her personification of the Columbia River as a natural force that resists the wayfarers' invasion. It seems "like some of those Greek streams that Homer tells of, which had so much personal feeling against individuals. I felt as if we were going to be punished for an audacious attempt, instead of rewarded for what might otherwise have been considered a brave one" (68). By invoking both personal experience and classical mythology, Leighton challenges the self-congratulatory tone of exploratory heroics that tend to make, as Bruce Greenfield has claimed, "personal testimony to the beauty and grandeur of the land itself into a transcendent authority for the viewer's presence"—and for claims to the land.[86]

Although Leighton, like Victor, expresses a fascination with metaphors of power, her representation of the relation between man and nature inverts the scenario of man facing a passive, often feminized nature that invites fantasies of contentment and mastery. In Leighton's version, the freedom of the narrative self is not dependent on the submission of the natural other, but rather on the latter's strength and its possibilities for resistance, on its ability to represent man's alter ego. Only in a "vigorous and unsubdued" state can nature trigger the self's "own slumbering potential" (70)— a statement that resembles Lippincott's observations on feeling power in powerlessness in the Yosemite Valley.

Like Victor, Leighton distances herself from the missionary rhetoric applied to Indians, which in the official culture seems to have become closely associated with the feminine sphere of influence. Her attitude is not informed by evangelical zeal but by primitivism. To her, Indians are admirable as embodiments of a primitive consciousness close to nature, childishly guided by a wilderness instinct that, in a later period of human time, is all but obliterated by the repressions necessary to form civilized man. However, nowhere in Leighton's text can the return of the primitive be represented other than in aesthetic terms of nature admiration, or in the admiration of the freedom of native life (85). The narrator herself cannot go native. She never becomes a participant, but remains an observer.

For Leighton and many others, civilization and Indianness are mutually exclusive categories. Civilization—not "whiteness"—denotes culture, history, and development in time, whereas Indianness is associated with "blood," nature, and timelessness. Civilization, not "white blood," taints Indian "purity"—an observation that casts a contradictory light on the narrator-traveler's presence, which is described as innocent and noninterventionist, detached from the civilizing mission. Thus the Leightons trust only "real" Indians as canoe paddlers: "If half-civilized Indians had been offered, or those that had had much intercourse with the whites, I should have hesitated more to trust them; but he was such a pure Indian, it seemed as if he were as safe as any wild creature" (119).

As in the narratives of her female contemporaries, encounters with Indian people center mainly on women. But Leighton's narrator sees more than the marks of an oppressed gender in tribal women's lives. It is the spirit of freedom that she acknowledges in the Indian wife and daughter of the white pioneer Angus McDonald. McDonald's wife—probably Catherine McDonald, the author of a travel narrative of her own[87]—cannot bear staying indoors and wanders about half the year with her band, and his daughter "spoke, too, of disliking to be confined" (76). Both exhibit a power of agency and cultural choice that for various reasons remains unacknowledged by most other women travelers writing about native women.

The fact that Indians relate to the white presence on their own terms is evidenced by Leighton's observation that some old women, "stiff old Indians," seem to take no notice whatsoever of the presence of white people (145). Attending the burial of a native girl, she wonders how "they had tolerated us so long, as they dislike being observed; but they seemed to feel that we sympathized with them" (147). She also registers the lack of gendered spheres in the tribal societies she encounters, as when she witnesses a dance "performed wholly by women and children, although in the dress of warriors. Some of them carried arms, others only green boughs" (87). Watching native women gathering the kamas-root, she realizes the importance of women's work within the tribal economy, which is reflected in the particularities of matrilocal social organization (61). Old Indian women doing hard work in all weathers compare favorably to "civilized women of the same age, who are generally helpless" (162). Unlike other women travelers who denounced native women's work roles as a mark of oppression, Leighton regards the female ability to perform rigorous physical labor as an asset. Moreover, she stresses that native women can attain positions of leadership, and she reminds her readers that Britain is also ruled by a woman (174).

Leighton's narrative is atypical among those of her contemporaries on account of her unusually sensitive observations on intercultural encounters, which address the problematic privileging of visualism in representing cultural others. Although the book seems to have been well received, at least by the philanthropic quarter, within the context of an emerging Indian-reform movement, its treatment of the subject—or rather, the way it avoids the debate over the Americanization of Indian or Chinese people—suggests that Leighton located her narrative outside of the movement. In fact, her primitivism is directly opposed to the evangelical Protestantism of the home-mission and the Indian-reform movement, which supported the complete transformation of tribal people into individual, propertied, family-oriented Americans, and which favored the destruction of tribal structures, cultural beliefs, and ways of life as the only possibility for Indian survival (see chapter 5).

Rather than being part of the debate over Indian reform, Leighton's writing anticipated the vogue of primitivist romanticization of the West, and especially southwestern Indians, which finds its climax in the first decades of the twentieth century. Of course, as discussed in the following chapter, women's missionary zeal is often closely linked to primitivist longings. However, together with Helen Hunt Jackson's work, Leighton's text also illustrates that women's narratives do not constitute one uniform tradition of women's writing. Rather, the discourses in which, or in reference to which, women locate their narratives are diverse and heterogeneous. Neither the home-mission movement nor the Indian-reform movement were unified platforms for debate, but were instead sites for conflicting and contesting arguments.

Missionaries, Reformers, and
New Women, 1890–1930

The narratives of Susan Wallace, Caroline Leighton, and Libby Beaman[1] illustrate how by the 1870s women were relating to the American West in terms of their interest in history, botany, zoology, and ethnology. Indeed, the end of the 1870s marked the beginning of many women's public activities in academic fields associated with westward expansion. At about this time, Native American women also began speaking out for their people in public. The Paiute Sarah Winnemucca was among those who lectured both in the East and the West for Indian reform, and her lectures became the basis for her autobiographical work, *Life Among the Piutes,* published in 1883.[2] Also writing about the lives of Native American women was the Omaha Susette LaFlesche, whose work was published in the *Woman's Congress* by the Association for the Advancement of Women (AAW), founded in 1873 by Julia Ward Howe.

During the financial depression of the mid-1870s, another woman associated with the AAW, Alice Fletcher, had gone on the lecture circuit giving talks on American history. Fletcher's biographer, Joan Mark, has explained this growing interest in history and in voluntary organizing, especially on the part of women, with a "search for order" in the face of industrialization and immigration, which had emerged as increasingly pressing problems. Boston women's clubs, Mark suggests, were convinced that foreign immigrants needed to be brought to order. Moreover, the club women sought to find in American history a sense of mission, and they subsequently initiated the first campaigns for historic preservation in Boston in 1876.[3]

Michael Kammen has stressed the particular role played by

women as custodians of tradition in the United States at a time when history in general "became the core of civil religion during the spiritual crisis of the Gilded Age." Their enthusiasm for Native American antiquities, he suggests, played an especially noteworthy part in the development of efforts for historic preservation. Indeed, in 1885, Alice Fletcher became the primary patron of excavation and preservation at the Serpent Mound in Ohio. In 1886, Mary Hemenway of Boston commissioned and subsidized a Southwestern Archaeological Expedition. She also promoted John Fiske's writings and lectures on the history of America, and at the turn of the century, a group of women formed the Colorado Cliff-Dwellings Association and launched an effort to establish Mesa Verde as a national park.[4]

Alice Fletcher's most popular topics had to do with prehistoric or "Ancient America," as she titled a series of lectures she presented in 1879. While Americans were still moving westward into the territories, New Englanders, it seems, went backward, searching for explanations of their destiny in American history.[5] As the plea for the preservation of mounds and prehistoric artifacts grew louder, researchers initiated some of the first American archaeological and anthropological studies. In the course of researching her lectures, Alice Fletcher became involved in the emerging discipline of anthropology, and when the director of the Peabody Museum of Archaeology and Ethnology at Harvard encouraged her to study at the museum, she accepted "the flattering implication that she might become a scientist in her own right." At the time, a friend of Fletcher's, the astronomer Maria Mitchell, was urging women to pursue careers in the observational sciences, and Fletcher recognized that ethnography could be one of them.[6] In 1881, at age 42, she adopted the cause of "serving science" and embarked on the first of many field trips, taking a step without precedence by living among the Sioux. Her field notes and collections of artifacts formed the basis of more than a hundred articles and monographs that highlighted her original theories on music and symbolic ritual systems.

In 1885, Matilda Coxe Stevenson founded the Women's Anthropological Society of America, whose original members included Alice Fletcher. Its brief written history explained the need for such an organization until "the time when science shall regard only the work, not the worker" and emphasized that members had "no desire to perpetuate a distinction of sex in science."[7] Other women, like Florence Merriam Bailey and Martha Maxwell, embarked on careers as ornithologists, naturalists, and taxidermists, trying to make a living by traveling, writing, and establishing observational sciences as a professional field for women.[8]

Women continued to write about the West in the last part of the nineteenth century, and most of their travel narratives and other writings deal with the present and future of the West. Many were designed as promotional guidebooks.[9] At the same time, some women writers seem to have been more interested in history and in revealing the romantic potential of an American frontier past in historical novels.[10] Other trends were the romanticization of the Hispanic past in women's novels[11] and the popularity of women's travels in, and historical works on, Mexico.[12] Also in the 1880s, women writers had a disproportionately high share in the evolving market for children's books and stories with a focus on the American West.

Of course, women's special focus on history was part of an increased general interest in American history, and especially the history of the American frontier, which reflected the contemporary search for an American myth of unity.[13] However, book reviews of the 1880s and 1890s show that some, although not all, women's historical and fictional works were still received in terms of a sexual division of labor. Eliza Scidmore's *Alaska,* for example, was described in gendered terms as a book more entertaining than instructive, "as Miss Scidmore has the feminine faculty for gossipy and chatty talk on matters that interest her."[14]

By the 1880s, women's western writings, like women's writing in general, had become diversified, informed by the contradictory trends within the discourses of femininity and the rhetoric of westward expansion and empire building. These contradictions emerged with full force in the western narratives of women teachers and missionaries on Indian reservations, most of them written retrospectively in the first decades of the twentieth century.

chapter 5

The West as a Female Mission?

White Women and the

Transformation of the American Indian

American westward expansion, with its concomitant official proclamations of manifest destiny and America's mission, entailed not
only a history of war against the indigenous people of the continent, but also, especially since the last quarter of the nineteenth
century, a legacy of policies designed to incorporate them into the
United States through Christianization and Americanization. The
same policies applied, although in a somewhat modified form, to
the Hispanic Americans of the Southwest, whose otherness, posing a threat to national unity, demanded a "second conquest."[1]
Reduced to small reserves of the least desirable lands and made
dependent upon allocations of essential supplies and support from
the federal government, Indians were placed under enormous
pressure to transform themselves into Americans. The rhetoric legitimating this cultural transformation was that of "Indian reform," which drew on liberal discourses invoking Indians' emancipation from dependency and superstition, and their ultimate
incorporation into American life as citizens. The move for Indian
reform gathered force in the last quarter of the nineteenth century
and culminated in the Dawes Allotment Act of 1887, which prescribed the transformation of Indians into Christian yeoman farmers living on individual allotments of land. The ability of individuals to handle private property was regarded as the prerequisite of
American civilization.

To accelerate the process of culture change, and to counter-
act the conservative influence of their parents, Indian children
were sent to boarding schools far from their reservation homes.
Indians were prohibited from speaking their native languages and

practicing their cultures. No form of internal tribal government was authorized until 1934, when the Indian Reorganization Act reinstated some degree of tribal authority.[2] Within this context of Indian transformation toward the end of the nineteenth century, both women and ideologies of womanhood played significant and conflicting roles as agents and tools of Americanization.

This chapter focuses on women's participation in the development and implementation of federal Indian policies, and analyzes the ways in which narratives of women missionaries and teachers on Indian reservations in the American West engaged with the discourses of Indian transformation and Americanization. My purpose is to locate women's western narratives in (or against) a context of conflicting discourses on westward expansion in late-nineteenth-century American culture: home mission and strenuosity, and primitivism and progressivism. Interestingly, most of the texts discussed previously, whether written by women in the frontier army or by western travelers, have suggested the impossibility of Indian transformation and have distanced themselves from the rhetoric of Indian reform.

Since the late eighteenth century, Indian assimilation had been effected by federal lawmakers and officials as well as Christian missionaries, who differed in their emphases. Government officials and tribal leaders focused their attention on legal matters, while missionaries concerned themselves "with the subtler nuances of the female role."[3] As historians of women have pointed out, white women missionaries had been active among Indians and Hispanics in the American West since the early nineteenth century, the most well known being Narcissa Whitman and Eliza Spalding. Mission superintendents believed and expected that women would provide a benevolent influence, serve as moral and religious examples to their students, and would impart a knowledge of academic and domestic subjects while also helping to run the missions through their skills in cooking, sewing, nursing, and housekeeping.[4] Of course, women missionaries had to be married; only as wives could they embark on their mission, conveyed to them from the Protestant pulpit, to carry light to the "heathens" all over the world. Others performed their missionary work as Catholic nuns.[5] In general, the way gender ideology was applied to

missionary work reflected the sexual division of labor in missionary families.[6]

In the postwar years, under Grant's peace policy, Protestant missionaries received their greatest chance to play a significant role in
the West's religious development.[7] In these years, single women
came in increasing numbers to the western territories as mission
teachers, even if administrators, ministers, and missionaries still
viewed married missionaries as best suited for the task.[8] Significantly, after the Civil War, this missionary emphasis on the role of
women in Indian transformation was increasingly adopted by federal lawmakers in Washington. This was one of the legacies of the
Women's National Indian Association, an organization that aimed
to influence federal Indian policy as an extension of religious and
moral duties. As Valerie Sherer Mathes has suggested, post–Civil
War westward expansion reinforced earlier formulations of wom-
en's social role. She points to William Fowler, who in his *Women
on the American Frontier* (1876) emphasized the important role of
women in frontier society, presenting frontier heroines as capable
of refining and humanizing society as they were of carrying civilization into the wilderness. A woman, he noted, was a "civilizer
par excellence." Fowler also drew attention to the idea that wom-
en's influence was necessary in effecting cultural change among
Indians.[9]

As a consequence of her obligations, the Victorian woman was
not only in charge of the destiny of every white American community, but she was also assigned the role of a special guardian of
American democracy. As the educator and reformer Catharine
Beecher had said years earlier, only the American woman, as "the
natural and appropriate guardian of the young . . . who has those
tender sympathies . . . who has that conscientiousness and religious devotion," could inspire in children the virtues "indis-
pensable to the safety of a democratic government like ours."[10]

Gender thus played a significant role in the rhetoric of Indian
reform, providing an important commentary on the way the Indian
problem demanded from Americans the definition and ordering of
relations of race, gender, and class. As Laura Ann Stoler has argued
in her studies on British colonialism in Asia, we cannot really
explain how racial boundaries and class distinctions are secured

without understanding how they are constituted in gender terms. The definition of women's roles in a culture is not merely a symbol of white male rule. On many colonial frontiers, white women became the excuse for—and the custodians of—racial distinctions that took the form of class-specific prescriptions for bourgeois respectability and sexual normalcy. Indian reformers' special focus on aspects of gender and sexuality suggests that these considerations were also crucial in the American context: reformers insisted on patrilineal relations of kinship and property inheritance, the abolition of polygamy, and the establishment of the nuclear family.[11] Moreover, the U.S. government's experience with Indian wars would be applicable not only to problems in overseas colonial administration but also to domestic affairs. A discussion of how women related to their cultural task by defining the boundaries and hierarchies of race, gender, nationality, and culture in the context of their work among Native Americans is therefore especially significant within the framework of westward expansion, where the issues of Americanness and of the direction of American national development are continuously addressed.

Women and the Rhetoric of Indian Reform

Helen Hunt Jackson was almost fifty years old when she became involved in the cause that would occupy her until her death in 1885. In November 1879, she had visited Boston and happened to attend a presentation by the Ponca chief Standing Bear; Susette LaFlesche, an Omaha woman known as Bright Eyes; and other Indians who told the tragic story of the Poncas' forced removal from their homeland along the Missouri River to Indian Territory. The case of the Ponca tribe sparked controversy and sympathy among eastern intellectuals and philanthropists, and helped carry along the movement for Indian-policy reform, in which a small group of dedicated Christian reformers had become active. The same year, the Boston Indian Citizenship Committee was organized to fight for the rights of the Ponca and other tribes.

Among the individuals involved was Jackson, who so far had shown no interest in either the abolition or the temperance movements in which white and black women had become so active

since the 1820s. Neither had she shown an interest in the movement for women's suffrage. Moreover, the travel letters she sent
from her first western journey had only commented negatively on
the presence of Native Americans. In the course of the Ponca controversy, however, this unlikely reformer began to embrace the Indian cause as her personal mission, and like many other women,
she became an interventionist and a disruptive presence for the
(male) lawmakers who were designing the policies for federal management of the West.[12]

Jackson embraced the cause by entering into a heated public
exchange with Secretary of the Interior Carl Schurz, becoming "a
one-person letter-writing campaign, taking on all comers from the
Denver Rocky Mountain News and *Harpers* to *The New York Times*
and *The Christian Advocate.*"[13] After intensive research at the As-
tor Library in New York City, in 1881 she published *A Century of
Dishonor,* an indignant account of government double dealings
with Native American tribes that stirred controversy and was denounced by the young Theodore Roosevelt as "capable of doing
great harm" when quoted by a "large class of amiable but maud-
lin fanatics."[14] As Mathes has pointed out, Jackson's efforts were
unique and distinct from the reform efforts undertaken by a growing number of eastern men and women in the 1880s. She was
"more of a muckraker than a missionary reformer." Although the
mainly female reformers who carried on her legacy were imbued
with evangelical Protestant Christianity and were strongly anti-
Catholic, "H.H." never fit this mold.[15] Neither did other women
who wrote about their reform efforts among Indians. With the exception of some missionaries, most women joined Jackson in de-
emphasizing the religious nature of their work. Instead, their mission was intricately related to discourses of femininity, or rather
feminism, in the context of the growing professionalization of
women and the reformulation of women's role in the 1890s.

Throughout the late 1860s and 1870s, church women formed
various regional organizations to propagate the work of missions.
Taking an active role in both foreign- and home-mission programs,
they had founded mission societies, raised money, collected and
distributed clothing, and sponsored educational programs designed to publicize the downtrodden condition of the "heathens"
and the needs of missionaries who ministered to them. Members of

the Women's National Indian Association (WNIA) likewise entered the reform arena through their religious commitments, using their right of petition as a political weapon.[16] Leading clergymen soon took notice of this group's work, but what had started out as a critique of America's unjust treatment of Indians and as a demand for the reform of federal Indian policy soon became a drive for the "reform" of Indian people. Whereas the focus of Jackson's work and of the WNIA's first petitions had been on the protection of Indian rights, the emphasis was increasingly laid on assimilation and the institutionalization of culture change.

Home-mission movements evolved not only in the East but also took hold in the new cities of the American West, where they assumed a slightly different form. Peggy Pascoe has explored how middle-class Protestant women since the 1870s joined together to try to establish what she calls the search for "female moral authority" in the American West.[17] In the process of interpreting the "home" as the ideal Christian home of Victorian rhetoric, home-mission women stretched the conventions of Victorian women's identification with morality and the home almost beyond recognition, associating it with the moral authority of women rather than the patriarchal control of men (33). However, while home-mission women in western cities ran against a double moral standard as protectresses of the victims of male immorality, challenging local hierarchies of gender and race, eastern women saw themselves as coworkers with male reformers in the task of reforming America.[18] Consequently, assuming the role of civilizer was a badge of conformity for eastern mission women, but the same role brought western women in conflict with their communities.

The rhetoric of home-mission women ultimately featured not only the need to establish the moral authority of women over men, but also the necessity to impose social control on potentially disruptive underclasses, including the women in need of protection. Thus women's evangelical activism in the field of Indian reform complemented rather than contested male political power. The WNIA's position on Indian policy was clearly based on the conviction that law, education, and citizenship were the tools needed to rescue Indians from the "oppression" they were seen to suffer in their separate existence on reservations. Moreover, women reformers' views were shaped by a sense of the impending closure of the western frontier. A memorial letter accompanying the 1882 petition contained the insight "that the commercial interests of our land are fast coming to demand a just and speedy settlement of the Indian question."[19]

After an initial meeting in 1883, concerned citizens gathered every October at Lake Mohonk, New York, calling themselves the "Friends of the Indians" and working for the "liberation" of Indians who, in their terminology, had been entrapped in tribalism and communalism and prevented from developing the individualism and "manhood" that characterized American society. Their rhetoric invoked the apocalyptic vision of the Indian facing either extermination or civilization, making Indian transformation a necessity. The group's approach also involved an interpretation of American history as a legacy of injustice: a weak government had been manipulated by unscrupulous white men who tricked Indians out of their land. As Patricia Limerick has noted, reformers believed that they could declare their independence from this flawed past and make a fresh start by focusing their attention on abolishing the reservation system, the main impediment to Indians' liberation through civilization, Christianity, and economic opportunity.[20]

Despite the gendered division of work, both men's and women's Indian organizations shared the basic belief that Indians had to change in order to survive in an American culture that at that time was seen, in the jeremiadic tradition described by Sacvan Bercovitch, as an aggressive civilization in need of redemption through the gentle touch of philanthropic humanitarianism. But this gentle touch ironically involved aggressive paternalistic interventions into cultural lifeways, with no intention of protecting the tribal rights that would obstruct white America's encroachment on tribal territory.[21] Richard Slotkin identifies two tendencies or "moods" of Gilded Age paternalism: the "masculine" style, which emphasized the sternness of necessity, and the "philanthropic" style, which invoked the perfectionist idealism and charity of antebellum reformers. Scenarios of conflict thus stood against scenarios of gentle tutelage and development. Both approaches, however, shared the essential doctrine of white supremacy, the necessity of a (transitional) regime of control, and the need for strong institutions. The philanthropic faction, however, was denigrated as

"effeminate . . . she-men," in whose system of thought "effeminate" sentiments allegedly had taken precedence over "manly"
strength in the ordering of politics; their philanthropy was associated with more violent and disruptive "female" states of mind,
such as irrationality, hysteria, and madness.[22] Critics of philanthropic reform thus used the influential presence of women in
Indian-reform activism as the target of their attacks.

Ultimately, the rhetoric of the philanthropic reformers showed
as much concern with paternalistic control and power as that of
their critics. Although the language of liberation initially dominated their propaganda, a focus on control soon entered the discussion. After all, Indian reform had become a topic at a time when
westward expansion took on an urgency as never before. Men like
Roosevelt and Turner had impressed Americans with the awareness that the reservoir of cheap, undeveloped land was exhausted,
and that with the loss of the agrarian frontier, America might be
losing the material conditions that had underwritten its form of
republican democracy. In Roosevelt's West, Indians were the representatives of an antiprogressive principle—the few who stood in
the way of the many. Ridiculing the "sentimentalists" who sought
to "preserve" the Indians, he believed that as a race they were not
inclined to adapt to the economic imperatives of the agrarian stage
of civilization. In his vision, Darwinian economics would eliminate, through starvation, both the Indians and the underclasses of
whites who would not adjust to the necessity of strenuous labor to
earn their bread.[23]

The "Friends of the Indians" likewise maintained that "[t]hree
hundred thousand people have no right to hold a continent and
keep at bay a race able to people it and provide the happy homes of
civilization."[24] Herbert Welsh of the Indian Rights Association declared: "We cannot stop the legitimate advance of emigration and
civilization if we would . . . and, we add most emphatically, we
would not if we could; but, on the other hand, we strenuously
oppose unlawful violent or ill-advised acquisition of Indian lands
whether by the Government or individuals."[25] Even while they
insisted that their proposed reforms obeyed "the laws which grow
naturally out of the family," the reformers admitted that they
would have to "force law" upon the Native Americans they were
seeking to transform.[26] Indian reform was therefore part of an effort

of economic and political centralization in the larger culture, and the regulation of a federal Indian policy that could assert control over Indians as imperial subjects became part of a more centralized management of the American West.

Significantly, the reformers' ideology, targeted at the refashioning of the gender, ethnic, and economic identities of Native Americans, was anachronistic in several ways. Not only did their ideology emphasize paternalistic family values and domesticity at a time when women increasingly sought work and professions outside of the home, but reformers also tried to impart the values of capitalism to Indian people in a manner that ignored contemporary economic and social developments. Their focus lay on a rural model of life anchored in the ideal of the yeoman farmer, which by the end of the nineteenth century was increasingly threatened by urbanization and industrialization. Trying to contain Indians in an anachronistic pastoral state, reformers denied them the possibility of adapting to modern American life, and ignored the dependence of reservation economies on the national market.

Another distinguishing mark of this reform movement was its insistence on individual salvation. Protestant evangelism could view individual development and the stimulation of labor only within the context of the family.[27] Both Indian and white women were thus essential and instrumental in bringing about Indian transformation. Carl Schurz formulated the goals of Indian policy in 1881: "Nothing will be apt to raise the Indians in the scale of civilization than to stimulate their attachment to permanent homes, and it is the woman that must make the atmosphere and form the attraction of the home. She must be recognized, with affection and respect, as the center of domestic life."[28] Merial Dorchester, a special agent in the Indian School Service, also emphasized that the answer to successful assimilation lay with Indian women.[29]

By the 1870s, women's missionary-training schools had been established, and growing numbers of ambitious single women were recruited for service on Indian reservations.[30] Others heeded the call for Indian transformation by becoming professional teachers in Indian schools or by taking positions as field matrons for the U.S. government. Established by Congress in 1891 as a counterpart to the farm-training program for Indian men, the civil-service field-matron program employed women to teach domestic skills to Indian women.[31]

Female missionaries were encouraged to focus especially on the establishment of proper gender relations. Some described their service as distinct from that of men and emphasized their gender-specific role, as in Isabel Crawford's explanation that "God called women . . . not to go into all the world and preach the Gospel, but to go into all the world and teach it in a simple womanly way."[32] Sue and Kate McBeth, Presbyterian missionaries on the Nez Perce Reservation in the 1870s, insisted that the father and husband must assume "his proper place at the head of his family," and they warned against the dangers of cohabiting in the same longhouse. They also attacked polygamy, easy divorce, "permissive" child rearing, and the "false ideas of dignity and labor" that kept Indian men out of the fields and Indian women out of their households.[33]

Women missionaries on the western frontiers and women reformers in the East also had to configure their roles as the upholders of moral and religious values and the instruments of cultural change. They not only carried the gospel to the "heathen" women of the American West, but they were also encouraged to bring domestic and material American culture to the tribes, to teach them how to make and keep an American home, how to prepare American food, make American clothing, and care for the sick. Consequently, they had to contest with Indian men and women over the management of Indian lives, homes, and the education of the children. White women, as missionaries and teachers, became maternal colonizers who went between Indian children and their parents, preventing the continuance and development of traditional parenting skills and contributing to a process that disinherited whole generations of Indian parents and children. Contradicting its own ideology, Indian reform ultimately robbed children of their family, establishing government schools and churches as the final authorities over their lives. Moreover, white women not only "domesticated" Indian girls and women in order to enable them to run their own households the American way; they also trained them with a view to their potential as domestics for white families in the West.[34]

Home-mission writers dealing with Indians often analyzed the position of women in Indian societies, reducing vast tribal differences to one single Indian society. Powerful images of Indian women as drudges and mistreated wives symbolized this society's shortcomings. Wrapped up in their own cultural notions, home-mission women "did not recognize sources of women's power apart from the Victorian ideals of female moral purity and the Christian home."[35] In contrast, several scholars have suggested that Indian women in some tribes enjoyed a freedom and social power unknown to nineteenth-century white women in America, including land ownership, independent control over property, and the opportunity to play culturally powerful roles in old age.[36]

As women's western narratives show, most of those who noted the allegedly low status of Indian women were not aware that they were observing cultures in transition. Mary Young has emphasized that this apparently low status of women was a direct negative result of culture change that had an impact on the work and, consequently, the status of Indian women. Forcing Indian men to become farmers meant obstructing the established system of gender relations. Since tribal women were induced to leave farming, their traditional activity in most tribes, they also no longer "owned" the land they farmed. Subsequently, long-term shifts from matrilineal to patrilineal inheritance patterns further weakened tribal women's status.[37] Rayna Green even suggests that Indian women's performance of hard labor, as well as Indian polygamy—the bone of contention for so many white women—were directly related to contact with whites. The trade with white people, at least in some tribal complexes, "had increased the amount of work for which women were responsible, because they alone had the skill to tan the hides of deer, elk, and buffalo. It may even have been the case that polygamy, which so repelled whites, actually proliferated as a result of the fur trade."[38]

With the arrival of white people in the West, tribal women found their lives changed as they played new and often powerful roles in relations with the newcomers. Although many Indian women, abused by white (and native) men, became trade items, slaves, or prostitutes, some assumed important roles as interpreters and guides. As wives and concubines of mountain men, fur traders, and some of the first settlers, Indian women also were go-betweens, playing an important mediating role between the cultures. And they became warriors—in words and deeds—in defense of their cultures, and many gained fame and economic power in both tribal and white cultures as artists and craftswomen.[39] By imposing Victorian American gender patterns on tribal women, home-mission women thus inadvertently helped to destroy the sources of Indian women's social power.[40] In their quest to replicate Euro-American gender patterns in Indians, reformers and missionaries also endangered the variety of Indian women's activities and roles, which had already suffered a disruption through changes in traditional survival patterns. In consequence, they threatened to erase any alternative gender roles that defied not only the stereotype of the drudging squaw but also the white ideal of feminine domesticity.[41]

Together with the control over Indian resources, the transformation of gender identities became the mainstay of Indian reform.[42] The strong focus of reformers and lawmakers on the nuclear family and on gender ideology reveals the growing concern for the moral and social well-being of the nation, which was traditionally seen as dependent on the institution of the family. These anxieties find their expression especially in the institutionalization of welfare politics at the beginning of the twentieth century. In his annual message to Congress in 1906, President Roosevelt endorsed government activism in the arena of social welfare on the theory that the modern industrial state has to assume a supervising role in the interest of stabilizing and securing family life. Women's individual aspirations were to be sacrificed in favor of their paramount obligation to the perpetuation of family, class, and nation.[43] Roosevelt translated these concerns adroitly into a national alarm about racial suicide and decline.[44]

The implementation of Indian reform on the reservations and in off-reservation boarding schools took place at a time when the very functions of government were changing. In the late nineteenth and early twentieth centuries, federal, state, and municipal governments increased their roles in social welfare and economic life. Progressive Era policymakers sought ways to regulate and rationalize business and industry, and to improve schools, hospitals, and other public services. By the early twentieth century, government began to assume some of the substantive functions of the home. Social policy, formerly the province of women's voluntary work, became public policy, and women's organizations turned their efforts toward securing legislation, passing on to the state the work of social policy that they found increasingly unmanageable. However, in the field of Indian reform, missionaries and teachers saw themselves taking over the role of the government long into the twentieth century.[45]

Although it seems that both men's and women's Indian organizations shared the same basic beliefs, the development and institutionalization of federal Indian policies may, nevertheless, have received a certain gendered slant due to the increasing participation of women. Peggy Pascoe suggests that alternative female voices came particularly from women who lived with Indian tribes in the 1880s and 1890s as missionaries, teachers, and anthropologists.[46] For example, Alice Fletcher, whose work among the Omaha drew the attention of the WNIA to the tribe, noted some limitations of home-mission images. As a government-allotment agent trying to convince Indians that the land allotments of married couples should be one unified parcel, she was "more than once interrupted by the remark that our laws showed that 'the white man had neither love nor respect for his women!' "[47] Not as preoccupied with threats to female moral authority as many home-mission women, Fletcher also worried that Indian women had been told to give up their healthy outdoor work and had lost control over their property.

At the founding conference of the International Council of Women in 1888, Fletcher expressed doubts about the benefits of constricting Native American women to an exclusively private, dependent domestic space. Nevertheless, even Fletcher could not escape the prevalent cultural ideology of domesticity, and she told her audience that she had realized "how much woman has given of her own freedom to make strong the foundations of the family and to preserve the accumulations and descent of property in order that the pressure of want should be removed." Women's sacrifices were necessary for "the development of civilization," and yet she craved for her "Indian sisters" her audience's help, patience, and labors "to hasten the day when the laws of all the land shall know neither male nor female, but grant to all equal rights and equal justice."[48]

Toward the end of the nineteenth century, white women were present in increasing numbers on Indian reservations as missionaries, teachers, and government officials, playing a significant role in the practical implementation of federal Indian policies and often choosing a special approach to their task. The fact that during the last two decades of the nineteenth century the focus of Indian policy was increasingly laid on Indian women and on Indian education may even have been related to the high proportion of women in the Indian Service. However, the question whether the concomitant focus on Christianity and domesticity was connected exclusively to women's presence in the field remains debatable, and one needs to ask how much power and authority women had over the ideas that they were to spread on Indian reservations. Barbara Welter even argues that women's involvement in missionary work expanded at the same time as the significance of the endeavor itself was declining, and that the expansion of women's missionary work did not necessarily expand women's influence.[49] Nevertheless, beginning in the 1870s, an increasing number of single women chose the missionary and the Indian service as professional opportunities and an alternative to domesticity, therefore contradicting in their own personal and professional lives the domestic ideology they were expected to propagate among Indian and Hispanic peoples of the West.

As the case of anthropologist and reformer Alice Fletcher suggests, becoming involved in federal Indian-policy reform was also a direct reflection of the restricted professional options women had in late-nineteenth-century America. Unable to gain access to salaried positions within the emerging academic discipline of anthropology, Fletcher accepted a position as an allotment agent for the U.S. government. She was thus forced to conduct research while simultaneously endorsing the government's policy of mandating property ownership, agriculture, and education as the means to assimilate Native Americans into white society.[50] Fletcher's example also illustrates how the egalitarian discourse of feminism can reinforce inequalities among women. Her feminism may have motivated her to support the campaign to amend the Dawes Act to give "80 acres to every man, woman, & child, irrespective of age or relation," in order to secure native women's right to property. Native women reformers themselves vigorously demanded and supported the allotment of individual parcels of property.[51] However, Fletcher's professional need for achievement also led her to encourage the establishment of an all-male governing committee among the Nez Perce when they ceded unallotted acres to the U.S.

government in 1893, inadvertently contributing to Nez Perce wom-
en's loss of property. Even if female reformers supported Indian
women's right to an allotment of land, one scholar cautions, Indian
policy was ultimately formulated with little regard for women who
might wish to farm their allotments by themselves. Even though
they received land under the revised Dawes Act, Indian women
were to be provided instruction only in household duties. Consequently, land owned by women who were not deemed "able-
bodied" enough to farm was readily passed into white hands.[52]
Women like Alice Fletcher, who endorsed the quest for female
independence in their own lives, thus became unwitting agents in
the transformation of economically independent tribal women into
domestic dependents.

White Women Missionaries in the Dakotas

Women missionaries' letters and journals reveal the immense dis-
crepancies between ideologically informed role expectations, their
actual work, and the Indians' reactions to their missionary efforts.
Although married women missionaries initially saw themselves as
their husbands' coworkers, joining in a common professional task,
they often found that for practical or ideological reasons, they had
to revert to established patterns of gendered work and separate
spheres.[53] Often, missionary women, especially those with children, had to expend all of their energy on the needs of their own
families, and they had to realize that they gained little recognition
for their overall work.[54] Nonetheless, an important and probably
distinct part of their ministry, like that of single women missionaries, was visiting Indian women in their homes and establishing
intercultural ties on a personal and domestic level. Some women
even found that Protestants could only hope to succeed in their
educational endeavors by avoiding instead of engaging religious
topics.[55]

In 1875, Mary Clementine Collins went to Dakota Territory to
serve as a missionary teacher. Because she had hoped to be sent to
Micronesia, she reluctantly accepted the assignment among "those
horrid Indians." Ten years later, in 1885, she felt that she "must go
out further . . . to leave all and go alone—the only white woman—

out among Sitting Bull's wild people."[56] She had come to the Sioux, she explains, to teach the women sewing, "better house-keeping methods," and medical care, but she had never been in danger of going native. As a teacher, she must never become one of them: "Always kind, always true, always sympathetic, but never an Indian" (62).

As she wrote in the mission paper *Iapi Oaye* (The Word Carrier) of August 1880, she and her Dakota coworker Winyan soon found that "our work must mainly be done at their homes." At first the Dakota woman would not let her go visiting alone, but as they both had their housework to do and could not always go together, she finally let her "go to the nearest houses without her. . . . I would stay 2 or 3 hours each time, going from house to house, talking with those I met, telling them how to do many things; how to be better housekeepers and better wives and mothers, asking them to come to school, and visiting the sick" (71–72).

Missionary women in the West, by reporting to and writing for eastern home-mission audiences, remained linked to home-mission discourses and were able to influence policy discussions by making suggestions for political reforms based on their own experience. Thus Collins, at the request of the Indian commissioner, in 1886 wrote a short treatise titled "Practical Suggestions on Indian Affairs," in which she outlined her ideas on Indian transformation, adopting the rhetoric of female moral authority. The great need, as she saw it, was for "clean, conscientious white workers; even with the common laborers sent out to work on the reservations, profanity, licentiousness, and drunkenness should not be permitted" (71–72). The reform of the Indian, she proposed, had to be preceded by the reform of the white man; Indian transformation was intricately linked to the moral regeneration of (male) white America. "May the Lord help us," she wrote in a letter in 1887, "to battle successfully against all the sin of the Indians and the sin of our Nation. I feel so weak and helpless when I see so much that is wrong" (73–74).

Among the most severe tests of Collins' ability to effect cultural change were the events leading to the massacre of hundreds of Sioux by U.S. soldiers at Wounded Knee in the winter of 1890–91. In an article of November 1890, she blamed Sitting Bull for the instigation of hostilities (75), and she discredited him and other leaders as pretenders who spread the hope of the return of the Messiah (76). Collins did not confine her comments to the female and domestic sphere in which she had initially located her task. In a maternalistic fashion, she assumed the authority to speak for or against Indian women and men, demanding the suppression of disruptive Indian men in order to ensure the redemption of the whole community. Her Dakota subjects are like children in need of constant help, who will "go backward if there is not a strong head and a strong heart to stand by them continually; they cannot hold their own against the inroads of a wild rush of godless men into the country" (80–81).

In 1892, when Beatrice Alicia Ramsay Stocker was sent to the Pine Ridge Reservation as a missionary for the Board of Foreign Missions of the Presbyterian Church, she was as surprised, and probably as dismayed, as Collins about not being sent to a foreign mission. Born in Rome, Italy, in 1858, she was a cosmopolitan who had lived in England, Germany, and New Zealand before coming to the United States in the early 1890s, where she went to live near her brother in Kearney, Nebraska. From Kearney and Pine Ridge, she wrote letters to her sister Caroline in Italy, which are preserved in the American Indian collection of the Presbyterian Church in Philadelphia.[57]

Stocker's letters are particularly interesting because they are written by a woman apparently unfamiliar with the American blend of Victorianism and home-mission ideals connected with Indian reform. In a letter written in February 1892, she grounds her determination to become a missionary in a powerful conversion experience that she links to an American brand of Christianity. Apparently, it was only in the United States that Beatrice Stocker had found her missionary calling. She had been on a quest for a purpose in life, for a personal calling and profession, which seems to have been at least partially answered by the decision to become a missionary. Her letters reveal a self constantly probing and chiding itself, although not without humorous self-mockery. Until she had her conversion experience, she claims, "my religion never took an aggressive form; now I begin to feel a responsibility for all over whom I have any influence, and for some I am horribly afraid" (43).

The expectations linked to her missionary career reveal Stocker as a world traveler longing for foreign lands and for the exotic. Like

Collins, she definitely had not located her mission in the American West: "My own leaning is towards work among educated and devoted young women in colleges, preparing for the foreign fields. And after some years of that I think I should like to be sent to a Christian college in Japan" (43). When she heard of her assignment to the Pine Ridge Reservation in South Dakota, she admits she was "a little dismayed" at first. In a letter to her future colleague Jennie Dickson, she wrote that her original goal had been to "get into a place where among superior and intellectual people I might find scope for all my capabilities—probably in some of the great centres of civilization" (41). This woman's decision to become a missionary was less informed, one begins to suspect, by the evangelical idea of a feminine mission than by a female quest for self-fulfillment, knowledge, and a purpose in life.

Soon, however, Stocker's curiosity got the better of her, and she set herself to the task of learning about Indians, adjusting her own incorrect notions: "I used to suppose that the Indians were all degraded and incomprehensible savages; that was my miserable ignorance, helped by the prejudices of others equally ill-informed" (44). One book instrumental in her change of mind was Jackson's *Century of Dishonor,* which is like a revelation: "I don't think there can be anything sadder in history. It is a perpetually recurring tale of removing them from their rich lands and smiling villages as the greed of advancing white settlers coveted their wealth; of treaties shamelessly violated year after year towards these helpless people, who bore all with a most marvellous patience, dignity, and loyalty." Westward expansion presents itself as the story of white invasion into an innocent Arcadia. Images of massacres involving women and little children, of removals and cruel uprootings, stick most powerfully in her mind. Indians are uprooted exiles, homeless in a wilderness, whose fate is best described in Longfellow's *Evangeline* (44).

Stocker's view of the Indian question, informed as it is by a critical view of American westward expansion, contrasts significantly with the interventionist rhetoric of home-mission women. However, she soon puts herself on a platform with the WNIA, perceiving Indian reform as the task of emancipating oppressed Indians: "it is hoped that the dark days of their wrongs are ended.

They are to be educated and given industrial and agricultural training, and allowed to go where they please, be absorbed in the nation
and have the privileges and responsibilities of citizens" (45). Despite her critical assessment of America's earlier dealings with its
indigenous inhabitants, this European immigrant apparently cannot see assimilation other than as a freedom of choice and as a
privilege. But rather than locating her task within a national American endeavor, Stocker seems to have envisioned the more individualist possibility that her broad and general education and talents
might finally be applied to a useful and fulfilling purpose.

The way she expresses her enthusiasm may illuminate the moti-
vations that brought many single women of her time into the missionary field. Becoming a missionary seems to have been one of the
few alternatives, besides teaching, open to single women; here they
could gain a measure of financial and personal independence and
find meaning in their lives while fulfilling a "higher duty" in accordance with traditional ideals of femininity. Here the broad, generalist scope of women's education might be focused into channels
other than marriage and motherhood: "The article said that no gift
or knowledge one might possess would fail to tell here—that is just
what I desire! Even gardening and poultry raising and all my miscellaneous proclivities may be turned to account for my brother the
Red Man. Isn't it superb?" (45).

Stocker's first letter from Porcupine, Pine Ridge Agency, in January 1893, reveals the dry humor, mostly directed at herself, with
which she glosses over her insecurity and unease in her new surroundings. Baffled by her own "stupidity" in learning the Dakota
language, she has written a poem: "The bother of it is, it is not
worth the paper it is written upon, for it was upon a tragic occurrence here, and on enquiring closer, I find I have got the circumstances incorrectly." The joke, however, is not solely on her, but on
the paradoxical relation of poetry and "facts": "I think I shall stop
writing poems till I get a better grasp of the facts. Perhaps then I
shall find them quite too unpoetical to set forth" (47). She had
written about the suicide of a young, pregnant Dakota woman and
had gotten her facts wrong by having the suicide take place on New
Year's Day: "then how could I bring in that line about 'wandering
by the frozen stream' when I find the gulley was dry?" To top off

the unsuitable nature of the reservation environment for the conventions of poetical language, the assumed cause of the suicide—Sioux polygamy—does not lend itself to poetic practice.

Her own maternalist feelings towards the Sioux, which were more of the nurturing kind, are set off against the more paternalist approach of her female colleague, who is "a strong, decided, masterful character, and . . . has some success with the men. She says Indians like to be ruled and controlled." This approach, however, does not seem to be suited to the control of Indian women: "The women are very bad. Many girls as soon as they are old enough make it their ambition to corrupt the men, who fall to them only too easily one after the other" (47). Stocker's perspective differs significantly from that of home-mission women who targeted men, especially non-Christian or Catholic, as the violators and abusers of women. Rather, she defines women's sexuality as dangerous to the cultural redemption of the Sioux. At times it seems as if the missionary felt compelled to describe women and gender relations in this manner in order to elevate her own task into a work of moral purification.[58] Ultimately, however, Stocker locates her personal mission less in the transformation of Indian women than in the teaching of Indian children and the care for Indian babies, who "are exactly like white babies in their ways" (47).

Stocker was initially enthusiastic about "the whole marvellous romance of missions. . . . It is a glorious thing to be a missionary, even in this despised, abandoned, barren field of S. Dakota: a doorkeeper in the house of my God, but what must it be to be an evangelist like Dr. Pentecost" (49). Soon, however, she regards her mission as far inferior to that of famous missionaries in India: she never heard "of the naked blacks that Livingston found, sinking to such shameless beast lives as these wretched, pampered, corrupted Indians" (50). But this image of the corrupted Indian who resists missionary teachings does not fit into the official ideology of the civilizatory mission: "We daren't write of the facts to our various missionary societies and magazines. . . . I envy those missionaries whose people are eager to learn but whether it be I or they, the work of Christ prospers there, and I don't deserve any better field than this, because for years I was lukewarm and doubtful—'offended'" (50–51).

As her interpretation of the events at Wounded Knee reveals,

Stocker had no stake in the distinctly American mission connected with westward expansion, which conceptualizes the transformation of the American Indian in nationalistic terms. In her history of Indian-white relations, white Americans are the perpetrators and main aggressors, and missionary work is a partial redemption of American sins. But missionary work also necessitates interventionist methods in the battle against tribal customs.

Stocker's colleague militantly fights the construction of a dance house near the Presbyterian mission, and with her methods she is obviously more successful than the male Indian agent: "Miss Dickson sent for the old hostile chief and fought it out with him. She forbade him in the name of the Lord to do one stroke towards that dance house—dared him to begin. And he did not dare. . . . If the Agent had a quarter of her pluck we should have no dance houses atall. He has the authority, and she has not" (52). And yet the Sioux do not stand by passively. They are given a voice, expressing their own views of the white women. Thus they are seen to develop strategies to control the impact of the white women on their tribal structures, assigning them a place in the community. The two white women are not only assigned a slot in the Sioux band as "prayerwomen," but they are also incorporated into their system of kinship: Sioux women visiting the missionaries refer to them as their relatives.

Anticipating her colleague's impending departure, Stocker's greatest fear was to be alone, and she asked her father in England to let one of her stepsisters come out to live with her as a companion—a plan that, it seems, is never realized. The vision of this companionship in terms of a same-sex marriage significantly inverts traditional gender roles: with her usual dry humor, Stocker slips into the role of a (male) pastor in need of a wife. As she explains to her sister, "the girl need not be any more of a missionary or a Presbyterian than she wants to. . . . When I am pastor here I want a wife, so to speak. I want her to share the housekeeping, play the organ, keep me company, and prevent my reverting to the wild type." She would also be "more lovable and loving to my poor dear Indians" if she had her sister to keep her warm: "I have been on my guard among strangers so many, many years and often stifling my feelings, if I had any, that I am too grave and cold and cautious to be taking hearts by storm as I ought. If the Board sends me a stranger, I might fall in love with her, or perhaps not. Anyhow it wouldn't make such a home feeling as a sister" (57).

The candor with which Stocker envisions female companionship in terms of a marriage, of "keeping each other warm" and "falling in love," suggests that neither she nor her sister perceive these same-sex relationships as unconventional or disrespectable. That this relationship is perceived as asexual is underlined in the following remark: "The happiest marriage I could imagine seems thin and flat compared with the missionary calling. And even if he were a devoted missionary, the worldly part, and trouble in the flesh would interfere. We single women travel so light, and we can give all the heart we have to our Indians" (59). Nevertheless, Stocker does not view nurturing as a natural female gift, given her own struggle with the emotional part of her missionary task.

In the course of her mission, she eventually describes herself as having "quite lost that anxious, almost guilty feeling of being in the wrong place, that always haunted me till I became a missionary" (59). She has found her place, which definitely does not lie with the white people of the territory. After these letters, Beatrice Stocker disappears from sight; her letters in the collections of the Presbyterian Church end with the dissolution of the Foreign Board's missionary efforts among Indians.

Elaine Goodale Eastman among the Sioux

In 1886, Elaine Goodale, a young woman of genteel New England upbringing and some literary reputation as a published child poet, went to Dakota Territory as a teacher in a small, isolated village on the Great Sioux Reservation. She described her experience in numerous articles in eastern magazines and newspapers. Later in her life, she apologetically disparaged these journalistic pieces, referring to them as "propaganda rather than literature."[59] In 1891, shortly after she witnessed the events at Wounded Knee, Goodale married the Sioux physician Charles Alexander Eastman, with whom she collaborated on nine books, most of which were published under his name. She was also the author of seven more books published under her own name, and she continued to write on Indian affairs until her death in 1953. In the late 1930s, she wrote her memoirs, which were based on her earlier journalistic pieces and which, like so many women's reminiscences of the time, remained unpublished until 1978, when Kay Graber edited the manuscript for the University of Nebraska Press under the title *Sister to the Sioux.*

Elaine Goodale Eastman opens her reminiscences by describing her family background as the daughter of a "book-farmer" and of a genteel New England woman who implanted in her children a taste for wide and varied reading and a love of knowledge. This information undoubtedly serves to explain the unconventional course of her life. Like Frances and Metta Fuller, Elaine and her sister Dora had become published poets before their teens. A college education was beyond the family's financial means, but as Eastman suggests, this was just as well: "The truth is that I had grown up a nonconformist, indifferent to fashion and disliking the prescribed figure, firmly molded of steel and whalebone, upon which alone the costume of the period could successfully be created" (15). It is therefore understandable, she suggests, that she accepted a teaching position at the Hampton Normal and Agricultural Institute, a vocational boarding school for black and Indian students in Virginia.[60] The position was still within the bounds of acceptable feminine occupation: Hampton Institute was based not only on the values of work and self-help, but also on the gendered division of work roles. Manual labor for a female teacher thus meant the sewing room at Hampton, where Goodale soon "absorbed the prevailing gospel which exalted self-help and manual efficiency" (18).[61]

As a pronounced individualist, however, the young woman only partly fit into the order of things at a school where military discipline and a rather puritanical religious atmosphere reigned. Religion never seems to have played an important part in her upbringing. Nevertheless, it was at Hampton that she developed the humanitarian beliefs—based on the assumption of human equality and the denial of human difference—that would inform her future life and work (20). She became an ardent propagandist for the Hampton educational experiment, bravely writing against "reverend senators and other solemn graybeards, who in those days regularly inveighed against the shocking waste of public funds in a futile attempt to civilize a 'horde of filthy savages.' As well, they exclaimed, send coyotes and rattlesnakes to school as vicious

Apaches and stolid Sioux!" (21). Indian reform emerges not as a dominant movement in the culture, but as a passionately contested cultural territory and a site for cultural conflict.

Eastman's retrospective presentation of 1880s Indian-reform goals underscores the author's basic support of the reform movement dominated by men (she does not mention the WNIA), which asserts that "a handful of primitives whose own way of life had been made impossible by our countrymen's advance could survive and prosper only through adaptation to the modern world. They must walk steadily forward to economic and political independence" (22). The key to this goal was education, and it was in the field of Indian education that women like her became involved, leaving their own distinctive mark.

Where Eastman disagreed with the male reformers was in her approach to Indian transformation. She privileged the local reservation school over the military-style eastern boarding school, and like Sarah Winnemucca, who established a reservation school for Paiute children, she became active in establishing and championing reservation day schools. She defined the Indian village, the Indian community, and the isolated homestead as the center of change, in contrast to others, like Richard H. Pratt, who favored the total removal of Indian students from their home communities. The day school, she argued, is the community's "object lesson in civilization," where the "neatly kept rooms, the neatly dressed teacher, the regular hours, [and] countless details are seen and studied and more or less unconsciously imitated." Americanization is defined in terms of spreading American material and moral culture.[62] The teacher, in Eastman's model of Indian education, becomes a social engineer, pitting her/his influence against that of the conservative Indian home. As Ruth Alexander has noted, what is notably absent from her arguments are "any pleas based on nurture or caring for the child's security and emotional stability by keeping him close to home—arguments that would have been common today."[63] Like Beatrice Stocker, Eastman seems to have had difficulties with the nurturing role assigned to women.

In the 1880s, reformers focused almost exclusively on the Indians of the northern plains. In 1885, burning to see the "Indian country," Goodale went on a tour of the Sioux agencies in Dakota Territory, the home of most of her Hampton pupils, whose language she had begun to study. Her friend, the future geologist Florence Bascom, was ready to "share in the adventure," and the two women traveled under the protection of Herbert Welsh of the Indian Rights Association. As Eastman explains with a certain degree of distancing, these " 'friends of the Indians,' or 'eastern sentimentalists,' as they were called, hoped to reach some compromise with land-hungry westerners on the opening of the Great Sioux Reservation, and to this end conferred with leading Dakotans in Pierre, the capital" (24). In fact, Welsh had gone to persuade the Sioux to accept the allotment of their land.

In the country of the Sioux, Eastman found her vocation. During a visit to a "forlorn little community," she determines to open a school, feeling pleaded to by the chief and the "mute appeal of the neglected little folk who clustered shyly about us. . . . Here was a clear call to the heart of the ardent young girl—a call which she then and there silently promised herself to answer" (26). Her mission to the Indians is not conceived as an active intervention; rather she sees herself called upon for help by the Sioux themselves.

In the meantime, her "letters from the field, hurriedly written in longhand with no opportunity to polish, were already appearing in New York and Boston papers." Mailed during the trip, they "described in detail the semibarbaric spectacle of Indian camp and council, new to most readers, not forgetting to stress the effects of mission training with its promise for the future" (28). Her "letters" thus built on the attraction of the exotic, "the semibarbaric spectacle," and the discourse of the civilizing mission in order to attract attention—and donations—to the cause. These articles appeared in the *Boston Weekly Adviser,* the *New York Evening Post,* and the *Southern Workman,* and although they mainly supported the assimilationist thrust of Indian reform, they also expressed Eastman's skepticism about the policies of land cession and allotment.

Eastman returned to the East with firm convictions about her future mission: "Meantime, one young woman came home in spirit deeply committed to her task as she saw it. She had made up her mind to begin at the beginning, in the heart of a newly transplanted, leaderless, bewildered little community. Others could carry on in more solidly established institutions where there was ample support and companionship." Eastman fashions herself as a pioneer: "Few, perhaps, would care to blaze a new trail in the obscure corner of a wild land, among recent 'enemies' speaking an unintelligible dialect." Behind these considerations "lurked, no doubt, a taste for adventure and a distinct bent toward pioneering, possibly handed down through a long line of early American forebears" (29). Faced with the necessity of supporting herself and the limited prospects of employment for women, Eastman carved out a profession for herself, authorizing her writing and her work by an altruistic motive. What is more, she found it necessary to legitimate her professional achievements not only by hinting at her devotion to the welfare of others but also by grounding it in an American pioneering legacy.

The latter seems to have been a common strategy for nineteenth-century women, adopted not only by other teachers on Indian reservations, such as Flora Gregg Iliff, but also by community activists like Jane Addams, who also rooted her professional ambition, defined as a will to serve, in her pioneer ancestors.[64] Women like Eastman did not authorize their maternalist colonialism in terms of ideology but in terms of a sense of service. Of course, this idea of service is part of the ideology of true womanhood. And it is with the cultural discourse of femininity that women like Eastman struggled, claiming the "mission" and the "call" instead of the quest for influence and authority—especially since women of the 1880s, as Ruth Alexander suggests, could not fashion themselves as "self-made" women.[65]

Eastman's dilemma was even more complex, since she identified herself not only as a teacher but also as a writer standing between art and a cause. She had addressed the dilemma in a review of Helen Hunt Jackson's *Ramona* and in an obituary on the occasion of the novelist's death in 1885. Although Eastman claimed in the review that Jackson's novel did not present the Indian problem adequately, and she criticized its wholesale condemnation of white people, in the obituary she implied that Jackson, who through her art "made the Indian cause the cause of humanity," could teach "that art may be obedient to the high demands of conscience, and still be art."[66] Apparently wishing that she, too, could have created art, Eastman wrote in 1937 that: "I sometimes wonder that no effort was made to launch me upon the journalistic or purely literary career for which I had shown most fitness and which would seem to offer so much more of congenial association and tangible reward than the obscure and ill-paid pioneer work which I, in fact, under-took at this point."[67]

Although teaching at Hampton was within the bounds of re-spectable feminine employment, the young woman's plans to es-tablish a reservation school created a stir of protest. In her mem-oirs, Eastman describes herself defending "the hopes and schemes of a mere girl of twenty-two who proposed to create a little center of 'sweetness and light'—so ran the intellectual jargon of the day—in a squalid camp of savages" (30). The writer of the 1930s dis-tances herself from the home-mission ideology of the 1880s, the "intellectual jargon of the day," rooting her own work less in con-ceptions of her feminine role than in her individualistic and non-conformist attitude. Like many other female writers of western reminiscences, Eastman also impresses upon her readers the out-rageous nature of her western journey by emphasizing the almost insurmountable resistance of her family against her going West: "Dire consequences were freely predicted in case we persisted, ranging from attacks by the savages to the cut direct from 'Society' on our return to civilization" (31). By dwelling on these scenes of home opposition, Eastman stresses the enormity of her undertak-ing as a rebellious act.

In 1886, the narrator found herself back in Sioux country, this time as a government teacher sharing work with a female friend. Until their own house was finished, the two women resided as guests in the rather unconventional family of a full-blooded Santee Sioux missionary married to a "kindly German hausfrau." In East-man's memoirs, one gradually becomes accustomed to these fre-quent marriages between well-educated Indian men and white women, foreshadowing her own marriage to a Santee Sioux. Intro-duced by this couple to the "strange new world of an Indian reser-vation," the two women come to see the latter as "two distinct worlds existing side by side, now in dramatic opposition, now intimately mixed. There were already a few Dakotas at home in the white man's world and superior in most respects to the frontier white men. There were also a good many of both races who be-longed about as much to one as to the other" (33). In this environ-ment, hierarchies of race and class become blurred and permeable, with educated Indians gaining superiority over uneducated white frontiersmen.

In retrospect, Eastman distanced herself from the discourses of femininity and the evangelical brand of the mission ideology, but her first move toward a better acquaintance with the Sioux remained within the domestic and missionary sphere: the two women organized a "church sewing-circle" for Indian women as a venue to get closer to the Indian community as a whole. Whereas Stocker had focused on Sioux women in terms of their allegedly uncontrolled sexuality, Eastman represents them repeatedly as paragons of modest and respectable femininity (34). They are at the same time sensuous, talking freely and jokingly about sexuality— the reason why "prim-lipped mentors" had advised Eastman not to learn the language, assuring her she "would often prefer not to understand what was being said" (35).

The first thing the two white women taught their Sioux neighbors is reminiscent of one of the tropes of women's narratives of army life. Although women teachers' narratives do not contain any "darkening-of-the-window" scenes, they are still concerned with the theme of privacy. Thus Goodale and her colleague aimed to instill in their neighbors a respect for the white concept of privacy, that is, "to knock before entering and to refrain from a preliminary peep in at the window." On the whole, though, neighborly relations were based on a system of reciprocity revolving around food and homes. Just as their native guests showed dignity and propriety when dining at their table, the two women, when they called among the tepees, "accepted whatever refreshment was offered and strictly observed the native conventions" (37–38).

In the school environment, however, the women set about the task of transforming Indian children, focusing at first on their external appearance. The boys had their long hair cut and were given new suits to wear, while the girls were supplied with dress materials and were taught to make their own (40). "Eastern well-wishers" added their share of American material culture by supplying boxes and barrels of used clothing. The children were enrolled under their father's name and given the name of "an eastern friend" for the teacher's personal use. Lessons were varied by "intervals of marching, singing, calisthenics" (41).

Not only did the new naming practice privilege patrilineal structures of kinship and inheritance, but the whole schoolroom experience was designed to inculcate in the students a sense of the gendered domains of white culture, which Eastman sees reciprocated in the children's Sioux upbringing: the boys draw horses on their slates, while the girls design patterns for beadwork—presumably traditional work roles reinforced by the white women teachers.[68] The boys were taught to cultivate vegetables in the school gardens, and the narrator, brought up on a farm, ironically violated the gender norms she was teaching by showing some of the men how to milk: "This meant wrestling with an excited calf and a slopping bucket, as I had seen my father do, loftily ignoring a splashed frock and the delighted howls of a ring of masculine spectators" (42).

Like Stocker and her colleague, the young Eastman discouraged the practice of Indian dances, trying to supplant them with community suppers, magic-lantern shows, and "other wholesome diversions." Indian dances, she explains, are the special target of church workers and government employees because they "not only involve paint and Dakota dress, but revival of war games, late hours, and a general relaxation of all rules" (43). Tribal traditions were deemed dangerous, felt to be beyond the civilizers' control. Female missionaries and teachers thus acted energetically as social directors on Indian reservations, trying their hands at a kind of social engineering in the service of Indian transformation. As generalists and jack-of-all-trades, they also performed medical services for the Indian community, introducing elements of white health care, although as Eastman claims, they undertook nothing to discourage the activities of medicine men.

In retrospect, however, Eastman condemns the wholesale transformation of Indian culture, speaking up against the needless rejection of "everything characteristically native without regard to intrinsic values" by "a few strait-laced individuals" fifty years ago. She herself had been taken to task by a clergyman for habitually wearing moccasins. She adds: "I am sure that same clergyman—if he had ever heard of it—would have rebuked me even more severely for taking part in an inter-camp game of 'shinny' with a hundred or more yelling and excited men and women!" Perhaps, she muses, "we placed undue emphasis on surface indications of conformity," although she is convinced that they help "to bolster up the courage of the new convert and effectively advertise his change of heart" (43). On the one hand, she is convinced that the suppression of native funeral customs had been for the better, since the custom of burning, burying, or giving away all one's possessions in the event of a death in the family "did no one any good" (56). On the other hand, she appreciated the Omaha, or grass, dance as an "exotic spectacle" and critically questions the categorical prohibition of native dances: "We were expected to frown upon all 'heathen spectacles,'" she recalls with a hint of sarcasm, "but could not help knowing that the modern round dance in which men and women publicly embrace was a shocking thing in the eyes of our ceremonious Dakotas" (59).

One may speculate that women like Eastman may have been attracted to the Indian cause since they themselves felt similarly held back and kept in a state of dependence. Barbara Babcock has suggested that for radical and disaffected women of the early twentieth century, "issues of race, ethnicity and class came to stand in for gender; feminism was transformed into a preoccupation with other cultures, other differences and inequalities, and an advocacy of cultural relativism."[69] Eastman's memoir is a case in point. Skirting the issue of women's rights, she asserts her authority in the field of Indian education. Nevertheless, she is constantly forced to reconcile the potentially conflicting identities of woman and government worker. On the Sioux Reservation, she suggests, two different cultural standards of feminine behavior met, although without clashing, as when the young white teacher exhibited behavior that was diametrically opposed to Sioux norms of femininity, which prohibited unchaperoned meetings with men (49–50). Moreover, her loyalty to the basic tenets of the Indian-reform ideology continuously competed with her concern for the preservation of certain cultural traditions. Although her memoirs formulate a strong belief in the necessity of Indian transformation, this conviction is often subverted by descriptions of personal encounters and interactions with traditional Sioux, relations that seem to have affected the educator more than those she educated.

In 1888, Eastman traveled over the "vast open spaces" of the Great Sioux Reservation, mostly with Sioux families, and to the dismay of an Indian Service official who was shocked by her temerity. Later, she remembers that she "often spent the night in a well-filled tipi, entirely surrounded by men, women, children, and dogs, all without the slightest self-consciousness. The etiquette of the tipi is strict." The respectability of her undertaking needs to be underscored: "The privacy of each is inviolable, and no Dakota would think of transgressing, even by a look, that invisible barrier" (65).

A year later, she uses her summer vacation to "still further consolidate my influence among the 'wilder' element" (94) by going on a deer hunt with some conservative Sioux. She had no little difficulty, she writes, in persuading the two wives of the hunter to carry her tent and baggage and to allow her to ride alongside on her pony. She avoids commenting negatively on the existence of polygamy and defends traditional female Sioux roles. Revising the image of the Indian woman as slave and drudge, she claims that the women's labors were "cheerfully performed. I have never seen them treated as 'slaves' or 'beasts of burden,' but always as equals and companions. They laughed and chatted freely with husbands and near relatives . . . advised and scolded them much as women do their menfolk all over the world" (104). Nevertheless, Eastman cannot go as far as assuming these traditional roles herself, that is, by carrying her own baggage. The white woman is dependent on the tribal women's skill and strength and covets the "privilege" of being able to accompany them. Neither does she assume the Sioux women's custom of riding astride but instead clings to the Victorian side-saddle, "even in the wilderness" (95).

Traveling through Nebraska, the Indian hunting group is stared at by "gaunt women, in ugly calico frocks and sun bonnets." Ranchers bring them chicken, eggs, and green corn, and the Sioux men are urged to give a dance, but "Nebraskans couldn't raise enough money to tempt them" (98). Had she earlier condemned frontiersmen as land-hungry speculators, she now admires the "courage of these pioneers," although she would never exchange her life among the Sioux for one among them: "The Sioux were on the whole living better at the time and showed some contempt for the white man's poverty" (99). She registers with amusement that she was accosted by white strangers who, puzzled by her presence and position in the hunting party, ask her: " 'Can you talk American?,' 'Why, you've been to school, I guess!,' or 'Were both your parents white folks?' " (107–8) In contrast to many of her contemporaries, who denied any temptation to go native, Eastman represents herself as a white woman who can blend herself, at least externally, into any group, Indian or white, and who revels in her own Indianized appearance (108).

Writing in the 1930s, Eastman was, of course, well aware of the wave of optimism surrounding the Indian New Deal, which had been stimulated by John Collier, an advocate of cultural pluralism instead of assimilation, who became commissioner of Indian affairs in 1933. She could then support at least a measure of Indian self-determination, yet castigate earlier Indian policies in whose implementation she had become involved.[70] She was, however, critical of Collier's New Deal, and in 1934 she wrote in an article for the *New York Times* that Collier's objective was "clearly not to assimilate but to perpetuate Indians and Indianism,"[71] again voicing her skepticism about any policy of segregation.

Eastman's writing and career illustrate the fact that women's involvement in the political debates and events of the day had many sides. Some women started writing memoirs of life in the army, strenuously avoiding the impression that they may have meddled in military politics, but others like Eastman defied standards of female modesty, speaking up as authorities and taking a public stance. This does not mean that the discursive pressures connected with ideals of femininity were absent from Eastman's public writings. However, her conception of womanhood was no longer limited to either a disinterested domestic femininity or a domesticity empowered by the evangelical mission. Rather, Eastman represented her feminine role in terms of a conflict between two guiding principles: the voice of individual conscience and the voice of social pressure. This individualism also informs her self-representation as a woman capable of living in two worlds, and her general approach to the issue of Indian transformation.

Significantly, Eastman's self-representation hardly ever draws on the privilege of innocence. Instead, she emphasizes the necessity of individual responsibility and accountability. Also significant is the fact that throughout her memoirs, her involvement in the Indian-reform effort is continuously justified, a necessity linked closely to her identity as a woman. Discourses of femininity seem to have forced her to repeatedly explain why a young woman with a promising writing career chose the Indian cause instead, and entered into personal relations with native people that may have been read by a white audience as potentially disrespectable or immoral. This also ties in with her repeated focus on the moral integrity of the Sioux, critically targeting the religious- and race-conscious rhetoric of female moral authority.

Interestingly, Eastman's memoirs end with her marriage to the Sioux Charles Eastman. Authorized by the figure of the headstrong, unconventional young woman pioneering the field of Indian education for women, the text obviously could not accommodate the story of the wife who subordinated her own career to that of her husband. Eastman had to legitimize not only her marriage to an Indian shortly after the events at Wounded Knee, but also her reversion to a traditional white feminine role. Though she had not "consciously considered marriage with a Dakota," she had "closely observed several such marriages which appeared successful. The idea certainly did not repel me in any way" (169). Eastman's apologia, of course, reinforces the transgressive nature of the marriage. As Brian W. Dippie has put it, the phenomenon of transculturation "represented a male-oriented escapist fantasy," fully elaborated in the romantic tale of Pocahontas's rescue of John Smith. In the case of relations between Indian men and white women, however, "propriety held that only the lower order of females would voluntarily choose an Indian paramour."[72]

As the narratives of Collins, Stocker, and Eastman show, the female civilizing mission was more complicated than either the story of women serving selflessly or that of authoritarian Victorians imposing white middle-class standards on powerless and oppressed groups. None of the white women who wrote their western stories in the context of Indian reform, and who re-wrote themselves in their texts from a distance of time and space, fits the mold of official Indian-reform ideology. Eastman, in particular, avoided its religious connotations, stressing individualism and nonconformity. Flora Gregg legitimized her mission in Indian country by her desire for knowledge, which had been awakened by a combination of primitivism and mysticism.[73] Nevertheless, these women represented the maternalist version of a colonialist project undertaken in the service of the civilizing mission.

Discourses of the civilizing mission also surface in the autobiographical texts written by assimilated Indians such as Charles Eastman and Sarah Winnemucca, where the appeal to white society for the privilege of education and literacy is an important message.[74] However, most of the texts composed by Indian women reveal a rather contradictory and critical view of Indian transformation. Even if, as Pascoe has suggested, a small group of minority women targeted by women's home-mission movements "enthusiastically adopted the Victorian search for female moral authority,"[75] the autobiographical narratives of Sarah Winnemucca and Zitkala Sa distance themselves from female and male brands of Indian cultural transformation, providing a critical context for white women's narratives of their benign missions among Native Americans.

From 1900 to 1903, the *Atlantic Monthly* published a series of reminiscences by the Sioux writer Zitkala Sa. The recollections of her childhood, the conflicted assimilation process, and her professional development must have seemed unusual at a time when other Indian intellectuals were either expressing their commitment to religious and cultural conversion, or trying to avoid the topic altogether in their attempt to establish the social and cultural legitimacy of Indian life. But then, the home-mission movement was already on the wane—even if the policies the movement had inspired were being implemented on Indian reservations with full force—and American intellectuals were in the process of rediscovering their earlier fascination with the primitive. In the early twentieth century, Indian intellectuals were forming political organizations, bringing together diverse and often conflicting Pan-Indian agendas.[76] Indeed, Zitkala Sa's recollections foreshadow themes of the Pan-Indian political movement in which she, under her English name Gertrude Bonnin, would play an instrumental role, focusing on the search for an Indian identity between two cultures, and retaining a strong sense of identity as a tribal woman. Zitkala Sa's stories were reprinted in book form in 1921 as *American Indian Stories*.

The context in which Zitkala Sa's personal narrative first appeared suggests yet another framework beyond that of Indian reform: the concurrent (re)discovery of the (South)West, which in the minds of some Americans was linked to a new appreciation of western landscapes. When they appeared in the *Atlantic Monthly*, Zitkala Sa's narratives were framed by Harriet Monroe's "The Grand Cañon of the Colorado" and "Arizona," as well as by Sharlot

Hall's and Mary Austin's stories of the Southwest. Zitkala Sa's bitter indictment of federal assimilation policies that were destroying Indian cultural knowledge, integrity, and identity not only anticipates a tentative political turn in federal Indian policy towards Indian self-determination but also a revision of earlier attitudes toward tribal cultures—to which she herself contributed actively. Her account of her tribal childhood, contrasted with the harsh, inhuman discipline of an Indian boarding school in the East, may also have addressed a tendency in American readers to again look to the West as a source of personal freedom and of closeness to nature. It is certainly no coincidence that the *Atlantic Monthly,* around the turn of the century, put a new and special focus on the literature of the American West, which at the same time revised and subtly reinforced the tenets of American expansionism.

Although her autobiographical narrative rejects the female involvement in Indian education as just another version of working the "civilizing machine," Zitkala Sa's later essays, stories, and political activism stress the importance of white women's involvement in the Indian cause. In an essay on "America's Indian Problem," she represents women's activism for Indian rights—with an obvious reference to Helen Hunt Jackson's work—as a powerful and positive cultural force: "A long century of dishonor followed this inheritance of somebody's loot. Now the time is at hand when the American Indian shall have his day in court through the help of the women of America" (186).[77] And in a short story about land fraud on the Sioux Reservation, an old chief appeals for help by addressing a letter "to a prominent American woman." When he is thrown in prison, she appears to him, in multiplied form, as a vision: "Lo, his good friend, the American woman to whom he had sent his message by fire, now stood there a legion! A vast multitude of women, with uplifted hands, gazed upon a huge stone image. Their upturned faces were eager and very earnest. The stone figure was that of a woman upon the brink of the Great Waters, facing eastward." American women have the power to turn the Statue of Liberty, who now not only welcomes the immigrants from Europe but also directs her attention westward: "It was she, who, though representing human liberty, formerly turned her back upon the American aborigine. Her face was aglow with compassion. Her eyes swept across the outspread continent of America, the home of the red man." The West is reclaimed as Indian land whose inhabitants ask for civil rights and justice. For a brief moment, the old man glimpses into a future in which the "light of liberty penetrated Indian reservations," a future which, the story suggests, lies both practically and symbolically in the hands of American women.[78]

Innocents Abroad: Two Field Matrons on the Klamath River

As some women's accounts illustrate, women in the Indian Service were often assigned positions of responsibility and power because men would not accept unattractive, low-paid posts in isolated places. They also suggest that the work done by women in the Indian Service was performed, with few exceptions, within the domestic framework of women's work, and that women's cultural authority on Indian reservations was necessarily limited. When they wrote about their experiences, women in the Indian Service assumed an ambiguous stance toward the rhetoric of the home mission, often focusing on a personal process of learning rather than on the work of Indian transformation. Significantly, in the period in which these women performed their work on Indian reservations, the search for female moral authority lost much of its special rhetorical power, which was now channeled into the institutionalization of reform impulses in the so-called Progressive Era.[79] Women's victories in this area led to what Paula M. Baker has called the "domestication of politics," which distinguished many of the reforms of the Progressive Era. Ironically, when Victorian culture lost its hegemony in the years after 1890, the ground beneath home-mission women's feet began to shift, and they ultimately lost their cultural authority in American society, deferring it to the government.[80]

Nevertheless, at about the same time that home-mission women's cultural authority seemed to decline, domestic ideologies were being institutionalized in federal reform programs. The establishment of the field-matron position for women in the 1890s is a case in point. The fact that the practical implementation of Indian policy was increasingly left in the hands of female teachers, field matrons, and nurses reflects the marginality of Indian affairs in early-twentieth-century American culture. This development found its special expression in the account I will discuss next, which draws on the ironies implied in women's work for the Indian Service and which paradoxically inverts the home-mission ideology. Although many women still felt empowered by the rhetoric of female moral authority, their work in the Indian Service and their search for personal independence, by the beginning of the twentieth century, obviously put them in opposition to an increasingly anachronistic home-mission ideology. This irony, reflected in the marginal power assigned to field matrons on Indian reservations, informs the self-parodic account of two women who went West in search of adventure and professional opportunities.

In her autobiographical narrative, first published in 1916, the Yurok woman Lucy Thompson refers to "two lady matrons on the Klamath River" sent by the government to "look after the interests of the Indians" (23). Undoubtedly these women were Mary Ellicott Arnold and Mabel Reed, who recorded their two years as field matrons on the Klamath Reservation in a book titled *In the Land of the Grasshopper Song: Two Women in the Klamath River Indian Country in 1908–09*. First published in 1957, the book reads like a twentieth-century female version of Mark Twain's *Innocents Abroad* and *Roughing It* combined.

Field matrons were sent to reservations by the Bureau of Indian Affairs from 1891 through the 1930s. Unlike the government teachers who primarily taught Indian children, field matrons were explicitly charged with training Indian women to follow the nineteenth-century ideal of middle-class "true womanhood." As Helen Bannan has pointed out, the program also "institutionalized American reformers' beliefs about Indian women (as culturally degraded opponents of assimilation); gender ideology (emphasizing women as natural civilizers sharing an idealized separate sphere); and the process of social change (as a simple matter of presenting the allegedly superior American cultural norm and teaching others to follow it)."[81] The way to the Indian led not only through the Indian home, which in the eyes of the reformers still needed to be established, but it also led against the Indian woman as the conservative barrier to Indian assimilation.

In the field, however, matrons were confronted with reservation realities that made the envisioned transformations next to impossible. Indian women's traditional work roles had already undergone considerable change.[82] Many field matrons found much of their energies devoted to health care. But here, as Bannan convincingly argues, also lay the crucial limitations of their position, since only a few of the women were trained nurses. Thus, "as the twentieth century's demand for expertise replaced the nineteenth century's idealistic support for well-intentioned philanthropy, field matrons appeared increasingly anachronistic." By the 1920s, the position "had come to reflect the persistently low estimate of the social and market worth of domestic labor."[83]

When Mary Ellicott Arnold and Mabel Reed recorded their experiences as field matrons in northern California, they did not care to mention that they were veterans of a New York model tenement project, and that their activities had included organizing cooperatives and land-settlement projects.[84] Instead, the reader comes to know two New Jersey women—properly dressed in pleated skirts—who traveled westward anxious to learn about Indian life. As if by coincidence, they were offered appointments as field matrons to the allegedly "roughest field in the United States," which for them was "the chance we had been hoping for" (13).

If seen in relation to Lucy Thompson's *To the American Indian,* the narrative of a Klamath woman who, as a member of the tribal aristocracy and of a secret society, spoke from a position of cultural authority, Arnold and Reed's narrative barely scratches the surface of Klamath Indian traditional culture. The field matrons' access to Klamath cultural knowledge was as limited as the possibilities for cultural change allowed by their position, although the transformations the two women may have actually effected among the Klamath River Indians are hard to judge. Their schools and Sunday schools, they claim, were a popular success; the people enjoyed singing hymns together and learning the three R's, asked them for medicine, and consulted them in their roles as government representatives in intertribal conflicts as well as government affairs. The two women also introduced some rituals of white culture, such as a Christmas tree and a marriage ceremony.

However, in their account they continually express their awareness of both their own personal limitations and the limitations of a government position that is so filled with ideological baggage, so anachronistic, and so vague about actual procedures. One is even forced to acknowledge that ultimately, the two women's account is less about change among the Klamath Indians than about the transformation taking place within the two narrators.[85] Their book centers on the impact of cultural encounters and the power of cultural change—on white, not Indian people. Like Eastman's and Iliff's narratives, *In the Land of the Grasshopper Song* focuses less on teaching Indians than on learning from Indians. It deals with the limitations of cultural authority, the circumscribed power two white women have as representatives of the U.S. government, and the possibility of turning these limitations into assets. Ultimately, it is a story about cultural identity, which is seen as contingent, fluid, and flexible, and which leaves its mark on language—a language that in its imitation of native reasoning mirrors the act of straddling cultures.

In the Land of the Grasshopper Song is full of laughter, mirth, and often-sarcastic humor. From the beginning, Arnold and Reed viewed their field-matron positions rather critically, and they profess having only a vague sense of the ideology shaping their indistinctly defined task. The first touch of irony is that they have to go in search of the Indians they have come to transform. That they are supposed to represent not only white womanhood but white culture as a whole adds another note of irony, since they present themselves as unconventional "new" women opposed to the domestic values of true womanhood that they are charged to impress upon Indian women.

Discourses of femininity are adopted only to be parodied and subverted; the women's self-representation as marginalized "heathen" rebels in their home community ultimately enables them to go native and define themselves as Indians, in direct opposition to the ideology of the field-matron program. As they parody themselves as naive innocents, whom it becomes to learn rather than to teach, they engage critically with a paternalistic ideology of Indian reform that leaves the civilizing to women, conferring upon them a power they do not actually have—and do not desire in the form it is offered. As noted in many women's narratives, self-parody forms a strong force in destabilizing colonial discourses of authority and power. Arnold and Reed explicitly draw on this strategy in their account, reflecting insecurity about their undefined power as government agents.

Arnold and Reed's narrative of travels and life in the Klamath

River country intricately maps the cultural and social spaces assigned to races and genders. It also shows that the process of westward expansion can by no means be grasped as a linear process.
The "white man's country" does not cover the whole terrain;
rather, the women find pockets of isolated Indian community life
untouched by the affairs of their white neighbors. At the time of
their account (1908–1909), the so-called Rivers country, which
had seen a great influx of whites during the gold rush of 1852, had
again become a native space in which white influence was limited
(9).

Significantly, the two women locate their text not only within
(or against) discourses of the civilizing mission. Their implied reference is also the literature of the "wild West." Although all around
them was "gold country, the land of the saloon and of the six-
shooter . . . the account given in these pages is not of these occurrences but of everyday life on the frontier in an Indian village, and
what Indians and badmen did and said when they were not engaged in wiping out their friends and neighbors." As in Kirkland's
narrative, the explicit focus is on the ordinary, quotidian aspects of
life in the West. Expectations connected with the female civilizing
mission are immediately deflated as the narrators describe themselves as "the only white women" in Indian country who were
"most of the time quite scared enough to satisfy anybody" (9–10).
The main value of their story, they claim, lies in "the authentic
account it gives of the customs and habits of thought of Indians
who could remember what life was like before the coming of the
white man, and its picture of conditions in what was the last of the
old frontier" (10). What the narrative ignores is the official history
of Klamath-white relations—the history of treaties, wars, and dis-
possessions. Rather, it focuses on the more subtle layers of Indian-
white relations—the everyday discriminations and prejudices, the
negotiations of power and authority between whites and Indians,
and the social relations within Indian communities.

Studying the Indian way of life acquired special meaning for
Arnold and Reed, who saw their positions not as extensions of
their female sphere but as part of their personal quests for a place
in life. Teaching Indians seems like a pretext for personal self-
development and the search for a new female identity. Although
the late-nineteenth-century discourse of femininity, coupled with

a nationalist discourse of expansion, officially legitimized Arnold and Reed's field-matron service, it recedes behind the narrators' desire to understand Indian people in their own right. Nevertheless, the shadow of Victorian womanhood follows them whenever they travel in "white man's country," where white men expect them to act like "ladies."

Going into Indian country meant trespassing into white territory first, where the two women encountered male hostility and generally felt unwelcome. In the white world of northern California, femininity was not an asset but a fault. As white women, easterners at that, they could hardly count on voluntary male assistance. Going to Indian country also meant leaving a part of their white female world behind: they carefully folded their voluminous pleated skirts and wrapped up their elaborate trimmed hats, stashing them away in a trunk to be left behind. Instead, they wore divided skirts that "seemed to be the right length, just a little below our ankles," cowboy or rubber hats, and high boots. Vestiges of their old appearance accompanied them in the form of "serviceable-looking shirtwaists and white, starched collars" (16). Women's self-representations on the basis of dress seem almost inevitable in their western narratives, serving as markers of transformations and transgressions (or their absence) and as signals of comic self-parodies that destabilize colonial discourses of authority.

At their first place of activity, they are still "Innocents Abroad in the Land of the White Man," where "everybody . . . draws you aside and tells you quite scandalous things about everybody else" (31). This is a land where whites, people of mixed blood, and Indians live together, with each group in its own place. It is a world with clear hierarchies of race and gender. Asked whether there were no Indians in Somesbar, an old pioneer answers: "Well, I don't hold much with Indians. . . . Saw all the Indians I ever want to see in Arizony. . . . Only good Indian is a dead Indian, that's what I say. Apaches are bad hombres and they're bad medicine. I'd kill an Apache soon as I got a sight of him" (34). An old woman replies: "Why, yes, of course, there are Indians. But they know their place and the men here see that they keep it" (36–37). The two women also note dryly how Indian women and their children in racially mixed marriages are excluded from eating at the table with their white husbands. With a wry humor that underscores their detachment from the racist and misogynist pretensions of this patriarchal white world, in which they feel like intruders (35), they describe how "Old Bob married a squaw. But his wife and his son and his daughter did not eat at the table with Bob. Old Bob was white. . . . only white people ate with Old Bob Elliott" (101).

When an Indian woman asks them whether they are "school-marms," they find a clue to one of their problems: "Schoolmarms! A nice familiar occupation that everyone understands. It's bad enough for us to be women. No one thinks much of women in this country. And no one likes them. And missionaries are worse. We simply can't be missionaries. And government agents are worst of all. No wonder people won't look at us or speak to us." Ironically, they are forced to fashion a role for themselves that detracts from their authority as government agents and is more in accord with traditional configurations of womanhood: "schoolmarms are safe" (41).

They decide to live in the Indian rancheria of Kot-e-meen, where they cause a ripple among the villagers, being "the most talked-of individuals in two hundred miles" (47). Once they move into the house rented to them by a half-Indian family, there is no longer any need for them to introduce themselves to the villagers. What they do not know yet is that they have been adopted by their landlords, a family in which the stereotypical image of Indian polygamy is stood on its head. At the center of the family stands Essie, "a full-blood Indian, small and dark, with a soft, low voice and very pretty manners," a woman with a son and two husbands, one of them a half blood and the other a full blood. Considering this family arrangement, the two white women ask with barely veiled amusement "whether we were exercising the civilizing influence for which the Government is paying us thirty dollars a month and traveling expenses. But we couldn't help being impressed by the way Essie carried off the situation. Socially, she put her two husbands on the map" (48).

As Essie and her husbands take them on a round of calls in the area, they briefly wonder about the propriety of this evident sanctioning of polygamy: "How would the Indian Department and the Northern Indian Association look upon our chosen companions, not to mention Bishop Moreland, who evidently considers us members of his flock and has sent us forty Bibles" (51). But then, they muse, "why exclude Essie, who sports two husbands, and include Sam, who regularly breaks the law by selling illicit whiskey to the Indians?" (52). The questions, humorously subverting the serious intentions of evangelical reformers, turn out to be purely rhetorical. The problem is solved in favor of Essie, who serves as intercultural mediator, and the two women soon find they "like very much being members of the Essie family" (54).

Ever since they had come to the country, they had been wondering why it was not more "like the westerns you read in books and magazines." Compared with the terrific pace set in Westerns, things are taken much more leisurely on the Rivers. Most of the shootings or knifings they hear about are "a long way off" or "up river." What really concerns people and what they talk about most are "river crossings and what happened the last ti postheree (high water) and salmon smokes and bears and eels and Indian gambles and, of course, apruan (Indian devils), and things like Indian marriage" (58–59). In the manner of Caroline Kirkland, the narrators revise and deflate literary notions about the wild West by assuming the position of insiders participating in the flow of daily life at the rancheria. At the same time, they paradoxically adopt the hyperbolic style of western journalism perfected by Mark Twain.

While the two women were still learning and not yet teaching, they were mapping the new territory, and especially their adoptive family, in terms of race and gender in order to make sense of the confusing blurring of well-established categories. Mart, "who was white, for all his Indian grandmother . . . had a white way of doing things. You couldn't think of Mart as an Indian." On the other hand, Essie was "small and dark and very Indian. Or was she? No other Indian woman was quite like Essie." Familiar categories blur, making room for new, more fluid boundaries. Personally the two white women prefer being with Essie and Les to being with Mart: "Mart was white. Working in the garden wasn't an adventure to Mart. It was a chore. Crossing the river in the dugout wasn't an adventure to Mart, as it was to Essie and Les and ourselves. It was a chore." Arnold and Reed have their own place on this chart, categorizing themselves with the "Indian" side of the family (63).

Language vividly reproduces the two women's charting of the territories of race and gender, marking boundaries as fluid and uncertain. The white women, posing as naive innocents, have become students concerned with identity, piecing together fragments of local knowledge and personal observation that constantly challenge one another. People do not conform to generalizing local information: "in this country, Sam Frame tells us, the man rides ahead on his horse and his woman walks behind with the load. But when the Essie family went over to the Forks, we noticed that it was Essie who rode and Les who walked. . . . But Les is Indian and Essie is Indian. Yet she rides and he walks" (64).

As Caroline Leighton noted in her travels at Puget Sound, married Northwest Indian women achieved and enjoyed an independence not shared by white women in the region. Arnold and Reed also found the lives of white married women in the West stultifying compared to the freedom of Indian women. As they have one of Essie's cousins explain, there are definite advantages for Indian women in an Indian marriage: "Woman marry white man . . . stay home all day and cook. Woman marry Indian, take her baby on her back when she want to, and go along trail." Mary and Mabel are fully convinced: "Certainly Mrs. Hilding doesn't leave home from year's end to year's end. Women who marry Indians pack their babies on their backs, take the other children, and go to all the dances while the men stay home and tend house" (163). They also come to better understand the sexual division of labor in an Indian ranchería, which reverses the divisions established in white culture. Thus only men would work on the interior decoration of the two women's house while, in a manner echoing Fuller's narrative, the white women's preoccupation with the ornamental is critically scrutinized by the practical-minded Indian women who run the business of daily life (172).

Gradually the women start attending to their professional duties, fashioning themselves now as "Innocents Abroad on the Professional Trail." The two schoolmarms open two Sunday schools and are properly equipped with horses. Their riding adventures provide a never-ending series of comic self-representations. They are not exactly ideal Sunday-school teachers, but "on every Sunday at nine, you may observe what were once considered the somewhat heathen members of the Episcopal Church of Somerville, New Jersey, in specklessly clean shirtwaists, mounted on their steeds" (89). Somewhat disrespectfully, they record singing " 'Onward, Christian Soldiers' and 'Little Children, Can You Tell' until the walls shake and the dust rises from the floor in clouds" (90). The singing is followed by Klamath drumming and song.

As soon as the two women hold school for the Klamath children, the narrators claim, they attract an unexpectedly large number of men and women. They explain the Indian women's fascination for arithmetic by their training as basket weavers, which teaches them a feeling for design (93).[86] Their scholars' thirst for knowledge and the speed with which they learn amaze their teachers. Mary teaches the Klamath men arithmetic, who by their fast intelligence soon surpass the instructor: "A wonderful time was had by all, that is, with one exception. While the class shouted with laughter and yelled and stamped as they competed for the answers, the unfortunate instructor, who has always been extremely poor at mental arithmetic, strove in mental anguish to arrive at the correct amount before anyone else could get there" (94).

Arnold and Reed's narrative suggests that there was not much that white people could teach the Indians on the Rivers. Studying geography and history American-style with her students even has its pitfalls for Mary, who finds that "the more I tell of the history and traditions of the whites, the more I question whether they are fit subjects on which in [sic] instruct the Indians." The class is shocked about what she tells them of ancient Rome, and fairy tales have equally dubious effects: "Lewis Hilding, aged twelve, wept over the story of Little Red Riding Hood and kept saying in a trembling voice, 'But the old woman. The wolf got the old woman.'" White history is too bloody, she concludes with characteristic understatement, after "the quiet, peaceful life we had here on the Rivers, with only an occasional panther and a few shootings and knifings at the Forks of Salmon" (97).

Interactions with Indians function on Indian terms, not those made by the field matrons (70). Assuming a native perspective, the two women look back to the first impression they must have made on the Klamath Indians: "When we had first come to Kot-e-meen, our manners were very bad. We talked too much. We lacked reserve and dignity. We were much too polite. Now we knew how to behave" (110). It is not the Indians who need to be reformed, but the white women.

White men on the Rivers, however, seem to think differently. When two white Forest Reserve men call on them, the women have to remap the boundaries of their world and adapt their behavior accordingly: "Now Mr. Hunter and Mr. Wilder are white men. They take us seriously, and coming to call on us was an occasion. The Indians do not take us at all seriously. We are just friends of theirs. But to Mr. Hunter and Mr. Wilder we are not only white women, we are ladies—the kind who have Sunday schools, and never say a bad word, and rustle around in a lot of silk petticoats." The two women have some difficulties conforming to these expectations, yet they do the best they can and "listen to what they say and try to act as though we never, never did such unladylike things as ride trails and cross rivers" (181). Womanhood represents a flexible code of behavior, an act performed differently in different situations. White men, especially, impose rigid standards of behavior on women. But then, traveling through white man's country each time confronts them with yet another part of the gender ideology: "Any man who travels in this country can be sure of warmth and comfort and companionship, although maybe a little unsavory. But women have not much chance in this white man's country" (250).

Increasingly they refer to themselves as Indians, claiming that "when it comes to a trouble or a quarrel, Mabel and I are not white. We are Indian" (224). Yet when they change their place of activity from Kot-e-meen to I-ees-i-rum in Karok country, they feel extremely white. The villagers make them feel that they belong "to a different race" (167). Soon, however, they are befriended by an older Klamath man, and Indian visitors drift in and out of their house again (170). At I-ees, the men in particular enjoy singing the hymns at Sunday school, having little need of Mary's and Mabel's guiding voices. And the singing is a far greater success than it ever was at Kot-e-meen: "But the Lord have mercy on the people who wrote the words in our Episcopal hymnbook. They will not do. They simply will not do. 'Veiled in time the Godhead see, Hail the Incarnate Deity.' When the Indians are completely stampeded, we hold up everything and compose entirely new words. The Lord Bishop better not try visiting this parish." These irreverent women were certainly unlikely missionaries. Instead of converting and Americanizing Indians, their Sunday school effects the opposite: "Suddenly we did not feel white at all. We felt Indian, just as we had felt at Kot-e-meen" (173).

By the end of their narrative, Arnold and Reed have become a part of the Klamath people. When they refute the idea of a special Indian "odor" repeatedly addressed by western travelers, they include themselves in the stereotyped group (219). Although as government officials they are charged to "look out for things" during the performance of a ceremonial dance in order to avoid and avert bloodshed, they seem more interested in the dance itself, immersing themselves, in a manner reminiscent of Summerhayes' account, in a spectacle of sight and sound that is subtly described as an erotically charged experience: "The naked, gleaming bodies, the gorgeous headdresses, the wavering white deerskins, with their bright beadwork tongues, and the deep guttural chant made our breath come quick. There was an excitement in it that we had never felt before" (279). Detaching themselves from the maternalist implications of their official task, they cast themselves as non-interventionist presences who avoid interfering with tribal ceremonial practices.

The two women present themselves not only as unlikely missionaries but also as unlikely government officials. It is certainly not in keeping with Indian Service regulations that they join a hunting party outside of the hunting season. They explain that they are "not much in sympathy with the game laws as they affect the Indian. To our mind, the Indian's hunting code is much better than the white man's. No Indian kills for sport or can understand such a point of view. He kills only for food, and he safeguards the game in his district much more effectively than does the white man's law" (98). In the same way, Arnold and Reed can barely restrain themselves from joining in the Klamath fun of gambling: "If we had not been field matrons and representatives of the Government, not to mention our somewhat tenuous relations with the bishop and his forty Bibles, we would have bet the bottom dollar in our little buckskin bag" (108). They even attempt to back Indian gambling in order to distract Indians from attending white dances which, in their opinion, tend to support rather low moral standards.

In times of conflict, of Indian "growls," the two women are called upon to help in the settling of trouble. But irony barely veils their feelings of inadequacy. Their white authority is especially demanded in medical and legal cases, the very fields in which they, and white women in general, lacked expertise. Ultimately their interventions are those of the powerless with inadequate access to medical and legal knowledge and authority. As field matrons, they ironically represent white law among Indians, the very law which keeps them as women powerless within white society—where they are mainly subjects, not agents, of the law. Nevertheless, they have to uphold at least a semblance of authority. They apply ingenuity: "It might be white law that we represented but we approached it with Indian tactics" (191).

One of these tactics is listening. Indian voices are heard so often that at times the narrators themselves shift to the Klamath Indian way of speaking English—in a version that is, of course, already translated by and through the white women. Sometimes native voices may even win over white voices. For example, an Indian man's rationalization of the custom of paying money for his future wife must appear plausible to both narrators and readers, just as a similar explanation had convinced Alice Fletcher: " 'You see,' he pointed out, 'you must have a good deal of regard for a woman if you are willing to pay money for her. . . . Now white way you only pay two dollars for a woman, and you pay it to the Government instead of to her family. You can't have much respect for a woman that you can get for two dollars' " (198). But in land-claims issues, the superior power of white men has to be conceded; in white man's country the Indian hardly has a chance (267). There the white women's power to defend Indians amounts to almost nothing: "Was there any chance at all for the Indian in this white man's country?" (271).

After almost two years, the two women are ordered away from the Rivers, hoping they will be able to come back "if, by any wild chance, the Indian Department should approve our plan of a much broader method of meeting the needs of the Indian on the Klamath. But this is quite uncertain" (298). What these needs might actually have been is never revealed. Rather, Arnold and Reed focus on their own need for interactions with Indians, and it would have been interesting to hear the Indian story of the two women's stay in Klamath land. Lucy Thompson mentions their activities only once, suggesting that the two field matrons were more actively interventionist than they cared to admit: they were closing down the liquor sale to Indians.[87] How much did the women actually change in Indian country? And how much were they changed when they left? The end of the book does not provide any clues: "We were no longer members of the Steve family or the Essie family. . . . We were white people in the white man's country. We were down below" (313).

The women who wrote about their experiences in the Indian Service took a critical stance toward the rhetoric of both the home mission and Indian reform, focusing as much on personal growth through learning as on the transformation of tribal people. In their narratives, all of them written in the twentieth century, the vocabulary of self-control used by, for example, the memoirists of army life is abandoned. The power of institutional authority invested in their own selves replaces the focus of earlier writers on the power of internalized mechanisms of control, and is in turn contested by discourses of femininity and the quest for the self. In addition, some of them describe an experience of transculturation.[88] Finally, as these women's western narratives show, female self-representations are closely connected to the description of Indian-white interactions, which challenge clear-cut boundaries of race and culture.[89]

Reminiscing the Old West, Creating the New

As this study demonstrates, women's western narratives reacted to, contributed to, and generated a whole range of cultural discourses on westward expansion and the American West. There was no single, unified "male" western narrative that women writers could refer to as a model or as a target. Rather, the way Americans represented westward expansion and the West to themselves seems to have been part of a series of cultural narratives that were kindled and fed continuously by diverse and changing cultural concerns. Seen through women's western accounts, the American West emerges as a fiercely contested cultural terrain. Fought over in fact as well as in fiction, it was as much about control as it was about freedom, as much about women as it was about men, as much about the exploitation of nature as it was about its preservation, as much about white hegemony as it was about cultural pluralism.

These various strands of the story of the American West came together at a particular moment in history—around the turn of the twentieth century—and emerged, seemingly frozen in a popular formula, as what we know as the genre of the Western. Despite its remarkable formulaic persistency, this western genre nevertheless continued to incorporate and reflect the various and changing cultural discourses that generated it in the first place, and women writers continued to bring the West alive in their stories of life and travel in the region.

As I have emphasized repeatedly, many of the texts I discussed were written in the twentieth century and engaged in some way or another with a popular western formula. It is also clear that women writers had conflicted relations with "wild" West conventions, as evident in their preoccupation with issues of control (over self and others), cultural development, and personal quests. The narratives of women in the frontier army steadfastly resisted the romance associated with cowboys or outlaws, while others like Arnold and Reed parodied its conventions, replacing it with accounts of intercultural encounters, even examples of transculturation.

To be sure, the first decades of the twentieth century brought forth a large number of women's western novels and stories—I am thinking here especially of the novels of Willa Cather, Dorothy Scarborough, Edna Ferber, and of other women's prairie and frontier novels.[90] But women also continued the tradition of what I have called women's "western narratives" in the form of personal accounts that engage with and contribute to twentieth-century (men's and women's) western writing. Women writers like Mary Austin, Ida Meacham Strobridge, and Mabel Dodge Luhan became major voices in establishing the Southwest as a distinct cultural region by writing essays of personal encounters with Southwestern landscapes and cultures.[91] Others remained minor contributors to the western story, but their voices were appreciated by smaller, local audiences, and some reached a larger audience with their reminiscences of life and travel in the Old West. Significantly, these texts continued to exhibit, with some modifications, the discursive constraints and rhetorical strategies that mark the accounts of women travelers and settlers, army women, and teachers and missionaries on Indian reservations discussed in my study. Most of the narratives seem to fall into two categories: those that continue to dramatize the story of an eastern woman, most often a young bride, going west,[92] and those that describe growing up female in the Old West, bringing new narrative paradigms and angles of vision to the story of women's engagement with the rhetoric of west-ward expansion.[93]

Many of these texts locate themselves in reference to the popular literature of the "wild" West, drawing on its romantic and nostalgic elements at the same time that they aim to revise stereotypes, especially with respect to western women's lives and work. Many texts also focus on the representation and defense of western masculinity, defining themselves in relation to chivalric, gallant cow-punchers. Women who wrote about growing up female in the Old West often used the trope of the double life to describe the contradictions between their feminine roles as both cowgirls and as educated "ladies."

Women who grew up and lived on the frontier in the 1870s and 1880s had as much to tell as their predecessors, but many of those who wrote their reminiscences in the 1920s were forced to realize that the receptivity of audience and publishers for their personal stories had, at least temporarily, vanished. Alice Baldwin, who accompanied her officer husband to the Indian frontier in 1867, encountered difficulties in publishing her memoirs—and then published them only as an appendix to her husband's life story. Lou Roberts, who wrote the story of her life with a Texas Ranger, and Ella Elgar Bird Dumont, a Texas woman who experienced the changing fortunes of the hunting and cattle frontier in Texas, both tried unsuccessfully to publish their reminiscences in the late 1920s, and neither of the memoirs was published in the authors' lifetimes. Lily Klasner's reminiscences of her childhood and youth in New Mexico before and during the famous Lincoln County War seem to have experienced the same fate. Written between 1925 and 1929, they were not published until 1972. Mary Hallock Foote's reminiscences of life in California, Colorado, and Idaho mining camps in the 1870s and 1880s, also written in the 1920s, were also declined by publishers.

The writings of women like Sharlot Hall, an Arizona ranch-woman, poet, and historian, reflect a need for reconciling two different Wests, which are related to some women's divided roles as female cultural critics and western promoters. Although in her private writings, Hall describes the ranch West as culturally barren and deeply patriarchal, in her public writings Hall extols Arizona as a new land full of opportunities. Like Frances Fuller Victor, she seems to have found no place for feminism in her historical and promotional work.[94] Her travel narratives, guided by the intention to put Arizona on the map, naturalize the territory and aim to trigger desire for its untapped resources. In the process, discourses of femininity (and feminism) are suppressed. Nevertheless, the female traveler and narrator cannot retreat completely behind a statistical, objectivist language, continuously establishing her presence as an opinionated, enthusiastic observer and rambler in the country.[95] In Lilian Whiting's promotional travel narrative of 1906, the narrator-traveler is even authorized as a 'he' or 'one.' This refusal, or difficulty, of women writers to continue to pose as gendered subjects is paralleled by the tendency in western women's accounts to extol male role models to the exclusion of their mothers' worlds.[96]

Although discourses of femininity may have lost their hegemony in these texts, they have not lost their influence as discursive constraints. They have, however, lost their subversive potential within the framework of discourses of westward expansion and empire building. With the exception of Mary Austin's essays, stories, and autobiographical writings, discourses of femininity had not yet been replaced by the language of feminism in women's western writing of the early twentieth century. And as Austin's example shows, the fashioning of a feminist persona in her autobiography does not counterbalance her consistent celebration and naturalization of Anglo-American westward expansion. Even if this persona, in the manner of her female predecessors, seeks out Indian knowledge and aims to create a softer, more culturally sensitive version of white westering by entering into personal relations with Indian people, she still needs to establish her superiority as a cultural authority.[97]

Although I do not lament the passing of constricting discourses of femininity in women's western writings (which is an isolated phenomenon at best), I have aimed to point to their contradictory potential both to subvert and reinforce colonialist discourses. I would suggest that the same applies to the present-day language of feminism, which still has to critically face its own legacy of racialist and colonialist exclusions and incorporations of minority men and women in its versions of the American national narrative of westward expansion. The exclusive focus on gender can veritably lead down a blind alley, reducing the complexity of relations within and between cultures to the sex-gender system.

I believe that the study of women's western narratives within the frameworks of both the discourses of femininity/feminism and the discourses of westward expansion and empire building is relevant and profitable for American studies in general, enabling us to gain new insights into the complex negotiations that were generated in American culture by the fact and idea of territorial expansion. Expansionism required the continuous and ongoing mapping of the territories of culture and nationality, of gender, race, and class. American culture itself emerges not as a unified whole but as a shifting set of relations and dialogues between margins and centers that demand negotiations of power and authority. Women's western narratives draw our attention to the continuous significance of America's margins—women, minorities, cultural hinterlands—for the creation and maintenance of its cultural centers as well as the definition of multiple and often conflicted American identities.

Conclusion

In my study of women's western writings and the discourses of westward expansion, I have avoided restricting women's texts to a single, unified narrative, aiming to do justice to the heterogeneity of the material and its discursive frameworks. What has, nevertheless, surprised me is the remarkable persistence of networks of allusions, motifs, and tropes, of common constraints and concerns that seem to weave disparate women's narratives about the West together—private and public texts, diaries and reminiscences, contemporary fiction and memoirs written long after the fact. Discourses of femininity surface as pressures and constraints in the production and reception of most of these texts, leading to divisions of labor between male and female writers on the West, and resulting in a tradition of feminine apologia and professions of marginality. Women writers profess to restrict themselves to a personal, subjective, and necessarily limited vision, and to distance themselves from politics, statistics, and imperial visions of adventurous enterprise. Set in the context of westward expansion and empire building, however, their poses of innocence and marginality can be interpreted as strategies of an "anti-conquest," which Mary Pratt has identified as the basis of European accounts of travel in the realm of colonialism.

Nevertheless, a closer look at the representational practices in women's western narratives reveals a basic inconsistency and instability resulting from the dynamic relation between problems of female self-representation and the representation of western people and landscapes. Women writers persistently avoided the implications of mastery contained in sweeping, panoramic visions of landscapes: women on the overland trails, like explorers placing themselves on hills and mountain tops, looked back instead of forward, transforming the "prospects" stretched before them into a landscape of memory. Denying any desire for control—except for the control over their own powers of representation—their attempts to adopt scientific or artistic modes of description often ended in declarations of incompetence or in self-parodic mockery. These female writers exposed themselves as locatable, embodied presences in their texts, which contrasts with the way male writers fashioned themselves as explorers, hiding as disembodied presences behind the objectivist language of scientific authority or the mode of merely visual contact with the land.

What is also remarkably persistent in women's western narratives is the configuration of the West as an extremely insecure terrain where American culture and politics had a rather precarious hold. Whether in the accounts of overland travelers or army travelers, representations of western nature are clearly related to the Native American presence on the land. I have tried to underscore this link in each chapter by moving from the discussion of women's western landscapes to that of women's encounters with western people. What struck me most about women's representations of these intercultural encounters was the recurrence of tropes like the "darkening-of-the-window" scene, which address the problematics not only of the white presence in the Indian country, but also of the female gaze, and which destabilize personal as well as cultural visions of imperial control.

Other recurrent strategies that counter discourses of female powerlessness are the reduction of Indian people to dress and appearance, the link drawn between race and aesthetics, the description of Indian women as drudges and slaves, and the representation of Indian men as effeminate dandies or aesthetic objects—strategies that distance and disempower Native American people as well as their cultures. Especially in post–Civil War narratives, the "first white woman" topos emerges as a powerful tool that establishes white hegemony in Indian country by highlighting the respectable and legitimate foundations of white expansion. Women writers thus adopted many representational practices that can be identified as part of colonialist discourses, using them in the service of their own empowerment. In this context, the rhetoric of women's rights in connection with the representation of Indian women often fulfills rather dubious functions. Detracting from both white patriarchy and white colonialism, it deflects attention from the relations of unequal power between Indians and whites. Nevertheless, due to the unstable foundations of female strategies of self-fashioning and self-authorizing, women's narratives of personal encounters with Indian men and women also potentially disrupt these assumptions of imperial control by representing Indians as speakers, commentators, and agents who asserted power over their own lives as well as those of white men and women.

White women, as presences in and as writers on the West, were instrumental in the cultural task of defining the boundaries and hierarchies of race, gender, nationality, and culture in the American nation. Women's western narratives, whether they reached a larger audience or only a private circle of addressees, participated in this project in a unique way that affirmed white women's difference as well as their implication in the national enterprise. The women's texts I have analyzed have directed my attention away from simplistic assumptions about the differences between men's and women's writing, guiding the discussion towards a closer consideration of the complex issues of power and authority within texts, whether written by men or women. They have also helped me to think about American territorial expansion and the American national narrative in less exceptionalist, more globalist terms.

In its insistence on issues of power, control, and authority and in its concern with representational practices, my study is obviously informed by the increasing focus within recent literary and cultural studies on issues of language, representation, and power. This has also led me to draw attention to the ways in which power inscribes itself in women's texts in the form of discursive pressures and rhetorical tropes. At the same time, I have found myself wondering, throughout the whole study, about the ideological implications of my argument: if power writes itself into our language, how can we resist, and, more important, how can we take responsibility for the violence implied in our speech acts and, consequently, our behavior? If both discourses of femininity and discourses of empire building persistently write themselves into women's texts, is there no way out from this circular entrapment, this "complicity," in discourse? Are the primary structuring elements of women's discourse—especially the persistent practice of othering, of masking history and racial conflict through gender conflict—essentially, as Peter Mason has argued in the context of European representations of America, a reflection of "the primary structuring elements of discourse as we know it"?[98]

In this context, Mary Pratt's concepts of the anti-conquest and contact zones have proven to be of inestimable value, helping me to put women's discourses into a broader perspective and to continuously conceptualize and address matters of responsibility, choice, and agency in women's texts. I have come to look at discourses of both femininity and empire building not as ideological constraints imposed from above, but as rhetorical pressures and imaginative possibilities that were constantly addressed, rationalized, engaged, and resisted, even created, in women's narratives. Like women's identities, women's texts are subject to control, positioned ambiguously within systems of power and authority. They are therefore also subject to their writers' belief in their own agency and freedom. Even if women writers profess to have limited claims to authority, they nevertheless authorize themselves in their works both as members of their culture, and, especially, as individuals.

Notes

Introduction

1. H. N. Smith, "Symbol and Idea," 27–28. See also Brumm, *Geschichte und Wildnis*, 23.

2. Greenfield, *Narrating Discovery*, 1–3.

3. See Lewis, *American Adam*, 1, 5–6.

4. See Dippie, "American Wests"; Pomeroy, "Toward a Reorientation." The idea of the West as a colony of the East has been critically reconsidered in recent years by the "new western history," which sees the West as "a scene of intense struggles over power and hierarchy, not only between the races but also between classes, genders, and other groups within white society." See Worster, "Beyond the Agrarian Myth," 21.

5. See Miller, "The Romantic Dilemma in American Nationalism and the Concept of Nature," in *Nature's Nation*, 199, 204; Rogin, "Nature as Politics," 5–30, esp. 13; Mitchell, *Witnesses*, xiv–xv, 5, 9. Lee Clark Mitchell has identified, in the writings of nineteenth-century Americans, a deep sense of foreboding, an "apprehension of doom," and a feeling of ambivalence toward westward expansion even among those who participated "in the nation's triumphant conquest of the wilderness." He argues that the contradictions of empire building created "alternative attitudes" among Americans who increasingly deplored the wastefulness inherent in pioneering, attitudes that eventually opened the way to preservationist policies and to an appreciation of the diversity and autonomy of Native American cultures. See also Fussell, *Frontier*, 210.

6. Greenfield, *Narrating Discovery*, 1–2.

7. Rogin, *Fathers and Children*, xvi, 297.

8. Slotkin, *Regeneration through Violence*, 4–5.

9. Slotkin, *Fatal Environment*, 52–53, 79–80, 30, 47. See also Pearce, *Savagism and Civilization*. Roy Harvey Pearce has shown how the cultural creation of an American self, and of the specificity of American national identity, from colonial times into the mid-nineteenth century, has depended on the Indian as an idea. In this he has anticipated recent Americanist and cultural studies that have pointed to the notion of "the other" and to negative class, race, and gender categories as important factors in shaping national identities. See also Pease, "National Identities," and Parker et al., *Nationalisms and Sexualities.* Slotkin is obviously indebted not only to Pearce, but also to Roland Barthes, whose definition of myth as "depoliticized

speech" and as a discourse that "transforms history into nature" provides a guiding premise for his study (Barthes, *Mythologies,* 143, 129).

10. Ickstadt, "Painting," 3–4.

11. Rogin, "Nature as Politics," 15. Rogin contends that both pastoral and wilderness ideals "liberate the white male in agrarian space from social conflict in historical time" (16–17).

12. Perry Miller, Albert K. Weinberg, and Sacvan Bercovitch identify the rhetoric of Manifest Destiny as a persistent trend in American history and as part of a cultural consensus. Frederick Merk assumes a nationalistic propaganda machine operated by certain influential spokespersons of the era. Slotkin's study exposes as mythmakers a controlling entrepreneurial group within a metropolitan-based expansion system, in whose interest the West was systematically conquered and managed. Laurence M. Hauptman points to the impact of curriculum materials on the "indoctrination of state values" in schoolbooks as ideal vehicles for transmitting the mythology of the frontier. See Miller, *Errand into the Wilderness;* Weinberg, *Manifest Destiny;* Bercovitch, "Fusion and Fragmentation"; Merk, *Manifest Destiny;* Hauptman, "Mythologizing Westward Expansion."

13. Kolodny, "Turning the Lens," 331.

14. Bercovitch, "Problem of Ideology," 635.

15. Bercovitch, *American Jeremiad,* 155–60, 180. See also Girgus, *Desire and the Political Unconscious.*

16. Mary Pratt has critically highlighted the ideas of community that underlie most of the thinking about language, communication, and culture that is done in the academy. Descriptions of interactions between people, she claims, "readily take it for granted that the situation is governed by a single set of rules or norms shared by all participants." See Pratt, "Arts of the Contact Zone," 37, 38.

17. Jehlen, "Archimedes," 579.

18. Fiedler, *Vanishing American,* 50.

19. See Baym, "Melodramas."

20. Stegner, *The Sound of Mountain Water,* 195.

21. Graulich, " 'O Beautiful for Spacious Guys,' " 187.

22. Ben-Zvi, " 'Home Sweet Home,' " 219.

23. Kolodny, *Lay of the Land,* 6, 8, 14, 22, 58. In a work less concerned with the frontier myth than with the significance of American masculinity in the literature of the American Renaissance, David Leverenz has argued that the classic male writers of the tradition find their most original voices in responding to the pressures and conflicts of American manhood. See Leverenz, *Manhood,* 3.

24. Ben-Zvi, " 'Home Sweet Home,' " 220.

25. Lander, "Eve among the Indians," 198, 202–3.

26. Smith-Rosenberg, *Disorderly Conduct,* 107–8.

27. In a recent article, Carroll Smith-Rosenberg points in this direction by establishing eighteenth-century white women writers' agency in authorizing Euro-Americans as true Americans and de-legitimizing Indian claims to America. See her "Subject Female."

28. Jane Tompkins has pointed out that the privileging of certain modes of male writing banished the phenomenally successful female writers like Harriet Beecher Stowe. Tompkins assumes the existence of two distinct, gendered writing and publishing cultures, especially in her study of the Western, excluding women as authors of the genre. See her *Sensational Designs,* 3–39, 122–46, 147–85. See also Tompkins, *West of Everything,* 37–45; "West of Everything."

29. See Jeffrey, *Frontier Women*; Faragher, *Women and Men*; Schlissel, *Women's Diaries*; Myres, *Westering Women*; Riley, *Female Frontier, Women and Indians,* "Women on the Great Plains," and *Women in the West*; Armitage and Jameson, *Women's West*; Schlissel, Ruiz, and Monk, *Western Women*; Norwood and Monk, *The Desert is No Lady*; Allen, *Traveling West*; Cronon et al., "Women and the West"; Malone, *Women on the Texas Frontier*; Thurman, *Women in Oklahoma*; and Levy, *They Saw the Elephant.*

30. Susan Armitage concludes that women's (private) texts construct an alternative to the (public) male vision of the frontier: "Women's literature will illuminate the private, domestic, interior side of the frontier experience which the myth has ignored" ("Women's Literature," 10). See also Armitage, "Through Women's Eyes," 9–18; Stoeltje, " 'A Helpmate for Man Indeed.' " On literary stereotypes of western women, see Atkins, "Women on the Farming Frontier"; Heatherington, "Romance Without Women"; Fairbanks, *Prairie Women*; Meldrum, "Women in Western American Fiction"; Armitage, "Reluctant Pioneers," in Stauffer and Rosowski, *Women,* 40–51; McKnight, "American Dream, Nightmare Underside," in Lee and Lewis, *Women,* 25–44.

31. See Pascoe, "Western Women," 41; Fryer, "Anti-Mythical Journey"; Hampsten, *Read This Only to Yourself*; Andreadis, "True Womanhood Revisited"; Schlissel et al., *Far From Home*; Jeffrey, *Frontier Women*; Faragher, *Women and Men*; Schlissel, *Women's Diaries.*

Myres, in *Westering Women,* is rather critical of this interpretation. Earlier studies on western women were motivated by the same questions. William Forrest Sprague (*Women and the West*)and Dee Brown (*Gentle Tamers*) see the emancipatory effect of the frontier on women in the fact that they had been accorded the vote in western states earlier than in the East, and in the idea that women gained in prestige in the West on account of their initially small numbers. Both write the history of western women as a continuous and progressive history of emancipation.

32. Personal Narratives Group, ed., *Interpreting Women's Lives,* 7, 8. On women's private writings, see also Buss, " 'The Dear Domestic Circle.' "

33. Brodzki and Schenck, *Life/Lines,* x. See also Benstock, *Private Self*; Smith, "Who's Talking/Who's Talking Back?"; Lensink, "Diary"; Culley, *A Day at a Time;* Hampsten, *Read This*; Gannett, *Gender and the Journal.*

34. In contrast, Elizabeth Hampsten (*Read This*) found in western women's letters a negation of the natural environment and of a regional sense of place. But as Vera Norwood points out, Kolodny's and Hampsten's analyses are not so different, "for each finds women's basic languagescape comprised of the same metaphors: the interior circle of home and family." In expansion of Kolodny's argument, Norwood suggests that women were "engaged in a 'muted' discussion of personal power acceptable only in the context of their submission to roles husband and father allowed them." The fact that a woman writes mostly about family life in her diary "may not be taken to imply that she has no interest in or attachment to the outside world, but only that she is restricted from expressing that attachment by the form in which she is communicating" ("Women's Place," 163–64).

35. See Davidson, *Revolution.*

36. The term "adventurous enterprise" was used, in reference to Washington Irving, by Peter Antelyes in his *Tales of Adventurous Enterprise.*

37. Greenfield, *Narrating Discovery,* 10. See also Hulme, *Colonial Encounters,* 2. In recent years, especially since the formal end of European colonialism, a new field of cross-cultural study, commonly termed postcolonial studies, has devoted

itself to re-examining the history, politics, psychology, and language of colonization. In his pioneering work on orientalism, Edward Said has pointed to the ways in
which Westerners have imagined other cultures and have created, in their academic
and imaginative writings, the subjects of imperialism and colonialism. He has also
helped to show how the conventions of imperialism continue to linger after the end
of European colonialism. In his recent *Culture and Imperialism,* Said has expanded
his focus by demonstrating how culture—in different forms, but especially in the
form of the canonical novels of the Western tradition—and politics cooperated to
produce a system of domination, a "consolidated vision" that affirmed the European right and obligation to rule. For an excellent introduction to modern European
and Euro-American colonial discourse, see Spurr, *Rhetoric of Empire.*

38. Greenfield, *Narrating Discovery,* 11. See also Martin Green, *Great American
Adventure,* viii.

39. Greenfield, *Narrating Discovery,* 2; Pratt, *Imperial Eyes,* 4, 7.

40. Kolodny, "Letting Go," 9, 13, 5. David J. Weber (*Spanish Frontier*) also defines frontiers as zones of interaction between different cultures, as places where
the cultures of the invader and the invaded contend with one another and with their
physical environment.

41. Greenfield, *Narrating Discovery,* 106; Pratt, *Imperial Eyes,* 201–8; see also
Goetzmann (*Exploration and Empire,* 224), who links the increasing scale of the
work of landscape artists who accompanied expeditions after the Civil War to the
new purposes and technologies of exploration itself. Thus the huge canvases,
which often provided panoramic views of the landscape, can be attributed to the
new physical vantage points from which the explorers saw the country—as surveying parties atop lofty mountains.

42. Greenfield, *Narrating Discovery,* 83–84, 102. See also Spengemann, *Adventurous Muse,* 49, 69.

43. Goetzmann, *Exploration and Empire;* Pomeroy, *In Search of the Golden West.*

44. Balandier, *Sociologie Actuelle,* quoted in Spurr, *Rhetoric of Empire,* 5–6.

45. Pamela Regis has shown that the scientific discourse of natural history that
developed in North America in the late eighteenth century was an important force
in the de-historicization and naturalization of America and its indigenous inhabitants. Natural-history description specifically incorporates human beings as natural
objects. The representations of human beings produced by this method have come
to be called "manners-and-customs" descriptions, which as Mary Pratt has noted
(as antecedents of ethnography proper) "codify difference" and "fix the Other in a
timeless present." Pratt points to the mutual engagement between natural history
and European economic and political expansionism. Bruce Greenfield has found
natural historical description, together with more personal narrative modes of representation, at work in narratives of discovery in North America, and recent studies
dealing with the interactions between literary and scientific discourses in the nineteenth century also point to the ongoing legacy of the discourse of natural history in
nineteenth-century literature. See Regis, *Describing Early America,* 3, 11, 23; Pratt,
"Scratches," 120, 121, 127; Pratt, *Imperial Eyes,* 15, 38–39, 33–34, 32; Greenfield,
Narrating Discovery, 12, 15–16, 26; Scholnick, *American Literature and Science.*

Part 1

1. See Martineau, *Society in America* (1837) and *Retrospect of Western Travel*
(1838); Trollope, *Domestic Manners* (1832).

2. In addition, Holley kept a diary (*Texas Diary*) of her second stay in Texas from 1835 to 1838, in which she was less enthusiastic about Texas as a terrestrial paradise.

3. Touristic travel was made possible by the completion in 1825 of the Erie Canal, which opened Minnesota, Wisconsin, Michigan, and other Great Lakes states to settlement.

Chapter 1

1. The same strategy of understatement and relationing of feminine writing as opposed to masculine writing is adopted by Catharine M. Sedgwick in her novel *Hope Leslie* (1827), in which she sets her work off from James Fenimore Cooper's *Last of the Mohicans* (1826). Sedgwick underrates her own writing by seeing herself "at an immeasurable distance" from the "mighty master of fiction," who has at his disposal "magician's enchantments," while she herself has to be guided by "accuracy" and "details" (143). The only merit she claims "is that of a patient investigation of all the materials that could be obtained" (6). See also Jameson, *Winter Studies,* viii, xi.

2. Kirkland's stated model was the English writer Mary Russell Mitford's *Our Village* (1824–32), a series of sketches of village life. As Sandra Zagarell has pointed out in her introduction to *A New Home* (xxviii), the village sketch provided an alternative to romantic-based formulas and dramatic plots. Developed primarily by women, the new genre displayed what Zagarell terms a "protoethnographic sensitivity," an observation that can also be applied to the regionalist writings of Sarah Orne Jewett, Rose Terry Cooke, and Mary Wilkins Freeman. See also Elizabeth Ammons' introduction to the work of Rose Terry Cooke in *'How Celia Changed Her Mind,'* xx–xxi. On regionalism as a female tradition, see Douglas, "Literature of Impoverishment," and Donovan, *New England Local Color Literature.*

3. See Hoffman, *Winter in the West,* and Judge James Hall, *Letters from the West.*

4. Stevenson, *Victorian Women,* 9. See also Birkett, *Spinsters Abroad.*

5. See Robinson, *Wayward Women,* x.

6. Foucault, "Truth and Power," in *Foucault Reader,* 61. In his *History of Sexuality,* Foucault claims that in the confessional, "the agency of domination does not reside in the one who speaks (for it is he who is constrained), but in the one who listens and says nothing; not in the one who knows and answers, but in the one who questions and is not supposed to know" (61–62).

7. Gillian Brown argues for a discussion of domestic ideology not only in the context of women's culture and literature but also as a development within its supposed antitype: the history of individualism, allegedly a male domain. Historicizing domestic ideology "as a passage in liberal individualism" demonstrates the role of domestic ideology in updating and reshaping individualism within nineteenth-century American market society (*Domestic Individualism,* 1).

8. Stevenson, *Victorian Women,* 11.

9. Ibid., 6.

10. Aiken, *Isak Dinesen,* 9, 39.

11. Lawrence Buell ("American Literary Emergence") has even considered nineteenth-century American literature as bearing the marks of a postcolonial literature, which leads him, however, to play down the colonialist implications of American political, cultural, and literary history.

12. Mills, *Discourses of Difference,* 23.

13. This unfavorable reception must have confronted Kirkland with the dangers of writing about dwelling in the West, especially as a woman writer, still an anomaly in nineteenth-century American society. Kolodny has noted that Kirkland composed her next book, *Forest Life,* under constraints unknown to its predecessor, which caused her to subdue her satire and apply more self-restraint (*Land Before Her,* 148–49). See also Zagarell's introduction, xvii.

14. Quoted in Osborne, *Caroline Kirkland,* 52–55.

15. H. N. Smith, *Virgin Land,* 263.

16. Ibid.

17. See Zagarell's introduction to *A New Home,* xxvii; Kolodny, *Land Before Her,* 133.

18. Authenticity and the claim to the true representation of the West have been continuous issues surrounding western writing since the early nineteenth century. Thus the self-proclaimed Westerner Daniel Drake had attacked the Easterner J. F. Cooper, and the New Englander James Freeman had taken the Westerner James Hall to task for ignorance of western character. See Edwin Fussell, *Frontier,* 13.

When Hall described his literary work as a Westerner in his *Legends of the West,* he promised "accurate descriptions of the scenery and population." Hall's protest against his *Wilderness and the War-Path* being bound together with Kirkland's *Western Clearings* (1845) is telling in this respect: "I beg you not to inflict so great an injury upon me, and so great a disgrace upon my book. *The Western Clearings* is a wretched composition—a vile piece of humbug. If the authoress was ever in the West, she has failed to convey the slightest idea of the country or its people" (quoted in Osborne, *Caroline Kirkland,* 81–82).

19. Zagarell, introduction, xxviii–xxix.

20. H. N. Smith, *Virgin Land,* 263.

21. Zagarell, introduction, xxxii.

22. H. N. Smith, *Virgin Land,* 251.

23. See Marx, "Pastoralism," 36–69.

24. Kolodny, *Land Before Her,* xiii.

25. Pratt, *Imperial Eyes,* 159–60.

26. See Pratt, 160–61.

27. See Welter, "Cult of True Womanhood," 165.

28. Zagarell, introduction, xxxv.

29. Ibid., xv–xvi; Welter, "Cult of True Womanhood," 152.

30. Linda Kerber has argued that the "cult" of true womanhood can mean "an ideology imposed on women, a culture created by women, a set of boundaries expected to be observed by women" ("Separate Spheres," 17–18). Domesticity was, as Robert L. Griswold put it, more of a "cultural system" than a dogmatic set of principles women slavishly adhered to ("Anglo Women," 15). And literary critics like Jane Tompkins and Joanne Dobson ("The Hidden Hand") have analyzed women's domestic novels in terms of the subtle ways in which novelists manipulated the conventions of both domesticity and the novel.

31. Cott, *Bonds of Womanhood.* See also Baker, "Domestication of Politics."

32. DuBois and Ruiz, introduction to *Unequal Sisters,* xiii. See also Gordon, "On 'Difference' "; Higginbotham, "African-American Women's History and the Metalanguage of Race."

33. See Hewitt, "Beyond the Search for Sisterhood," 2; Jensen and Miller, "Gentle Tamers"; Pascoe, "Western Women at the Crossroads." See also the articles in *Western Women: Their Land, Their Lives* and *The Women's West,* which expand the

traditional focus of the nineteenth-century frontier by including the experiences of American Indian women, Mexicanas, and Hispanas. For a critique of the feminist inclination to subsume all women into the sisterly category of "woman" despite differences of race, class, and historical condition, or on the other extreme, to establish the token image of the "Third World Woman," see Trinh, *Woman, Native, Other,* 79–116. Laura Donaldson has also drawn attention to the potential for violence and racism within feminist criticism's "denial of the diverse experiences and genders of the global community of women" (*Decolonizing Feminisms,* 2).

34. Kolodny, *Land Before Her,* 98–99. Kolodny sees this familial fantasy related to Farnham's biography: Eliza Burhans had early lost her mother and had been separated from her brother and sisters. In 1835 she followed her sister Mary to Illinois, where she married the New England attorney Thomas Jefferson Farnham. For these biographical details, see also Madeleine B. Stern's introduction to Eliza Farnham's *California In-Doors and Out,* x–xi.

35. Quoted in Fussell, *Frontier,* 182.

36. This judgment is probably based on her later work and on her reputation as an independent California farmer after the death of her husband in 1848, an experience described in *California In-Doors and Out* (1856). In another work, *Woman and Her Era* (1864), she asserts the theory of woman's (spiritual) superiority over man on account of the "higher complexity" of her organism.

37. Kolodny, *Land Before Her,* 104.

38. Farnham's naturalization and sentimentalization of Indian extinction resembles her husband's argument in one of his travel narratives. However, she seems to have resisted the imagery of natural violence implicit in his view of westward expansion. In 1843 he had written that the Indians of Illinois and Iowa "dwindle" away "at the approach of the whites. A melancholy fact. The Indians' bones must enrich the soil, before the plough of civilized man can open it." In the order of nature, he asserted, "the plough must bury the hunter." See Thomas Farnham, *Travels,* 146, 148.

39. Novak, *Nature and Culture,* 47.

40. See Fussell, *Frontier,* 184; Albert J. von Frank, *Sacred Game,* xii, vii, 114.

41. Kolodny, *Land Before Her,* 117–20.

42. Fuller here invokes the discussions led in 1830s and 1840s America about the linking of architecture with wilderness landscapes, and about the relation between nation, landscape, and architecture, which had its expression in the landscape gardener Downing's vision "of an America visually and morally defined through a union of picturesque landscape and architecture." See Foster, *Civilized Wilderness,* 63.

43. See White, "Trashing the Trails," 33–34.

44. See Bercovitch, "Fusion and Fragmentation."

45. See Mitchell, *Witnesses,* xiii–xiv.

46. Rosowski, "Margaret Fuller," 129.

47. See Antelyes, *Tales of Adventurous Enterprise,* 42.

48. See Billington, *Westward Expansion,* 299.

49. Maddox, *Removals,* 6, 10–11, 174, 176, 178.

50. Thoreau, *Maine Woods,* 133.

51. Maddox, *Removals,* 145.

52. Farnham, *Life in Prairie Land,* 173.

53. Babcock, " 'A New Mexican Rebecca,' " 403, 429.

54. Fuller rates Catlin's book as "far the best," finding him "true to the spirit of

the scene," while other travel narratives lack poetic force: "we believe the Indian cannot be looked at truly except by a poetic eye" (23). Irving's books have a "stereotype, second-hand air. . . . His scenery is only fit to be glanced at from dioramic distance; his Indians are academic figures only. He would have made the best of pictures, if he could have used his own eyes for studies and sketches" (24–25).

55. See Maddox, *Removals*, 132.

Chapter 2

1. See Schlissel, *Women's Diaries*, 19–20, 35; Kolodny, *Land Before Her*, 232; Starr, *Americans and the California Dream*, 3–19; Billington, *Westward Expansion*, 323–24.

2. Starr, *Americans and the California Dream*, 15, 21.

3. Annette Kolodny has pointed to the fact that throughout the 1850s, despite the habit of identifying that decade exclusively with the overland emigration, areas east of the Missouri River continued to be newly settled. Domestic novelists such as Maria Susanna Cummins refer to this emigration as the historical framework of their fiction. As in Kirkland's and other women's travel narratives, overland emigration is relegated to the background, "as if trying to consolidate imaginatively the meaning of what had already transpired" (Kolodny, *Land Before Her*, 229–30).

4. See Schlissel, *Women's Diaries*, 58.

5. In Fanny Fern's (Sara Willis Parton's) novel *Ruth Hall* (1855), one female character refuses to go to California with her husband and is deserted. When he finally asks her to send him the passage money for the journey home, she looks into her purse and hisses the word "N-e-v-e-r." See *Ruth Hall and Other Writings*, 107–9. Western expansion is only indirectly a family affair in most domestic novels. Maria Cummins, in *The Lamplighter* (1854), has only young, and mostly single, men go: "Among the wanderers, we hope,—ay, we believe that there is many a one who is actuated, not by the love of gold, the love of change, the love of adventure but by the love he bears his mother,—the earnest longing of his heart to save her from a life of toil and poverty" (118–19). The West is a "wilderness" which "has proved to many a greedy emigrant a land of falsehood and deceit." The gold rush is even associated with war: "You know how the war-cry went forth to all lands, and men of every name and nation brought their arms to the field of fortune" (422). See also Kolodny, *Land Before Her*, 161–226, on the way women writers of the 1850s chose the Midwest as the setting of their novels, thus distancing themselves from the emigration to the Far West.

6. Schlissel lists more than eight hundred diaries and day journals published or catalogued in archives (11). See also Myres, *Westering Women*, xix.

7. While Jeffrey and Schlissel suggest frontier women's continuity with the East, Myres argues that the western experience engendered new roles for women. See Jeffrey, *Frontier Women*, 26, 61–78; Myres, *Westering Women*, 7–11, 165, 269.

8. See especially Myres, *Westering Women*, 98–99.

9. See Schlissel, *Women's Diaries*, 111–14. Glenda Riley argues that as women's views of themselves changed as a result of their frontier experience, their images of Indians changed, too. Women, she argues, discarded stereotypes and prejudices about Indians more easily than men, and came to see that their prejudices about native life were unfounded. See *Women and Indians* xiii–xiv, 140–42, 164, 167–69.

10. Fender, *Plotting the Golden West*, 7–8.

11. See Schlissel, *Women's Diaries*, 10. Myres argues against Schlissel, estab-

lishing women as participants in the decision-making process (*Westering Women,* 99–102).

12. Before Lorena Hays went overland to California in 1853, she had read, besides novels and religious periodicals, "some in the beauties of Washington Irving," William Clark Larrabee's *Lectures on the Scientific Evidences of Natural and Revealed Religion* (1850), the memoirs of August Hermann Francke, Grace Greenwood's *Greenwood Leaves,* and John Charles Frémont's *Report to Congress.* A few years later, she read Elisha Kent Kane's *Arctic Exploration.* See Hays, *Land of Gold,* 67–69, 172, 275–76.

13. Gabriel, introduction to *A Frontier Lady,* xi.

14. Kate Dunlap records a similar incident in her diary of an 1864 journey to Montana, where an "old chief" forbids the emigrants to camp on the tribe's pasture, "claiming that all this land belonged to the Sioux, that God had given it to them and we must move. After a long debate with him and among ourselves we concluded to go on." Shortly afterwards, Dunlap notes how the picturesque sights along the way "fill the mind with wonder at the vastness and magnificence of God's creation," discrediting previous Indian claims by declaring the country to be God's creation (*Montana Gold Rush Diary,* B-16, B-18).

15. Fender, *Plotting the Golden West,* 92.

16. The tribal people on this next to last part of the journey along the Humboldt River, which included the Shoshoni, Paiute, and Ute, were considered among the most troublesome on the entire trail. They were usually lumped together by the emigrants under the epithet of "Digger Indians," since they subsisted primarily by digging for roots. See Myres, *Ho for California,* 165.

17. See Greenfield, *Narrating Discovery,* 73; Turner, *Frontier in American History,* 3.

18. Fender, *Plotting the Golden West,* 89.

19. See Carpenter, "Trip Across the Plains," 155.

20. See Schlissel, *Women's Diaries,* 187, 197. See also Frances Fuller Victor's title story in her collection *The New Penelope* (1877).

21. For this view of the western journey, see Mansur, "MS Letters" 48–57; Megquier, *Apron Full of Gold.*

22. Schlissel, *Women's Diaries,* 111, 115.

23. Ward, *Prairie Schooner Lady,* 65–66, 168, 76.

24. Sallie Hester reports a similar experience: "When we left St. Joe my mother had to be lifted in and out of our wagons; now she walks a mile or two without stopping, and gets in and out of the wagons as spry as a young girl" ("Diary of a Pioneer Girl," quoted in Levy, *They Saw the Elephant,* 6).

25. See Norwood, *Made From This Earth,* xix, chapter 1.

26. Mary Richardson Walker, "Diary," 4.

27. Pratt, *Imperial Eyes,* 201ff.

28. See Rob Wilson, *American Sublime,* 69ff., 74, 4.

29. Ibid., 37.

30. Luzena Wilson, "49er," quoted in Levy, *They Saw the Elephant,* 4.

31. Frink, "Journal," quoted in Levy, *They Saw the Elephant,* 3–4.

32. Schlissel, *Women's Diaries,* 77.

33. Riley (*Women and Indians,* 167–69) argues that women routinely bartered and traded with Indians in their attempts to provide food, clothing, and other commodities for those people who depended on their succor, and that they often formed relationships for mutual support. Although I basically agree with her—the

emigrants' dependence on Indian support is much more central in women's than in men's diaries—I want to emphasize that women's diaries also make us aware of the fact that these interactions did not take place in a power vacuum.

34. Lorena Hays seems to have been in the same process of sorting out her impressions when she remarked on the Kansa or Caw Indians: "They are quite civilized, only live 2 or 3 miles from Kanzas. The women are in town every day. They get drunk" (*Land of Gold,* 148). Of course, this phenomenon must be considered in the context of the event-oriented, immediate, and always incomplete nature of a travel diary. See Margo Culley's introduction to *A Day at a Time,* 20–21.

35. Riley, *Women and Indians,* 131–32, 182, 197.

36. On the politics of race and sexual morality in a colonial context, see Stoler, "Making Empire Respectable."

37. See Person, "American Eve," 670; Kolodny, *Land Before Her,* xv, 70–71; Maddox, *Removals,* 96–98, 110–11, 171.

38. Lorena Hays, when walking some way ahead of the wagons with her mother, met a group of Sioux men who apparently enjoyed the women's fright. One of them, she records, "wished to frighten me seeing that I looked rather timid, but I did not like the strange, wild expression of his countenance, and since then I have felt more aversion to their presence than before" (*Land of Gold,* 174). Mollie Sanford, on her journey to Colorado in 1860, was surrounded by Indian men who, evidently amused by her consternation, took hold of her braids, "took their hunting knives and made every demonstration of cutting them off, or scalping, I did not know which" (*Mollie,* 123).

39. Lamar, foreword to *Down the Santa Fe Trail,* xvii.

40. Pratt, *Imperial Eyes,* 149.

41. Ibid., 152.

42. See H. N. Smith, *Virgin Land,* 208–9.

43. See Goetzmann, *Exploration and Empire,* 36–40.

44. See Pratt, *Imperial Eyes,* 201–5.

45. Susan Magoffin has long been considered the first Anglo-American woman to travel to New Mexico. Marian Meyer has shown in a recent biography, however, that she was preceded by Mary Donoho (*Mary Donoho: New First Lady of the Santa Fe Trail*).

46. On these political beliefs of the Mexican upper class, see Starr, *Inventing the Dream,* 16.

47. See Lamar, foreword to *Down the Santa Fe Trail,* xi, xxx.

Part 2

1. See Utley, *Indian Frontier,* 37.

2. Ibid., 13, 72. See also Trachtenberg, *Incorporation of America,* chapter 1.

3. Trachtenberg, *Incorporation of America,* 19–20. Goetzmann, *Exploration and Empire,* 232, 355–56.

4. Trachtenberg, *Incorporation of America,* 20; Slotkin, *Fatal Environment,* 36.

5. Limerick, *Legacy of Conquest,* 39.

6. See Churchill, *Over the Purple Hills* and *Active Footsteps.* See also Bennion, *Equal to the Occasion,* 85–87.

7. Michael Kammen has cautioned that for many groups in America, national memories have been less compelling or determinative than the feel for regional traditions. He notes a tension between national memory and local allegiance not

evident before the 1870s, and he argues that place-specific activities involving the invention of local traditions served as the strongest impulse to create tradition as moments of self-definition. See his *Mystic Chords of Memory,* 37, 141–45, 215–23. See also Mitchell, *Witnesses,* 67.

Chapter 3

1. Utley, *Indian Frontier,* 31; see also Prucha, *Great Father,* chapter 3.

2. Utley, 39–40; see also Prucha, chapter 7.

3. Utley, 40–41.

4. Ibid., 43–45, 46.

5. The term "Five Civilized Tribes" has been applied since the nineteenth century to the Creek, Cherokee, Choctaw, Chickasaw, and Seminole nations to denote their high stage of "civilization."

6. Prucha, *Great Father,* 150.

7. See Utley, *Indian Frontier,* 96.

8. Sherry Smith's work on the military's perceptions of Indians provides an important illustration of my argument. See *The View from Officers' Row,* 2, 7–10, 106, 111–14.

9. Utley, *Indian Frontier,* 101, 125; Prucha, *Great Father,* chapter 10; Dippie, *The Vanishing American,* 144–46.

10. Utley, *Indian Frontier,* 129–32.

11. Frances Carrington, *My Army Life,* 61–62.

12. See Fougera, *With Custer's Cavalry*; Roberts, *Summer on the Plains*; Brown, *Letters from Fort Sill.*

13. Limerick, *Legacy of Conquest,* 195.

14. The Bozeman Trail had been built through the Powder River hunting grounds of the Sioux to link the new mining regions of Montana with the Oregon Trail near Fort Laramie. See Prucha, *Great Father,* 154.

15. In 1912, Elizabeth Burt wrote the story of her life in the army on the basis of her diaries. The manuscript with the title "An Army Wife's Forty Years in the Service, 1862–1902" is in the holdings of the Library of Congress and was published in excerpts in Mattes, *Indians, Infants and Infantry.* Quotes from Burt's manuscript are from Mattes' edition.

16. On December 21, 1866, Lieutenant William Fetterman, ignoring the admonitions of Carrington not to go beyond the protective range of Fort Phil Kearny, was ambushed by Indian warriors. He perished with his whole command in what became known as the "Fetterman Massacre." See Prucha, *Great Father,* 154.

17. Utley, *Indian Frontier,* 99–108.

18. See McDermott's introduction to *My Army Life,* xix–xx, xxvi.

19. See Slotkin, *Fatal Environment,* part 7; Leckie, *Elizabeth Bacon Custer,* 29; Stewart, introduction to *'Boots and Saddles,'* ix. For a contemporary fellow officer's critical view of Custer, see *Life in Custer's Cavalry: Diaries and Letters of Albert and Jennie Barnitz,* edited by Robert M. Utley.

20. See Leckie, *Elizabeth Bacon Custer,* 261–63, 270–71; Stewart, introduction, xxiii.

21. Leckie suggests that Custer, after her husband's death, discovered that her domestic role as widow, although inflated by Americans at large, did not necessarily translate into cultural power. Her activities centered on the memorials commemorating her husband, and only in this domestic capacity did she assume a

public role, avoiding the male domain of politics. However, by publishing her reminiscence of her private life with Custer, she expanded her personal influence and infused her domestic role with public power (*Elizabeth Bacon Custer,* 223, 237–42, 246).

22. *Harper's New Monthly Magazine* (May 1885): 813.

23. The reviewer for the May 1885 issue of *The Dial* grounds the book's merit also in its unpretentiousness, and Custer's second book is praised in similar terms in the same magazine. See *The Dial* (May 1885): 19 and (May 1888): 14.

24. See Lander, "Eve among the Indians," 198, 202–3.

25. King, "Heroines of the Army," *The Dial* (Feb. 1, 1893): 80.

26. See Robert and Eleanor Carriker's introduction to *An Army Wife,* 14–15; Steinbach, *A Long March,* 192.

27. Susman, *Culture as History,* 29–30; Norris, "The Frontier Gone at Last," 53–61. Norris aims to create a new vision of international commerce and peace out of the end of the American frontier. See also Gerould, *Aristocratic West.*

28. Slotkin, "Nostalgia and Progress," 608–9.

29. Susman, *Culture as History,* 34, 36.

30. Trachtenberg, *Incorporation of America,* 24; Denning, *Mechanic Accents.*

31. Trachtenberg, *Incorporation of America,* 24ff.

32. Lears, *No Place of Grace,* xiii, 98–99. See also Douglas, *Feminization of American Culture.*

33. Lears, *No Place of Grace,* xiii, 101–2.

34. See Drinnon, *Facing West,* 279–332.

35. Lears, *No Place of Grace,* 44–45.

36. Cawelti, *Six-Gun Mystique* and *Adventure, Mystery, and Romance.* See also Etulain, "Origins of the Western," 56–60. Peter Bischoff traces the emergence of the Western back to the first captivity narratives of the seventeenth century; thereafter, he argues, the Western historically diversified into various types. He defines the Western as a receptacle of an American collective ideology, a social theory, and a utopian wish image. See "The Western: A Critical Survey," 247. None of these scholars, however, takes note of how the encoding of gender functions as one of the most important strategies of the genre in the construction of an American national mythology: If the Western is a form of national self-definition, why does the story of American identity have to be a story of male violence, conquest, and extermination?

37. Tompkins, *West of Everything,* 37–45; "West of Everything," 357–77.

38. Faith Jaycox expresses a similar critique in her "Regeneration Through Liberation," 5–12. Stephen Tatum presents another argument against Tompkins' clear-cut divisions. Rather than providing an "antithesis" or an "answer" to the domestic novel, the Western "appropriates in classic imperialist fashion certain conventions and features of the domestic novel and the cult of domesticity in order to dramatize in the adventure narrative two things: an emergent masculine version of the cult of domesticity; and actions by male westerners to preserve the cult of domesticity endangered by women's departure from traditional morality and the private sphere" ("Literature Out-of-Doors," 301).

39. See Myres, "Army Women's Narratives," 177–79; Miller, "Foragers, Army Women, and Prostitutes," 142; Cheryl J. Foote, *Women of the New Mexico Frontier,* chapter 2.

40. See Myres, "Army Women's Narratives," 177; Stallard, *Glittering Misery,* chapter 2.

41. See Custer, *'Boots and Saddles,'* chapter 17.

42. For example, Abbie Gardner-Sharp's reminiscence of the Spirit Lake Massacre of 1857 in Iowa and her captivity among the Sioux was published in 1885 and went through seven editions until 1918 (*History of the Spirit Lake Massacre*). In a recent analysis of Indian-white coexistence on the American frontier, June Namias has shown that visual, literary, and historical accounts of the capture of Euro-Americans by Indians are commentaries on the uncertain boundaries of gender, race, and culture. She demonstrates that these captivity materials portray anxieties about gender and ethnicity on the frontier and in American society, pointing out the vulnerability of the family and the social fabric on the frontier (*White Captives*, 82–91, 272–73).

43. See Stallard, *Glittering Misery*, 23; Myres, "Army Women's Narratives," 181.

44. See Utley, *Indian Frontier*, 161.

45. Lou Roberts, who enjoyed fishing and hunting near the Texas Rangers' camp while her husband was chasing Indians or outlaws, had made an "up-to-date riding habit" in which no part of her legs was visible (*A Woman's Reminiscences*, 12).

46. On officers' self-defenses and their wives' defenses of army activities, see Sherry Smith, *View from Officers' Row*, 129, 132–33.

47. "If a historian only looked at the public record," Lensink writes, "Emily Hawley's role as secretary of the local Soldiers Relief Society in Iowa would indicate support for the war effort. . . . But Emily Hawley's comments about the war in her diary . . . tell a different story" (*'A Secret to Be Burried,'* 97–98).

48. Welter, "Cult of True Womanhood," 151–75. Lawrence J. Friedman argues that the early nineteenth-century construction of American womanhood particularly emphasized the idea of female malleability (*Inventors of the Promised Land*, 119).

49. Tatum, "Literature Out-of-Doors," 301. Jane Tompkins also points to the preoccupation of Westerns with self-discipline and the suppression of pain (*West of Everything*, 12, 56, 84).

50. See Leckie, *Elizabeth Bacon Custer*, 110–36.

51. See, for instance, Alderson and Smith, *A Bride Goes West*, 193.

52. Lears, *No Place of Grace*, 12–13.

53. See Steinbach, *A Long March*, xiii, 48. Alice Grierson's private letters uncover a similarly troubled story of an army marriage (*The Colonel's Lady on the Western Frontier*).

54. See Alexander, *Cavalry Wife*. See also Canfield, "An Army Wife."

55. The plural "we" and the assumption of uncontested authority also predominates in another contemporary account, Teresa Viele's *Following the Drum* (1858), which is exuberantly expansionist in its filibustering enthusiasm for the annexation of Cuba (60–61) and all of Mexico (105, 111), extolling the qualities of "Anglo-Saxon endurance" (144). The same expansionist fervor is expressed in Mrs. William L. Cazneau's (Cora Montgomery's) *Eagle Pass*.

56. One of the narratives that depicts a family's adaptation to the Hispanic culture of New Mexico is Marian Russell's *Land of Enchantment*. But even here, acculturation to Hispanic life is accompanied by images of Euro-Americans as "sturdy pioneers" and trailblazers, and by a pervasive rhetoric of Indian hating.

57. Utley, *Indian Frontier*, 55–56, 58, 60.

58. See Mattes, *Indians, Infants, and Infantry*, 58–59.

59. See Scott, *Karnee*, 31.

60. See Utley, *Indian Frontier*, 47, 71; Mattes, *Indians, Infants, and Infantry*, 92.

61. See here especially the difference in Eveline Alexander's description of the

(peaceful) Indian Territory and of Colorado, where her husband's campaign against the Utes centered on forcing the tribe back on a reservation. See also Frances Boyd's spiritualization of the West as exhilarating, morally ennobling nature in Nevada and New Mexico, a western landscape configured as detached from human history at the same time as the frontier army is deployed in controlling the Indian populations of the area.

62. See Hays, *Land of Gold*, 174.

63. See Victor, *Eleven Years*; Tallent, *Black Hills*.

64. Slotkin, *Fatal Environment*, 325, 351, 363–69, 32.

65. Fougera, *With Custer's Cavalry*, 137.

66. See Tylor, *Primitive Culture*.

67. For further illustration of this observation, see Edgerton, *Governor's Wife*. Although men's private letters from the military also reveal domestic concerns, they seldom re-create the material aspects of their home life. See Utley, *Life in Custer's Cavalry*.

68. Sitka had been the scene of the chief activities of the Russian American Company until the transition in 1867, when Alaska became a possession of the United States, and the fort in Sitka was put under military rule. However, there was neither civil law nor protection for the civilian population of Russians and Tlingit Indians, the latter of whom, together with the Chilkat, remained hostile to the U.S. occupation for quite some time. See Andrews, *Story of Sitka*, 80–82.

69. Eliza Rudamah Scidmore, who visited Sitka in 1883, fills in historical details completely left out by FitzGerald. She points to the colorful history of Sitka before the American takeover, characterized by a flourishing social life surrounding the Russian governor's castle and the Greek Orthodox church. She also puts the responsibility for the ensuing decline of Sitka and the flaring up of Indian violence upon the American military (*Alaska*, 157ff., 161, 183, 217).

70. See Mourning Dove, *Mourning Dove*, 58–59; Miller's introduction, xxi. See also Marion T. Brown (*Letters*), who wrote from Fort Sill in 1886: "It had never occurred to me that Indian children ever laughed or cried" (21).

71. This skepticism also informs Lane's narrative, framed by the beginning of Indian wars in the Southwest and the end of Indian wars after the Massacre of Wounded Knee in 1890–91 (*I Married a Soldier*, 191).

72. See Greenblatt, *Marvelous Possessions*, 17–19. Greenblatt draws these connections in relation to sixteenth-century narratives of the New World and to medieval admiration for the wonders of pagan art.

73. See Babcock, " 'A New Mexican Rebecca,' " 385. These issues of the aesthetic appropriation of non-Western others were also raised by Edward Said, although without much attention to issues of gender. However, he had pointed to the phenomenon that the other is frequently represented as female and thus subject to domestication (*Orientalism*, 206–7).

74. "Strikers" were enlisted men who worked for an officer during their off-duty hours; some men were said to have performed all kinds of domestic labor for officers' families, including doing the laundry (Stallard, *Glittering Misery*, 29–30).

75. Torgovnick, *Gone Primitive*, 192.

76. See especially *Mourning Dove*, 70–78. Sherry Smith has argued that officers' wives in general avoided the subject, while officers often used Indian women's childbirth practices, outdoor lives, and work roles as vehicles to reprove civilization and its women, and to criticize white middle-class women's unproductive indoor life (*View from Officers' Row*, 64).

77. In this I obviously differ with Glenda Riley, who argues that white women achieved a degree of warmth and closeness with Native Americans that white men could not parallel. She assumes basic differences in men's and women's perceptions, not in their access to discourse and language, and pays no attention to power relations (beyond those involving gender) surrounding women's texts (*Women and Indians*, 175, 178, 182). In contrast, Sherry Smith finds that one cannot argue that army wives proved more compassionate toward Indians than officers. She found that officers' wives rarely pursued friendships with Indian women, and that they restricted their sympathetic comments about individuals to prominent Indian leaders. Possibly, she speculates, Indian women did not even welcome intimacy with army wives; they may have returned white women's sentiments, seeing them as their inferiors (*View from Officers' Row*, 66–78).

78. *Mourning Dove*, 19–20.

79. Donaldson, *Decolonizing Feminisms*, 64.

80. Sherry Smith has found, especially in frontier officers' private correspondence, evidence of large-scale sexual relations between officers and female Indian captives. Indian women were evidently seen as "the spoils of war, as sexual conveniences, as powerless and depersonalized objects." In general, however, a conspiracy of silence reigned on these matters in both official and private documents, a silence in which officers' wives joined in their own narratives. As Shirley Leckie has pointed out, Elizabeth Custer, for example, must have been interested in avoiding the issue of her husband's infidelity and of his alleged sexual liaison with a Cheyenne captive, who was even rumored to have had a child with Custer. Thus she also circumvented the issue—if she knew about it—of the sexual coercion of Indian women by frontier officers who, ironically, were officially devoted to rescuing white women from a similar fate. See Sherry Smith, *View from Officers' Row*, 82–83; Leckie, *Elizabeth Bacon Custer*, 117, 253. In my own readings of women's western narratives, I have found the same conspiracy of silence about male white violence against Indian women. Exceptions are Sarah Winnemucca Hopkins' and Mary Austin's autobiographies (Winnemucca Hopkins, *Life Among the Piutes*; Austin, *Earth Horizon*, 267). For an interpretation of Hopkins' autobiographical narrative in terms of its authorizing strategies and the way the text engages issues of race, gender, and sexuality, see Georgi-Findlay, "Frontiers of Native American Women's Writing."

Chapter 4

1. Pomeroy, *Golden West*, 3–30.
2. Ibid., xv–xvii, chapter 1.
3. Susan Sutton Smith, "Sara Jane Clark Lippincott," 14.
4. See Coultrap-McQuin, *Doing Literary Business*.
5. Whitaker, *Helen Hunt Jackson*, 12.
6. See Odell, *Helen Hunt Jackson*, 64–66.
7. *Atlantic Monthly* 13 (Dec. 1878): 778.
8. Hubbard, "Helen Hunt Jackson," *The Dial* 6 (Sept. 1885): 109–10.
9. Lippincott, *New Life in New Lands*, 28. Railroads offered Indians free rides, perhaps to induce them to protect instead of harm the new means of transportation. See Athearn, *Westward the Briton*, 22.
10. In the year 1871, woman suffrage leaders Susan B. Anthony and Elizabeth Cady Stanton went on their lecture tour through the West. See Beeton and Edwards,

"Susan B. Anthony's Woman's Suffrage Crusade," 5–15. Possibly Sara Lippincott also gave lectures to finance her travels. Women's rights were a subject especially in Utah and Wyoming, where women had received the vote but were temporarily in danger of losing it again.

11. See Athearn, *Westward the Briton*, 12, 16–30.

12. Prucha, *Great Father*, 169–70.

13. Starr, *Americans and the California Dream*, 175.

14. On the problematic Indian-white relations in California, see Utley, *Indian Frontier*, and Starr, *Inventing the Dream*, 23, 51–52.

15. Starr, *Americans and the California Dream*, 181, 183. See also Demars, *The Tourist in Yosemite*.

16. For an overview of women's Yosemite narratives, see Sargent, "Literary Ladies" and *Pioneers in Petticoats*.

17. See Yelverton, *Zanita*; Logan, "Does it Pay to Visit Yo Semite," 498–509.

18. Muir, *Letters to a Friend*, 80–81.

19. Hunt's travel letters from the Yosemite Valley were reprinted in *Ah-Wah-Ne Days*. See pp. 32, 38–39, 46, 53–63.

20. See Sargent, *Pioneers in Petticoats*, 12–13.

21. Quoted in Sargent, "Literary Ladies," 131.

22. Lydia Lane seems to refer to Johnson's book when she notes in her account of army life that she had been traveling "at least eight thousand miles in an ambulance" (*I Married a Soldier*, 192).

23. See also Schivelbusch, *Railway Journey*.

24. One of the many local pioneer histories that were written toward the end of the century similarly draws upon the "first white woman" topos. Annie Tallent's *Black Hills* (1899) is authorized by her narrative of personal involvement in the miners' invasion of the Black Hills. The presence of a "delicate woman, wholly unused to exposure" (49) highlights the respectability of the undertaking, redeeming the gold-seekers from the stain of lawlessness and greed: instead of outlaws, they were in fact the avant-garde of civilization, of "thrift and enterprise" (12).

25. Cummins, *Story of the Files*, 8.

26. Quoted in Cummins, 17.

27. Franklin Walker, *San Francisco's Literary Frontier*, 6, 11.

28. Ibid., 14.

29. "Dame Shirley" (Louise A.K.S. Clappe) was the author of *The Shirley Letters*, which were published serially in *The Pioneer* in 1854–55. They were republished as *The Shirley Letters: Being Letters Written in 1851–1852 from the California Mines.*

30. See Walker, *San Francisco's Literary Frontier*, 74, 106–7, 131.

31. Egli, *No Rooms of Their Own*, xxi.

32. Victor, quoted in Martin, *Bit of A Blue*, 30.

33. Ibid., 31.

34. Haslam, *Voices of a Place*, 21.

35. Victor, quoted in Martin, *Bit of A Blue*, 42.

36. From the beginning of American expansion into California, the Far West seems to have raised issues of women's rights, work, and profession. See the letters written by California women who had come to California with high hopes of earning a "competency" (Fischer, *Let Them Speak*).

37. See Martin, *Bit of A Blue*, 67. For biographical details, also see Mills, "Emergence of Frances Fuller Victor," 309–36.

38. Victor, quoted in Martin, *Bit of A Blue,* 58.

39. Victor, "Manifest Destiny," 148.

40. Although this work has been acknowledged by such frontier historians as William H. Goetzmann as an important historical source, there still seems to be confusion about the gender of the author. Goetzmann's *Exploration and Empire* is only one instance in which Victor's first name is misspelled as "Francis" (140).

41. Victor, quoted in Martin, *Bit of A Blue,* 76.

42. See Mary Hallock Foote, *In Exile*; *Led-Horse Claim.*

43. Victor, *New Penelope,* 57–58.

44. Quoted in Martin, *Bit of A Blue,* 162.

45. Ibid., 196.

46. Ibid., 196.

47. Ibid., 55.

48. Ibid., 197.

49. Sargent, foreword, *Mother Lode Narratives,* 11.

50. Herr, *Jessie Benton Frémont,* 392–99.

51. Ibid., 1–3.

52. Ibid., 4.

53. Starr, *Americans and the California Dream,* 98–99, 367.

54. Frémont, *Mother Lode Narratives,* 13–14.

55. Ibid., 33–34.

56. See, for example, "My Grizzly Bear," in *Mother Lode Narratives,* esp. 26–27.

57. *Mother Lode Narratives,* 64. See also Herr and Spence, *Letters,* 188.

58. Only recently it has come to my attention—unfortunately too late for this publication—that at about the same time, a Hispanic woman wrote a novel about the conquest of California that shows the loss of land to American squatters: Maria Amparo Ruiz de Burton's *The Squatter and the Don,* 1875/1885, reprinted, Houston: Arte Público Press, 1993. The novel focuses on a white woman who represents ambivalence and a strong sense of social and economic justice with respect to the squatters (portrayed as a crass and vulgar group of men), and who has a vision of multicultural coexistence. See Rebolledo and Rivero, *Infinite Divisions,* 11–12.

59. For Clifford's biography, see Cheryl J. Foote. "'My Husband Was a Madman.'"

60. Ibid., 199–202, 221.

61. Clifford, *Overland Tales,* 224, 228.

62. Clifford, "An Officer's Wife in New Mexico," in *Overland Tales,* 370–72.

63. Clifford, "Crossing the Arizona Deserts," in *Overland Tales,* 304.

64. See Franklin Walker, *Literary History,* 123–24; Starr, *Inventing the Dream,* 55–63.

65. Clifford, "La Graciosa," in *Overland Tales,* 13.

66. As the anthropologist Edward P. Dozier pointed out, Indian ancestry was marked among most Hispanos of the nineteenth century. The upper-class group who claimed "pure" Spanish ancestry in actuality "represented the ricos or wealthy strata of the society rather than a group with any legitimate claim to descent from pure Spanish ancestors" (*Pueblo Indians,* 91). This establishment of class hierarchies in terms of race and ancestry in Clifford's story may thus, at least partially, be retraced to contemporary Hispanic self-fashioning.

67. See Shrode, "Journal," 263–64. Similar practical considerations guide Lydia English's representation of the Southwest in her travel diary of 1875 ("By Wagon From Kansas").

68. See English, "By Wagon from Kansas," 378, 384.

69. Susan Wallace, quoted in Lew Wallace, *An Autobiography,* 920–21.

70. For biographical information on Susan Wallace, see McKee, *'Ben-Hur' Wallace,* 27, 64, 116–17, 140–56, 229; Morsberger and Morsberger, *Lew Wallace,* 257–96.

71. Other works by Susan Wallace include *The Storied Sea* and *Along the Bosphorus and Other Sketches.*

72. See Cheryl Foote, *Women of the New Mexico Frontier,* xviii, 117–46; Babcock and Parezo, *Daughters of the Desert,* 9–13.

73. Goetzmann, *New Lands,* 366–67.

74. Cheryl Foote, *Women of the New Mexico Frontier,* 118.

75. For this interpretation, see Morsberger and Morsberger, *Lew Wallace,* 289.

76. Archaeological and anthropological scholarship has established that the present-day Pueblos are the descendants of the prehistoric town builders and derive from different prehistoric traditions indigenous to the area (see Dozier, *Pueblo Indians,* 31–43).

77. *Estufas* are underground Puebloan ceremonial chambers or kivas that serve as clan buildings and centers of religious ceremonies. Since in many Pueblo cultures women are not initiated into certain societies, they also do not join these sacred club-houses, which gave the impression to visitors that the kivas are men's clubs. See Parsons, "Waiyautitsa of Zuni," in Babcock, *Pueblo Mothers and Children,* 90. Visits to these sites seem to have been a favorite pastime for Anglo visitors, who associated them with mysterious Montezuma legends. See Eveline Alexander, *Cavalry Wife,* 107–8.

78. In 1986, a new tribal constitution replaced the term "Papago," Spanish for "bean eater," with "Tohono O'odham," or "desert people," as the official name of the tribe. See *Arizona Daily Star,* Fri., Apr. 23, 1993, 16A.

79. LaFarge, *Pictorial History,* 144.
The Pima had raised wheat so successfully that the grain they supplied to the American troops was vital to the army's success in that part of the Southwest. They also served the U.S. Army as scouts. It was only after white settlers began irrigating upstream on the Gila River, diverting water from the Indian farmers, that the Pima became dependent on food rations from the government. By the end of the century, they had been transformed from skillful and prosperous farmers into wards of the government.

80. See Mary Mathews, *Ten Years in Nevada*; Wilson, *'49er*; Moynihan et al., *So Much to Be Done.*

81. See Emma Adams, *To and Fro*; Sanborn, *Truthful Woman.*

82. Starr, *Americans and the California Dream,* 50.

83. *The Dial* (Mar. 1884): 286.

84. Ibid., 285.

85. See Boller, *Among the Indians* (1868); Bowles, *Across the Continent* (1865); Wilkes, *Narrative of the United States Exploring Expedition* (1856). The influence of Emerson's emphasis on self-trust on women is especially marked toward the end of the century. See Grierson, *Colonel's Lady,* 190; Kofalk, *No Woman Tenderfoot,* 32–33; Caffrey, *Ruth Benedict.*

86. See Greenfield, *Narrating Discovery,* 96.

87. Winona Adams, "An Indian Girl's Story," 3–17.

Part 3

1. See Wallace, *Land of the Pueblos;* Leighton, *Puget Sound;* Beaman, *Libby.*

2. See Hopkins, *Life Among the Piutes.*

3. Wiebe, *Search for Order;* Mark, *Stranger,* 18–31.

4. Kammen, *Mystic Chords,* 12, 188, 266–69. See also Norwood, *Made From This Earth,* 143–44.

5. Lilian Whiting emphasizes this distinction between the antiquarian concerns of New England women and the political activism of Colorado women in her promotional travel narrative *Land of Enchantment,* 22–24. This is also one of the texts by women in which the prophetic poetry of Emerson, extolling human power and progress, provides a guiding philosophy.

6. Mark, *Stranger,* 32, 41. See also Abel, "Anthropologist," 21.

7. Quoted in Cheryl Foote, *Women of the New Mexico Frontier,* 120, 127–8.

8. See Kofalk, *No Woman Tenderfoot;* Bonta, *Women in the Field;* Benson, *Martha Maxwell.*

9. See Scidmore, *Alaska;* Jenness, "Indian Territory." World travelers Mary E. Hitchcock and Edith van Buren even went to the Klondike via the Yukon River route for their 1898 touring season, recording the experience "in order to show women who feel inclined to make the trip exactly what they may expect" (Hitchcock, *Two Women in the Klondike,* 4).

10. See Barr, *Remember the Alamo;* Catherwood, *Romance of Dollard* and *Old Kaskaskia.*

11. See Heaven, "Chata and Chinita"; Atherton, *Before the Gringo Came, Californians,* and *Splendid Idle Forties.*

12. See *The Dial* (Nov. 1888): 164; Blake and Sullivan, *Mexico;* Hale, *Mexico.*

13. See Frederick Jackson Turner's review of Theodore Roosevelt's *Winning of the West* in *The Dial* (Aug. 1889): 71–73. See also the series of articles on American history by John Fiske and Thomas Wentworth Higginson in *Harper's Monthly* (1881 ff.).

14. See *The Dial* (July 1885): 76–77.

Chapter 5

1. Deutsch, *No Separate Refuge,* 63.

2. On federal Indian policy, see Prucha, *Great Father.* D. W. Meinig puts Indian policy into the broader context of various internal territorial strategies that illustrate that the United States "was certainly in fact an empire, and made use of a variety of territorial strategies in the management of captive peoples." The United States, he claims, was "an unusually severe imperial state, not just because of its enormous and ever-expanding material power, but because it was intolerant of cultural diversity in territorial form" ("Strategies of Empire," 17).

3. Young, "Women, Civilization, and the Indian Question," 106.

4. See Peterson, "Patient, Useful Servants," 105.

5. See Peterson, " 'Holy Women' and Housekeepers"; Sister Blandina Segale, *At the End of the Santa Fe Trail.*

6. Cheryl Foote, *Women of the New Mexico Frontier,* 5–6; Whitman, *Letters.* Although Whitman assumed the role of teacher to Indian children and women, the initial plans of the missionaries did not envision any special proceedings for Indian

women (41). The missionary woman's focus was on religious teaching. Domestic training of women and girls was complementary and followed practical consider- ations: Indian girls were needed as domestic helpers at the missions in order to relieve the missionary women "from so many worldly cares and perplexities" and to enable them to spend their time "in seeking the immediate conversion of these dear heathen to God" (43). Whitman even interprets the death of her little daughter as a sign of God "that most of my time should be spent in teaching school, which I could not do without her having been exposed to the contaminating influence of heathenism and very much neglected" (91).

7. Cheryl Foote, *Women of the New Mexico Frontier*, 3–4; Pearce, *Savagism*, 61.

8. See Stright, "A Missionary Teacher's First Winter in Jemez," in Niederman, *Quilt of Words*, 49–66; Foote, *Women of the New Mexico Frontier*, 5–6.

9. See Mathes, *Helen Hunt Jackson*, 9–10.

10. See Beecher, *Duty of American Women*, 3, 65, quoted in Deutsch, *No Separate Refuge*, 68.

11. Stoler, "Carnal Knowledge and Imperial Power," 51–101. See also Hall, "Missionary Stories," in Grossberg et al., *Cultural Studies*. Hall defines religion and the missionary discourse as key discursive terrains for the articulation of axes of power and thus for the construction of a national identity (241). In the debates over slaves or freed blacks, she argues, English men and women were as much con- cerned with constructing their own identities as with defining those of others, and those identities were always classed and gendered as well as ethnically specific (242).

12. Even Frances Fuller Victor had become involved. In 1877, she republished *River of the West* with a new text on the history of the Sioux war. Although in her travel narratives she had privileged white progress over Indian survival, this new text contained a multiplicity of (male) voices, white and Indian, and voiced the critique of an inhuman Indian policy expressed by Jackson and other "Friends of the Indians," trying to balance it with the views of western settlers interested in the speedy solution of the "Indian problem" (*Eleven Years*, 10–11).

13. Dorris, introduction to *Ramona*, ix.

14. Theodore Roosevelt, quoted in Dorris, introduction, v. Dorris attributes the quote to Roosevelt's *Winning of the West*, 68–69, 81–82.

15. Mathes, *Helen Hunt Jackson*, xvi.

16. As Paula Baker has shown, from the time of the Revolution, women used, and sometimes pioneered, methods for influencing government from outside elec- toral channels, using the home as a basis for political action. In looking at the relation between women and politics, she argues, one has to assume a more inclu- sive definition of politics that can take into account how much nineteenth-century women's voluntary work was part of the political system ("Domestication of Poli- tics," 621–22).

17. Pascoe, *Relations of Rescue*, xvi–xvii, 9.

18. In 1883, the WNIA moved from a focus on propaganda to more direct mission- ary activities because, in the words of Amelia Quinton, "Providence has answered our prayers by bringing the gentlemen's Indian Rights Association into existence . . . thus leaving our own society free to devote . . . a portion of our work to uplifting Indian homes" (quoted in Prucha, *American Indian Policy*, 138).

19. See Prucha, *American Indian Policy*, 135–36.

20. See Limerick, *Legacy of Conquest*, 196–98.

21. On the pervasive rhetoric of the jeremiad in American culture, which not only allowed for but actually elicited social criticism, see Bercovitch, *American Jeremiad.* See also Slotkin, *Fatal Environment,* 316–17.

22. Slotkin, *Fatal Environment,* 316–17, 342–43.

23. Slotkin, "Nostalgia and Progress," 609, 617–18.

24. Lyman Abbott, quoted in Prucha, *American Indian Policy,* 160.

25. Quoted in Prucha, *American Indian Policy,* 180.

26. Janiewski, "Learning to Live 'Just Like White Folks,' " 168.

27. Prucha, *American Indian Policy,* 158, 159, 153, 155.

28. Quoted in Janiewski, "Learning to Live," 167.

29. In 1889, Dorchester wrote in her special report: "No uncivilized people are elevated till the mothers are reached. The civilization must begin in the homes. . . . It is very clear . . . that the elevation of the woman is . . . the key to the situation. Children start from the plane of the mother rather than that of the father" (quoted in Herring, "Their Work," 70).

30. See Herring, "Their Work," 70.

31. See Herring, "Their Work," 75; Bannan, *'True Womanhood.'*

32. Quoted in Herring, "Their Work," 73.

33. Janiewski, "Learning to Live," 170.

34. At many missions, Indian children were part of the "mission family," living and working with the missionaries as domestic helpers. See Lockwood, "Letters," 218–19; Whitman, *Letters,* 57, 120.

35. Pascoe, *Relations of Rescue,* 56–58.

36. Ibid., 58. See also Kidwell, "Power of Women."

37. See Young, "Women, Civilization, and the Indian Question," 101ff.

38. Rayna Green, *Women in American Indian Society,* 48–49.

39. See van Kirk, *'Many Tender Ties.'*

40. Pascoe, *Relations of Rescue,* 58.

41. See Buchanan, *Apache Women Warriors;* Stockel, *Women of the Apache Nation,* 15.

42. See Janiewski, "Learning to Live," 179–80.

43. This interpretation of Roosevelt's institutionalization of welfare politics is based on Chesler, *Woman of Valor,* 60.

44. Roosevelt said in his message that "there is nothing so vitally essential to the welfare of the nation . . . as the home life of the average citizen . . . wilful sterility is, from the standpoint of the nation, from the standpoint of the human race, the one sin for which the penalty is national death, race death" (*State Papers,* 377). In "The Strenuous Life," Roosevelt's rhetoric similarly privileges race over gender; women are called to work in the service of the race: "When men fear work or fear righteous war, when women fear motherhood, they tremble on the brink of doom" (4).

45. Baker, "Domestication of Politics," 620–21, 639–41; Elm and Hatch, " 'Ready to Serve,' " 204.

46. Pascoe, *Relations of Rescue,* 58.

47. Quoted in Pascoe, *Relations of Rescue,* 59.

48. Quoted in Janiewski, "Learning to Live," 173.

49. See Welter, " 'She Hath Done What She Could,' " 111.

50. See Mark, *Stranger,* 62–63, 66, 82–83; Abel, "Anthropologist," 21.

51. See Green, *Women in American Indian Society,* 70ff. Indian women like Sarah Winnemucca also campaigned for Indian citizenship.

52. Janiewski, "Learning to Live," 174–75.

53. See Cheryl Foote, *Women of the New Mexico Frontier,* 5–9, 28; Herring, "Their Work," 73.

54. See Walker, "The Diary." Narcissa Whitman also found her work increasingly shifting from the conversion of Indians to the care of her family (*Letters,* 207).

55. Foote, *Women of the New Mexico Frontier,* 10. Herring, "Their Work," 78.

56. Quoted in Olsen, "Mary Clementine Collins," 60, 61.

57. Stocker, "A Doorkeeper," 38–40.

58. As Sarah Deutsch has written with respect to female missionaries in the Hispanic Southwest, these women had to conceive adventures that would place them on a level with foreign missionaries: "The scene had to be dark, and not just beautiful, just as the New Mexican had to be childlike, or the missionaries had no function" (*No Separate Refuge,* 71).

59. Quoted in Graber's introduction to Eastman, *Sister to the Sioux,* xi.

60. In 1868, Samuel Chapman Armstrong had initiated the establishment of the Hampton Normal and Agricultural Institute as a vocational boarding school for black students, to which in 1878 was added an Indian department for the education of former prisoners of war—Kiowa, Comanche, Cheyenne, and Arapaho—under the direction of Richard Henry Pratt. See Eastman, *Sister to the Sioux,* 16–7; Ludlow, "Indian Education."

61. In her memoirs, Eastman does not mention that in her second year at Hampton, she also taught natural history and botany, striving to correct, as she wrote in an 1885 article, "crude or false notions of animal and plant life and to encourage habits of exact observation," thus devaluing tribal people's relationship with the natural world as part of a superstitious practice (quoted in Ruth Ann Alexander, "Finding Oneself," 12).

62. Quoted in Alexander, "Finding Oneself," 21.

63. Nevertheless, Ruth Alexander sees Eastman's approach as basically family-centered and in accordance with her own educational background ("Finding Oneself," 23).

64. Iliff, *People of the Blue Water;* Addams, *Twenty Years at Hull House,* 35.

65. Alexander, "Finding Oneself," 24.

66. Quoted in Alexander, "Finding Oneself," 13–14. Alexander points to Eastman's continuing fascination with Jackson.

67. Quoted in Graber's introduction to Eastman, *Sister to the Sioux,* xi–xii.

68. Minnie Braithwaite, a teacher on the Navajo Reservation at the beginning of the twentieth century, made a startling discovery when she saw the pictures drawn by her pupils "of animals in the most intimate of corral animal life" ("Minnie Braithwaite Jenkins," in Morgan and Strickland, *Arizona Memories,* 162).

69. Babcock, introduction to *Pueblo Mothers and Children,* 4.

70. By the 1910s, the failure of the policies pursued since the 1880s had become evident. Rather than achieving self-sufficiency, tribal people had become dependent on money acquired through leasing their land to whites. But even the Indian New Deal of the 1930s, which guaranteed "religious and social freedom" and counteracted the earlier focus on assimilation and individualization by emphasizing the importance of tribal organization, implemented paternalistic policies concerning land and resources, placing ownership in the hands of male household heads and continuing to emphasize women's primary role as domestic (Janiewski, "Learning to Live," 175–77).

Frederick Hoxie wrote that by the early 1900s, influential scholars and policymakers had given up the push for assimilation and relegated Indians again to the periphery of American life. The attention of white Americans returned to Indian land and resources (*Final Promise*, 33–34, 39, 113, 173, 187). See also Limerick, *Legacy of Conquest*, 200–211.

71. Quoted in Dippie, *Vanishing American*, 319.

72. Dippie, *Vanishing American*, 259, 257.

73. Iliff, *People of the Blue Water*, 3–4.

74. See Eastman, *From the Deep Woods*; Hopkins, *Life Among the Piutes*.

75. Pascoe, *Relations of Rescue*, 111.

76. See Hertzberg, *Search for an American Indian Identity*.

77. Zitkala Sa, *American Indian Stories*, 186.

78. Zitkala Sa, *American Indian Stories*, 173, 179–80.

79. As Pascoe has pointed out, in 1901 the Women's National Indian Association dropped the word "Women's" from its title. The earlier emphasis on female morality was replaced by the focus on cooperation across gender lines (*Relations of Rescue*, 177–78).

80. Baker, "Domestication of Politics"; Pascoe, *Relations of Rescue*, 192. In a recent study, Theda Skocpol has detailed how women's voluntary groups effected a work of persuasion among local, state, and federal governments. She argues that by the early twentieth century, the United States had become very close to creating a "maternalist" welfare state to benefit women and children (*Protecting Soldiers and Mothers*).

81. Bannan. *'True Womanhood.'* See also Emmerich, "'Civilization' and Transculturation."

82. Bannan, *'True Womanhood,'* 5; Rayna Green, *Women in American Indian Society*, 54.

83. Bannan, *'True Womanhood,'* 10–12, 15, 17–18, 20.

84. Ibid., 9.

85. Emmerich suggests that despite the failure of domestic instruction in promoting assimilation among Indian women, the field-matron program had the unexpected and ironical effect of "civilizing" Anglo-American women through connections to tribal culture ("'Civilization' and Transculturation," 44–45).

86. Lucy Thompson supplies an additional explanation for the Klamath Indians' easy grasp of arithmetic: the Klamath have a native system of counting that, since it is not based on writing, demands the practice and exercise of mnemonic skill (*To the American Indian*, 90).

87. Thompson, *To the American Indian*, 23.

88. See Bannan, "Newcomers to Navajoland," 165–67. Bannan argues that the experiences of "voluntary exiles" on the Navajo Reservation may be compared to those of protagonists in captivity narratives, a comparison designed to revise the stereotype of women's fear of Indians, which is not very convincing, however.

89. The strategies of emphasizing self-growth and the possibilities of transculturation for a female self resurface in accounts written by women who worked on Indian reservations as traders and nurses. See Gillmor and Wetherill, *Traders to the Navajos*; Faunce, *Desert Wife*; Forster and Gilpin, *Denizens of the Desert*.

90. See, for example, Cather, *O Pioneers!*, *My Antonia*, *Death Comes for the Archbishop*; Scarborough, *The Wind*; Ferber, *Cimarron*; Ostenso, *Wild Geese*; Roberts, *The Great Meadow*; Gordon, *Green Centuries*. For women's western stories of the time, see the anthologies *Westward the Women*, edited by Vicki Piekarski, and *She Won the West*, edited by Marcia Muller and Bill Pronzini.

91. See Austin, *Land of Little Rain,* and Luhan, *Edge of Taos Desert.* Idah Meacham Strobridge's works were recently collected and reprinted in *Sagebrush Trilogy.*

92. See, for example, Strahorn, *Fifteen Thousand Miles*; Alderson and Smith, *A Bride Goes West*; Richards, *A Tenderfoot Bride*; Bunton, *A Bride on the Old Chisholm Trail.*

93. See Sarah Bixby-Smith, *Adobe Days*; Ellis, *Life of an Ordinary Woman*; Bennett, *Old Deadwood Days*; Cabeza de Baca, *We Fed Them Cactus*; Cleaveland, *No Life for a Lady*; Wilbur-Cruce, *Beautiful, Cruel Country.*

94. See especially her historical essay "Story of Early Arizona."

95. See Hall, *Sharlot Hall on the Arizona Strip.*

96. See Cleaveland, *No Life for a Lady*; Bennett, *Old Deadwood Days.*

97. I am here referring particularly to Austin's assumption of a role of translator and special guardian of the West for both western Indian peoples and an eastern public in her *Land of Little Rain.* I am also referring to her celebration of Anglo-Saxon westward pioneering and her biologistic notions of race expressed in her autobiography *Earth Horizon.* See Richard Drinnon's chapter on Austin in his *Metaphysics of Indian-Hating.*

98. Mason, *Deconstructing America,* 9.

Bibliography

Primary Sources

Adams, Emma Hildreth. *To and Fro, Up and Down in Southern California, Oregon, and Washington Territory, with Sketches in Arizona, New Mexico and British Columbia.* Cincinnati, Chicago, St. Louis: Cranston & Stowe, 1888.

Adams, Winona, ed. "An Indian Girl's Story of a Trading Expedition to the Southwest about 1841." *Sources of Northwest History* 11 (1930): 3–17.

Addams, Jane. *Twenty Years at Hull House, with Autobiographical Notes.* New York: Macmillan, 1910.

Alderson, Nannie T., and Helena Huntington Smith. *A Bride Goes West.* 1942. Reprint, Lincoln: University of Nebraska Press, 1969.

Alexander, Eveline M. *Cavalry Wife: The Diary of Eveline M. Alexander, 1866–1867.* Edited by Sandra L. Myres. College Station: Texas A & M University, 1977.

Arnold, Mary Ellicott, and Mabel Reed. *In the Land of the Grasshopper Song: Two Women in the Klamath River Indian Country in 1908–09.* 1957. Reprint, Lincoln: University of Nebraska Press, 1980.

Atherton, Gertrude. *Before the Gringo Came.* New York: J. Selwin Tait, 1894.

——. *The Californians.* London, New York: J. Lane, 1898.

——. *The Splendid Idle Forties: Stories of Old California.* New York: F. A. Stokes, 1902.

Austin, Mary. *Earth Horizon: An Autobiography by Mary Austin.* 1932. Reprint, Albuquerque: University of New Mexico Press, 1991.

——. *The Land of Little Rain.* 1903. Reprint, Albuquerque: University of New Mexico Press, 1974.

Bailey, Mary Stuart. "A Journal of Mary Stuart Bailey, Wife of Dr. Fred Bailey from Ohio to California, April–October 1852." In Myres 1980.

Baldwin, Alice. *An Army Wife on the Frontier: The Memoirs of Alice Blackwood Baldwin 1867–1877.* Edited by Robert C. and Eleanor R. Carriker. Salt Lake City: University of Utah Library, 1975.

Barr, Amelia. *Remember the Alamo.* New York: Dodd, Mead, 1888.

Beaman, Libby. *Libby: The Sketches, Letters & Journal of Libby Beaman, Recorded in the Pribilof Islands, 1879–1880. As Presented by her Granddaughter Betty John.* Tulsa, Okla.: Council Oaks Books, 1987.

Bennett, Estelline. *Old Deadwood Days.* New York: J. H. Sears & Co., 1928.

Biddle, Ellen McGowan. *Reminiscences of a Soldier's Wife.* Philadelphia: J. B. Lippincott Co., 1907.

Bird, Isabella L. *A Lady's Life in the Rocky Mountains.* New York: G. P. Putnam, 1878. Reprint, New York: Ballantine, 1960.

Bixby-Smith, Sarah. *Adobe Days.* Cedar Rapids: Torch Press, 1925.

Blake, Mary Elizabeth, and Margaret Frances Sullivan. *Mexico: Picturesque, Political, Progressive.* Boston: Lee and Shepard, 1888.

Boller, Henry A. *Among the Indians: Eight Years in the Far West, 1858–1866. Embracing Sketches of Montana and Salt Lake.* Philadelphia: T. E. Zell, 1868.

Bonnin, Gertrude. See Zitkala Sa.

Bowles, Samuel. *Across the Continent: A Summer's Journey to the Rocky Mountains, the Mormons, and the Pacific States, with Speaker Colfax.* Springfield, Mass.: Samuel Bowles & Co.; New York: Hurd and Houghton, 1865.

Boyd, Mrs. Orsemus Bronson (Frances A.). *Cavalry Life in Tent and Field.* 1894. Reprint, Lincoln: University of Nebraska Press, 1982.

Brown, Marion T. *Letters from Fort Sill, 1886–1887.* Edited by C. Richard King. Austin, Tex.: Encino Press, 1970.

Bunton, Mary Taylor. *A Bride on the Old Chisholm Trail.* San Antonio, Tex.: Naylor Company, 1939.

Bunyard, Harriet. "Diary of a Young Girl." In Myres 1980.

Burt, Elizabeth. "An Army Wife's Forty Years in the Service, 1862–1902." Reprint, in excerpts, in Mattes.

Cabeza de Baca, Fabiola. *We Fed Them Cactus.* Albuquerque: University of New Mexico Press, 1954.

Canfield, Sarah E. "An Army Wife on the Upper Missouri: The Diary of Sarah E. Canfield, 1866–1868." Edited by Ray M. Mattison. *North Dakota History* 20 (Oct. 1953): 190–220.

Carpenter, Helen. "A Trip Across the Plains in an Ox Wagon, 1857." In Myres 1980.

Carrington, Frances C. *My Army Life: A Soldier's Wife at Fort Phil Kearny with An Account of the Celebration of 'Wyoming Opened.'* 1910. Reprint, Boulder, Colo.: Pruett, 1990.

Carrington, Margaret I. *Ab-Sa-Ra-Ka, Land of Massacre: Being the Experience of an Officer's Wife on the Plains.* Philadelphia: Lippincott, 1868. Reprint, as *Ab-Sa-Ra-Ka; Or, Wyoming Opened: Being the Experience of an Officer's Wife on the Plains. With an Outline of Indian Operations and Conferences Since 1865* by Col. Henry B. Carrington. Philadelphia: J. B. Lippincott, 1890.

Cather, Willa. *Death Comes for the Archbishop.* New York: A. A. Knopf, 1927.

——. *My Antonia.* 1918. Reprint, Boston: Houghton Mifflin, 1977.

——. *O Pioneers!* Boston: Houghton Mifflin, 1913.

Catherwood, Mary Hartwell. *Old Kaskaskia.* Boston, New York: Houghton, Mifflin, 1893.

——. *The Romance of Dollard.* New York: The Century Co., 1889.

Cazneau, Mrs. William L. (Cora Montgomery). *Eagle Pass or Life on the Border.* 1852. Reprint, Austin, Tex.: The Pemberton Press, 1966.

Churchill, Caroline N. *Active Footsteps.* Colorado Springs: Mrs. C. N. Churchill, 1909.

——. *Over the Purple Hills.* Chicago: Hazlitt and Reed, 1877.

Cleaveland, Agnes Morley. *No Life for a Lady.* 1941. Reprint, Lincoln: University of Nebraska Press, 1969.

Clifford (McCrackin), Josephine. *'Another Juanita' and Other Stories*. Buffalo, N.Y.: Charles Wells Moulton, 1893.

——. *Overland Tales*. San Francisco: A. L. Bancroft & Co., 1877.

——. *'The Woman Who Lost Him' and Tales of the Army Frontier*. Pasadena, Calif.: George Wharton James, 1913.

Cooke, Lucy Rutledge. *Crossing the Plains in 1852: Narrative of a Trip from Iowa to 'The Land of Gold,' as Told in Letters Written During the Journey*. Fairfield, Wash.: Ye Galleon Press, 1988.

Cummins, Maria. *The Lamplighter*. Boston: J. P. Jewett, 1854.

Custer, Elizabeth. *'Boots and Saddles,' Or, Life in Dakota with General Custer*. 1885. Reprint, Norman: University of Oklahoma Press, 1961.

——. *Following the Guidon*. New York: Harper & Brothers, 1890.

——. *Tenting on the Plains or General Custer in Kansas and Texas*. New York: Charles L. Webster & Co., c1888, 1889.

Dame Shirley (Louise A.K.S. Clappe). *The Shirley Letters: Being Letters Written in 1851–1852 from the California Mines*. Salt Lake City, Utah: Peregrine Smith Books, n.d.

Dumont, Ella Elgar Bird. *An Autobiography of a West Texas Pioneer: Ella Elgar Bird Dumont*. Edited by Tommy J. Boley. Austin: University of Texas Press, 1988.

Dunlap, Kate. *The Montana Gold Rush Diary of Kate Dunlap*. Edited by S. Lyman Tyler. Denver: Fred A. Rosenstock Old West Publishing; Salt Lake City: University of Utah Press, 1969.

Dyer, Mrs. D. B. *'Fort Reno,' or Picturesque 'Cheyenne and Arrapahoe Army Life': Before the Opening of 'Oklahoma.'* New York: G. W. Dillinham, 1896.

Eastman, Charles. *From the Deep Woods to Civilization*. 1916. Reprint, Lincoln: University of Nebraska Press, 1977.

Eastman, Elaine Goodale. *Sister to the Sioux: The Memoirs of Elaine Goodale Eastman 1885–91*. Edited by Kay Graber. Lincoln: University of Nebraska Press, 1978.

Edgerton, Mary. *A Governor's Wife on the Mining Frontier: The Letters of Mary Edgerton from Montana, 1863–1865*. Edited by James L. Thane, Jr. Salt Lake City: University of Utah Library, 1976.

Ellis, Anne. *The Life of an Ordinary Woman*. 1929. Reprint, Lincoln: University of Nebraska Press, 1980.

English, Lydia E. "By Wagon From Kansas to Arizona in 1875: The Travel Diary of Lydia E. English." Edited by Joseph W. Snell. *The Kansas Historical Quarterly* 36 (winter 1970): 369–89.

Farnham, Eliza Woodson. *California In-Doors and Out*. 1856. Reprint, Nieuwkoop: B. De Graaf, 1972.

——. *Life in Prairie Land*. 1846. Reprint, New York: Arno Press, 1972.

——. *Woman and Her Era*. 2 vols. New York: A. J. Davis & Co., 1864.

Farnham, Thomas. *Travels in the Great Western Prairies, The Anahuac and Rocky Mountains, and in the Oregon Territory*. 1843. Reprint, New York: Da Capo Press, 1973.

Faunce, Hilda. *Desert Wife*. 1928. Reprint, Lincoln: University of Nebraska Press, 1981.

Ferber, Edna. *Cimarron*. New York: Grosset & Dunlap, 1929.

Fern, Fanny. *Ruth Hall and Other Writings*. Edited by Joyce W. Warren. New Brunswick: Rutgers University Press, 1986.

Fisk, Elizabeth Chester. *Lizzie: The Letters of Elizabeth Chester Fisk, 1864–1893.* Edited by Rex C. Myers. Mountain Press Publishing, 1989.

FitzGerald, Emily McCorkle. *An Army Doctor's Wife on the Frontier: The Letters of Emily McCorkle FitzGerald from Alaska and the Far West, 1874–1878.* Edited by Abe Laufe. Pittsburgh: University of Pittsburgh Press, 1962. Reprint, Lincoln: University of Nebraska Press, 1986.

Foote, Mary Hallock. *A Victorian Gentlewoman in the Far West: The Reminiscences of Mary Hallock Foote.* Edited by Rodman W. Paul. San Marino, Calif.: Huntington Library, 1972.

——. *In Exile, and Other Stories.* Boston: Houghton Mifflin, 1894.

——. *The Led-Horse Claim: A Romance of a Mining Camp.* Boston: J. R. Osgood, 1883.

Forster, Elizabeth, and Laura Gilpin. *Denizens of the Desert: A Tale in Word and Picture of Life Among the Navaho Indians.* Edited by Martha A. Sandweiss. Albuquerque: University of New Mexico Press, 1988.

Fougera, Katherine Gibson. *With Custer's Cavalry: From the Memoirs of the Late Katherine Gibson.* Caldwell, Idaho: Caxton Printers, 1940.

Frémont, Jessie Benton. *A Year of American Travel.* New York: Harper & Bros., 1878.

——. *Mother Lode Narratives.* Edited by Shirley Sargent. Ashland, Ore.: Lewis Osborne, 1970.

Frizzell, Lodisa. *Across the Plains to California in 1852.* Edited by Victor Hugo Paltsits. New York: New York Library, 1915.

Fuller, Margaret. *Summer on the Lakes.* 1844. Reprint of second edition, 1856. Edited by Arthur B. Fuller. New York: Haskell House Publishers, 1970.

Gardner-Sharp, Abbie. *The History of the Spirit Lake Massacre and Captivity of Miss Abbie Gardner.* 1885. Reprint, Des Moines, Iowa: Homestead Printing, 1918.

Gerould, Katherine Fullerton. *The Aristocratic West.* New York: Harper & Brothers, 1925.

Gibson, Katherine Garrett. See Fougera.

Gillmor, Frances, and Louise Wade Wetherill. *Traders to the Navajos: The Story of the Wetherills of Kayenta.* Boston: Houghton Mifflin, 1934.

Gordon, Caroline. *Green Centuries.* New York: Bantam, 1941.

Greenwood, Grace. See Sara Lippincott.

Gregg, Josiah. *The Commerce of the Prairies.* 1844. Reprint, edited by Milo Milton Quaife. New York: The Citadel Press, 1968.

Grierson, Alice Kirk. *The Colonel's Lady on the Western Frontier: The Correspondence of Alice Kirk Grierson.* Edited by Shirley A. Leckie. Lincoln: University of Nebraska Press, 1989.

Hale, Susan. *Mexico.* New York: G.P. Putnam's, 1891.

Hall, Judge James. *Letters from the West.* London: Henry Colburn, 1828.

Hall, Sharlot. *Sharlot Hall on the Arizona Strip: A Diary of a Journey Through Northern Arizona in 1911.* Edited by C. Gregory Crampton. Flagstaff: Northland Press, 1975.

——. "Story of Early Arizona." *Arizona Magazine* (Dec. 1906): 3–10.

Haun, Catherine. "A Woman's Trip Across the Plains in 1849." In Schlissel.

Hays, Lorena L. *To the Land of Gold and Wickedness: The 1848–59 Diary of Lorena L. Hays.* Edited by Jeanne Hamilton Watson. St. Louis: The Patrice Press, 1988.

Heaven, Louise Palmer. "Chata and Chinita: A Novel of Mexican Life." *Overland Monthly* 7–10 (Jan. 1886–Dec. 1887).

Herndon, Sarah Raymond. *Days on the Road: Crossing the Plains in 1865.* 1882. Reprint, New York: Burr Printing House, 1902.

Hitchcock, Mary E. *Two Women in the Klondike: The Story of a Journey to the Gold-Fields of Alaska.* New York: G. P. Putnam's Sons, 1899.

Hoffman, Charles Fenno. *A Winter in the West.* 1835. Reprint, Ann Arbor, Mich.: Microfilm Productions, 1966.

Holley, Mary Austin. *Texas: Observations, Historical, Geographical and Descriptive. In a Series of Letters, Written during a Visit to Austin's Colony, with a view to a permanent settlement in that country, in the Autumn of 1831.* Baltimore, Md.: Armstrong and Plaskitt, 1833.

——. *The Texas Diary, 1835–1838.* Edited by James P. Bryan. Austin: University of Texas Press, 1965.

Hopkins, Sarah Winnemucca. *Life among the Piutes: Their Wrongs and Claims.* Edited by Mrs. Horace Mann. 1883. Reprint, Bishop, Calif.: Sierra Media, 1969.

Hubbard, Sara A. "Helen Hunt Jackson." *The Dial* 7 (Sept. 1885): 109–110.

Hunt, Helen. See Helen Hunt Jackson.

Iliff, Flora Gregg. *People of the Blue Water: A Record of Life Among the Walapai and Havasupai Indians.* 1954. Reprint, Tucson: University of Arizona Press, 1985.

Jackson, Helen Hunt. *Ah-Wah-Ne Days: A Visit to the Yosemite Valley in 1872.* San Francisco: Book Club of California, 1971.

——. *Bits of Travel at Home.* Boston: Roberts Brothers, 1878.

——. *Ramona.* 1884. Reprint, New York: Signet, 1988.

Jameson, Anna. *Winter Studies and Summer Rambles in Canada.* 3 vols. London: Saunders and Otley, 1838.

Jenness, Theodora R. "The Indian Territory." *Atlantic Monthly* (Apr. 1879): 444–52.

Johnson, Laura Winthrop. *Eight Hundred Miles in an Ambulance.* Philadelphia: J. B. Lippincott Co., 1889.

Kirkland, Caroline. *A New Home—Who'll Follow? Or, Glimpses of Western Life. By Mrs. Mary Clavers. An Actual Settler.* New York and Boston: Francis, 1839. Reprint, edited by Sandra A. Zagarell. New Brunswick: Rutgers University Press, 1990.

——. *Forest Life.* 1842. Reprint, Upper Saddle River, N.J.: Literature House, 1970.

Klasner, Lily. *My Girlhood Among Outlaws.* Edited by Eve Ball. Tucson: University of Arizona Press, 1972.

Lane, Lydia Spencer. *I Married a Soldier.* 1893. Reprint, Albuquerque: University of New Mexico Press, 1987.

Leighton, Caroline. *Life at Puget Sound, with Sketches of Travel in Washington Territory, British Columbia, Oregon, and California, 1865–1881.* Boston: Lee and Shepard; New York: Charles T. Dillingham, 1884.

Lippincott, Sara (Grace Greenwood). *New Life in New Lands.* New York: J. B. Ford, 1873.

Lockwood, Cassandra Sawyer. "Letters of Cassandra Sawyer Lockwood: Dwight Mission, 1834." *Chronicles of Oklahoma* 33 (summer 1955): 202–32.

Logan, Olive. "Does it Pay to Visit Yo Semite." *Galaxy* 10 (Oct. 1870): 498–509.

Ludlow, Helen W. "Indian Education at Hampton and Carlisle." *Harper's New Monthly Magazine* 62 (Apr. 1881): 659–75.

Luhan, Mabel Dodge. *Edge of Taos Desert: An Escape to Reality.* 1937. Reprint, Albuquerque: University of New Mexico Press, 1987.

Magoffin, Susan. *Down the Santa Fe Trail and Into Mexico: The Diary of Susan*

Shelby Magoffin 1846–1847. Edited by Stella M. Drumm, 1962. Reprint, Lincoln: University of Nebraska Press, 1982.

Mansur, Abby. "MS Letters Written to Her Sister, 1852–1854." In Fischer.

Martineau, Harriet. *Society in America*. 2 vols. London: Saunders and Otley, 1837.

———. *Retrospect of Western Travel*. 3 vols. 1838. Reprint, New York: Greenwood Press, 1969.

Mathews, Mary. *Ten Years in Nevada, or, Life on the Pacific Coast*. Buffalo, N.Y.: Baker, Jones & Co., 1880.

Megquier, Mary Jane. *Apron Full of Gold: The Letters of Mary Jane Megquier from San Francisco, 1849–1856*. Edited by Robert Glass Cleland. San Marino, Calif.: Huntington Library, 1949.

Moodie, Susanna. *Roughing It in the Bush; or, Forest Life in Canada*. 1852. Reprint, Toronto: McClelland & Stewart, 1962.

Mourning Dove (Hum-ishu-ma). *Mourning Dove: A Salishan Autobiography*. Edited by Jay Miller. Lincoln: University of Nebraska Press, 1990.

Muir, John. *Letters to a Friend, written to Mrs. Ezra S. Carr, 1866–1879*. New York: Houghton Mifflin Co., 1915.

Norris, Frank. "The Frontier Gone at Last." In *Responsibilities of the Novelist*. New York: Doubleday, Page, & Co., 1903, 53–61.

Ostenso, Martha. *Wild Geese*. New York: Dodd, Mead, and Co., 1925.

Powers, Mary Rockwood. *A Woman's Overland Journey to California*. Edited by W. B. Thorsen. Fairfield, Wash.: Ye Galleon Press, 1985.

Richards, Clarice E. *A Tenderfoot Bride: Tales from an Old Ranch*. 1920. Reprint, Lincoln: University of Nebraska Press, 1988.

Roberts, Annie Gibson. *A Summer on the Plains, 1870: From the Diary of Annie Gibson Roberts*. Edited by Brian Pohanka. Mattituck, N.Y., and Bryan, Tex.: J. M. Carroll & Co., 1983.

Roberts, Mrs. D. W. (Lou Conway). *A Woman's Reminiscences of Six Years in Camp With the Texas Rangers*. Austin, Tex.: State House Press, 1987.

Roe, Frances M. A. *Army Letters from an Officer's Wife, 1871–1888*. 1909. Reprint, Lincoln: University of Nebraska Press, 1981.

Roosevelt, Theodore. *State Papers as Governor and President, 1899–1909*. New York: Scribner's, 1926.

———. "The Strenuous Life." In *Works* 12. New York: Scribner's, 1926.

———. *The Winning of the West*. New York: Scribner's, 1926.

Royce, Sarah. *A Frontier Lady: Recollections of the Gold Rush and Early California*. 1932. Edited by Ralph Henry Gabriel. Reprint, Lincoln: University of Nebraska Press, 1977.

Rudd, Lydia Allen. "Notes by the Wayside en Route to Oregon, 1852." In Schlissel.

Russell, Marian. *Land of Enchantment: Memoirs of Marian Russell along the Santa Fe Trail*. 1954. Reprint, Albuquerque: University of New Mexico Press, 1981.

Sanborn, Kate. *A Truthful Woman in Southern California*. New York: D. Appleton, 1893.

Sanford, Mollie Dorsey. *Mollie: The Journal of Mollie Dorsey Sanford in Nebraska and Colorado Territories, 1857–1866*. Lincoln: University of Nebraska Press, 1959.

Scarborough, Dorothy. *The Wind*. New York: Harper & Row, 1925.

Scidmore, Eliza Ruhamah. *Alaska: Its Southern Coast and the Sitkan Archipelago*. Boston: D. Lothrop and Co., 1885.

Scott, Lalla. *Karnee: A Paiute Narrative*. Reno: University of Nevada Press, 1966.

Sedgwick, Catharine Maria. *Hope Leslie; Or, Early Times in the Massachusetts.* 1827. Edited by Mary Kelley. Reprint, New Brunswick, N.J.: Rutgers University Press, 1987.

Segale, Sister Blandina. *At the End of the Santa Fe Trail.* Milwaukee, Wis.: Bruce, 1948.

Shrode, Mrs. Maria. "Journal." In Myres 1980.

Steele, Eliza. *A Summer Journey in the West.* 1841. Reprint, New York: Arno Press, 1975.

Stewart, Catherine. *New Homes in the West.* 1843. Reprint, Ann Arbor: University Microfilms, 1966.

Stocker, Beatrice A. R. "A Doorkeeper in the House of God: The Letters of Beatrice A. R. Stocker, Missionary to the Sioux, 1892–1893." Edited by Anne Marie Baker. *South Dakota History* 22 (spring 1992): 38–63.

Strahorn, Carrie Adell. *Fifteen Thousand Miles by Stage: A Woman's Unique Experience during Thirty Years of Path Finding and Pioneering from the Missouri to the Pacific and from Alaska to Mexico.* 2 vols. 1911. Reprint, Lincoln: University of Nebraska Press, 1988.

Strobridge, Idah Meacham. *Sagebrush Trilogy: Idah Meacham Strobridge and Her Works.* Reno: University of Nevada Press, 1990.

Summerhayes, Martha. *Vanished Arizona.* 1908. 2nd ed., 1911. Reprint, Lincoln: University of Nebraska Press, 1979.

Tallent, Annie. *The Black Hills; or, The Last Hunting Grounds of the Dakotahs: A Complete History of the Black Hills of Dakota from their First Invasion in 1874 to the Present Time.* St. Louis, Mo.: Nixon-Jones Printing Co., 1899.

Thompson, Lucy. *To the American Indian: Reminiscences of a Yurok Woman.* 1916. Reprint, Berkeley, Calif.: Heyday Books, 1991.

Thoreau, Henry David. *The Maine Woods.* 1864. Reprint, Boston: Houghton Mifflin, 1906.

Traill, Catharine Parr. *The Backwoods of Canada: Being Letters from the Wife of an Emigrant Officer, illustrative of the domestic economy of British America.* 1836. New ed., London: Charles Knight & Co., 1846.

Trollope, Frances. *Domestic Manners of the Americans.* 1832. Reprint, New York: Dodd, Mead, and Co., 1901.

Tylor, Edward B. *Primitive Culture: Researches into the Development of Mythology, Philosophy, Religion, Language, Art and Custom.* 1865. Reprint, London: J. Murray, 1920.

Victor, Frances Fuller. *All Over Oregon and Washington: Observations on the Country, Its Scenery, Soil, Climate, Resources, and Improvements.* San Francisco: John H. Carmany & Co., 1872.

———. *Eleven Years in the Rocky Mountains and Life on the Frontier: Also a History of the Sioux War, and a Life of Gen. George A. Custer With Full Account of His Last Battle.* Hartford, Conn.: Columbian Book Company, 1877.

———. "Manifest Destiny in the West." *Overland Monthly* 3 (Aug. 1869): 148–59.

———. *The New Penelope and Other Stories and Poems.* San Francisco: A. L. Bancroft & Co., 1877.

———. *The River of the West: Life and Adventure in the Rocky Mountains and Oregon.* 1870. Reprint, Missoula: Mountain Press Publishing Company, 1983.

Viele, Mrs. (Teresa). *'Following the Drum': A Glimpse of Frontier Life.* 1858. Reprint, Austin, Tex.: Steck-Vaughn Co., 1968.

Walker, Mary Richardson. "The Diary of Mary Richardson Walker, June 10–December 21, 1838." Edited by Rufus E. Coleman. *Sources of Northwest History* 15. Missoula: State University of Montana, n.d.

Wallace, Lew. *An Autobiography.* 2 vols. New York: Harper & Brothers, 1906.

Wallace, Susan. *Along the Bosphorus and Other Sketches.* Chicago: Rand, McNally & Company, 1898.

———. *The Land of the Pueblos.* New York: John B. Alden, 1888.

———. *The Storied Sea.* Boston: J. R. Osgood, 1883.

Ward, Harriet Sherrill. *Prairie Schooner Lady: The Journal of Harriet Sherrill Ward, 1853.* Edited by Ward G. De Witt and Florence Stark De Witt. Los Angeles: Westernlore Press, 1959.

Whiting, Lilian. *The Land of Enchantment: From Pike's Peak to the Pacific.* 1906. Reprint, Albuquerque, N.M.: Sun Books, 1981.

Whitman, Narcissa. *The Letters of Narcissa Whitman.* Fairfield, Wash.: Ye Galleon Press, 1986.

Wilbur-Cruce, Eva Antonia. *A Beautiful, Cruel Country.* Tucson: University of Arizona Press, 1987.

Wilkes, Charles. *Narrative of the United States Exploring Expedition, During the Years 1838, 1839, 1840, 1841, 1842.* New York: G. P. Putnam, 1856.

Wilson, Luzena. *'49er: Memories recalled years later for her daughter Correnah Wilson Wright.* Mills College, Calif.: Eucalyptus Press, 1937.

Winne, Caroline Frey. "Letters of Caroline Frey Winne from Sidney Barracks and Fort McPherson, Nebraska, 1874–1878." Edited by Thomas R. Buecker. *Nebraska History* 62 (spring 1981): 1–46.

Winnemucca, Sarah. See Hopkins, Sarah Winnemucca.

Yelverton, Therese. *Zanita: A Tale of the Yosemite.* N.p: 1871.

Zitkala Sa (Gertrude Bonnin). *American Indian Stories.* Washington: Hayworth Publishing House, 1921.

Secondary Sources

Abel, Marianne. "Anthropologist with a Mission." *Women's Review of Books* 6 (Sept. 1989): 21.

Aiken, Susan Hardy. *Isak Dinesen and the Engendering of Narrative.* Chicago: University of Chicago Press, 1990.

Alexander, Ruth Ann. "Finding Oneself through a Cause: Elaine Goodale Eastman and Indian Reform in the 1880s." *South Dakota History* 22 (spring 1992): 1–37.

Allen, Martha Mitten. *Traveling West: 19th-Century Women on the Overland Routes.* El Paso: Texas Western Press, 1987.

Ammons, Elizabeth. Introduction to *'How Celia Changed Her Mind' and Selected Stories,* by Rose Terry Cooke, edited by Elizabeth Ammons. New Brunswick: Rutgers University Press, 1986.

Andreadis, Harriette. "True Womanhood Revisited: Women's Private Writings in Nineteenth-Century Texas." *Journal of the Southwest* 31 (summer 1989): 179–204.

Andrews, C. L. *The Story of Sitka.* Seattle, Wash.: Shorey Book Store, 1922.

Antelyes, Peter. *Tales of Adventurous Enterprise: Washington Irving and the Poetics of Western Expansion.* New York: Columbia University Press, 1990.

Armitage, Susan. "Reluctant Pioneers." In Stauffer and Rosowski.

———. "Through Women's Eyes: A New View of the West." In Armitage and Jameson.

———. "Women's Literature and the American Frontier: A New Perspective on the Frontier Myth." In Lee and Lewis.

Armitage, Susan, and Elizabeth Jameson, eds. *The Women's West*. Norman and London: University of Oklahoma Press, 1987.

Athearn, Robert G. *Westward the Briton: The Far West, 1865–1900*. Lincoln: University of Nebraska Press, 1953.

Atkins, Annette. "Women on the Farming Frontier: The View from Fiction." *Midwest Review* 3 (spring 1981): 1–10.

Babcock, Barbara A. " 'A New Mexican Rebecca': Imagining Pueblo Women." *Journal of the Southwest* 32 (winter 1990): 400–437.

———, ed. *Pueblo Mothers and Children: Essays by Elsie Clews Parsons 1915–1924*. Santa Fe, N.Mex.: Ancient City Press, 1991.

Babcock, Barbara A., and Nancy J. Parezo. *Daughters of the Desert: Women Anthropologists and the Native American Southwest, 1880–1980. An Illustrated Catalogue*. Albuquerque: University of New Mexico Press, 1988.

Baker, Paula. "The Domestication of Politics: Women and American Political Society, 1780–1920." *The American Historical Review* 89 (June 1984): 620–47.

Bannan, Helen M. "Newcomers to Navajoland: Transculturation in the Memoirs of Anglo Women, 1900–1945." *New Mexico Historical Review* 59 (1984): 165–85.

———. *'True Womanhood' on the Reservation: Field Matrons in the United States Indian Service*. Working Paper No. 18. Tucson, Ariz.: Southwest Institute for Research on Women, 1984.

Barthes, Roland. *Mythologies*. Translated by Annette Lavers. New York: Hill & Wang, 1972.

Baym, Nina. "Melodramas of Beset Manhood: How Theories of American Fiction Exclude Women Authors." *American Quarterly* 33 (summer 1981): 123–39.

Beeton, Beverly, and G. Thomas Edwards. "Susan B. Anthony's Woman Suffrage Crusade in the American West." In Riley 1982.

Bennion, Sherilyn Cox. *Equal to the Occasion: Women Editors of the Nineteenth-Century West*. Reno: University of Nevada Press, 1990.

Benson, Maxine. *Martha Maxwell: Rocky Mountain Naturalist*. Lincoln: University of Nebraska Press, 1986.

Benstock, Shari, ed. *The Private Self: Theory and Practice of Women's Autobiographical Writings*. Chapel Hill: University of North Carolina Press, 1988.

Ben-Zvi, Linda. " 'Home Sweet Home': Deconstructing the Masculine Myth of the Frontier in Modern American Drama." In Mogen et al.

Bercovitch, Sacvan. *The American Jeremiad*. Madison: University of Wisconsin Press, 1978.

———. "Fusion and Fragmentation: The American Identity." In *The American Identity: Fusion and Fragmentation*, edited by Rob Kroes. Amsterdam: Amerika Instituut, Universiteit van Amsterdam, 1980, 19–45.

———. "The Problem of Ideology in American Literary History." *Critical Inquiry* 12 (summer 1986): 631–53.

Bercovitch, Sacvan, and Myra Jehlen. *Ideology and Classic American Literature*. Cambridge: Cambridge University Press, 1986.

Berkhofer, Robert F., Jr. *The White Man's Indian: Images of the American Indian from Columbus to the Present*. New York: Knopf, 1978.

Billington, Ray Allen. *Westward Expansion: A History of the American Frontier*. New York: Macmillan, 1974.

Binder, Wolfgang, ed. *Westward Expansion in America (1803–1860)*. Erlangen: Palm & Enke, 1987, 3–30.

Birkett, Dea. *Spinsters Abroad: Victorian Lady Explorers*. New York: Basil Blackwell, 1989.

Bischoff, Peter. "The Western: A Critical Survey." *Literatur in Wissenschaft und Unterricht* 22 (1989): 247–70.

Bonta, Marcia Myers. *Women in the Field: America's Pioneering Women Naturalists*. College Station: Texas A & M University Press, 1991.

Brodzki, Bella, and Celeste Schenck, eds. *Life/Lines: Theorizing Women's Autobiography*. Ithaca: Cornell University Press, 1988.

Brown, Dee. *The Gentle Tamers: Women of the Old Wild West*. 1958. Reprint, Lincoln: University of Nebraska Press, 1968.

Brown, Gillian. *Domestic Individualism: Imagining Self in Nineteenth-Century America*. Berkeley: University of California Press, 1990.

Brumm, Ursula. *Geschichte und Wildnis in der amerikanischen Literatur*. Berlin: E. Schmidt, 1980.

Buchanan, Kimberly Moore. *Apache Women Warriors*. El Paso: The University of Texas, 1986.

Buell, Lawrence. "American Literary Emergence as a Postcolonial Phenomenon." *American Literary History* 4 (fall 1992): 411–42.

Buss, Helen M. " 'The Dear Domestic Circle': Frameworks for the Literary Study of Women's Personal Narratives in Archival Collections." *Studies in Canadian Fiction* (1989): 1–17.

Buzard, James. *The Beaten Track: European Tourism, Literature, and the Ways to Culture, 1800–1918*. Oxford: Clarendon Press, 1993.

Caffrey, Margaret M. *Ruth Benedict: Stranger in This Land*. Austin: University of Texas Press, 1989.

Carriker, Robert and Eleanor. Introduction to *An Army Wife on the Frontier*, by Alice Baldwin.

Cawelti, John G. *Adventure, Mystery, and Romance: Formula Stories as Art and Popular Culture*. Chicago: University of Chicago Press, 1976.

——. *The Six-Gun Mystique*. Bowling Green, Ohio: Bowling Green University Popular Press, 1970.

Chesler, Ellen. *Woman of Valor: Margaret Sanger and the Birth Control Movement in America*. New York: Simon and Schuster, 1992.

Cott, Nancy F. *The Bonds of Womanhood: 'Woman's Sphere' in New England, 1780–1835*. New Haven: Yale University Press, 1977.

Coultrap-McQuin, Susan. *Doing Literary Business: American Women Writers in the Nineteenth Century*. Chapel Hill: University of North Carolina Press, 1990.

Cronon, William, Howard R. Lamar, Katherine G. Morrissey, and Jay Gitlin. "Women and the West: Rethinking the Western History Survey Course." *Western Historical Quarterly* 17 (July 1986): 269–90.

Culley, Margo, ed. *A Day at a Time: The Diary Literature of American Women from 1764 to the Present*. New York: Feminist Press, 1985.

Cummins, Ella Sterling. *The Story of the Files: A Review of Californian Writers and Literature*. San Francisco: Co-operative Printing Co., 1893.

Davidson, Cathy N. *Revolution and the Word: The Rise of the Novel in America*. New York: Oxford University Press, 1986.

Demars, Stanford E. *The Tourist in Yosemite, 1855–1985*. Salt Lake City: University of Utah Press, 1991.

Denning, Michael. *Mechanic Accents: Dime Novels and Working-Class Culture in America.* London and New York: Verso, 1987.

Deutsch, Sarah. *No Separate Refuge: Culture, Class, and Gender on an Anglo-Hispanic Frontier in the American Southwest, 1880–1940.* New York: Oxford University Press, 1987.

Dippie, Brian W. "American Wests: Historiographical Perspectives." *American Studies International* 27 (Oct. 1989): 3–25.

——. *The Vanishing American: White Attitudes and U.S. Indian Policy.* Middletown, Conn.: Wesleyan University Press, 1982.

Dobson, Joanne. "The Hidden Hand: Subversion of Cultural Ideology in Three Mid-Nineteenth-Century Women's Novels." *American Quarterly* 38 (summer 1986): 223–42.

Donaldson, Laura E. *Decolonizing Feminisms: Race, Gender, and Empire-Building.* Chapel Hill: University of North Carolina Press, 1992.

Donovan, Josephine. *New England Local Color Literature: A Women's Tradition.* New York: Ungar, 1983.

Dorris, Michael. Introduction to *Ramona,* by Helen Hunt Jackson. 1988.

Douglas, Ann. *The Feminization of American Culture.* New York: Knopf, 1979.

——. "The Literature of Impoverishment: The Women Local Colorists in America 1865–1914." *Women's Studies* 1 (1972): 3–45.

Dozier, Edward P. *The Pueblo Indians of North America.* Prospect Heights, Ill.: Waveland Press, 1983.

Drinnon, Richard. *Facing West: The Metaphysics of Indian-Hating and Empire-Building.* 1980. Reprint, New York: Schocken Books, 1990.

DuBois, Ellen Carol, and Vicki L. Ruiz, eds. *Unequal Sisters: A Multicultural Reader in U.S. Women's History.* New York: Routledge, 1990.

Egli, Ida Rae, ed. *No Rooms of Their Own: Women Writers of Early California.* Berkeley, Calif.: Heyday Books, 1992.

Elm, Adelaide, and Heather S. Hatch, comps. " 'Ready to Serve': Elsie Prugh Herndon Among the Pima and Papago. A Photo Essay." *The Journal of Arizona History* 30 (summer 1989): 193–208.

Emmerich, Lisa A. " 'Civilization' and Transculturation: The Field Matron Program and Cross-Cultural Contact." *American Indian Culture and Research Journal* 15 (1991): 33–48.

Etulain, Richard W. "Origins of the Western." In *Critical Essays on the Western American Novel,* edited by William T. Pilkington. Boston: G. K. Hall, 1980, 56–60.

Fairbanks, Carol. *Prairie Women: Images in American and Canadian Fiction.* New Haven: Yale University Press, 1986.

Faragher, John Mack. *Women and Men on the Overland Trail.* New Haven: Yale University Press, 1979.

Fender, Stephen. *Plotting the Golden West: American Literature and the Rhetoric of the California Trail.* Cambridge: Cambridge University Press, 1981.

Fiedler, Leslie. *The Return of the Vanishing American.* New York: Stein & Day, 1968.

Fischer, Christiane, ed. *Let Them Speak For Themselves: Women in the American West, 1849–1900.* Hamden, Conn.: Shoe String Press, 1977.

Fisher, Dexter. "Zitkala Sa: The Evolution of a Writer." *American Indian Quarterly* 5 (Aug. 1979): 229–38.

Foote, Cheryl J. " 'My Husband Was a Madman and a Murderer': Josephine Clifford

McCrackin, Army Wife, Writer, and Conservationist." *New Mexico Historical Review* (Aug. 1990): 199–224.

———. *Women of the New Mexico Frontier, 1846–1912.* Niwot: University Press of Colorado, 1990.

Foster, Edward Halsey. *The Civilized Wilderness: Backgrounds to American Romantic Literature, 1817–1860.* New York: Free Press, 1975.

Foucault, Michel. *The History of Sexuality: An Introduction.* Translated by Robert Hurley. New York: Vintage Books, 1978.

———. "Truth and Power." In the *Foucault Reader,* edited by Paul Rabinow.

Friedman, Lawrence J. *Inventors of the Promised Land.* New York: Knopf, 1975.

Fryer, Judith. "The Anti-Mythical Journey: Westering Women's Diaries and Letters. A Review Essay." *The Old Northwest* 9 (spring 1983): 77–90.

Fussell, Edwin. *Frontier: American Literature and the American West.* Princeton, N.J.: Princeton University Press, 1965.

Gannett, Cinthia. *Gender and the Journal: Diaries and Academic Discourse.* New York: State University of New York Press, 1992.

Georgi-Findlay, Brigitte. "The Frontiers of Native American Women's Writing: Sarah Winnemucca's *Life among the Piutes.*" In *New Voices in Native American Literary Criticism,* edited by Arnold Krupat. Washington, D.C.: Smithsonian Institution Press, 1993, 222–52.

Girgus, Sam. *Desire and the Political Unconscious in American Literature: Eros and Ideology.* New York: St. Martin's Press, 1990.

Goetzmann, William H. *Exploration and Empire: The Explorer and the Scientist in the Winning of the American West.* 1966. Reprint, New York: Norton, 1978.

———. *New Lands, New Men: America and the Second Great Age of Discovery.* New York: Viking Penguin, 1986.

Gordon, Linda. "On 'Difference'." *Genders* 10 (spring 1991): 91–111.

Graulich, Melody. " 'O Beautiful for Spacious Guys': An Essay on the Legitimate Inclinations of the Sexes." In Mogen et al.

Green, Martin. *The Great American Adventure.* Boston: Beacon Press, 1984.

Green, Rayna. "The Pocahontas Perplex: The Image of Indian Women in American Culture." *Massachusetts Review* 16 (autumn 1975): 698–714.

———. *Women in American Indian Society.* New York and Philadelphia: Chelsea House Publishers, 1992.

Greenblatt, Stephen. *Marvelous Possessions: The Wonder of the New World.* Chicago: The University of Chicago Press, 1991.

Greenfield, Bruce. *Narrating Discovery: The Romantic Explorer in American Literature, 1790–1855.* New York: Columbia University Press, 1992.

Griswold, Robert L. "Anglo Women and Domestic Ideology in the American West in the Nineteenth and Early Twentieth Centuries." In Schlissel, Ruiz, and Monk.

Hall, Catherine. "Missionary Stories: Gender and Ethnicity in England in the 1830s and 1840s." In *Cultural Studies,* edited by Lawrence Grossberg et al. New York: Routledge, 1992.

Hampsten, Elizabeth. *Read This Only to Yourself: The Private Writings of Midwestern Women, 1880–1910.* Bloomington: Indiana University Press, 1982.

Haslam, Gerald. *Voices of a Place: Social and Literary Essays from the Other California.* Walnut Creek, Calif.: Devil Mountain Books, 1987.

Hauptman, Laurence M. "Mythologizing Westward Expansion: Schoolbooks and the Image of the American Frontier before Turner." *Western Historical Quarterly* 8 (July 1977): 269–82.

Heatherington, Madelon E. "Romance Without Women: The Sterile Fiction of the American West." *The Georgia Review* 33 (1979): 643–56.

Helly, Dorothy O., and Susan M. Reverby, eds. *Gendered Domains: Rethinking Public and Private in Women's History.* Ithaca, N.Y.: Cornell University Press, 1992.

Herr, Pamela. *Jessie Benton Frémont: A Biography.* New York: Franklin Watts, 1987.

Herr, Pamela, and Mary Lee Spence, eds. *The Letters of Jessie Benton Frémont.* Urbana: University of Illinois Press, 1993.

Herring, Rebecca. "Their Work Was Never Done: Women Missionaries on the Kiowa-Comanche Reservation." *Chronicles of Oklahoma* 64 (spring 1986): 69–83.

Hertzberg, Hazel W. *The Search for an American Indian Identity: Modern Pan-Indian Movements.* Syracuse: Syracuse University Press, 1971.

Hewitt, Nancy. "Beyond the Search for Sisterhood: American Women's History in the 1980s." In DuBois and Ruiz.

Higginbotham, Evelyn Brooks. "African-American Women's History and the Meta-language of Race." *Signs* 17 (winter 1992): 251–74.

Hoxie, Frederick. *A Final Promise: The Campaign to Assimilate the Indians, 1880–1920.* Lincoln: University of Nebraska Press, 1984.

Hulme, Peter. *Colonial Encounters: Europe and the Native Caribbean, 1492–1797.* Cambridge: Cambridge University Press, 1987.

Ickstadt, Heinz. "Painting, Fiction, and the Rhetoric of Westward Expansion." In Binder.

Janiewski, Dolores. "Learning to Live 'Just Like White Folks': Gender, Ethnicity, and the State in the Inland Northwest." In Helly and Reverby.

Jaycox, Faith. "Regeneration Through Liberation: Mary Austin's 'Walking Woman' and Western Narrative Formula." *Legacy: A Journal of Nineteenth-Century American Women Writers* 6 (spring 1989): 5–12.

Jeffrey, Julie Roy. *Frontier Women: The Trans-Mississippi West. 1840–1880.* New York: Hill & Wang, 1979.

Jehlen, Myra. "Archimedes and the Paradox of Feminist Criticism." *Signs* 6 (1981): 575–601.

Jensen, Joan M., and Darlis A. Miller. "The Gentle Tamers Revisited: New Approaches to the History of Women in the American West." *Pacific Historical Review* 49 (May 1980): 173–212.

——, eds. *New Mexico Women: Intercultural Perspectives.* Albuquerque: University of New Mexico Press, 1986.

Kammen, Michael. *Mystic Chords of Memory: The Transformation of Tradition in American Culture.* New York: Knopf, 1991. Reissued, New York: Vintage Books, 1993.

Kerber, Linda. "Separate Spheres, Female Worlds, Woman's Place: The Rhetoric of Women's History." *Journal of American History* 75 (June 1988): 9–39.

Kidwell, Clara Sue. "The Power of Women in Three American Indian Societies." *Journal of Ethnic Studies* 6 (fall 1978): 113–22.

Kofalk, Harriet. *No Woman Tenderfoot: Florence Merriam Bailey, Pioneer Naturalist.* College Station: Texas A & M University Press, 1989.

Kolodny, Annette. *The Land Before Her: Fantasy and Experience of the American Frontiers, 1630–1860.* Chapel Hill: University of North Carolina Press, 1984.

——. *The Lay of the Land: Metaphor as Experience and History in American Life and Letters.* Chapel Hill: University of North Carolina Press, 1975.

——. "Letting Go Our Grand Obsessions: Notes Toward a New Literary History of the American Frontiers." *American Literature* 64 (Mar. 1992): 1–18.

——. "Turning the Lens on 'The Panther Captivity': A Feminist Exercise in Practical Criticism." *Critical Inquiry* 8 (winter 1981): 329–45.

LaFarge, Oliver. *A Pictorial History of the American Indian.* New York: Crown, 1957.

Lamar, Howard. Foreword to *Down the Santa Fe Trail,* by Susan Magoffin.

Lander, Dawn. "Eve among the Indians." In *The Authority of Experience: Essays in Feminist Criticism,* edited by Arlyn Diamond and Lee R. Edwards. Amherst: University of Massachusetts Press, 1977, 194–211.

Lears, T. J. Jackson. *No Place of Grace: Antimodernism and the Transformation of American Culture.* New York: Pantheon, 1981.

Leckie, Shirley A. *Elizabeth Bacon Custer and the Making of a Myth.* Norman: University of Oklahoma Press, 1993.

Lee, L. L., and Merrill Lewis, eds. *Women, Women Writers and the West.* Troy, N.Y.: Whitston Publishing, 1980.

Lensink, Judy Nolte. "The Diary as Female Autobiography." In *'A Secret to Be Burried': The Diary and Life of Emily Hawley Gillespie, 1858–1888.* Iowa City: University of Iowa Press, 1989, 378–95.

Leverenz, David. *Manhood in the American Renaissance.* Ithaca, N.Y.: Cornell University Press, 1989.

Levy, JoAnn. *They Saw the Elephant: Women in the California Gold Rush.* Hamden, Conn.: Archon, 1990.

Lewis, R.W.B. *The American Adam: Innocence, Tragedy, and Tradition in the Nineteenth Century.* Chicago: University of Chicago Press, 1955.

Limerick, Patricia. *The Legacy of Conquest: The Unbroken Past of the American West.* New York: Norton, 1987.

Limerick, Patricia, Clyde A. Milner II, and Charles E. Rankin, eds. *Trails: Toward a New Western History.* Lawrence: University Press of Kansas, 1991.

Maddox, Lucy. *Removals: Nineteenth-Century American Literature and the Politics of Indian Affairs.* New York and Oxford: Oxford University Press, 1991.

Malone, Ann Patton. *Women on the Texas Frontier: A Cross-Cultural Perspective.* El Paso: Texas Western Press, 1983.

Mark, Joan. *A Stranger in Her Native Land: Alice Fletcher and the American Indians.* Lincoln: University of Nebraska Press, 1989.

Martin, Jim. *A Bit of A Blue: The Life and Work of Frances Fuller Victor.* Salem, Ore.: Deep Well Publishing Co., 1992.

Marx, Leo. "Pastoralism in America." In Bercovitch and Jehlen.

Mason, Peter. *Deconstructing America: Representations of the Other.* New York: Routledge, 1990.

Mathes, Valerie Sherer. *Helen Hunt Jackson and Her Indian Reform Legacy.* Austin: University of Texas Press, 1990.

Mattes, Merrill J. *Indians, Infants and Infantry: Andrew and Elizabeth Burt on the Frontier.* Denver, Colo.: Old West Publishing, 1960.

Maxwell, Margaret E. *A Passion for Freedom: The Life of Sharlot Hall.* Tucson: University of Arizona Press, 1982.

McDermott, John. Introduction to *My Army Life,* by Frances Carrington.

McKee, Irving. *'Ben-Hur' Wallace: The Life of General Lew Wallace.* Berkeley: University of California Press, 1947.

McKnight, Jeannie. "American Dream, Nightmare Underside." In Lee and Lewis.

Meinig, D. W. "Strategies of Empire." *Culturefront: A Magazine of the Humanities* 2 (summer 1993): 12–18.

Meldrum, Barbara Howard. "Women in Western American Fiction: Images, or Real Women?" In Stauffer and Rosowski.

Merk, Frederick. *Manifest Destiny and Mission in American History: A Reinterpretation.* New York: Vintage Books, 1963.

Meyer, Marian. *Mary Donoho: New First Lady of the Santa Fe Trail.* Santa Fe, N.Mex.: Ancient City Press, 1991.

Miller, Darlis A. "Foragers, Army Women, and Prostitutes." In Jensen and Miller.

Miller, Perry. *Errand into the Wilderness.* Cambridge, Mass.: Harvard University Press, 1956.

——. *Nature's Nation.* Cambridge, Mass.: Harvard University Press, 1967.

Mills, Hazel E. "The Emergence of Frances Fuller Victor–Historian." *Oregon Historical Quarterly* 62 (Dec. 1961): 309–36.

Mills, Sara. *Discourses of Difference: An Analysis of Women's Travel Writing and Colonialism.* London and New York: Routledge, 1991.

Mitchell, Lee Clark. *Witnesses to a Vanishing America: The Nineteenth-Century Response.* Princeton, N.J.: Princeton University Press, 1981.

Mogen, David, Mark Busby, and Paul Bryant, eds. *The Frontier Experience and the American Dream: Essays on American Literature.* College Station: Texas A & M University Press, 1989.

Morgan, Anne Hodges, and Rennard Strickland, eds. *Arizona Memories.* Tucson: University of Arizona Press, 1984.

Morsberger, Robert E., and Katharine M. *Lew Wallace: Militant Romantic.* New York: McGraw-Hill, 1980.

Moynihan, Ruth, Susan Armitage, and Christiane Fischer Dichamp, eds. *So Much to Be Done: Women Settlers on the Mining and Ranching Frontier.* Lincoln: University of Nebraska Press, 1990.

Muller, Marcia, and Bill Pronzini, eds. *She Won the West: An Anthology of Western and Frontier Stories by Women.* New York: William Morrow and Co., 1985.

Myres, Sandra L. "Army Women's Narratives as Documents of Social History: Some Examples from the Western Frontier, 1840–1900." *New Mexico Historical Review* 65 (Apr. 1990): 175–98.

——. "Evy Alexander: The Colonel's Lady at McDowell in Arizona." *Montana: The Magazine of Western History* 24 (July 1974): 26–38.

——. *Westering Women and the Frontier Experience 1800–1915.* Albuquerque: University of New Mexico Press, 1982.

——, ed. *Ho for California! Women's Overland Diaries from the Huntington Library.* San Marino, Calif.: Huntington Library, 1980.

Namias, June. *White Captives: Gender and Ethnicity on the American Frontier.* Chapel Hill: University of North Carolina Press, 1993.

Niederman, Sharon, ed. *A Quilt of Words: Women's Diaries, Letters and Original Accounts of Life in the Southwest, 1860–1960.* Boulder, Colo.: Johnson Books, 1988.

Norwood, Vera. *Made from This Earth: American Women and Nature.* Chapel Hill: University of North Carolina Press, 1993.

——. "Women's Place: Continuity and Change in Response to Western Landscapes." In Schlissel, Ruiz, and Monk.

Norwood, Vera, and Janice Monk, eds. *The Desert is No Lady: Southwestern Landscapes in Women's Writing and Art.* New Haven: Yale University Press, 1987.

Novak, Barbara. *Nature and Culture.* New York: Oxford University Press, 1980.

Odell, Ruth. *Helen Hunt Jackson.* New York: Appleton, 1939.

Olsen, Louise P. "Mary Clementine Collins, Dacotah Missionary." *North Dakota History* 29 (Jan. 1952): 59–81.

Osborne, William S. *Caroline Kirkland.* New York: Twayne, 1972.

Parker, Andrew, Mary Russo, Doris Sommer, and Patricia Yaeger, eds. *Nationalisms and Sexualities.* New York: Routledge, 1992.

Pascoe, Peggy. *Relations of Rescue: The Search for Female Moral Authority in the American West, 1874–1939.* New York and Oxford: University of Oxford Press, 1990.

———. "Western Women at the Cultural Crossroads." In Limerick, Milner, and Rankin.

Pearce, Roy Harvey. *Savagism and Civilization: A Study of the Indian and the American Mind.* Revised edition of *The Savages of America,* 1953. Berkeley: University of California Press, 1988.

Pease, Donald E. "National Identities, Postmodern Artifacts, and Postnational Narratives." *boundary 2* 19 (1992): 1–13.

Person, Leland S., Jr. "The American Eve: Miscegenation and a Feminist Frontier Fiction." *American Quarterly* 37 (winter 1985): 668–85.

Personal Narratives Group, ed. *Interpreting Women's Lives: Feminist Theory and Personal Narratives.* Bloomington: Indiana University Press, 1989.

Peterson, Susan. " 'Holy Women' and Housekeepers: Women Teachers on South Dakota Reservations, 1885–1910." *South Dakota History* 13 (fall 1983): 245–60.

———. "Patient, Useful Servants: Women Missionaries in Indian Territory." In Thurman.

Piekarski, Vicki, ed. *Westward the Women: An Anthology of Western Stories by Women.* Albuquerque: University of New Mexico Press, 1984.

Pomeroy, Earl. *In Search of the Golden West: The Tourist in Western America.* 1957. Reprint, Lincoln: University of Nebraska Press, 1990.

———. "Toward a Reorientation of Western History: Continuity and Environment." *Mississippi Valley Historical Review* 41 (Mar. 1955): 579–600.

Pratt, Mary Louise. "Arts of the Contact Zone." *Profession* (1991): 33–40.

———. "Fieldwork in Common Places." In *Writing Culture: The Poetics and Politics of Ethnography,* edited by James Clifford and George E. Marcus. Berkeley: University of California Press, 1986.

———. *Imperial Eyes: Travel Writing and Transculturation.* London and New York: Routledge, 1992.

———. "Scratches on the Face of the Country; or, What Mr. Barrow Saw in the Land of the Bushmen." *Critical Inquiry* 12 (autumn 1985): 119–43.

Prucha, Francis Paul. *American Indian Policy in Crisis: Christian Reformers and the Indian, 1865–1900.* Norman: University of Oklahoma Press, 1976.

———. *The Great Father: The United States Government and the American Indians.* Abridged ed. Lincoln: University of Nebraska Press, 1986.

Rabinow, Paul, ed. *The Foucault Reader.* New York: Pantheon, 1984.

Rebolledo, Tey Diana, and Eliana S. Rivero. *Infinite Divisions: An Anthology of Chicana Literature.* Tucson: University of Arizona Press, 1993.

Regis, Pamela. *Describing Early America: Bartram, Jefferson, Crèvecoeur, and the Rhetoric of Natural History.* De Kalb: Northern Illinois University Press, 1992.

Riley, Glenda. *The Female Frontier: A Comparative View of Women on the Prairie and the Plains.* Lawrence: University Press of Kansas, 1988.

——. *Women and Indians on the Frontier, 1825–1915*. Albuquerque: University of New Mexico Press, 1984.

——. "Women on the Great Plains: Recent Developments in Research." *Great Plains Quarterly* 5 (spring 1985): 81–92.

——, ed. *Women in the West*. Manhattan, Kans.: Sunflower University Press, 1982.

Robinson, Jane. *Wayward Women: A Guide to Women Travellers*. New York: Oxford University Press, 1990.

Rogin, Michael Paul. *Fathers and Children: Andrew Jackson and the Subjugation of the American Indian*. 1975. Reprint, New Brunswick, N.J.: Transaction Publishers, 1991.

——. "Nature as Politics and Nature as Romance in America." *Political Theory* 5 (1977): 5–30.

Rosowski, Susan J. "Margaret Fuller, an Engendered West, and *Summer on the Lakes*." *Western American Literature* 15 (Aug. 1990): 125–44.

Said, Edward. *Culture and Imperialism*. New York: Knopf, 1993.

——. *Orientalism*. 1978. Reprint, New York: Vintage Books, 1979.

Sargent, Shirley. "Literary Ladies." *Pacific Historian* (May and Aug. 1965): 97–101, 129–32.

——. *Pioneers in Petticoats: Yosemite's Early Women 1856–1900*. Los Angeles: Trans-Anglo Books, 1966.

Schivelbusch, Wolfgang. *The Railway Journey: Trains and Travel in the Nineteenth Century*. New York: Urizen Books, 1979.

Schlissel, Lillian. *Women's Diaries of the Westward Journey*. New York: Schocken Books, 1982.

Schlissel, Lillian, Byrd Gibbens, and Elizabeth Hampsten. *Far From Home: Families of the Westward Journey*. New York: Schocken Books, 1989.

Schlissel, Lillian, Vicki L. Ruiz, and Janice Monk, eds. *Western Women: Their Land, Their Lives*. Albuquerque: University of New Mexico Press, 1988.

Scholnick, Robert J. *American Literature and Science*. Lexington: University Press of Kentucky, 1992.

Skocpol, Theda. *Protecting Soldiers and Mothers*. Cambridge, Mass.: Harvard University Press, 1993.

Slotkin, Richard. *The Fatal Environment: The Myth of the Frontier in the Age of Industrialization, 1800–1890*. New York: Atheneum, 1985.

——. "Nostalgia and Progress: Theodore Roosevelt's Myth of the Frontier." *American Quarterly* 35 (1981): 608–37.

——. *Regeneration through Violence: The Mythology of the American Frontier, 1600–1860*. Middletown, Conn.: Wesleyan University Press, 1973.

Smith, Henry Nash. "Symbol and Idea in *Virgin Land*." In Bercovitch and Jehlen.

——. *Virgin Land: The American West as Symbol and Myth*. 1950. Reprint, New York: Vintage Books, 1957.

Smith, Sherry L. *The View from Officers' Row: Army Perceptions of Western Indians*. Tucson: University of Arizona Press, 1990.

Smith, Sidonie. "Who's Talking/Who's Talking Back? The Subject of Personal Narrative." *Signs* 18 (1993): 392–407.

Smith, Susan Sutton. "Sara Jane Clark Lippincott." In *American Women Writers: A Critical Reference Guide from Colonial Times to the Present,* vol. 3, edited by Lisa Mainiero. New York: Ungar, 1979.

Smith-Rosenberg, Carroll. *Disorderly Conduct: Visions of Gender in Victorian America*. New York and Oxford: Oxford University Press, 1985.

——. "Subject Female: Authorizing American Identity." *American Literary History* 5 (fall 1993): 481–511.

Spengemann, William C. *The Adventurous Muse: The Poetics of American Fiction, 1789–1900*. New Haven: Yale University Press, 1977.

Sprague, William Forrest. *Women and the West: A Short History*. 1940. Reprint, New York: Arno Press, 1972.

Spurr, David. *The Rhetoric of Empire: Colonial Discourse in Journalism, Travel Writing, and Imperial Administration*. Durham: Duke University Press, 1993.

Stallard, Patricia Y. *Glittering Misery: Dependents of the Indian Fighting Army*. 1978. Norman: University of Oklahoma Press, 1992.

Starr, Kevin. *Americans and the California Dream, 1850–1950*. New York: Oxford University Press, 1973.

——. *Inventing the Dream: California Through the Progressive Era*. New York: Oxford University Press, 1985.

Stauffer, Helen Winter, and Susan J. Rosowski, eds. *Women and Western American Literature*. Troy, N.Y.: Whitston Publishing, 1982.

Stegner, Wallace. *The Sound of Mountain Water*. New York: Dutton, 1980.

Steinbach, Robert H. *A Long March: The Lives of Frank and Alice Baldwin*. Austin: University of Texas Press, 1989.

Stevenson, Catherine Barnes. *Victorian Women Travel Writers in Africa*. Boston: Twayne, 1982.

Stewart, Jane R. Introduction to *'Boots and Saddles'*, by Elizabeth Custer.

Stockel, H. Henrietta. *Women of the Apache Nation: Voices of Truth*. Reno: University of Nevada Press, 1991.

Stoeltje, Beverly J. "'A Helpmate for Man Indeed': The Image of the Frontier Woman." *Journal of American Folklore* 88 (Jan.–Mar. 1975): 25–41.

Stoler, Laura Ann. "Carnal Knowledge and Imperial Power: Gender, Race, and Morality in Colonial Asia." In *Gender at the Crossroads of Knowledge: Feminist Anthropology in the Postmodern Era*, edited by Micaela di Leonardo. Berkeley: University of California Press, 1991.

——. "Making Empire Respectable: The Politics of Race and Sexual Morality in 20th-Century Colonial Cultures." *American Ethnologist* 16, 4 (Nov. 1989): 634–60.

Susman, Warren I. *Culture as History: The Transformation of American Society in the Twentieth Century*. 1973. Reprint, New York: Pantheon Books, 1984.

Tatum, Stephen. "Literature Out-of-Doors." *American Literary History* 5 (summer 1993): 294–313.

Thurman, Melvena K., ed. *Women in Oklahoma: A Century of Change*. Oklahoma City: Oklahoma Historical Society, 1983.

Tinling, Marion. *Women into the Unknown: A Sourcebook on Women Explorers and Travelers*. New York: Greenwood Press, 1989.

Tompkins, Jane. *Sensational Designs: The Cultural Work of American Fiction, 1790–1860*. New York and Oxford: Oxford University Press, 1985.

——. "West of Everything." *South Atlantic Quarterly* 86 (1987): 357–77.

——. *West of Everything: The Inner Life of Westerns*. New York and Oxford: Oxford University Press, 1992.

Torgovnick, Marianna. *Gone Primitive: Savage Intellects, Modern Lives*. Chicago: University of Chicago Press, 1990.

Trachtenberg, Alan. *The Incorporation of America*. New York: Hill & Wang, 1982.

Trinh, T. Minh-Ha. *Woman, Native, Other: Writing Postcoloniality and Feminism*. Bloomington: Indiana University Press, 1989.

Turner, Frederick Jackson. "The Significance of the Frontier in American History." In *The Frontier in American History*. 1920. Reprint, New York: Holt, Rinehart, and Winston, 1963.

Underhill, Ruth M. *Papago Woman*. 1979. Reissued, Prospect Heights, Ill.: Waveland Press, 1985.

Utley, Robert M. *The Indian Frontier of the American West 1846–1890*. Albuquerque: University of New Mexico Press, 1984.

——, ed. *Life in Custer's Cavalry: Diaries and Letters of Albert and Jennie Barnitz 1867–1868*. New Haven, Conn.: Yale University Press, 1977.

van Kirk, Sylvia. *'Many Tender Ties': Women in Fur-Trade Society in Western Canada, 1670–1870*. Winnipeg: Watson & Dwyer, 1980.

von Frank, Albert J. *The Sacred Game: Provincialism and Frontier Consciousness in American Literature, 1630–1860*. Cambridge: Cambridge University Press, 1985.

Walker, Franklin. *A Literary History of Southern California*. Berkeley: University of California Press, 1950.

——. *San Francisco's Literary Frontier*. New York: Alfred A. Knopf, 1939.

Weber, David J. *The Spanish Frontier in North America*. New Haven, Conn.: Yale University Press, 1992.

Weinberg, Albert K. *Manifest Destiny: A Study of Nationalist Expansion in American History*. Baltimore, Md.: Johns Hopkins Press, 1935.

Welter, Barbara. "The Cult of True Womanhood, 1820–1860." *American Quarterly* 18 (1966): 151–75.

——. " 'She Hath Done What She Could': Protestant Women's Missionary Careers in Nineteenth Century America." In *Women in American Religion*, edited by Janet Wilson James, Philadelphia: University of Pennsylvania Press, c 1978, 1980.

Whitaker, Rosemary. *Helen Hunt Jackson*. Boise, Idaho: Boise State University Western Writers, 1987.

White, Richard. "Trashing the Trails." In Limerick, Milner, and Rankin.

Wiebe, Robert. *The Search for Order, 1877–1920*. New York: Hill & Wang, 1967.

Wilson, Rob. *American Sublime: The Genealogy of a Poetic Genre*. Madison: University of Wisconsin Press, 1991.

Worster, Donald. "Beyond the Agrarian Myth." In Limerick, Milner, and Rankin.

Young, Mary E. "Women, Civilization, and the Indian Question." In *Clio Was a Woman: Studies in the History of American Women*, edited by Mabel E. Deutrich and Virginia C. Purdy. Washington: Howard University Press, 1980.

Zagarell, Sandra A. Introduction to *A New Home*, by Caroline Kirkland.

Index

About the Author

Brigitte Georgi-Findlay is an associate professor of American literature at the University of Bremen, Germany. She is a generalist in American literature and culture with specializations in minority literatures, women's literature and gender studies, and the literature and history of the American West.

Georgi-Findlay holds a doctoral degree in English and French from the University of Heidelberg, Germany. Between 1991 and 1993, she was a visiting scholar at the University of Arizona, sponsored by the American Council of Learned Societies and the German Research Association.

Georgi-Findlay is the author of two books, both published in German: *The Image of the American Indian in American Literature* (1982) and *Tradition and Modernism in Contemporary Native American Literature* (1986). She has also published articles on Native American literature and women's western literature. Her current project is a study of American travel abroad.